DRYLAND FORESTRY

DRYLAND FORESTRY

Planning and Management

Peter F. Ffolliott
University of Arizona
Tucson, Arizona

Kenneth N. Brooks, Hans M. Gregersen, and Allen L. Lundgren
University of Minnesota
St. Paul, Minnesota

JOHN WILEY & SONS, INC.

New York • Chichester • Brisbane • Toronto • Singapore

Library of Congress Cataloging in Publication Data:
Ffolliott, Peter F.
   Dryland forstry / Peter F. Ffolliott ; and Kenneth N. Brooks,
Hans M. Gregersen, and Allen L. Lundgren.
     p.   cm.
   Includes bibliographical references.
   ISBN 0-471-54800-6 (cloth)
    1. Arid regions forestry. 2. Arid regions agriculture.
  3. Sustainable forestry. 4. Sustainable agriculture. I. Title.
SD410.3.F46 1994
634.9'0915'4—dc20   95-27699

Printed in the United States of America

10 9 8 7 6 5 4 3 2 1

CONTENTS

PREFACE

The topic of forestry in the dryland regions of the world involves many technical and social disciplines. Unfortunately, it is infrequent that a "specialist" can be called upon to help solve every forestry-related problem. To be of value, therefore, foresters and others interested in the planning, implementation, and management of forestry projects must have some knowledge of a great number of topics. With this in mind, the primary objective of this book is to present the kinds of information required to understand and integrate biophysical and socioeconomic components into environmentally sound, sustainable forest management practices in dryland environments. To achieve this objective, this book furnishes:

- Basic knowledge of important disciplines involved in the practice of forestry in the dryland regions of the world.
- Forest management practices appropriate to specific situations.
- Practical experiences to problem solving in planning and implementing forest management practices in dryland environments.

The book has been organized into five parts, each of which addresses a specific set of issues that relate to forestry and the management of trees and shrubs for multiple benefits and sustainable development of dryland regions.

- Part I is important in obtaining an appreciation of sustainable development in dryland regions by considering use of these lands for livestock production, small-scale agricultural crop production, watershed values and management of water resources, and wildlife, recreation and tourism, and amenity plantations. The role of forestry in the sustainable development of dryland regions—the focus of the book—and opportunities for investment, employment, and income generation in relation to forestry also are presented.
- Part II is concerned with the planning and assessing of forestry projects. Integrating dryland forestry into the multiple use concept also is introduced.
- Part III consists of technical considerations in dryland forestry, including nursery operations and the improvement of planting stock, the establishment and management of rainfed and irrigated forest plantations, and the management of natural forests and woodlands.
- Part IV presents special topics, which, in many instances, are the purposes of dryland forestry activities. These topics include fuelwood production,

agroforestry systems, windbreak plantings and sand dune stabilization, soil erosion and control measures, and the rehabilitation of saline environments.

- Part V concludes the book by considering issues related to implementing and supporting dryland forestry activities. Involvement of rural people in these activities, monitoring and evaluation, and forestry extension programs are considered.

This book has been written as a text for upper-level and graduate students in forestry-related, conservation, and natural resource curricula. The information presented pertains to dryland environments in both the United States and elsewhere in the world. Much of the material presented in the book has been the basis for formal college courses in the United States and training courses for national and international participants.

The book also is a general reference for planners, decision makers, managers and technicians, and administrators concerned with the management of natural forests and woodlands and forest plantations in relation to sustainable development and improvement in the livelihoods of rural people in the dryland regions of the world.

The International System of Units (Système International d'Unités, SI), informally called the metric system (centimeters, cubic meters, grams), is used throughout the book. Exceptions are found where the original relationships or data were presented in English units (inches, cubic feet, pounds) and conversions to the metric system would be awkward. To help in the conversion process, a table of common metric-to-English conversions is presented in Appendix I.

PETER F. FFOLLIOTT

Tucson, Arizona

KENNETH N. BROOKS

HANS M. GREGERSEN

ALLEN L. LUNDGREN

St. Paul, Minnesota

DRYLAND FORESTRY

1 Introduction

In many dryland regions of the world, forestry has not been practiced on a sustainable basis. Exceptions can be found in some drylands of developed countries, where capital investments have been sufficient to make forestry economically justifiable. Even in these cases, however, applications of forestry often are "extrapolations" from forestry practices in the moist tropical and other temperate regions, which can lead to ineffective and inefficient land management.

Natural forests and woodlands, and forest plantations in dryland regions are capable of providing multiple benefits to people living in these areas. Furthermore, introduction of trees and shrubs into agricultural and livestock production systems can enhance production of goods and services, and can provide environmental protection at the same time. Production and environmental protection are both essential for sustainable development to occur.

Appropriate policies, planning procedures, implementional methods, managerial strategies, and extension programs are required to apply forestry on a sustainable basis in dryland regions. A necessary background to an appreciation and proper use of this information includes a recognition of what characterizes dryland environments and the "constraints" that these environments place on the practice of forestry. It also is necessary to know where the dryland regions are found throughout the world, what forestry applications in dryland environments entail, and what critical problems are confronted by people concerned with the management of forests and woodlands in dryland regions. Answers to these and related questions are found in this introductory chapter.

DRYLAND ENVIRONMENTS

Drylands are diverse in terms of climate, soils, vegetation, animals, and people's activities. Because of this diversity, no practical characterization or definition of *drylands* can be made. One binding feature of all drylands in the world, however, is aridity.

Aridity

Aridity results from the presence of dry, descending air. Therefore, aridity is found mostly in places where anticyclonic conditions are persistent, as is the case in regions lying under the anticyclones of the subtropics. The influence of subtropical anticyclones on rainfall increases with the presence of cool surfaces. Arid conditions also occur in the lee of major mountain ranges that disrupt the structure of cyclones passing over them, creating "rain shadow" effects. Rainfall also is hindered by the presence of greatly heated land surfaces. As a consequence, large areas of dry climate exist far from the sea.

Aridity can be expressed in a number of ways as a function of rainfall and temperature. One representation of aridity is the index used by the United Nations Educational, Scientific, and Cultural Organization (UNESCO), expressed as the ratio of average annual precipitation (P) to average potential evapotranspiration (PET), the latter calculated by Penman's method, taking into account atmospheric humidity, solar radiation, and wind (Baumer and Salem 1985).

Three bioclimatical zones with varying degrees of aridity can be delineated by this index: *hyperarid* (< 0.03), *arid* (0.03 < 0.20), and *semiarid* (0.20 < 0.50). Of the total land area in the world, hyperarid zones cover 4.2 percent, arid zones 14.6 percent, and semiarid zones 12.2 percent. Almost one-third of the total land area of the world, therefore, is considered to be characterized by aridity. These lands, together with their *subhumid* margins (0.50 < 0.75), collectively comprise the "drylands" of the world.

Hyperarid zones comprise regions with sparse annual and perennial vegetation and scattered shrubs. True nomadic pastoralism frequently is practiced. Annual rainfall is low, rarely exceeding 100 mm. Rains are infrequent and irregular, with sometimes no rain for several years.

Arid zones are characterized by pastoralism and little farming, except where irrigation is possible. Vegetation typically is sparse, comprised of annual and perennial grasses, other herbaceous plants, shrubs, and small trees. Rainfall variability is high, with annual amounts ranging between 100 and 300 mm.

Semiarid zones often can support rainfed-sustained levels of agricultural production. Sedentary livestock production occurs. Native vegetation includes a variety of grasses and grasslike plants, forbs and half-shrubs, and shrubs and trees. Annual rainfall varies from 300 to 800 mm, depending upon the relative occurrences of summer and winter rains.

Climate

Dryland environments are characterized by inadequate, variable rainfall. Some of these environments have excessive heat, while others are cold, dry areas. However, contrasts in climate occur, such as in Tibet and Mongolia. Three major types of climate, *Mediterranean*, *Tropical*, and *Continental*, are found in the drylands of the world. Rainy seasons in a Mediterranean climate, as exists in Rabat, Morocco, for example, are in autumn and winter (Figure 1.1a). Summers are hot with no rains, while winter temperatures are relatively mild. Rainfall occurs during the summer in Sennar, Sudan, an area typical of a Tropical climate (Figure 1.1b). The greater the distance from the equator, the shorter the rainy season. Winters are long and dry. In a Continental climate, illustrated by Alice Springs, Australia, rainfall is

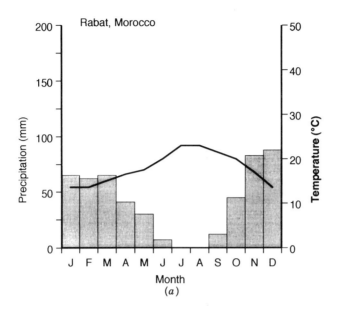

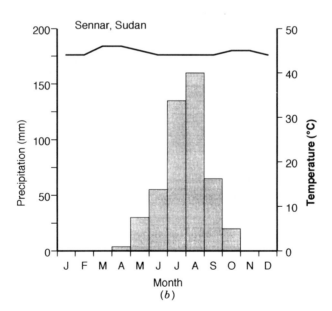

Figure 1.1. Annual precipitation and temperature in (a) Rabat, Morocco, (b) Sennar, Sudan, and (c) Alice Springs, Australia (adapted from the Food and Agriculture Organization of the United Nations (1989a)

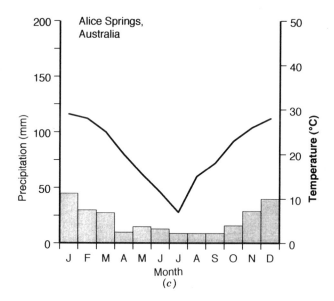

Figure 1.1. *(Continued)*

distributed evenly throughout the year, although there is a tendency toward greater summer rainfall (Figure 1.1c).

Modifications of the three major types of climate are found throughout the dryland environments. Two rainfall periods occur in Tucson, Arizona, in the Sonoran Desert of the southwestern United States, one in the hot summer and another in the cool winter (Figure 1.2). Although total annual rainfall frequently is less than 300 mm, its distribution into two seasons of the year partly explains the relatively dense cover of small trees, shrubs, and other herbaceous species that are common to the Sonoran Desert.

Variability of rainfall is characteristic of most dryland regions that must be recognized in the planning and management of agricultural and natural resources. Example 1.1 illustrates some of the extremes in the variability of rainfall that are encountered in many of these areas.

Droughts

Although not unique to dryland environments, the occurrences and effects of droughts in dryland regions require special attention. A *drought* is a departure from average or normal conditions, in which shortage of water adversely impacts ecosystem functioning and the resident populations of people. Sometimes, the terms *drought* and *aridity* are used incorrectly. Aridity refers to the average conditions of limited rainfall and water supplies, not to the departures therefrom.

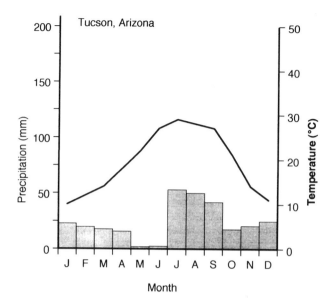

Figure 1.2. Annual precipitation and temperature in Tucson, Arizona (adapted from McGinnes 1988)

Example 1.1

Variability of Rainfall in Dryland Regions: Some Examples (Jackson 1989)
Rainfall variability and the presence of distinctive periods of droughts are characteristic of the dry tropics. Over two-thirds of Africa receives its annual rainfall during three months, with extremes being common. In Liberia, for example, the maximum annual rainfall recorded is 1,203 mm, the minimum is 123 mm, and the average is 461 mm. At Meru, Kenya, rainfall amounts in October have ranged from as little as 15 mm to as much as 1,386 mm.

Even in the most arid areas, rainfall can be quite variable. At the Red Sea station of Hurghada, the average annual rainfall is only 8 mm. In November 1991, however, 41 mm of rain fell in one day. More examples can be presented, but the point made is that average values of seasonal or annual rainfall do not necessarily provide a representative picture of the climatological conditions for many dryland regions.

It is known that droughts will occur in the future, but it is not possible to predict when they will occur or how long they will last. Because of uncertainties associated with droughts and the severity of their impacts, there are many special considerations in planning and management of forests, woodlands, and grasslands in dryland regions. Droughts are characterized by shortages of water, and usually shortages of food for people and forage for livestock, which can lead to unplanned use of agricultural and natural resources. If contingency planning is not undertaken to meet these shortages, serious degradation of land and resources can result. The topic of drought and suggestions for managerial strategies to minimize the effects of drought will be revisited throughout this book.

Geomorphology

Mountain massifs, plains, pediments, and deeply incised ravines and drainage patterns in the drylands display sharp changes in slope and topography, and a high degree of angularity. Rivers traverse wide floodplains at lower elevations and, at times, are subject to changes of course. Many of these landforms are covered by unstable sand dunes or sand sheets. Sand also inundates grazing lands, agricultural crops, and cities and villages.

Other geomorphical features influence soil formation and its characteristics, including the distribution of coarse and fine soil fractions from transportation processes, reworking, disposition by wind and water, and periodic inundation of floodplains. Among the beneficial effects of these influences are the replenishment of soil nutrients and leaching of accumulated salts in the soil.

Soils

Of primary importance for soils in the drylands are the water-holding capacity and ability to supply nutrients. Soil depth largely governs the amount of water that can be held in a soil profile. However, the depth of soils in drylands often is limited by a "hardpan" layer, restricting water-holding capacities. These hardpans, consisting of various materials depending upon the actions of climate and vegetation on parent rock, can be more or less continuous and occur between 5 and 60 cm below the surface.

Soils are characterized by the leaching of nutrients and intensive weathering of minerals. Natural soil fertility, therefore, is low. Because there is little accumulation of organic litter in dryland environments, organic matter content of the soils is low. This limited organic matter is lost quickly when soils are cultivated for agricultural crop production.

Water Resources

Most of the water that is available to people living in the drylands is found in large rivers that originate in areas of higher elevation. These rivers include the Colorado in the western United States, the Nile in the Sudan and Egypt, and the Tigris, Indus, Ganges, Senegal, and Niger. Local, but often limited, groundwater resources also are available to help support development of relatively small areas.

Recharge of groundwater resources in an area is dependent largely upon the amount, intensity, and duration of the rainfall and also soil properties, the latter including infiltration capacities and water-holding characteristics of the soil, which also influence the amount of surface runoff. Much of the rainfall is lost by evapotranspiration, and, as a result, groundwater is recharged only locally by seepage through the soil profile. Surface runoff events, soil moisture storage, and groundwater recharge generally are more variable and less reliable than in more temperate regions. Groundwater frequently is used at rates that exceed recharge.

Water that is available for use in many drylands is affected, to varying degrees, by salinity. Problems of salinity, well known in many other temperate regions, are more widespread and acute in the drylands (Armitage 1987). Although most soil contains some soluble salts, it is only when the accumulations of salts attain a harmful level to plants that a salinity condition has developed. In effect, therefore, plants define the salinity of soil in terms of their tolerances.

Mineralization of groundwater resources is also a common problem. The causes of mineralization include the evaporation from water surfaces and shallow groundwater, fossil brines from ancient lagoons and lakes, and airborne salts deposited by precipitation and in the form of dry fallout.

Vegetation

Many plants in dryland regions have adaptations that enable them to reproduce, grow, and survive in some of the harshest environments in the world. The extremes of dryland climates, often characterized by strong winds and wide fluctuations in temperature and precipitation, dictate, to a large extent, physiological adaptations and ecological requirements of plants in these regions. Some plants have evolved special root systems, while others have unique leaf characteristics that allow them to withstand prolonged periods of drought. Other plants simply lose their leaves when soil moisture conditions become too dry. Other adaptations are described in Example 1.2.

Example 1.2

Adaptations of Plants to the Dryland Environments of the Southwestern United States (Went 1955) Plants in the southwestern United States have adapted to their environments in many ways. For example, mesquite (*Prosopis velutina*) has roots from 10 to 30 m long that enable the plant to tap into underground lenses of fresh water. This morphological adaptation allows mesquite to occupy floodplains and other sites with relatively shallow groundwater and, in doing so, avoid stresses that other plants undergo during drought.

The evergreen creosote bush (*Larrea divaricata*) has a wide-reaching root system and special adaptations that reduce competition for soil moisture by surrounding plants. The evenly spaced pattern of creosote bush that is evident from above is due largely to excretion of toxic substances that kill other plants. Spacing of creosote bush is related to rainfall—the less the rainfall, the wider the spacing. Greater amounts of rainfall apparently leach the "poisons" from the soil, but with the greater amount of soil moisture is also a factor.

Annual plants have characteristics that enable them to survive. Seeds of some annuals remain dormant in the soil for many years and only germinate under special conditions. Many of the annuals in the southwestern United States have no morphological adaptations to withstand drought conditions, but they require a minimum of 10 to 20 mm of rainfall before they will germinate. Seeds lie dormant in the upper layers of the soil until a threshold amount of rainfall occurs. Apparently, the mechanism by which seeds discriminate between rainfall of more than the threshold amount is the amount of leaching required to remove inhibitors to germination.

Three plant forms, *ephemeral annuals*, *succulent perennials*, and *nonsucculent perennials*, are found in dryland environments. Ephemeral annuals, which appear after rains, complete their life cycle during a short season (±8 weeks). Ephemerals are small in size, have shallow roots, and, at times, form relatively dense stands and provide some forage. Succulent perennials store water, largely through the enlargement of parenchymal tissue and their low rates of transpiration, which then is consumed in periods of drought. Cacti are typical succulent perennials.

Nonsucculent perennials that withstand the stress of dryland environments are the majority of plants in these regions. Three forms of nonsucculent perennials, *evergreen*, *drought-deciduous*, and *cold-deciduous*, are found. Evergreen plants are active biologically throughout the year, drought-deciduous plants are dormant in the dry season, and cold-deciduous plants are dormant in the cold season.

Xeromorphological leaf structures, physiological controls of transpiration and metabolism rates, moisture and nutrient storage organs, and thorns are common in plants in the drylands. Such specializations becomes less pronounced as aridity becomes less severe and, consequently, conditions for plant establishment and growth become favorable. It is interesting that at the more "arid end" of the dryland environmental spectrum, only a few plants of the "specially" adapted provide food for people, although leaves and flowers of some plants are useful as supplements.

Land Use

Unconfined livestock production historically has been widespread in the drylands of the world and, undoubtedly, will continue as such into the future. Small-scale agricultural crop production—except where irrigation is possible, in which case larger-scale, more intensive agriculture is practiced—is found on sites favorable to this form of land use. Intensive forestry practices have been uncommon, although this has been changing recently, especially with the establishment of "energy plantations" for fuelwood. Interest in forestry as a sustainable land use has been gaining increased attention by both professional foresters and local people.

In formulating a role for forestry in dryland environments, a consultation to review and analyze this unique and enlarging role of forestry was organized largely by the Food and Agriculture Organization (FAO) of the United Nations in

1985. One outcome of this consultation, held in Saltillo, Cohahuila, Mexico, as a satellite meeting to the Ninth World Forestry Congress, was a recognition of the importance of "dryland forestry" as an emerging strategy in sustainable development (FAO 1989b, Salem 1988). It was felt that the intensification of tree and shrub management in these ecosystems, within the framework of environmentally sound planning, should help to ensure that the whole system will contribute effectively to the production of goods, services, and the wider aim of food security.

Consumptive and nonconsumptive wildlife uses, recreation and tourism, and amenity plantations of trees and shrubs also are important components in many efforts to attain sustainable development of dryland systems. Although it is not always possible to place monetary values on these components, they frequently make significant contributions to overall developmental activities and the general well-being of local people. It is necessary, therefore, to consider the varied roles that wildlife, recreation and tourism, and amenity plantations play in dryland regions when addressing issues related to land use.

People

Approximately 20 percent of the world's population lives in dryland environments. Almost 75 percent live in semiarid zones, 25 percent in arid zones, and only 1 percent in hyperarid zones. In general, the population densities are less than $1/km^2$ in the hyperarid zone, below $5/km^2$ in the arid zone, and about $10/km^2$ in the semiarid zone (FAO 1989a). The population in dryland regions is 72 percent agricultural, 7 percent animal-based, and 21 percent urban. Increasing populations of people moving into the commonly encountered spreading slums of urban areas is a major demographical feature of the drylands, however, as it is in other regions of the world.

People living in drylands are arranged roughly into *nomadic*, *seminomadic*, *transhumant*, and *sedentary* populations. Nomadic people are found in pastoral groups that depend upon livestock for subsistence and, whenever possible, farming as a supplement. Following the irregular distribution of rainfall, they migrate in search of pastures and water for their animals. Seminomadic people also are found in pastoral groups that depend largely upon livestock and practice agricultural cultivation at a base camp, where they return for varying periods of time. Transhumant populations combine farming and livestock raising during favorable seasons but seasonally migrate along regular routes when grazing diminishes in the farming area. Sedentary farmers practice rainfed or irrigated agriculture. Land use practices often are a combination of agricultural crop growing, and animal and wood production.

There frequently is no clear distinction between a farmer and a nomad, as the people living on marginal lands take into account the local limitations and adopt whatever land use is suitable. However, the delicate balance achieved by the traditional forms of land use is easily upset. A general deterioration of grazing lands in dryland ecosystems is an example of this. A main cause of degradation, often referred to as *desertification*, is overpopulation of people and animals, particularly in semiarid regions, where agricultural crop production and pastoralism become competitive, rather than complementary, forms of land use.

DRYLAND REGIONS OF THE WORLD

One-half of the world's countries have portions or all of their land in dryland environments, including hyperarid, arid, or semiarid zones (Figure 1.3). These lands and their subhumid margins account for 45 million km^2, or approximately one-third of the Earth's surface. It is here where land and environmental degradation is developing at an alarming rate and threatening the livelihood of 850 million inhabitants.

Large areas of drylands are located in North and South America, North Africa, the Sahelian region, Africa south of the equator, the Near East, and Asia and the Pacific. The climatological patterns, soils, vegetation, and major land uses of the countries in these dryland regions suggest the following common features (FAO 1989b).

Extremely dry to dry climates are found between the latitudes of 50° N and 50° S, a broad geographical band within which a wide range of extreme summer and winter temperatures occur, including hot summers and mild winters, hot summers and cold winters, and cool summers and cool winters. Hyperarid zones are located in Saharan Africa, northern and southeastern Saudi Arabia, Ethiopia, and Namibia. Arid and semiarid zones are more widespread, although there is a tendency for them to be found toward the western edges of the tropical and subtropi-

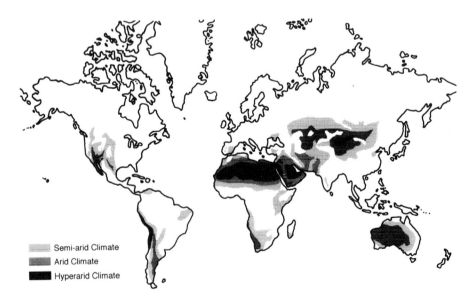

Figure 1.3. Dryland regions of the world (adapted from Dregne 1983)

cal areas of the continental masses, a feature that is marked particularly in southern Africa, the Americas, the Indian subcontinent, and, to some extent, Australia.

Prevailing winds are strong, unhampered by obstacles on the ground, and, as a result, aeolian erosion is common with frequent seasonal occurrences of dust storms. Soils are erodable, poorly structured, high in pH, and low in organic content. Salt deposits and, as mentioned above, salinization are common phenomena. Water from rainfall is lost through high rates of evaporation. Vegetation varies from woodlands and savanna-type woodlands to largely xerophytic, thorny trees and shrubs, through thorny shrubs to often halophytical or succulent steppes. This pattern is common in tropical conditions in all regions, while the vegetation is less thorny in subtropical and temperate conditions.

Populations of people are low in density, and pastoralism is the main agricultural pursuit. Rainfed agriculture is found in some of the more heavily populated semiarid zones, along with a variety of agroforestry practices. Irrigated agriculture, horticulture, and some forestry are practiced in locations where permanent rivers or sources of groundwater are available, for example, in North America, the Near East, and Asia. Wildlife is often a significant but frequently exploited resource.

Major causes of land and environmental degradation, especially desertification, are overgrazing by livestock and wildlife species, shifting agriculture, fuelwood harvesting, and, in the better-vegetated areas, wildfire or deliberate burning to reduce the density of competing vegetation or renew perennial forage species. This degradation is more pronounced in the Indian subcontinent, the Sahel, and in parts of North Africa and the Near East than in other areas, but degradation is noticeable, to some extent, in all of the dryland regions of the world.

FORESTRY IN DRYLAND REGIONS

Forestry in dryland regions, simply stated, is concerned with the management of trees and shrubs for conservation and sustainable development. Forestry in dryland regions differs in many ways from the commercial forestry practiced in moist tropical and other temperate ecosystems (Table 1.1), and, in many instances, its applications are broader in their scope. These applications include production of wood for fuel, poles, and building materials; horticultural practices for fruit and nut production; range management for fodder and forage production; forestry to modify microclimates for improved agricultural crop production; and protection forestry on lands susceptible to water and wind erosion. Many rural people combine these applications of forestry into combinations of land uses linked to their needs and social values. Dryland forestry, therefore, should be defined more broadly as management of trees and shrubs to improve the livelihood and quality of life for rural people in dryland environments. Dryland forestry includes traditional forestry practices, forestry practices unique to dryland environments, horticulture, livestock and wildlife management, and social science applications for analyzing cultural, institutional, and economic constraints and opportunities. It is

TABLE 1.1. Differences in Dryland Forestry and Commercial Forestry in Moist Tropical and Other Temperate Ecosystems

	Dryland Forestry	Commercial Forestry in Moist Tropical and Other Temperate Ecosystems
Purpose of management	Short-term, medium-term, and long-term sustained yield	Medium-term and long-term sustained yield
Management responsibility	Mostly local people, with technical assistance	Centralized (state) organization
Land ownership	Often privately owned, sometimes communal or state lands	Mostly state lands, also plantations in private sector
Areas of production	Mostly relatively small land holdings	Large tracts of land
Mode of production	Subsistence, commercial, or mixed	Largely commercial, occasionally subsistence
Destination of products	Often needs of local people	Country or region
Products	Large variety, not only wood products but also agricultural crops and fodder	Limited number, mostly timber and other commercial wood products

Source: Adapted from Wiersum (1988).

in this diverse context that policy-making must take place if sustainable development of forest resources in dryland systems is to be achieved.

The value of forestry in the dryland regions is difficult to evaluate monetarily or, more generally, economically. Many of the direct benefits from forestry are not derived through a marketplace. Development of reliable sources of fuelwood is one example. Over one-half of the wood that is cut is used as fuel, largely in people's homes. Much of this wood is not bought or sold in a market, but obtained directly from forests, woodlands, or plantations by family members responsible for this task. It is difficult, consequently, to place a monetary value on this wood, although imputed values might be estimated. However, there is little question that this wood can represent a major contribution to and provide a basis for long-term investments in conservation and sustainable development.

CRITICAL PROBLEMS

Practicing forestry on a sustainable basis is a challenge to people in dryland regions. In large part, the purpose of this book is to provide information that helps people solve the problems confronted. Three commonly faced problems are desertification, inadequate knowledge of forestry practices, and low levels of investment.

Desertification

Rapidly spreading desertification of drylands is a problem of worldwide dimensions. To some people, the term *desertification* incorrectly implies that the world's deserts are people-induced (El-Baz 1991). Some people suggest that *land degradation* is a more descriptive term than desertification, in that it better describes the processes of aeolian and fluvial erosion, soil salinization, and loss of vegetative cover. In their opinion, this term also clarifies relationships among climate, topography, soil structure and land use, hydrology, and vegetation in the dryland regions of the world. The more popular and generally recognizable term of *desertification* is deemed appropriate to discussions in this book, however.

The United Nations Environment Program (UNEP) has estimated that 35 million km^2 of the dryland regions of the world, an area approximately the size of both North and South America, are affected by desertification (FAO 1989b). Nearly 20 million km^2 of this area has been classified as being subjected to "high" and "very high" desertification risk. Equally important is the fact that 30,000 km^2 are reduced to a state of "uselessness" every year, a loss that is expected to continue into the future unless remedial actions are taken.

A map of the dryland regions of the world (Figure 1.3), when compared to a world map of desertification (Figure 1.4), shows a close correlation between the drylands and the locations of areas that are likely to be affected by desertification. This correlation is explained largely by the fragile dryland environments undergoing overgrazing by livestock, overcutting of fuelwood, and other excessive uses by people. In addition, the prevailing climate exerts a persistent stress on both soil and vegetative resources. As a result, relatively little disturbance can cause instability and imbalance, leading to desertification. Importantly, desertification is a human problem for people to put right.

Inadequate Knowledge of Forestry Practices

People can confront serious problems in attempting to introduce sustainable forestry into dryland regions because of inadequate knowledge of proper forestry practices. For example, knowledge about the potentials of indigenous tree and shrub species often is inadequate, leading local people to select exotic species to meet their fuelwood, fodder, and other requirements. However, exotic species can be selected that are poorly adapted to the site or that do not meet the needs for which they were intended.

Choosing tree or shrub species for afforestation can be difficult. Forest plantation establishment techniques also frequently are inadequate. There is little knowledge of improvement techniques for the planting stock currently used in forest plantations. Information on the biology and growth rates of plantation species is sparse. Ignorance of the silvicultural prescriptions for the important indigenous and exotic tree and shrub species must be overcome. Agroforestry opportunities and the performance of tree and shrub species to meet these opportunities are not well understood. Solutions to these and other related problems are what largely

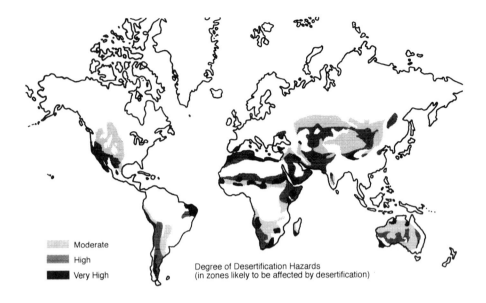

Figure 1.4. Desertification in the world (adapted from the UN 1977)

separates applications of forestry in the dryland regions of the world from forestry practices in the moist tropical and other temperate regions.

Compounding problems of inadequate knowledge of forestry practices is the fact that forestry, when practiced, is constrained by the climate itself. For example, low rainfall and its frequent concentration in a relatively short period must be faced. High temperatures and low relative humidities occur. Poor soils that are either heavily sandy (and, therefore, characterized by low cation exchange and water retention capacity) or are lateric in nature also are encountered. Forestry practiced successfully within these limitations is necessary for conservation and sustainable development in dryland regions.

Inadequate knowledge of forestry practices also translates into inadequate and incomplete technical references and extension services. In turn, it becomes difficult to inform professional foresters and rural people about the proper applications of forestry in dryland regions. This problem is being eliminated, to some extent, in educational and training programs for forests, but it frequently remains in the case of rural people, especially those in developing countries.

Many people have a tradition in agriculture that is not necessarily matched by a similar attitude toward forestry. This lack of appreciation of forestry can be a barrier to the initiation of forestry practices, particularly on marginal agricultural lands. Fortunately, this barrier often can be removed by providing guidance, through the education of people, extension services, and, most of all, by demonstrating the beneficial roles of trees and forests in demonstration plots established on a farmer's land.

Low Levels of Investment

The dryland regions of the world, in general, suffer from a vicious cycle of low productivity, low levels of investment, and, as a result, poverty. Investments, apart from those made for irrigated agricultural production, are relatively low. In The World Bank assistance projects in eastern and southern Africa in the middle 1980s, for example, interventions in areas that were rainfed, with less than 900 mm of rainfall, received only 15 percent of a total of $374 million in loans (Marples 1986). Irrigated areas, in contrast, received 26 percent of the loans, and areas with 900 mm or more of rainfall received 42 percent. Private investments by farmers also is minimal, largely because of the higher risk that is associated with erratic rainfall. This lack of investment has exacerbated the gap in agricultural-related productivity between the rainfed drylands and irrigated and wetter rainfed areas.

Low productivity, low levels of investment, and land degradation in rainfed regions are responsible for regional poverty and income disparities. The poverty and hunger that are prevalent in sub-Saharan Africa is, perhaps, the most poignant example. However, critical conditions are found elsewhere. Improving this situation requires that a variety of technical and institutional problems be solved, chief among them being to increase the levels of investment in appropriate agricultural, forestry, and agroforestry interventions. Others are to design strategies for risk management and implement programs for equitable land distribution and income.

Solutions to these and other critical problems, including the inherent problem of water scarcity, tenure considerations, and ineffective developmental policies, are required if sustainable forestry and, more generally, conservation and the sustainable development of dryland regions is to be achieved. Sustainable development of dryland regions is the topic of the chapters in the following part of this book.

REFERENCES

Armitage, F. B. 1987. *Irrigated forestry in arid and semi-arid lands: A synthesis*. International Development Research Center, Ottawa.

Baumer, M. C., and B. B. Salem. 1985. The arid zone. In FAO. 1985. Sand dune stabilization, shelterbelts and afforestation. *FAO Conservation Guide* 10, Rome, pp. 1–8.

Dregne, H. E. 1983. *Desertification in arid lands*. Harwood Academic Publishers, New York.

El-Baz, F. 1991. Desertification. *Geotimes* 36(2):52–54.

Falloux, F., and A. Mukendi (eds.). 1987. Desertification control and renewable resource management in the Sahelian and Sudanian zones of West Africa. *The World Bank Technical Paper* 70, Washington, D.C.

Food and Agriculture Organization of the United Nations (FAO). 1989a. Arid zone forestry: A guide for field technicians. *FAO Conservation Guide* 20, Rome.

Food and Agriculture Organization of the United Nations (FAO). 1989b. Role of forestry in combating desertification. *FAO Conservation Guide* 21, Rome.

Jackson, I. J. 1989. *Climate, water and agriculture in the tropics.* Longman, Singapore.

McGinnes, W. G. 1988. Climate and biological classifications of arid lands: A comparison. In Whitehead, E. F., C. F. Hutchinson, B. N. Timmermann, and R. G. Varady (eds.). 1988. *Arid lands: Today and tomorrow.* Westview Press, Boulder, Colorado, pp. 61–68.

Marples, S. 1986. Production and investment in marginal areas. In Davis, T. J. (ed.). 1986. *Development of rainfed agriculture under arid and semiarid conditions.* The World Bank, Washington, D.C., p. 87.

Salem, B. B. 1988. A strategy on the role of forestry in combating desertification. In Whitehead, E. F., C. F. Hutchinson, B. N. Timmermann, and R. G. Varady (eds.). 1988. *Arid lands: Today and tomorrow.* Westview Press, Boulder, Colorado, pp. 841–49.

United Nations (UN). 1977. *World map of desertification at a scale of 1:25000000.* United Nations Conference on Desertification, Nairobi, Kenya.

Went, F. W. 1955. The ecology of desert plants. *Scientific American* 192(4):68–75.

Wiersum, K. F. 1988. Outline of the agroforestry concept. In Wiersum, K. F. (ed.). 1988. *Viewpoints on agroforestry.* Agricultural University Wageningen, Netherlands, pp. 1–26.

PART I

Sustainable Development of Dryland Regions

2 Livestock Production and Management of Grazing Lands

Livestock production is a natural element of many dryland regions and a traditional land use of many societies. However, desertification can be accelerated where overgrazing occurs. Improvement of livestock grazing practices in these overgrazed areas, therefore, frequently is recommended, although these improvement measures must be acceptable to the herdsmen's way of life. It also is important that livestock grazing practices are compatible with other land uses, including agricultural crop production and forestry. To better understand the methods of livestock production and management of grazing lands, this chapter discusses the importance of proper grazing land use, grazing management, livestock nutrition, range improvement, and livestock improvement.

Underlying concepts of the methods of achieving sound management of grazing lands falls within the realm of *range management*. This term and other related terms are defined below. To place this chapter in a proper perspective, it also is helpful to look briefly at grazing lands that occur in some of the dryland regions of the world and to consider the types of management, problems, and opportunities that exist on these lands.

DEFINITIONS

Definitions of terms that relate to range management are presented as a starting point in this chapter (Holechek et al. 1989, Society for Range Management 1974). *Range management* is the manipulation of natural resources on rangelands to provide optimum combinations of goods and services for people on a sustained basis. It is based upon ecological principles and deals with husbandry of rangelands and range resources. *Rangelands* are areas on which native vegetation is predominantly herbaceous and woody plants suitable for grazing and browsing by domesticated livestock and wildlife and areas that are unsuitable for agricultural cultivation. *Pasturelands* also are grazing and browsing lands but differ from rangelands in that they usually are fenced and require periodic cultivation to maintain mostly introduced forage species and, sometimes, such agronomical inputs as fertilizers or irrigation water. *Forage* includes all of the herbaceous and woody plants that are available to grazing and browsing animals. *Grazing* is the consumption of forage, mostly grasses and forbs, by livestock or wildlife, while *browsing* is consumption of edible foliage and twigs from woody plants.

Stocking rate is the amount of land allocated to each animal unit for a grazing period. An *animal unit* is one mature (450 kg) cow or the equivalent, based upon an average daily forage consumption of 12 kg dry matter. *Proper* stocking refers to placing the correct number of animals in an area to achieve proper use at the end of a specified grazing period. *Proper use*, in turn, refers to the amount and timing of forage use of the current year's growth, which can maintain or improve the range condition, as long as the conservation of other resources is continued. *Range condition* refers to the current productivity of a rangeland in relation to what the rangeland is capable of producing naturally. *Range trend* expresses the direction of change in the range condition, that is, whether the rangeland is improving, remaining in the same condition, or declining.

Overstocking is placing too many animals on an area so that overuse will occur if allowed to continue through a planned grazing period. *Overuse* is the utilization of an excessive amount of the current year's forage growth. *Overgrazing* is continued overuse that will result in a deteriorated range condition. Overgrazing can be devastating to drylands and is a leading cause of desertification.

GRAZING LANDS IN DRYLAND REGIONS

Grazing lands, including rangelands and pasturelands, are found in deserts, grasslands, shrublands, and open forests and woodlands that support livestock and wildlife herbivores. Grazing lands also are derived after loss or removal of trees and shrubs, and on lands where agricultural cultivation has been abandoned. Grazing often occurs in combination with agricultural and forest crops in what is known generally as *agroforestry*, a topic to be discussed in detail in Chapter 16. It is not surprising, therefore, that grazing lands are diverse in terms of their potential to produce livestock and that the management of these lands also is varied, as can be illustrated in the southwestern United States, southern margins of the Sahara, and Australia.

Southwestern United States

Rangelands in the southwestern United States, while seemingly limitless, are fragile, easily damaged by improper use, and subject to droughts. The original vegetation on large portions of these lands was depleted by a combination of these factors (Herbel 1979). Vegetation on some of these lands has been improved in recent years through seeding of forage species, controlling undesirable plants, and implementing grazing systems that are more compatible to the biological capacities of the lands to sustain livestock production, principally cattle. Sometimes, sheep or goats are mixed with cattle to better utilize all of the classes of forage.

Grazing of livestock occurs in practically all elevational zones in the southwestern United States, but it is a dominant form of land use in the lower elevations of Arizona, New Mexico, western Texas, and the eastern portions of grasslands in Texas and Oklahoma. Much of Arizona and New Mexico is controlled federally and leased to private ranchers to graze livestock. Maximum production of forage and, as a consequence, livestock is not the only consideration in the management of public lands, however. Concern about aesthetics, destruction of wildlife habitats, and the balance of nature, at times, has been enough to restrict many projects to improve the grazing capacities of these lands. Environmental impact statements often must be prepared before improvement practices are initiated.

Concern for multiple benefits also limits management options to some extent on privately controlled grazing lands in the region (Martin 1975). However, with increasing demands for food throughout the world, increasing efforts are placed on the production of meat from lands not suitable for agricultural cultivation. The challenge, therefore, is to attain a proper balance among the biological limitations of a site, need for multiple use management on these lands, and increasing demands of consumers.

Southern Margins of the Sahara

Land use along the southern margins of the Sahara, a region commonly referred to as the "Sahel," is dependent entirely upon the vagaries of climate. In most years, rainfall is too low for the production of agricultural crops. In the southern wetter areas, it occasionally is possible to grow cash crops, although more commonly agricultural crops are restricted to sites that receive runoff of water from adjacent areas (Wickens and White 1979). Many of the people in the Sahel are pastoralists, however, which has a bearing on the present way of life in the area. These people, to survive, generally accept neither political nor geophysical boundaries and move with the rains to locate forage for their animals. Important livestock include camels, sheep, goats, cattle for human consumption, and horses and donkeys as beasts of burden.

There are three general systems of livestock management practiced in the Sahel, *sedentary, transhumance*, and *nomadic*. Livestock are kept at a permanent site throughout a year with sedentary systems. The number of animals is limited to the capacity of the grazing land to support livestock in the dry season. Should this number be exceeded, surplus livestock usually is placed in the care of a migratory herdsman belonging to either the owner's family or a traditionally nomadic tribe. The transhumance system also contains a permanent base, but the number of livestock and environmental conditions are such that a part of the annual forage resource is obtained elsewhere. The nomadic system has no permanent base and the herdsmen move freely in search of the best forage for their livestock. Changing conditions can induce individual herdsmen to change from one system to another, sometimes for short-term management considerations.

The principle of seasonal use of natural forage, regardless of the grazing system, is a guideline in the Sahel. Providing that stocking rates are within the grazing capacities of the land, application of this principle helps in obtaining maximum utilization with minimum environmental damage. Governments tend to disapprove of this approach because of difficulties in administration. Nevertheless, as a strategy of livestock production and management of grazing lands in the Sahel, it likely is the best.

Australia

Australia's drylands cover the vast central area of the continent, comprising nearly 70 percent of the total land surface of the country. Grazing lands in Australia are managed on a different basis than those in most of the other dryland regions of the world. Livestock enterprises are geared largely to monetary export, market-oriented systems, contrasting with subsistence systems in many dryland regions of the developing world (Wilson and Graetz 1979). Secondly, the livestock industry is organized on a sedentary basis. Individual units of this pastoral system are sheep or cattle "stations," which are leased from the state on a 35- to 40-year tenure and managed by one family. The size of these units vary from 25,000 to 100,000 ha. Interchange of sheep and cattle is limited largely by the climate, standard of fencing, supply of water, and expertise initially adopted in that area of Australia.

Management practices differ greatly among the major types of grazing lands in Australia. In the northern woodlands, for example, no form of grazing management is invoked, although a natural rotation occurs through grazing of these woodlands in the wet season and other lands in the dry season. These areas are grazed solely by cattle at relatively low intensities because of the low productivity and nutritive value of the forage. Continuous, yearlong grazing of sheep is practiced in most of the shrub woodlands, with some movement of sheep when lambs are weaned. The reduction of trees and shrubs to increase forage production and the control of erosion are the principal problems of vegetation management in the shrub woodland type. The arid woodlands are grazed almost entirely by sheep at a number restricted to that which can be carried safely in 3 out of 4 years. Control of sheep numbers is a principal management strategy, along with a provision of constructing livestock watering points.

Traditionally, sheep have grazed in the chenopod shrublands, also referred to as "saltbush" and "bluebush" country, although cattle numbers have increased in recent years. Some of these areas were degraded historically through overgrazing, a situation that is being "corrected" by conservative stocking of livestock with periodic adjustments according to forage availability. In the *Acacia* shrublands, also employed for the production of sheep and, to a lesser extent, cattle, careful management of tree and shrub densities is necessary in ensuring a balance between the woody and herbaceous strata; components of this strata are both important in furnishing fodder and forage to livestock. Management plans call for the restriction of livestock numbers when necessary, protection of sites from grazing in periods of shrub regeneration, and seeding by desirable perennial grasses. The tussock and hummock grasslands are both treeless communities, or almost so. These grasslands are grazed mostly by sheep, with the numbers controlled to coincide to the grazing capacities of the land. This latter point is the focus of management and livestock production throughout Australia, as it should be on grazing lands in dryland regions everywhere.

PROPER USE OF GRAZING LANDS

Grazing lands, particularly rangelands, are crucial for human subsistence, livestock production, and wildlife habitats. It is not surprising, therefore, that to obtain maximum grazing land benefits, multiple values should be developed concurrently to attain maximum grazing land benefits. Even when only grazing of livestock is emphasized, impacts on other values also must be considered. Otherwise, there can be unwanted effects.

The following sections explain some of the relationships of plants and grazing animals, providing a background to fundamental concepts of range management.

Plant Growth and Utilization

Plants are the focus of range management. For sustained use, the correct number of grazing animals must be balanced with available forage resources. To achieve this balance and, in doing so, properly manage grazing on rangelands, an understanding of plant physiology, morphology, and ecology is required. Forage plants are *primary producers*; that is, these plants synthesize food from sunlight at rates determined largely by their leaf surface areas and water availability to the plants. Soil nutrients, temperature, and physiological efficiencies of plants also are important.

Livestock, in turn, are *secondary producers*, since their productivity is determined by the rate at which energy is accumulated by plants and then converted into animal products. Maximum productivity of a grazing land is achieved by maximizing intakes of forage plants by livestock. However, plants are complex organisms that respond to grazing and a number of interrelated environmental factors and perturbations according to their genetic makeup. These relationships must be understood to develop appropriate management strategies for rangeland resources.

Grazing Influences on Plants   Plants grow by synthesizing their requirements from substances that are removed from the air and soil. Plant tissues, largely comprised of carbohydrates, fats, and protein, contain *enzymes* necessary for the functioning of tissue components. These enzymes are built of proteins containing nitrogen, phosphates, and sulfur, with specific minerals and other elements. Plants also build tissues for support and protection. These tissues are comprised mostly of cellulose, polysaccharides, and lignin. Additionally, plants synthesize sugars as energy reserves. Oils and proteins are accumulated for the same reason.

Nutrients are transported within a plant to maintain the necessary constructional and biochemical processes for growth. The fluid in which this transport takes place is essentially water, one of many roles of water in plant metabolism and growth.

Storage of food reserves, largely carbohydrates, is essential to plant survival in periods of dormancy, and to ensure that plants can grow and reproduce following dormancy. In general, food reserves are stored in the roots and stem bases of perennial herbaceous plants, roots and stems of woody plants, and seeds of annual plants.

Grazing reduces leaf areas of plants, at least temporarily, but the overall impact of grazing on plants depends largely upon the extent to which carbohydrate reserves are affected. The timing of grazing is important, with two periods being crucial—the period of active plant reproduction and the initial period of carbohydrate storage. Little is known about the critical levels of carbohydrate reserves that are necessary for most forage plants, although it is known that plant species vary greatly in their response to grazing. Responses to grazing are related to the phenology and morphology of plants, environmental conditions, and level of grazing.

Grasses respond differently to grazing than woody plants do, largely because of differences in the locations of meristematic tissue. Meristematic tissue in grasses is located at the base of stems, often close to the soil surface. In contrast, woody plants have meristematic tissue, or buds, at the ends of branches and, therefore, elevated above the soil surface, making them more susceptible to grazing. Appropriate levels of grazing on woody plants can stimulate lateral growth and increase forage production at the same time, however.

Methods of reproduction also affect responses of plants to grazing. Plants that reproduce by seeds, including most grasses and forbs, can recover from grazing, drought, and other disturbances if allowed to produce seeds. Annual plants reproduce only by seeds, which allows them to survive overgrazing and drought, and initiate growth when temperature and soil moisture are adequate. Repetitive overgrazing prevents grasses from producing seeds and, as a consequence, reduces plant productivity. However, seeds from some grass species remain viable for 10 years or more.

Some plants reproduce vegetatively by *rhizomes*, which are underground stems, or *stolons*, which are aboveground stems. Plants with rhizomes are more resistant to grazing and mechanical injury and, furthermore, able to store more carbohydrates than can be stored in seeds. These plants, therefore, have a competitive advantage over seedlings in early periods of growth and can respond more quickly to improved soil moisture conditions following dormancy.

Defoliation of plants by grazing early in a growing season is less injurious to plants than grazing late in a growing season. As a result, the timing of cessation of grazing often is more important than when grazing is initiated. In all situations, the greatest effects on the physiology of plants occur when the plants are under stress, for example, during droughts (Holechek et al. 1989, Pratt and Gwynne 1977).

Adaptations of Forage Plants   Forage plants on rangelands are subject to drought, fire, and defoliation by livestock. Various physiological and anatomical adaptations enable some of these plants to survive these influences. Plants adapt to water shortages by either evading a drought or resisting its effects. Evasion of drought can be achieved by annual plants completing their life cycles in a period of available water supply and passing the dry periods in seed form. Some perennials survive a drought by conserving water in an abundance of fibrous tissue. Many drought-resistant plants have large root systems that allow a sufficient intake of water when little is available. Some plants can regulate transpiration by restricting the size of their stomata. In other plants, the stomata are sunk into pits filled with hairs that slow air movement and reduce evaporation.

Most forage plants tolerate infrequent fires but vary in their response to repeated burning. Grasses and grasslike plants are less affected by fire than are woody plants, attributed in part to the protected location of their growing points. Despite their relative fire tolerance, however, grasses can be susceptible to damage in early stages of growth. Attributes of woody plants that lead to a resistance to fire include thickness of bark, size of root system, nature of regrowth, and degree of combustibility of stems. Fire can stimulate sprouting in many plants, ensuring their survival after burning.

Perennial grasses are susceptible to defoliation by livestock, but they are adapted to this situation because of the position of their growing points near the ground. Some grass species effectively resist defoliation by grazing because of the spiky nature of their leaves. It is not clear whether these adaptations are a response to grazing or drought, however.

Defoliation of Forage Plants by Livestock

Defoliation of forage plants by livestock has several effects. If grazing is allowed either too early in the growing season or too frequently throughout the grazing period, it lowers the production of dry matter by reducing the leaf areas and light interception, resulting in lower plant growth rates. However, sometimes defoliation can increase the rate of production. For maximum forage production, the leaf areas should be maintained close to the optimum throughout the growing season, which is achieved by avoiding severe defoliation and allowing livestock to graze the excess growth as it accumulates. There are exceptions, however. When a forage plant shifts from vegetative to reproductive development, intense grazing can prevent formation of flowering shoots, promoting further growth of leaves and production of secondary branches. Consequently, heavy grazing of forage plants can serve to substantially increase the production of dry matter for a time over extended grazing periods. However, there is a limit to which any plant can be grazed and still survive.

Information is needed about the percentages of foliage than can be removed from important forage plants without causing overuse and a reduction in range condition in order to determine the proper use of a rangeland. Proper use, or the *percent allowable use*, indicates the percentage of foliage that can be removed during a grazing period without damaging the forage plants. These values usually are determined through clipping and grazing trials, in which vegetative responses are monitored under different intensities of defoliation until thresholds of overuse are identified (Holechek et al. 1989, Pratt and Gwynne 1977, Stoddart et al. 1975).

Proper use factors vary with the forage species, season, climatological factors, associated plant species, type of livestock, and past grazing history. Therefore, once established for important forage species, proper use factors should be used only as guides to be altered as conditions change. In general, the drier the climate, the lower the proper use factors. Examples of proper use factors for important forage species vary from 25 to 35 percent in the southwestern United States to 35 to 45 percent in higher rainfall areas of the short-grass prairie of the central United States.

Competition is inevitable when livestock of different types that have similar diets graze a particular area. This competition increases as the number of livestock on the area increases, especially if the same type of livestock is involved. However, different types of livestock have different preferences for forage plants. Cattle, horses, and donkeys are more adapted to a grass diet, while sheep and goats utilize more forbs and shrubs, particularly when grass production is limited.

Competition also is present when livestock are introduced onto an area occupied by wildlife species, where feeding habitats and nutritional requirements of the livestock and wildlife are similar (Holechek et al. 1989, Heady and Heady 1982, Pratt and Gwynne 1977). Competition between livestock and wildlife is species specific and varies with the area, season, and kinds of plants that exist on the area. Some wildlife species avoid areas grazed by livestock. In some regions, for example, the savannas of Africa, indigenous wildlife species have developed feeding habitats that allow for a variety of animals to graze and browse together with little competition. Some animals graze or browse only certain plants, often at different heights or during different periods of time. Furthermore, animals with specialized feeding habitats can reduce plant densities of specific forage plants, which can reduce plant competition in general and favor the growth and development of other plants that provide suitable forage for other types of animals.

Condition and Trend of Grazing Lands

The concept of range condition serves to integrate the responses of a grazing land to management into one measure. It is an "index" of whether the principles of good range management and improvement have been applied properly. As defined above, *range condition* is the state of health of the rangeland, based largely upon what that grazing land is capable of producing naturally. Condition is expressed, somewhat arbitrarily, from excellent to poor. *Range trend*, on the other hand, is the direction of the change in rangeland condition. Trend is described as improving, stable, or deteriorating. Both of these definitions imply that an assessment of the rangeland is made at a specific point in time and in relation to a predetermined standard (Holechek et al. 1989, Pratt and Gwynne 1977, Stoddart et al. 1975).

A judgment of range condition is an appraisal of the difference between current plant cover and the plant cover required for the highest sustained level of productivity attainable under the prevailing ecological site conditions and best range management practices. In applying the concept of range condition, it is assumed that there is an "optimum" plant cover for the site. However, the nature of the optimum condition often is uncertain, especially on rangelands that have suffered long-term grazing misuse. In citing a standard of comparison, one should state whether this standard is known or assumed. Criteria to consider in the assessment of grazing land condition and trend include:

- *Ground cover*—herbaceous plant density, species composition, vigor, and litter accumulation.
- *Shrub and tree cover*—the above factors, and relative height and age measures.
- *Forage value*—nutritive value, bulk, seasonal variations, potential level of productivity, and palatability.
- *Soil features*—depth of soil, texture and structure, extent of erosion, nutrient status, microbial activity, and infiltrative properties.

Criteria reflecting the health and performance of livestock, degree of grazing and browsing, and presence of pests (e.g., the tsetse fly) also are important (Pratt and Gwynne 1977). All of these criteria should be evaluated together, as they all can affect the productivity of a rangeland ecosystem.

At times, assessments of range condition and trend are based upon the occurrence and productivity of *key forage species*, which are forage species that are palatable, nutritious, and abundant under conditions of "good" range management (Stoddart et al. 1975). When this is the case, careful selection of the key forage species is important. A plant should be considered on its own merits and not necessarily on the placement of the forage species in a successional hierarchy. What matters is productivity, persistence, palatability, and cover.

Methods of Measurement

Earlier methods of measuring range condition and trend placed an emphasis on the successional status of a rangeland. These methods express condition as a departure from a *climax vegetative type*. The climax approaches to measuring range condition assume that a climax or near-climax status represents an "excellent" range condition. Dyksterhuis (1949) classified rangeland vegetation by the climax approach, grouping plants according to their responses to grazing. His approach is based upon the fact that overgrazing results in a somewhat orderly and predictable change in composition of plant species on a rangeland subjected to continued "heavy" grazing pressure. Plants were grouped into three categories, *decreasers*, *increasers*, and *invaders*, with the relative percentages of plants in each category then used to classify range condition (Figure 2.1).

One problem with the climax approaches is the prerequisite of knowing and recognizing the climax vegetative type, a requirement that frequently is impossible to meet. This situation is particularly the case in dryland regions of the world that have undergone overgrazing for decades and even centuries. The potentials of these sites and climax vegetation that might exist if the sites are properly managed are difficult, if not impossible, to determine.

Site-potential approaches to measuring range condition emphasize potential forage production (Holechek et al. 1989, Pratt and Gwynne 1977, Stoddart et al. 1975). Criteria for classification are the contributions of key species to forage pro-

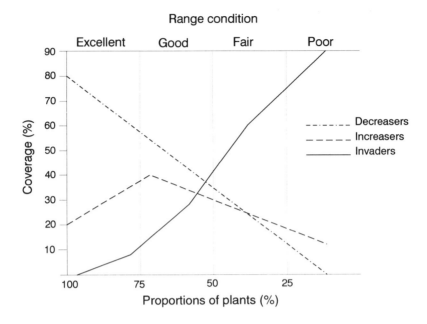

Figure 2.1. Percentages of decreasers, increasers, and invaders in Texas (adapted from Dyksterhuis 1949, by permission of the Society for Range Management)

duction on the site, plant vigor, litter accumulation, and occurrence of soil erosion. Range condition is determined by the value of the specific forage species becoming established, vigor of the more valued forage species, accumulation of litter, extent of soil erosion, and degree of forage utilization by the livestock. Arbitrarily, a range is considered to be in excellent condition when it has 75 percent or more of the possible forage production and in poor condition when the possible forage production is less than 25 percent. One advantage of this approach is that forage species are weighed in terms of their values to the site. However, a misjudgment of the ecological significance of the forage species can lead to errors in classification.

Other methods to classify range condition and trend incorporate the notion of measuring occurrences of forage species found in the early stages of succession and, therefore, can be indicative of prolonged misuse or drought. Some methods are based upon contributions of "desirable" and "undesirable" forage species, soil cover, and erosion condition (Example 2.1). There are methods that involve botanical analysis and an examination of soil resources on established sampling transects. From these measurements, an assessment is made of range condition and trend; that is, whether the land is improving, stable, or deteriorating. Regardless of the approach, the measurement of grazing land condition and trend should encompass the following principles (Pratt and Gwynne 1977):

- *Accuracy*—to facilitate a correct classification of range condition and trend 90 percent of the time, for example.
- *Flexibility*—to allow for an adjustment due to the kind of livestock present on the rangeland.
- *Rapidity*—to permit an evaluation of extensive rangeland areas in a relatively short period of time.
- On-site decision making.
- Statistical validity.
- A basis in ecological principles.

Example 2.1

USDA Forest Service Method for Determining Range Condition (USDA Forest Service 1969) The USDA Forest Service bases range condition on a numerical rating for vegetal composition, plant production, ground cover, and soil erosion. Vegetal composition is assigned a value from 0 to 60 points and classified as desirable, intermediate, or least desirable, based upon plant lists for specific rangeland areas. Plant production is evaluated by values between 0 and 40 points, with rangelands of high production given the highest values. Points for vegetal composition and plant production are summed to provide a vegetative rating, the maximum rating being 100 points.

Percentage of ground cover and soil erosion are evaluated individually and assigned values from 0 to 50 each. These values then are summed to obtain a soil rating, the maximum rating once again being 100 points. Point totals for either vegetation or soil are related to range condition as follows:

Points	Condition
81–100	Excellent
61–80	Good
41–60	Fair
21–40	Poor
< 21	Very poor

It is possible to derive different ratings for vegetation and soil. In these cases, the lower classification usually is used.

GRAZING MANAGEMENT

While grazing management furnishes the means for economic exploitation of a rangeland, improper grazing management can lead to its destruction. In properly implemented grazing management practices, livestock are manipulated to meet a designated purpose (e.g., production of meat) and in a manner that does not impact other land uses adversely. In general terms, the objective of grazing management is to achieve the maximum level of livestock production that, simultaneously, is commensurate to maintaining or improving the condition of the rangeland. The management of rangelands to achieve proper use by livestock should be aimed at the following:

- Rangelands should be stocked with the proper number of animal units.
- Grazing should be permitted only during the proper season.
- Grazing animals should be distributed appropriately on a rangeland.
- Rangelands should be stocked with the kind of animals that are best suited to the particular range.

Variables of Importance

Grazing management is implemented through the alteration of one or more of four variables, the species or type of livestock, number of livestock, distribution of livestock, and season of grazing. Knowledge of plant physiology, ecology of vegetative communities, and different species and types of livestock, their feeding habitats, and dietary requirements are all needed to properly manage rangelands.

Most rangelands can accommodate more than one type of animal, whether they are domesticated livestock or wildlife. The production of animal products and, consequently, a higher economic return often is attained by grazing more than one type of livestock or combining management of livestock and wildlife species (Holechek et al. 1989, Pratt and Gwynne 1977). This form of grazing is referred to as *mixed grazing* or *common use*. For example, inclusion of sheep or goats with cattle, while complicating management procedures, can increase livestock production without adversely impacting rangeland ecosystems (Example 2.2). In doing so, a better distribution of animals can be achieved on a rangeland, resulting in a more uniform use and increased utilization of available forage species.

Example 2.2

Mixed Grazing in Botswana: Improving Livestock Production by Combining Goats and Cattle (McLeod 1990) Introduction of goats and other small livestock into cattle operations can improve farmer's incomes, and can help to reduce overgrazing and soil erosion during periods of drought. In years with abundant rainfall and forage, goats and cattle are complementary in their grazing habitats. Cattle graze on grasses and forbs, and goats browse woody plants, allowing higher stocking rates than would be possible with only cattle.

During periods of drought, cattle overgraze rangelands, resulting in goats and cattle becoming more competitive because cattle are forced to eat more woody plants. Shrubs are less nutritious for cattle, which do not fare well on a diet of woody plants. In years of drought, thorny *Acacia* species, which are more drought resistant than grasses and forbs, provide considerable forage. As a result, farmers substitute goats for cattle and, consequently, increase their revenues in comparison to what they can achieve with cattle only during droughts. It also is suggested that heavy browsing of shrub species can help improve grass production indirectly, because shrub competition with grasses is reduced. Once the rains return, densities of shrubs are reduced, allowing grasses to better compete for soil moisture and nutrients.

The appropriate combinations of grazing animals on a rangeland are determined largely by the vegetative types present, topography, conditions of the rangeland, and economic requirements. From a standpoint of economics, cash flows sometimes can be increased by producing a variety of animal products, such as meat, milk, wool, or combinations thereof. Furthermore, the risks to farmers and herdsmen are reduced by diversifying production in this manner.

Stocking Rate

There is a limit to the number of livestock that a particular rangeland can support, regardless of the species, types, or combinations thereof. Overstocking should be avoided in most instances. When continued for a long period of time, overstocking likely will lead to overgrazing and rangeland deterioration. On the other hand, understocking reduces the productivity of a rangeland. Therefore, the initial task in properly implementing grazing management practices is to determine the *stocking rate*, and, if this stocking rate is deemed correct in the long run, the second task is to maintain this stocking rate on the rangeland in question (Holechek et al. 1989, Stoddart et al. 1975). In many situations, adjustments in stocking rates are required throughout long-term grazing periods, according to seasonal conditions and changes in the vegetative and animal types as the grazing land responds to the influence of grazing.

Maintaining proper stocking rates is difficult during periods of drought. How vegetative cover and, therefore, stocking rates are affected by drought is illustrated in Figure 2.2. To avoid overgrazing, stocking rates theoretically should be aimed at levels that are appropriate for periods in which forage is limited. Achieving these levels presents a managerial problem on most rangelands, largely because there is limited flexibility in grazing systems to allow for meaningful changes in stocking levels from year to year.

Initial stocking rates are calculated by analyzing the requirements of livestock along with the availability of dry matter and nutrient content of forage for the proposed grazing period. Competitive use of forage by wildlife also must be considered. The emphasis here is that these are initial approximations of stocking rates only. In practice, the response of a rangeland to an initially calculated stocking rate should be observed for a number of years and the stocking rate then should be

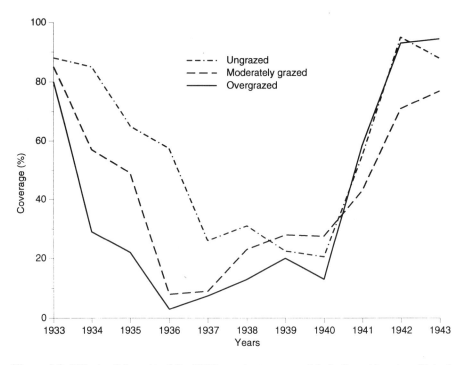

Figure 2.2. Effects of drought of the 1930s on short-grass prairie in the midwestern United States (adapted from Branson 1985, by permission of the Society for Range Management)

adjusted so that overgrazing does not occur. This adjusted stocking rate is the *carrying capacity* of the rangeland. A compromise between stocking rates in both "good" and "bad" years, weighed in favor of bad years, is chosen as the "best" estimate of stocking rate in most situations (Figure 2.3).

An initial estimate of carrying capacity is determined from the following equation for stocking rate:

$$\text{Stocking Rate} = \frac{(\text{Forage Production})\,(\text{Forage Utilization})}{\text{Forage Requirement}} \qquad (2.1)$$

To solve equation (2.1), estimates of forage production are required, the amount of forage to be utilized is specified by the manager to meet a managerial goal, and the forage requirement to support livestock must be known. Forage requirements vary with the species and type of livestock. A common approximation of the daily dry matter requirements for cattle is 2 percent of the body weight of the animal (Holechek et al. 1989, Stoddart et al. 1975). Horses and donkeys have a 50 percent higher requirement, and it frequently is assumed that between 5 and 7 sheep are equivalent to 1 animal unit.

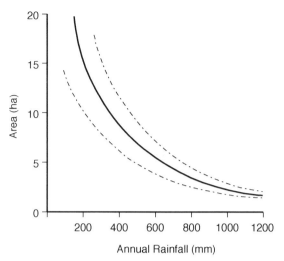

Figure 2.3. Area required to support livestock decreases with increasing annual precipitation, as illustrated on a natural grassland in East Africa (adapted from Pratt and Gwynne 1977)

Clipped sample plots, 1 m on a side, can be used to determine the weight of the standing herbaceous biomass, a measure of forage production. With this plot size, the forage weight in grams, when multiplied by 10, is converted to kilograms per hectare. Since clipped-plot samples are expensive and time-consuming to obtain, they often are employed with ocular estimates in a system of double sampling (Wilm et al. 1944). Forage utilization—the amount of forage that livestock are "allowed" to eat—is specified by the manager of the grazing land. The forage requirement—the amount of forage required to sustain the livestock—is obtained from studies.

Determining the carrying capacity for a rangeland is a difficult task because:

- Steep topography and distribution of water affect animal distributions on the rangeland, which, in turn, require that initial stocking rates be adjusted.
- The amount of forage produced in a year varies greatly with changes in rainfall patterns from year to year.
- Timing of forage removal affects the number of animals that are appropriate.
- Forage competition between grazing and browsing animals often is not quantified.
- Utilization of forage by small mammals and insects needs to be considered.

Determining carrying capacities of rangelands in dryland regions is particularly difficult because of the relatively large changes in forage production from year to year and the severe effects that drought has on forage production. Stocking rates should be flexible, so that the number of livestock can be decreased during dry periods and droughts and increased during wet periods and "favorable" conditions. Livestock owners often do not have this flexibility, unfortunately. The choices then become one of either overstocking during dry periods and drought or understocking during wet periods and favorable conditions.

It is through the control of movements, concentrations, and removal of livestock to achieve proper distributions of livestock that range management is practiced in dryland regions (Holechek et al. 1989, Stoddart et al. 1975). Proper distributions of animals on a rangeland to improve overall livestock production can be accomplished by:

- Distributions of salt blocks and mineral licks in different parts of a rangeland to encourage animal use in areas away from water.
- Development of water in areas where water limits animal use of available forage resources.
- Herding of animals, in which animals are moved to more effectively utilize forage without overgrazing portions of the rangeland.
- Use of fences.

Controlling the distributions of livestock and the timing and duration of range use are achieved within the framework of the grazing system used. Therefore, implementation of planned grazing systems is largely the basis for attaining proper distributions of livestock and, therefore, proper range management.

Grazing Systems

Grazing systems should be planned to restore the vigor of forage plants, allow "key" forage plants to produce seeds, allow for heavier use of a rangeland through more appropriate distributions of livestock, and increase the production of animal products (Child et al. 1987, Holechek et al. 1989, Stoddart et al. 1975, Vallentine 1990). In general, grazing systems fall into four main categories, namely, *continuous systems*, *seasonal systems*, *rotational systems*, and *balanced rotational systems*.

Continuous Systems As the name implies, in continuous grazing systems, livestock are kept on one area of land, on which they are allowed to freely move and graze. The distribution of livestock is "controlled" through the placement of salt blocks and mineral licks, and opening and closing of stock tanks, boreholes, and other water supplies. Unless they are confined by herding, livestock often adapt a form of rotational grazing on grazing lands with periodical shortages of water. Dry-season and wet-season grazing patterns can develop as separate entities. Continuous grazing in the absence of proper planning frequently leads to problems of overgrazing.

Seasonal Systems Livestock are confined to one area in the dry season and to another area in the wet season in seasonal grazing systems. A feature of these systems is that one area of land is grazed at the same time each year. Rangelands that typically suffer misuse are those which are grazed regularly in the wet season. Therefore, a seasonal grazing season is acceptable only when the wet-season grazing area is large in relation to the size of the dry-season grazing area and number of livestock.

Rotational Systems   The total area to be grazed is divided into a number of blocks in rotational grazing systems. These blocks are grazed separately in the order that seems appropriate. Grazing is rationed out in a "functional" manner, keeping the best forage for the most productive livestock. However, unless the systems are monitored, some of the blocks can be overused and others wasted. When grazing is proportioned equally among the blocks, the result is a balanced rotation.

Balanced Rotational Systems   In balanced rotational grazing systems, also referred to as *deferred rotational grazing systems*, a period of deferment is applied to each block, with successive grazing periods in a block deferred so that grazings take place at different times of the year (Figure 2.4). Each block is grazed for an equal period during a grazing season, which normally is 12 months on grazing lands in dryland regions. There are many variations of balanced rotational grazing systems, with selection of grazing cycle among the blocks determined largely by the condition of the grazing land, species and type of livestock, and rangeland management objectives.

The main reasons for the periods of grazing deferment in rotational and balanced rotational systems is to allow a buildup of food reserves in forage species and plants to set seeds. Under good grazing conditions, a deferred period of 1 year in 4 is sufficient. However, more frequent deferments (e.g., in alternate years) can be necessary on overgrazed lands. The durations of deferments are determined by the pattern of grazing and deferment. Typically, periods of from 3 to 4 months are set aside for resting of the grazing land. Regardless of their frequency and duration, to be effective, deferred periods should include a portion of the growing season for the forage plants.

The number of blocks into which a rangeland is divided in rotational and balanced rotational grazing systems is determined largely by the condition of the rangeland and availability of water. The blocks should have similar carrying capacities. Otherwise, livestock may rotate too quickly for proper periods of rest to be incorporated into the systems. Grazing systems of 4 or 5 blocks characterize situations with one rainy season in the year. Some form of compromise, taking into account the availability of water, condition of the grazing land, and species or type of livestock, is necessary in determining the number of blocks.

Other Systems   Other grazing systems also can be designed to satisfy specific objectives. Designing other grazing systems involves determining the frequency and duration of the periods of grazing and deferment, requirements for reserve grazing, and number of blocks to be delineated in systems derived largely from rotational and balanced rotational systems (Pratt and Gwynne 1977, Vallentine

Block	Year 1			Year 2			Year 3			Year 4		
	J-A	M-A	S-D	J-A	M-A	S-D	J-A	M-A	S-D	J-A	M-A	S-D
I	G			G					G			
II		G				G				G		
III			G				G				G	
IV				G				G				G

Figure 2.4. A four-block balanced rotational grazing system, showing the movement of livestock as each block is grazed in turn (G) for a period of 4 months. The complete cycle lasts 4 years, and then is repeated (adapted from Pratt and Gwynne 1977)

1990). The extent of flexibility that can be exercised in the management of the grazing systems also should be known. To a large extent, design of other grazing systems is based upon the four categories described above.

One other type of grazing warrants specific mention. *Short-duration grazing systems*, of which the "Savory grazing method" is one version (Savory 1983), involves essentially an overstocking of livestock on small pastures or paddocks, but then moving the livestock quickly before overgrazing occurs. Each area is grazed by livestock for a few days, after which it receives several weeks of nonuse. It is claimed that stocking rates can be increased by this method, and that this method emulates the patterns of grazing that were prevalent on bison ranges in North America and big-game rangelands of Africa. Although short-duration grazing systems have been controversial, they do result in a more uniform use of forage. However, some authorities have stated that the heavy concentrations of livestock can compact the soil and, as a consequence, result in reduced rainfall infiltration (Pluhar et al. 1987, Weltz and Wood 1986). Prior to adopting short duration or any other kind of new grazing system, it is recommended that the grazing systems be tested on a small scale or pilot study basis before applying them to large rangelands.

Other Considerations

Riparian ecosystems—the transition lands between aquatic and adjacent terrestrial ecosystems—require special care and planning when they are grazed by livestock. On many rangelands, riparian ecosystems (to be discussed in detail in Chapter 4) are the most productive forage-producing areas. Their proximity to water and favorable microclimates also make riparian ecosystems attractive to livestock and wildlife alike. As a result, riparian ecosystems are susceptible to overgrazing. Overgrazing along streambanks and on wet soils can degrade the vegetative community, lead to increased soil erosion, and cause the pollution of associated waters with excessive sediment, bacteria, and increased water temperatures. Therefore, a grazing strategy is needed to protect the vegetation, soil, and aquatic ecosystems that are unique to these areas. Some general guidelines to protect riparian ecosystems and allow for their continued use as important forage-producing areas include (Clary and Webster 1989):

- Grazing in periods (seasons) when succulent forage is more widespread on the range and not limited to riparian ecosystems is preferred. Livestock do not seek out the wetter areas when water is more readily available and early season grazing allows forage plants to regrow. Grazing in cooler periods when shade is not important tends to keep the livestock from concentrating on riparian sites. It is suggested that plants be utilized to the point where at least 10 cm of stubble is left.

- Avoid grazing riparian ecosystems in the hottest months, and avoid season-long grazing unless livestock use and distribution can be controlled.

- Late season grazing before plant dormancy has some of the same advantages as early season grazing, with the exception that a 15-cm stubble height should remain after grazing.

- Where fisheries are critical and streambanks are susceptible to erosion, stubble heights of 15 cm or more should be maintained following grazing.

These guidelines can not always be met in many developing country situations, or when droughts are severe and the vegetation of riparian ecosystems is the only forage available. However, if riparian ecosystems are overgrazed, their productivity will not be sustained, and the method of rehabilitating riparian sites is costly and time consuming. When riparian ecosystems become degraded, recovery usually requires structural measures to re-establish water levels, measures that must be followed by a period of nonuse by livestock. As a consequence, the benefits of wisely managing riparian ecosystems includes avoiding the costs and time needed for restoration.

Grazing strategies for dry periods, particularly periods of drought, are special problems to livestock producers and the managers of rangelands. Holechek et al. (1989) suggest that the grazing of livestock in dry seasons presents problems primarily because of lower quantities and qualities of forage. As dry seasons begin, grasses begin to cure, with pronounced losses in production and nutrient contents. Crude protein, digestible protein, phosphorus, and vitamin A contents can diminish dramatically. To cope in dry seasons, the following options can be considered to minimize stresses on livestock, rangelands, and people:

- *Provide complementary forage*—Agricultural crop residues or succulents that have had their thorns burned off can provide forage to complement native grasses and forbs.

- *Provide supplementary feed*—Stored feed, for example, harvested native grass or alfalfa hay, is used as supplementary feed in many of the industrial countries. This option often is not available in developing countries, although peanut and cottonseed meal have been used as protein supplements in some African countries.

- *Centripetal grazing*—The pattern of livestock grazing near water in dry seasons can be altered. Livestock can be forced to graze areas that are most distant from water early in the dry season and, as the dry season progresses, allowed to graze areas closer to water. Doing this reverses the normal pattern of livestock overgrazing areas near water first and then having to travel greater distances to find forage as the dry season continues, which also is a time when the physiological condition of the animals is the poorest.

If complementary forage or supplementary feed are not available, the only viable option in periods of extended drought is to reduce the number of livestock. However, a flexible grazing system and a set of management objectives, for example, use of mixed grazing practices (Example 2.2), can prolong the need to reduce livestock numbers. Nevertheless, livestock numbers ultimately must be reduced in most droughts.

Objectives and needs of livestock owners must be considered within the context of land tenure and natural resources management programs to successfully manage grazing. Land tenure conditions, whether common ownership, leasehold or permitting systems, or private ownership influence abilities to effectively implement environmentally sound grazing management practices. Confounding the problems of land tenure, the multiple use objectives of society often conflict with the economic conditions of the region and requirements of local people.

LIVESTOCK NUTRITION

The art of livestock nutrition, a key to proper management of grazing lands, is to balance the needs of livestock with forage resources available. It is not the purpose of this chapter to elaborate on the topic of livestock nutrition in detail. This information is found in standard references (Holechek et al. 1989, Pratt and Gwynne 1977, Stoddart et al. 1975). However, the concepts of livestock nutrition and the nutritive value of forage plants grown on rangelands are presented below.

Importance of Livestock Nutrition

Forage plants have different nutritive values to livestock. A measure of the nutritive value of plants can be obtained from knowledge of the *standard fractions* of crude protein, crude fiber, fat, ash, and carbohydrates. Laboratory procedures for estimating standard fractions are found in standard references. Standard fractions are used to measure nutritive values, because they are indicative of the nature of forage plants in a form that is related to the needs of livestock (Pratt and Gwynne 1977).

Protein and carbohydrate requirements are critical to the well-being of livestock. Livestock also need minerals and vitamins for skeletal development and to form body fluids. Minerals and vitamins, necessary only in small quantities, are essential for growth and development. All of the required quantities of nutrients should be present in the forage that the livestock consumes in a day. It is necessary to know the requirements for the maintenance and production of livestock in terms of gains in weight and amount of forage that the animal is likely to consume in order to assess the requirements of livestock.

One method of determining actual feeding requirements of livestock is the *balance method*. With this method, an animal is kept in a respiration chamber in which a balance between consumption and excretion of carbon and nitrogen is maintained (Stoddart et al. 1975, Pratt and Gwynne 1977). By feeding starch, protein, or other materials to the animal in addition to the maintenance ration, the amount of starch or protein required to form 1 km of animal fat is calculated. These values, combined with the percentage composition of the forage plants, indicate the weight of fat that forage plants should produce.

The amount of fat actually formed often is less than that predicted by the standard method, particularly in fibrous plant materials. Therefore, the *starch equivalent*, which is the amount of starch required to produce the same amount of fat as 100 km of a specified type of feed, is calculated. Alternatively, metabolizable and net energy can be determined through calorimetric studies. *Metabolizable energy* is the gross energy liberated when the feed is burned in a calorimeter, less the energy of excreta. *Net energy* is metabolizable energy less the energy of heat lost from the body. For comparative purposes, 1,000 J of metabolizable energy are equivalent approximately to 575 J of net energy for fattening.

Digestibility is important in livestock nutrition, because it is the link between the energy value and actual feeding value of the forage plants. In general, the digestibility of any nutrient in a plant can be obtained by subtracting the total weight of the nutrient in the feces from the total weight of the nutrient eaten by the animal. *In vitro* digestibility tests also can be made. The amount of a nutrient digested divided by the total amount of the nutrient in the feed, when multiplied by 100, is the *digestibility coefficient*. To determine the percentage of digestible nutrients, the percentage of nutrient in a feed source is multiplied by the corresponding digestibility coefficient and divided by 100.

Nutritive Value of Forage Plants

Forage plants grown on open grazing lands are the main source of inexpensive feed for livestock production. Livestock production by stall feeding on concentrates is not feasible in most dryland regions. It is necessary, therefore, to know the nutritive value of the forage plants, in addition to the selectivity of forage by livestock, to evaluate the value of a grazing land. Knowledge of intake of nutrients also is important.

Determination of the Nutritive Value   The nutritive value of forage is determined by a laboratory analysis of plant samples. From this analysis, patterns of change in the chemical composition is established throughout a plant's growing season. The nutritive value of perennial plants found on a rangeland varies depending upon the plant compositions, but it usually is sufficient for livestock maintenance for most years. However, where annual forage plants predominate, a major problem can be the lack of bulk, not poor nutritive value.

Although the nutritive values of important forage species can be estimated from data collected elsewhere, most often these data represent early stages of growth, when plants are relatively high in nutrients. Insufficient attention has been directed toward the postflowering stages of growth, a period that is critical in livestock production. Moreover, it usually is not possible to make comparisons among the data from different grazing lands and investigators, because most of the sampling is based on the physiological maturity of plants and the physiological stages of maturity are not uniform.

Selectivity of Forage   Livestock exhibit a marked degree of forage preferences, selecting among different forage species and various parts of the plants throughout a grazing period (Holechek et al. 1989, Stoddart et al. 1975, Vallentine 1990). Notwithstanding the deterioration that occurs in nutritive value as plant growth progresses in time, a relatively high protein content frequently is found in selected leaves. Frequent defoliation increases the percentage of protein in the plant as a whole for some forage plants.

Livestock can be fitted with esophageal fistula and used as sampling machines to determine plant selection. Because forage selection varies with the type of grazing land, stage of plant growth, grazing intensity, and livestock hunger, information obtained from fistular trials should not be applied generally. Nevertheless, these studies have illustrated how misleading "clipping" methods can be and, importantly, how poor the relationships can be between the forage offered and that actually consumed.

Intake of Nutrients   Livestock will not thrive unless the total intake of nutrients is sufficient. For most livestock, intake varies with the nature of the forage and the age of the animals. With mature zebu cattle in East Africa, for example, the average intake of dry matter is between 1 and 3 percent of the liveweight (Pratt and Gwynne 1977).

It is easy to measure the intake with stall-fed livestock, but the problem is more complicated with livestock on open grazing lands. Theoretically, a measure of intake can be obtained by sampling the forage resource before and after it is grazed. However, this measurement can be inaccurate on heterogeneous grazing lands. A better estimate is possible if the fecal output can be measured and related to digestibility of the forage grazed, that is:

$$\text{Intake} = 100 \times \frac{\text{Fecal Output}}{100 - \text{Digestibility}} \tag{2.2}$$

Intake of dry matter is limited by the amount of forage that can be gathered in the time allowed for livestock to graze, which typically is 8 to 10 hours. During the dry season, when forage is sparse, intake can be limited in terms of both forage bulk and the nutritive value of the forage. The stocking rate, therefore, should be based upon the number of livestock that can be fed on a rangeland during the dry season, unless supplementary feeding with preserved forage or concentrates can be accomplished.

Supplementary Feeding Livestock will lose body weight in submaintenance grazing situations that frequently characterize dry seasons. When this occurs, there can be benefits from supplementary feeding, although a careful analysis is necessary to economically justify this practice. Supplementary feeding is an expense that must be balanced against the weight gains obtained. Furthermore, supplementary feeding should be considered only as a short-term intervention in most situations.

Supplementary feeding for cattle operations generally is offered only to cows because the effects of low nutrition on fertility and milk production are pronounced. Supplementation increases milk production and, as a consequence, the growth of calves. Supplementary feeding of other classes of livestock also can be considered, but the decision to supplement depends upon the cost of feed and the value of the meat, milk, or other products derived from the livestock. When supplementary feeding is warranted, many forms of feed can be used. In general, the feed is designed to compensate for a protein deficiency. Urea frequently is utilized as a source of nitrogen. However, it is unwise initially to introduce urea at more than 2 percent of the total dry matter intake.

Water Two-thirds of the body weight of a growing animal is water. Water is vital to every cell in the body and to all body fluids. Without it, food and nutrients cannot be digested and utilized. Moreover, water has a vital role in the processes of heat regulation. Most livestock require access to water daily for maximum growth and optimum productivity, although their specific water requirements can vary.

A minimum water regime slows the rate at which food passes through an animal and helps to ensure maximum digestion when the intake is limited or low in quality. For many livestock species and types, a physiological mechanism exists to recirculate nitrogen and other materials that are normally excreted. This mechanism operates for most types of livestock only when the animal is on a relatively low protein diet and water intake is reduced. Utilization of metabolic nitrogen also has been demonstrated under conditions of low protein and restricted water.

Under conditions of starvation, unlimited water can be detrimental and, in some instances, can cause death. For example, under conditions of stress, sheep that graze in dryland environments should be allowed access to water only once a week (Pratt and Gwynne 1977).

RANGE IMPROVEMENT

Overgrazing can cause loss of valuable forage species on rangelands. When this situation has not progressed too far, it often becomes possible to improve water supplies and increase the availability of forage supplies. Overgrazing is commonplace in many dryland regions of the world and, as a consequence, efforts to improve range conditions have been initiated. Solutions to overgrazing involve a number of interrelated factors, some related to biophysical conditions of the rangeland and others related to social conditions and the traditions of local people (Example 2.3).

Example 2.3

Overgrazing in Kgalagadi, Botswana (McLeod 1990) Botswana has one of the most fragile environments in southern Africa. Its unreliable rainfall regimes average 450 mm annually, and its hot and dry winds contribute to annual evapotranspiration rates in excess of 2,000 mm. In the sandveld of the western region of Botswana, comprising the Kgalagadi, annual rainfall is little more than 200 mm, and the area is suitable only for grazing by livestock. Much of the area has deep sands, but water is near to the surface where pans have developed, resulting in villages being established around these pans. Supplementary minerals for livestock also are obtained from these pans, a necessity because of poor nutritive values of the grasses in the sandveld. As a consequence, overstocking of livestock occurs in close proximity to the pans, which has lead to overgrazing and major changes in compositions of plant species in this fragile ecosystem. The Kgalagadi as a whole is understocked, however, with vast areas supporting no cattle at all.

Range improvement has involved development of boreholes to encourage grazing away from pan areas and villages. However, much of the water in the Kgalagadi is saline. Desalinization treatments, therefore, are needed for development of domestic water supplies in the region. Unfortunately, these treatments are too costly for livestock producers. Furthermore, there is concern that increasing grazing of cattle in the more remote areas could intensify damage to the ecosystem. As a result, the government of Botswana is considering potentials of managing the land only for wildlife species, because wildlife generally graze lightly, and eat a wider variety of forage plants, are more selective in their eating habitats, and farmers potentially can earn more money from wildlife than cattle through tourism, safari hunting, and the harvest of meat and skins for local use. Considering this alternative provides additional options for correcting overgrazing.

A long-term perspective is needed for range improvement programs to be successful. It is essential that range-improvement methods be followed with range management practices that lead to sustainable resource use. Furthermore, range improvement programs should integrate the conflicting needs of livestock, plant communities on the rangelands in question, and people with the multiple uses that occur. However, range improvement measures will have only temporary benefits if the livestock are not managed properly.

An array of conditions frequently are considered for range improvement, from seriously degraded rangelands to lands that are in relatively "good" condition but in which there are opportunities for increasing forage production. Methods of range improvement include water development, removal of undesirable plants, and increasing forage production through the seeding of forage species.

Water Development

Provision of adequate water for livestock is one of the most important aspects of grazing land development in dryland regions. Available and potential sources of water always must be examined simultaneously with the availability of forage plants. When water supplies are limiting, a survey of water resources takes precedence over all other considerations in the planning of range improvement.

Water requirements of livestock depend upon the species or type of animal and ecological conditions of the rangeland. In situations of extreme aridity, livestock often are forced to graze as long as 3 days between waterings. Inevitably, cattle, sheep, and goats lose weight under these conditions. Cattle are particularly susceptible to water shortages because they should have water every day. Grazing as far as 25 km from their water source, livestock can develop an insatiable thirst, with death frequently resulting. With these conditions, economic returns are reduced greatly, and when the subsistence of a family is involved, they can be at the bare minimum.

In general, a daily requirement of 25 L of water per animal unit has become accepted as the minimum. Water consumption rises with many exotic animals or when animal liveweight or milk production is improved. Intake of meat-producing cattle, when grazed on areas close to water and allowed to drink twice a day, increases from 25 to 35 L per animal. The daily intake can rise to nearly 90 L per animal with high-grade milk-producing cows.

Livestock consume more water in hot, dry seasons than in cool, wet periods. Nevertheless, in planning for water supplies, it is the maximum seasonal utilization that determines the amount of water that must be provided on a rangeland. For example, if the daily water requirement rises to 20,000 L, the water supply must be capable of furnishing this quantity, even when the average for the year is only 5,000 L per day.

The most appropriate water development is determined through inventories and evaluations of the location and extent of both forage and water resources (Pratt and Gwynne 1977). Water developments in themselves can encourage overgrazing and rangeland degradation if not properly planned and implemented. Water should not be used to encourage grazing in situations where forage production is not sufficient to support the specified stocking rates.

Water development for livestock can involve the methods of water development that are described in Chapter 4. Some of the more commonly used methods include construction of stock tanks, drilling of wells, and development of water-harvesting systems. Stock ponds offer a system to trap and hold runoff that otherwise would be unavailable to livestock. Wells are a means of increasing available water supplies, but their drilling requires knowledge of the nature of groundwater aquifers and water quality and of the economics of drilling operations. Water-harvesting systems, widely used in dryland regions, provide a method of capturing seasonal rainfall and storing the water for use in dry seasons.

Vegetative Manipulations

Removal of *noxious* or other undesirable plants for purposes of favoring the establishment and growth of forage plants can be an objective of vegetative manipulations on rangelands. Noxious plants include unpalatable plants, both herbaceous and woody, and poisonous plants. Vegetative manipulations to remove these plants include the use of mechanical, chemical, and biological methods, and fire (Heady and Heady 1982, Vallentine 1990). Sometimes, more than one method of vegetative manipulation is needed. The removal of noxious plants frequently is followed by seeding of forage plants.

Noxious plants vary in their reaction to different methods of removal and, therefore, to apply a method without considering the plant species to be removed can be ineffective. No removal program results in permanent plant eradication, as re-encroachment from seeds or resprouting always is possible. Nevertheless, with careful supervision, removal of noxious plants can be achieved, which can increase the amount of available forage when linked to a maintenance program.

Seeding of Forage Species

The vegetative cover and forage production on some rangelands can be improved by the seeding of forage plants. Successful seeding of forage plants usually should be accompanied with soil treatments and, sometimes, fertilization (Holechek et al. 1989, Stoddart et al. 1975). Seeding of forage plants is expensive and, as a consequence, must be planned carefully.

Seeding of perennial grasses is preferred to other plants, with the exception of conditions in which the rainfall is too low and annual grasses have to be used. Seeding of mixtures of grass species frequently is preferred. These mixtures often contain annuals in addition to perennials, helping to cover the soil early in the growing season. Mixtures also can contain "tufted" species to provide a persistent cover and "creeping" species to quickly cover the soil. The sowing of mixtures can be difficult when seeds of the components are different in size, shape, and weight, however.

Seeding is not successful without seedbed preparation on many rangelands (Springfield 1976). Scratch plowing or the use of brush crushers often are used in seedbed preparation. On rocky sites, seedbed preparation may not be possible, in which case the seed is broadcast onto the ground. Regardless of the technique, soil cultivation and sowing of seed normally are prescribed early in the rainy season.

No grazing should be allowed on a seeded area during the period of establishment. However, "light" grazing may be permissible in the following season and, in fact, can benefit forage species. When a rangeland is grazed under a rotational system, the block or blocks that are rested should be those seeded. If the rangeland is not being grazed in rotation, the area to be seeded must be protected by fencing or other means. Seeded areas on rangelands that also are utilized by wildlife can not always be protected. In these situations, fences made of branches can be effective. Control of wildlife also might be achieved by closure of water supplies.

Selecting Range Improvements

Because of the costs of most range improvements, the available options must be considered carefully (Holechek et al. 1989). The magnitudes and distributions of the benefits and costs need to be ascertained, remembering the financial situations of local farmers and herders. In this regard, some of the following guidelines are helpful:

* Methods that have been successful locally are preferred over methods imported from other regions or countries.
* Small-scale pilot studies should be carried out on a trial basis before widespread applications of imported methods.
* Methods and subsequent changes in range management procedures must be compatible with local land tenure situations and the goals of livestock owners and others involved in land management.
* Methods that are used should be appropriate for the stage of rangeland deterioration or range condition.
* Appropriate range improvement methods should be carried out in locations in which the potentials for improvement are greatest.

LIVESTOCK IMPROVEMENT

Management considerations for improving livestock production involve a number of actions, many of which already have been covered in this chapter. In addition to improvement of rangeland vegetation, there are some decisions and management options that can be directed toward the selection, care, and breeding of livestock that can improve livestock production.

Options for improving livestock production include the development of combined production systems of forge and fodder for a variety of livestock species and types, that is, applications of the *common use* principle. Livestock should be selected that are best suited to the rangeland conditions on hand. The traits of importance for livestock to be produced in dryland regions include heat tolerance, traveling ability, water requirements, and efficiency for meat, milk, or wool production. Removal of nonbreeders, extending breeding lives of females, encouraging multiple births, supplemental feeding or flushing in breeding seasons, artificial insemination, and control of breeding seasons all help to improve livestock production.

A breeding program can be initiated to improve the performance of livestock. Through breeding, livestock of desired features (e.g., adaptability to climatological conditions, resistance to insects and disease, and higher levels of productivity) are sought. Individual animal characteristics that are heritable and can be affected by breeding include size, color, growth rate, temperament, mothering ability, and presence or absence of horns. Improved growth rate, one of the more important criterion in a breeding program, is one of the more complex and difficult of these characteristics to plan.

Livestock-breeding programs include maintaining or refining the livestock type, upgrading the type, crossbreeding, and multiple crossbreeding or rotational breeding. All of these categories of livestock-breeding programs have been used for the improvement of cattle breeds in dryland regions. There also are opportunities to improve performance of sheep and goats through livestock-breeding programs. However, it is important to recognize that a basic understanding of the control of inherent genes, combining both recessive and dominant characteristics, and varying their heritability are prerequisite to the development of any livestock improvement program.

SUMMARY

The importance of managing grazing lands for livestock production should be appreciated after completing this chapter. Livestock production is a natural element of many drylands and a traditional land use of many societies. However, it is important that the livestock grazing practices be compatible with agricultural crop production, forestry, and other land uses. After having read this chapter, you should be able to:

1. Explain the concepts of condition and trend of grazing lands and methods of measuring these indicators and their applications in determining grazing capacities and the response of rangelands lands to management.
2. Understand the variables of importance in grazing management, in how to estimate initial stocking rates, and in the categories of grazing systems and how these grazing systems are implemented.
3. Appreciate the importance of livestock nutrition and the roles of supplementary feeding and water in livestock production.

4. Describe the methods of water development, vegetative manipulations, and seeding of forage species in range improvement programs.
5. Recognize situations in which livestock improvement might be warranted.

REFERENCES

Branson, F. A. 1985. Vegetation changes on western rangelands. *Range Monograph* 2, Society for Range Management, Denver, Colorado.

Child, R. D., H. F. Heady, R. A. Peterson, R. D. Pieper, and C. E. Poulton. 1987. *Arid and semiarid rangelands: Guidelines for development*. Winrock International, Morrilton, Arkansas.

Clary, W. P., and B. F. Webster. 1989. Managing grazing of riparian areas in the Intermountain region. *USDA Forest Service, General Technical Report* INT-263.

Dyksterhuis, E. J. 1949. Condition and management of rangelands based on quantitative ecology. *Journal of Range Management* 2:104–15.

Heady, H. F., and E. B. Heady. 1982. *Range and wildlife management in the tropics*. Longman Group Limited, Essex, UK.

Herbel, C. H. 1979. Utilization of grass and shrublands of the south-western United States. In Walker, B. H. (ed.). 1979. *Management of semi-arid ecosystems*. Elsevier Scientific Publishing Company, New York, pp. 161–203.

Holechek, J. L., R. D. Pieper, and C. H. Herbel. 1989. *Range management: Principles and practices*. Prentice Hall, Englewood Cliffs, New Jersey.

McLeod, G. 1990. Mixed grazing to the farmer in semi-arid Botswana. *Splash* 6(1):15–16.

Martin, S. C. 1975. Ecology and management of southwestern semidesert grass-shrub ranges: The status of our knowledge. *USDA Forest Service, Research Paper* RM-156.

Pluhar, J. J., R. W. Knight, and R. K. Heitschmidt. 1987. Infiltration rates and sediment production as influenced by grazing systems in the Texas Rolling Plains. *Journal of Range Management* 40:240–44.

Pratt, D. J., and M. D. Gwynne (eds.). 1977. *Rangeland management and ecology in East Africa*. Robert E. Krieger Publishing Company, Huntington, New York.

Savory, A. 1983. The Savory grazing method. *Rangelands* 5:155–59.

Society for Range Management. 1974. *A glossary of terms used in range management*. Society for Range Management, Denver, Colorado.

Springfield, H. W. 1976. Characteristics and management of southwestern pinyon-juniper ranges: The status of our knowledge. *USDA Forest Service, Research Paper* RM-160.

Stoddart, L. A., A. D. Smith, and T. W. Box. 1975. *Range management*. McGraw-Hill Book Company, New York.

Vallentine, J. F. 1990. *Grazing management*. Academic Press, San Diego, California.

USDA Forest Service. 1969. *Range environmental analysis handbook*. Intermountain Region, USDA Forest Service, Ogden, Utah.

Weltz, M., and M. K. Wood. 1986. Short duration grazing in central New Mexico: Effects on infiltration rates. *Journal of Range Management* 39:365–68.

Wickens, G. E., and L. P. White. 1979. Land-use in the southern margins of the Sahara. In Walker, B. H. (ed.). 1979. *Management of semi-arid ecosystems*. Elsevier Scientific Publishing Company, New York, pp. 205–42.

Wilm, H. G., D. F. Costello, and G. E. Klippe. 1944. Estimating forage yield by double-sampling method. *Journal of the American Society of Agronomy* 36:194–203.

Wilson, A. D., and R. D. Graetz. 1979. Management of the semi-arid and arid rangelands of Australia. In Walker, B. H. (ed.). 1979. *Management of semi-arid ecosystems*. Elsevier Scientific Publishing Company, New York, pp. 83–111.

3 Small-Scale Agricultural Crop Production

Agriculture is practiced in the dryland regions of the world to produce food, fiber, and raw materials for people's use by the cultivation of agricultural crops, keeping of livestock under largely unconfined conditions, or combinations of both. Production of livestock for meat, milk, and other animal products in largely unconfined conditions on open rangelands was the topic of the previous chapter. Here, we are concerned with production of agricultural crops (e.g., cereals, legumes, and roots as a source of food for people). Annual and perennial grasses and other forage plants for livestock also are agricultural crops, although their production is not as commonly stressed as food for people in dryland farming.

FARMING PRACTICES

Systems to produce crops that provide food for people or forage for livestock are traditional agricultural practices in many dryland regions. Depending largely upon the capacities of land to produce agricultural crops and levels of capital investment made to do so, either *subsistence* or *commercial* farming is practiced. Subsistence farming is practiced on many lands, with most of the crops produced to meet the immediate needs of farm families. When a surplus is available, farmers often enter markets to obtain additional incomes, although the amounts of crops offered for sale generally fall short of that necessary for commercial attitudes to farming. Commercial farming requires large, diversified, well-defined marketplaces, infrastructures of roads and vehicles for transportation, and middlemen as agents or brokers. Large-scale commercial crop production rarely is possible in dryland regions without applications of large irrigation systems, facilities normally not available to subsistence farmers.

Small-scale subsistence farming is the focus of this chapter. These agricultural crop production systems are carried out at farm levels for mostly local benefits. Inputs and technologies used in small-scale subsistence farming practices differ considerably from those used in commercial farming practices, as indicated in Table 3.1. In attempting to sustain themselves, small-scale farmers often utilize land that also can be used to grow forage plants for livestock production or trees and shrubs for fuel and other wood products. Therefore, potential conflicts in land use are encountered commonly.

TABLE 3.1. Inputs or Technologies Used in Small-Scale Subsistence and Commercial Farming Practices

Input or Technology	Small-Scale Subsistence Farming Practices	Commercial Farming Practices
Land	Small (< 1–5 ha)	Large (10–100 ha or more)
Tools	Fire, axe, hoe, digging stick, machete	Tractors and implements, threshers, combine harvesters, etc.
Crops	Many species (5–80), little genetic improvement, wide genetic base	Few species (1–3), improved narrow genetic base
Animals	Several species (2–5)	Usually 1 or 2 species
Labor	Manual, human or animal power	Mechanical, petroleum fuels, electrical energy
Soil fertility maintenance	Fallows, ash, organic manures	Inorganic fertilizers, sometimes manures or soil amendments (lime and gypsum)
Weed control	Manual, cultural	Mechanical, chemicals (herbicides and petroleum-based products)
Pest management	Physical, cultural	Mainly mechanical and/or chemical, insecticides, fungicides, bactericides, nematocides, rodenticides
Crop management	Manual	Growth regulators for defoliation, control of flowering, fruit formation, etc.
Harvesting	Manual or simple tools	Tractors and implements, mechanical pickers, balers, threshers, combine harvesters
Postharvest handling and drying	Simple drying in and fire	Mechanical forced-air artificial drying with petroleum fuels, sometimes refrigeration

Source: Adapted from Okigbo (1991).

Small-scale farming can include one or two farmsteads with land holdings of a few hectares or involve an entire rural community in a cooperative effort extending over several hundred hectares. Rural people in many countries cannot be sustained without production from this type of farming. Unfortunately, small-scale subsistence farming is "at odds" with *sustainable* agriculture in many instances, regardless of how sustainable agriculture is defined. As a consequence, farmers are faced with the dilemma of increasing needs to feed their families with farming systems that, in themselves, are difficult to sustain.

Emphasis in this chapter also is placed on farming under rainfed conditions, although agricultural crop production with use of small, local, inexpensive irrigation systems also are considered. Rainfed areas in dryland regions generally remain underdeveloped in terms of agricultural crop production (Dregne 1983).

Nevertheless, rainfed drylands are the "backbone" of agriculture in many countries in North and sub-Saharan Africa and the Near East. Dryland areas comprise about 50% of all agricultural croplands in Mexico and Argentina.

AGRICULTURAL CROPS

Any listing of agricultural crops produced through subsistence farming practices in the dryland regions of the world is incomplete. Local uses of many plants are largely unknown, additional uses of native plants continue to be found (Hinman 1984), and improvements in cultivars are always a focus of investigations (Janick et al. 1981). Furthermore, thousands of plant species have been utilized historically by indigenous peoples, although a number of these species were used only in times of necessity.

Examples of plant species grown by people in subsistence farming in the dryland regions of the world, according to *crop type*, are presented in the following list (Janick et al. 1981, Spedding 1988). In reviewing this list of plants, it should be remembered that domestication of wild species has been common in many genera. Furthermore, a number of subspecies, varieties, races, and hybrids frequently occur, and innumerable cultivars exist.

- *Cereals*—rice (*Oryza sativa*), wheat (*Triticum aestivum*), maize (*Zea mays*), barley (*Hordeum vulgara*), oat (*Avena sativa*), rye (*Selale lereala*), sorghum (*Sorghum bicolor*), and millet (*Setaria* spp., *Panilum* spp., and others).
- *Legumes*—soybean (*Glycine max*), peanut (*Arachis hypogaea*), and beans and peas (*Phaseolus* spp., *Vicia* spp., *Vigna* spp. *Cajanus* spp., and others).
- *Root Crops*—potato (*Solanum tuberosum*), cassava (*Manihot esculenta*), sweet potato (*Ipomoea batatas*), and yam (*Dioscorea* spp.).
- *Stem and Leaf Vegetables*—cabbage (*Brassica oleracea*) and lettuce (*Lactuca sativa*).
- *Fruit and Seed Vegetables*—tomato (*Lycopersicon lycopersicum*), pepper (*Capsicum* spp.), okra (*Abelmoschus esculentus*), and pumpkin (*Cucurbita* spp.).
- *Fruit Crops*—grapes (*Vitus vinifera*), citrus (*Citrus* spp.), apple (*Malus pumila*), other temperate fruit such as peach (*Prunus perica*), and other tropical fruit including date (*Phoenix dactylifera*), fig (*Ficus carica*), and pomegranate (*Punica granatum*).
- *Nuts*—almond (*Prunus dulcis*) and pistachio (*Pistacia vera*).
- *Extractives and Derivatives*—beverage crops, including coffee (*Coffea arabica*), tea (*Camellia sinensis*), and vegetable oils, fats, spices, and flavorings.
- *Forage Crops*—alfalfa (*Medicago sativa*), clover (*Trifolium* spp.), and a large number of annual and perennial grasses preferred as forage by livestock.

Many of these plant species can be grown under rainfed conditions to obtain production levels necessary for subsistence. However, other plants require supplementary water to obtain yields that are sufficient to justify their production. Supplementary water is applied generally through use of small, local, inexpensive irrigation systems. *Water harvesting*, one example of such a system, provides irrigation water to subsistence farmers with a storage facility on a seasonal basis or for a longer period of time (Frasier and Myers 1983, Mollison 1990, Thames 1989). A discussion of water-harvesting techniques is found in Chapter 13.

Reliable, comprehensive estimates of the extent of dryland areas that are used for production of agricultural crop types and plant species in small-scale subsistence farming are difficult to generate. Many of the areas in question support a variety of *mixed cropping systems*, in which more than one crop type or plant species are grown on a piece of land simultaneously (Spedding 1988). Other areas are used largely in *agroforestry* practices, in which trees or shrubs are integrated components of agricultural crop or livestock production systems (MacDicken and Vergara 1990, Nair 1989). Agroforestry is the topic of Chapter 16. An indication of the relative importance of some crop types and plant species is obtained by looking broadly at the cultivated areas of the world that are used to produce crop types and plant species.

Cereal crops occupy the largest proportion of cultivated areas in the world (World Resources Institute 1990). Wheat, rice, and maize are cereal crops of dominance in both subsistence and commercial farming. Cereal crops are the primary source of food for people worldwide. Other crop types of significance, in terms of total land areas used in their production and their contributions to dietary energy intakes, include root crops, stem and leaf crops, and fruit and seed vegetables.

On a *per capita* basis, the areas of cultivated lands in the world likely will decline in the future, if projections of increasing populations are accurate. Expansions of cultivated lands, if they are to occur, will come at the expense of natural forests and woodlands, rangelands, and other lands that are both economically important and ecologically fragile. The impacts of expansions of cultivated agricultural areas in dryland regions can be significant.

CROPPING SYSTEMS

Cropping systems employed by subsistence farmers relate to local climatological constraints and people's needs, abilities, and perceptions of agriculture. Systems for agricultural crop production are endless in their characteristics and methods of implementation (Cox and Atkins 1979, Grigg 1974, Janick et al. 1981). However, for simplicity, the components of *settled agriculture* and *shifting cultivation* are used as a framework for the following discussion of small-scale cropping systems in the dryland regions of the world.

Settled Agriculture

Settled, or sedentary, agriculture is practiced on sites where soil fertility and precipitation and temperature regimes allow crops to be grown *in place* more or less continuously. Under rainfed conditions, one agricultural crop a year usually is grown in dryland regions at the time when rainfall amounts are sufficient. With supplementary water available through irrigation, however, production of two or more crops a year can be possible. Settled agriculture often is a key to the sustainable development of a region. In addition, it has been suggested that stable societies of people are difficult to maintain in the absence of settled agriculture (Mollison 1990).

Subsistence farmers engaged in settled agriculture in dryland regions must cope with soil erosion by the actions of water, wind, or both. Soil erosion is affected by physical structures and chemical properties of the soil, slope of the land, and the agricultural crop-production practices imposed. The kinds of crops planted, whether they are planted in *monocultures* or *associations*, and the sequences in which crops are planted and harvested are related to the magnitude of soil loss through erosion.

Subsistence farmers who experience excessive soil losses and, as a consequence, losses of soil nutrients often are forced to abandon their lands. These farmers frequently assume roles of shifting cultivators if they are forced to continue in subsistence farming.

Shifting Cultivation

Shifting cultivation, as the term implies, involves shifting to other pieces of land once the potentials of soil to produce agricultural crops at subsistence levels on the original land has been lost. In many countries in the moist tropics and other temperate regions, the cycles of shifting cultivation often include the clearing of relatively dense forest or woodland overstories; frequent burning of vegetation, with the resulting ash serving as fertilizer; and the planting of agricultural crops. Once soil fertilities deteriorate to the point of limiting crop production to unacceptable levels, farmers move to repeat the cycle elsewhere. Less dense trees and shrubs in dryland regions also are cleared in shifting cultivation, although less work generally is necessary in clearing operations (Example 3.1). The cut trees and shrubs often are gathered as a source of fuelwood. Burning may or may not be part of the cycle.

Example 3.1

Shifting Cultivation Systems: Two Examples (Spedding 1988) Any form of agricultural crop production removes elements from the soil and these have to be replaced. If these elements are not returned to the soil in one way or another, the eventual recourse for a farmer is to move to a "fresh" piece of land. This shifting commonly involves clearing of forests or woodlands, with the vegetation often burned. The resulting ash serves as an initial fertilizer and in some systems, such as the "chitamere" system of Zambia and the "hariq" system in the Sudan, branches and herbaceous vegetation are collected from the area to be burned on the newly cleared land. Stumps and boulders can restrict the amount and type of cultivation that is practiced, although it often is possible to cultivate around these obstacles with plenty of labor. Once elements in the soil have been removed to where levels of crop production become unacceptable, the farmer simply repeats the cycle by moving once again to another piece of land.

Shifting cultivation cycles move relatively slowly through time in the drylands in contrast with the moist tropics and other temperate regions. Farmers return to the same piece of land at longer intervals in a range of rotational fallowing systems (Spedding 1988). Largely regular rotational periods are followed on occasion. As populations of people increase, however, the lengths of fallow generally diminish and soil losses increase, as observed in parts of East Africa.

Shifting cultivation can progress toward settled agriculture, when necessary inputs of inexpensive fertilizer to produce crops at sustainable levels, are available on a continuing basis. Such is seldom the case with subsistence farming in dryland regions, however. A progression to uncultivated grasslands is more common. In some countries, shifting cultivation has become a method of extending areas of land cleared for livestock production (Spedding 1988). Shifting cultivation based upon annual crops evolves to perennial crops and often trees or shrubs on some sites.

Shifting cultivation represents a way for subsistence farmers in dryland regions to use marginal lands to produce agricultural crops in which soil fertilities are lost in relatively short periods of time or, in less likely situations, regeneration of natural vegetation is rapid. Nevertheless, relatively large expenditures of labor often are needed in initially preparing nonagricultural lands for the planting of crops. There are limits, though, to the extent to which these expenditures are worthwhile.

MANAGEMENT CONSIDERATIONS

In maintaining agricultural crop production in dryland regions, regardless of system, scale, or purpose, water supplies must be dependable and available. Other managerial considerations include controlling soil erosion when it becomes excessive, monitoring soil-nutrient levels, and limiting the impacts of pests.

Water Supplies

Water supplies that are available to dryland farmers generally are inadequate and unreliable. Frequently, however, farmers are concerned more with rainfall variability than with average rainfall amounts (Kanemasu et al. 1990). Farmers usually begin a growing season with a perception of what the rainfall pattern will be and then alter management based upon what rainfall actually occurs. It is important, therefore, that farmers have some understanding of rainfall patterns in order to make decisions necessary for sustainable crop production. Unfortunately, there most often is considerable uncertainty in predicting the amount and timing of rainfall, which gives the farmers little confidence.

One solution to the problems of inadequate and unreliable rainfall amounts is to irrigate, employing one of the systems that are described in Chapter 13. The systems to use if irrigation ultimately is selected depends largely upon:

- Reliable supplies and qualities of water.
- Infiltration and percolation rates, water-holding capacities, and chemical characteristics (for example, salinity and alkalinity) of the soil.
- Water requirements of planted crops.
- Evapotranspiration rates of the crops.
- Economic resources available to farmers, especially in moving water to the fields (Altieri 1988).

Another approach to alleviating the problem of sparse rainfall is to apply *runoff agricultural* practices, if the conditions are suitable. Runoff agriculture involves water harvesting, in which rainwater collected from hill slopes and catchments is stored and then used directly in agricultural crop production systems (NAS 1974, Thames and Ffolliott 1990). Runoff agriculture was developed almost 4,000 years ago to produce crops on lands receiving as little as 100 mm of annual rainfall. However, many techniques of runoff agriculture still are applicable today (Example 3.2).

Example 3.2

Runoff Agriculture: Some Techniques (NAS 1974, Thames and Ffolliott 1990)

Runoff Farming. Ancient runoff farms in the Negev Desert had several cultivated fields fed by watersheds of 10 to 50 ha. The watersheds were divided into smaller catchments of 1 to 3 ha that allowed runoff water to be collected in easily constructed channels on the hillsides, but were small enough to prevent uncontrollable amounts of water. Channels directed water onto cultivated fields, which were terraced and had stone spillways, so that surplus water in one field could be diverted to lower fields. Farmers dammed small channels between the catchment and the fields with rocks. By removing strategically placed rocks from channel walls, a farmer could guide the water to different fields at will.

Water Spreading. Water spreading is a simple means of using ephemeral flows of runoff water from the short, intense rainfall events that are common to dryland regions. These flows are diverted from their natural courses by ditches, dikes, or small dams, and spread onto adjacent floodplains or detained on valley floors where agricultural crops are grown.

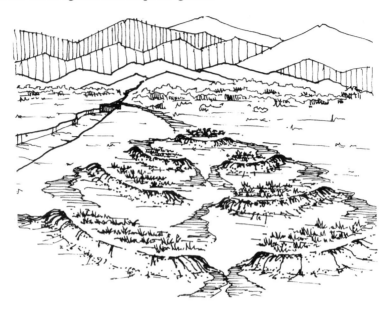

A water-spreading system (adapted from NAS 1974)

Microcatchment Farming. In microcatchment farming, small catchment areas are prepared in which one to several plants are grown on the low side. The rainfall collection areas range from 20 to 1,000 m^2, depending largely upon rainfall regimes and plant requirements. Microcatchment farming is used on complex terrain where other water harvesting methods are difficult to install. Microcatchments also are used to grow trees and shrubs in irrigated forest plantations, as discussed in Chapter 13.

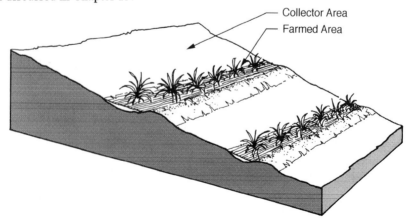

Contour catchment farming (adapted from Thames and Ffolliott 1990)

Contour Catchment Farming. Contour catchment farming, also referred to as *desert strip farming*, is a modification of microcatchment farming. Berms are erected along contours and the area between the berms treated, often only by clearing brush and vegetation, to serve as a rainfall collection area. Runoff from the catchment area is concentrated in a strip on the upslope edge of the berm, where crops or forage are planted.

Other solutions to the problem of inadequate water are to employ cropping practices that conserve water supplies and to plant drought-tolerant crops. Water-conserving cropping practices include mulching or no-tillage to lower evapotranspiration losses, terracing to reduce runoff rates, and the actions discussed below.

Soil Loss

Soil erosion is a natural phenomenon in dryland environments. Soil erosion at some level, therefore, is inevitable in dryland farming (Fryrear 1990, McCool and Renard 1990). However, subsistence farmers often accelerate rates of soil loss from generally marginal lands through use of improper cultivation practices. When this happens, remedial actions become necessary to sustain crop production.

Subsistence farmers experiencing excessive soil erosion by the actions of water frequently attempt to control this erosion by:

- Planting a protective crop cover, or providing a layer of crop residues or other organic materials, which facilitates infiltration of rainfall into the soil and, therefore, reduces runoff.
- Constraining surface runoff with physical barriers, for example, contour-bunds, terraces reinforced by rocks, ridges, or live barriers of natural or planted grasses and other herbaceous plants.
- Strip cropping with furrows in between.
- *Conservation tillage* techniques, a variety of "no-plow" systems to retain some crop residues on the surface of the land (Altieri 1988, Unger 1990).
- Rotating crops in time, which generally provides more soil protection than single-crop systems.
- Planting on contours.

A more detailed discussion of processes of soil erosion caused by the actions of water and vegetative control measures are presented in Chapter 18. Means of controlling soil loss by the actions of wind include:

- Planting of barriers of trees or shrubs in *windbreaks*, to be discussed in Chapter 17.
- Establishing artificial windbreaks from lathing or other fencing materials.
- Stubble mulching.

Soil Nutrients

Nitrogen, phosphorus, potassium, and other key nutrients are essential to plant growth. The primary sources of nutrients in dryland farming are the inherent soil nutrients (which often are relatively low), plant residues, animal wastes, legumes (which contain nitrogen-fixing bacteria in their root systems), nutrients in rainfall, and, when available, chemical fertilizers. Unfortunately, even soils that are fertile naturally can be depleted of nutrients by soil erosion, continuous agricultural cropping, or combinations of both. When this occurs, applications of *fertilizers*, which are anything added to increase the natural fertilities of soils, are considered. The choice of fertilizers to apply, considering not only commercially available inorganic fertilizers but also organic matter that has decomposed microbially, depends largely upon the availability, costs, and effects on plant performances.

Fertilizers provide nutrients to plants, which benefit from either inorganic or organic sources. Inorganic fertilizers can have side effects, however. In a long-term perspective, inorganic fertilizers can reduce diversities of microbes in the soil (Altieri 1988, Power 1990), and, importantly, they frequently are difficult to obtain and too expensive for subsistence farmers. In addition, improper applications of excessive nutrients can enter larger environments, causing pollution.

From an economic standpoint, organic matter (e.g., plant residues, animal wastes, and legumes) often is recommended instead of commercial inorganic fertilizers. However, applications of these less expensive and generally more readily available fertilizers also must be monitored to limit problems of pollution.

In many instances, erosion control measures are all that are needed to reduce the losses of nutrients necessary for plant growth. If nutrient losses persist and become excessive, however, other agricultural-management practices become necessary. Applications of fertilizers or crop rotations, either by themselves or in combination with fertilizers, might be prescribed. To illustrate rotational patterns that might be employed, agricultural crops that require high levels of nitrogen (for example, maize or sorghum) often are rotated with legumes (soybeans, or beans and peas) or crops that require smaller amounts of nitrogen, such as small grains. The cropping sequences in a rotation are likely to vary with climatological conditions, soil, economic factors, and traditional uses of the crops by local people.

Pests

Pests are organisms that reduce the availabilities, qualities, or values of agricultural crops to people. Examples of pests that confront subsistence farmers are insects, diseases, indigenous and domesticated animals, competing vegetation, and people themselves. Concern here is directed largely toward insects, diseases, birds, rodents when they reach "pest proportions," and competing vegetation.

Chemical pesticides developed from the 1940s to the present time are used widely in commercial farming throughout the world. However, the benefits that pesticides offer must be balanced against the detrimental impacts of direct contact when applying the chemicals and secondary effects on people through the food that they eat, the water that they drink, and, in general, damage to the environment (Altieri 1988, Brown 1978). Subsistence farmers may not be as concerned as they should be with these issues in attempting to provide food for their families. In spite of this apparent lack of concern, these farmers rarely are able to purchase and apply chemical pesticides effectively and, as a consequence, more commonly rely on alternative measures when it is necessary to control pests.

Indigenous plants known to possess pest-control properties often are planted. Some plants, like the neem tree (*Azadirachta indica*), have multiple forms of pest-control actions. Crop management practices, especially in terms of the arrangements of crops in time and space, also are used to reduce pest potentials (Figure 3.1). Many traditional cropping practices rely on crop rotations, including insertions of nonhost plants, to protect crops from specific pests. Sometimes, the least costly and most environmentally sound approaches to controlling pests involves the use of traditional mechanical control methods (Altieri 1988). These methods include:

- Removing competing vegetation (weeds) by hand or cutting down these plants with sickles.
- Covering competing vegetation with mulches to prevent their growth.
- Burning fields before planting to eliminate insects, diseases. and their respective hosts.
- Plowing, harvesting, and other tillage practices that reduce occurrences of specific pests.

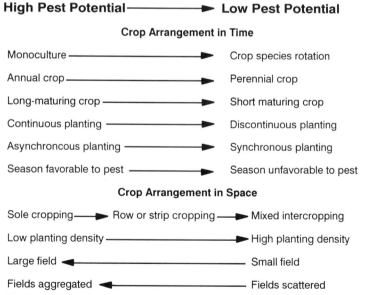

Figure 3.1. Potential pest problems in relation to crop arrangements in time and space (adapted from Altieri, M., *Environmentally sound small-scale agricultural projects, Guidelines for Planning Series,* © CODEL, Inc.)

Integrated pest management practices, a combination of chemical, biological, and mechanical-control techniques, can be the best way to control pests on commercial agricultural lands (Flint and vanden Bosch 1981). However, it is seldom that subsistence farmers in dryland regions are able to apply integrated pest management practices effectively, due largely to their limited financial resources and a lack in understanding of the complex ecological interrelationships involved.

TRADITIONAL MANAGEMENT PRACTICES

Through time, subsistence farmers throughout the world have used a variety of traditional management practices in attempting to overcome environmental constraints to agricultural crop production. These management practices often serve as a basis to improve upon managerial inputs and increase the levels of crop production by considering the perceptions in which subsistence farmers view their lands and resources. Examples of these practices are presented in Table 3.2, in reference to environmental constraints confronted by farmers and the objectives or processes involved.

TABLE 3.2. Traditional Agricultural Management Practices

Environmental Constraint	Objectives or Processes	Agricultural Management Practices
Limited space	Maximum utilization of land and resources	Intercropping, agroforestry, altitudinal crop zonation, farm fragmentation, rotational farming
Steep slopes	Erosion control, soil improvement, water conservation, diversification of production	Terracing, contour farming, living and dead barriers, mulching, leveling, continuous cropping with or without fallow cover, stone walls, planting so crops have maximum location advantage
Unreliable rainfall	Better use of available water	Use of drought-tolerant plant species, mulching, use of weather indicators, mixed cropping to better utilize rainfall at end of season, use of crops with short growing seasons
Flooding or excess water	Use of water bodies in integrated manner with agriculture	Raised-field agriculture, ditching of fields, diking
Excess water	Optimum use of available water	Control of floodwater with canals and checkdams, sunken fields dug to groundwater, "splash" irrigation, canal irrigation from wells, lakes, or reservoirs
Salinity or water logging	Lowering of water tables	Planting of appropriate tree or shrub species as part of agroforestry practices

TABLE 3.2. *(Continued)*

Environmental Constraint	Objectives or Processes	Agricultural Management Practices
Wind velocity, temperature, or radiation	Microclimatical amelioration	Shade reduction or enhancement, modifications in plant densities, use of shade-tolerant plant species, mulching, wind control with hedges, fences, other barriers, shallow plowing, weeding, minimum tillage, intercropping, agroforestry
Limited soil fertility	Sustain soil fertility and recycle organic material	Natural or improved fallow, crop rotations and intercropping with legumes, litter gathering, composting, manuring, green manuring, mounding with hoe, use of alluvial deposits, plowed leaves, branches, and other debris, burning of vegetation
Pests	Crop production, maintenance of low pest population levels	Overplanting allowing for some pest damage, scaring away pests, trapping, hedging, fencing, use of resistant plant species, mixed cropping patterns, enhancement of natural enemies, hunting, poisons or repellents, planting in times of low pest problems

Source: Adapted from Altieri (1987, 1988).

Management practices listed in Table 3.2 apply more directly to labor-intensive than capital-intensive farming. Many of the practices are relevant mostly to dryland environments and, therefore, appropriately discussed in this chapter. In these examples of traditional management practices, not only is agricultural crop production considered, but also production of livestock and, importantly, agroforestry and other combined production systems.

Performances of traditional or introduced systems of agriculture generally are evaluated in reference to *sustainability, stability, resilience,* and *equity* (Altieri 1988, Conway 1985):

- Sustainability relates to abilities of agricultural systems to maintain production through time in the face of ecological and social-economic constraints. Sustainability of small-scale agricultural systems also depends largely upon accessibility of technologies and resources to local farmers. Sustainability of crop production is limited in dryland regions, as discussed below.

- Stability expresses consistency of the levels of production from agricultural systems through time in relation to environmental, economic, and managerial conditions encountered.
- Resilience relates to abilities of agricultural systems to recover from perturbations, including problems of salinity, pests, flooding, or drought.
- Equity is a measure of how equitably both production from a farm (for example, yields of crops or income) and inputs to this production (land or labor) are distributed among farmers and consumers, and between men and women.

LIMITATIONS TO SUSTAINABLE AGRICULTURAL CROP PRODUCTION

Sustainable agricultural crop production can be defined arbitrarily either broadly or narrowly, although the definition used should specify the time and space scales being considered in either instance (Brown et al. 1987, Conway 1985). To be *sustainable* refers to long-term production with a minimum of resource depletion and environmental deterioration. To be sustainable also requires that crop production be viable economically and acceptable socially. With sustainable agriculture, food, fiber, and raw materials are provided in the "near-term" for today's populations, while conserving resource bases for use by future generations of people. A question frequently asked is, *Can small-scale subsistence farming systems in the dryland regions of the world become sustainable?* The answer, unfortunately, is *no* in many cases.

Sustainable crop production depends largely upon effectively managing the limited resources available and the capabilities of local people for doing so. There are a number of limitations to resources in dryland regions that collectively present a cause for concern in striving for sustainability on a small scale, however. Although identified originally for conditions in Africa (Antoine et al. 1993, Okigbo 1990, 1991), these limitations are applicable more generally to other dryland environments:

- *Climate*—Large portions of dryland regions are too dry for sustainable agricultural crop production. High rates of evapotranspiration, coupled with low and variable rainfall amounts often lead to periods of water deficits, which have serious implications on sustainable crop production (Kanemasu et al. 1990).
- *Water*—Water supplies generally are inadequate. At times, water that comes as rainfall can be collected and retained for subsequent use. Relatively small proportions of drylands are irrigable, and these areas are used largely in commercial agriculture.
- *Soils*—Soils in the dryland regions of the world are weathered or inherently low in fertility. If water is adequate, the use of fertilizer can enhance crop

production, although this practice generally is too costly in subsistence farming.

- *Energy*—There also is limited use of animals for work in small-scale subsistence agriculture. Over 80 percent of the energy used in African agriculture is human energy (Okigbo 1990, 1991). The most common source of energy in rural homes of many countries is wood, the increasing scarcity of which is affecting environmental qualities and people's nutritional status. Much of the food that is produced in dryland regions is nutritional only when cooked.
- *Crops*—Many crops produced in subsistence agriculture have remained largely unimproved genetically through time, although some progress in this regard has been made in recent years (Janick et al. 1981).
- *Human resources*—Human resources in dryland regions are large, more than 850 million people in total (FAO 1989). Large proportions of these people are illiterate, however. Levels of malnutrition also are high, especially among pregnant women and children. Many rural areas suffer from parasitical diseases, with health services and education frequently deficient.

When one considers these limitations to sustainable crop production, it is seen that small-scale subsistence farming, in general, contributes, in many instances, relatively little to the overall economic development of a region, even though the livelihoods of rural people are largely dependent upon these agricultural practices. Suggestions for increased institutional support, made largely in relation to large-scale, commercial agriculture, also can be appropriate here. They include:

- More effective political and administrative machinery to respond directly to needs of small-scale subsistence farmers.
- Improvements in education, training, research, and extension activities.
- Better marketing opportunities and pricing policies.
- More credits, cooperatives, and farmer organizational institutions.

SUMMARY

Small-scale subsistence farming is practiced in dryland regions to provide cereals, legumes, and roots as a source of food for people, and annual and perennial grasses as forage for livestock. Although these farming practices may contribute relatively little to the overall economic development of a region, the livelihoods of rural people can be dependent upon them. When you have finished reading this chapter, you should understand the:

1. General nature of the inputs and technologies that are used in small-scale subsistence farming in comparison to those in commercial farming practices.

2. Characteristics of settled agriculture and shifting cultivation.
3. Importance of water supplies, soil loss, soil nutrients, and pest control in maintaining agricultural crop production in dryland regions.
4. Traditional management practices that subsistence farmers throughout the world have used in attempting to overcome environmental constraints to agricultural crop production.
5. Limitations to sustainable agricultural crop production.

REFERENCES

Altieri, M. A. 1987. *Agroecology: The scientific basis of alternative agriculture*. Westview Press, Boulder, Colorado.

Altieri, M. 1988. *Environmentally sound small-scale agricultural projects: Guidelines for planning*. VITA Publication Services, Arlington, Virginia.

Antoine, P., E. Gilbert, P. Timmer, C. Ackello-Ogutu, and T. Bork. 1993. What is happening in Africa in the 1990s? In Seckler, D. (ed.). 1993. *Agricultural transformation in Africa*. Winrock International Institute for Agricultural Development, Arlington, Virginia, pp. 43–79.

Brown, A. W. A. 1978. *Ecology of pesticides*. John Wiley & Sons, Inc., New York.

Brown, B. J., M. F. Hanson, D. M. Liverman, and R. W. Merideth, Jr. 1987. Global sustainability: Toward definition. *Environmental Management* 2:713–19.

Conway, G. 1985. Agroecosystem analysis. *Agricultural Administration* 20:31–55.

Cox, G. W., and M. D. Atkins. 1979. *Agricultural ecology: An analysis of world food production systems*. W. H. Freeman and Company, San Francisco.

Dregne, H. F. 1983. *Desertification of arid lands*. Harwood Academic Publishers, New York.

FAO. 1989. Arid zone forestry: A guide for field technicians. *FAO Conservation Guide* 20, Rome.

Flint, M. L., and R. vanden Bosch. 1981. *Introduction to integrated pest management*. Plenum Press, New York.

Frasier, G. W., and L. E. Myers. 1983. Handbook of water harvesting. USDA Agricultural Research Service, *Agricultural Handbook* 600.

French, N., and I. Hussain. 1974. *Water spreading manual*. Range Management Record Number 1, West Pakistan Range Improvement Scheme, Lahore.

Fryrear, D. K. 1990. Wind erosion: Mechanics, prediction, and control. In Singh, R. P., J. F. Parr, and B. A. Stewart (eds.). 1990. *Dryland agriculture: Strategies for sustainability*. Springer-Verlag, New York, pp. 187–99.

Grigg, D. B. 1974. *The agricultural systems of the world: An evolutionary approach*. Cambridge University Press, New York.

Hinman, C. W. 1984. New crops for arid lands. *Science* 225:1445–48.

Janick, J., R. W. Schery, F. W. Woods, and V. W. Ruttan. 1981. *Plant science: An introduction to world crops*. W. H. Freeman and Company, San Francisco.

Kanemasu, E. T., J. I. Stewart, S. J. van Donk, and S. M. Virmani. 1990. Agroclimatic approaches for improving agricultural productivity in semiarid tropics. In Singh, R. P., J. F. Parr, and B. A. Stewart (eds.). 1990. *Dryland agriculture: Strategies for sustainability*. Springer-Verlag, New York, pp. 273–309.

McCool, D. K., and K. G. Renard. 1990. Water erosion and water quality. In Singh, R. P., J. F. Parr, and B. A. Stewart (eds.). 1990. *Dryland agriculture: Strategies for sustainability*. Springer-Verlag, New York, pp. 175–85.

MacDicken, K. G., and N. T. Vergara (eds.). 1990. *Agroforestry: Classification and management*. John Wiley & Sons, Inc., New York.

Mollison, B. 1990. *Peraculture: A practical guide for a sustainable future*. Island Press, Washington, D.C.

Nair, P. K. R. (ed.). 1989. *Agroforestry in the tropics*. Kluwer Academic Publishers, Boston.

NAS. 1974. *More water for arid lands: Promising technologies and research opportunities*. National Academy of Sciences, Washington, D.C.

Okigbo, B. N. 1990. Sustaining agricultural production in Africa. *Work in Progress*, United Nations University, 13(1):9.

Okigbo, B. N. 1991. *Development of sustainable agricultural production systems in Africa*. International Institute of Tropical Agriculture, Ibadan, Nigeria.

Power, P. W. 1990. Fertility management and nutrient cycling. In Singh, R. P., J. F. Parr, and B. A. Stewart (eds.). 1990. *Dryland agriculture: Strategies for sustainability*. Springer-Verlag, New York, pp, 131–49.

Spedding, C. R. W. 1988. *An introduction to agricultural systems*. Elsevier Applied Science, New York.

Thames, J. L. 1989. Water harvesting. In FAO. 1989b. Role of forestry in combating desertification. *FAO Conservation Guide* 21, Rome, Italy, pp. 234–52.

Thames, J. L., and P. F. Ffolliott. 1990. *Conservation and production practices in drylands*. FAO, Rome.

Unger, P. W. 1990. Conservation tillage systems. In Singh, R. P., J. F. Parr, and B. A. Stewart (eds.). 1990. *Dryland agriculture: Strategies for sustainability*. Springer-Verlag, New York, pp. 27–68.

World Resources Institute. 1990. *World resources, 1990–91*. Oxford University Press, New York.

4 Watersheds and Management of Water Resources

Watersheds and water resources on watershed lands play significant roles in the development of dryland regions. A watershed can furnish a diversity of primary wood products, contribute forage for livestock and wildlife species, and yield water for municipal, agricultural, and industrial developments. Because of scarcities and variabilities of water in dryland environments, management of watershed lands can be more challenging than in areas of water excess. However, the accumulated effects of past and often abusive use of the land that has resulted in degraded watersheds will continue to be felt in many countries for some time into the future. Recovery from watershed degradation is both slow and prolonged in dryland environments. It is urgent, therefore, for all concerned with management of watershed lands to understand the principles and concepts of watershed management and, more importantly, to develop ways of implementing land use practices that are compatible with watershed management principles.

DEFINITIONS

To help in understanding the roles of watersheds and watershed management in development of a country's resources, definitions of some terms are helpful (Brooks et al. 1991, Easter and Hufschmidt 1985). A *watershed* is a topographically delineated area that is drained by a stream system. It is considered to be a hydrologic unit, a physical-biological unit, or a socioeconomic unit. A *river basin* is defined similarly, but it is on a larger scale. For example, the Colorado River Basin, the Nile River Basin, and the Ganges River Basin include all lands that drain through these rivers and their tributaries into the ocean. In common usage, the term *watershed* refers to a smaller upstream catchment that is part of a river basin.

Watershed management is the process of formulating and implementing a course of action involving the manipulation of natural, agricultural, and human resources to achieve specific objectives on watershed lands, taking into consideration social, economic, and institutional factors operating within a river basin and other relevant regions. Watershed management also refers to the management of all of the resources on a watershed to maintain, protect, or, in some instances, increase high-quality water resources. Watershed management, therefore, should be viewed as multiple use management within the boundaries of a watershed. Emphasis in this chapter is placed on considerations related to the management of water resources. Discussions of the uses of other resources on watershed lands are topics of other chapters in this book, and Chapter 10 is oriented toward a discussion of multiple use management.

WATERSHED MANAGEMENT PRACTICES

Practices commonly associated with watershed management programs generally include those that prevent adverse impacts from occurring to soil and water resources, restore or rehabilitate watersheds from a poor, mismanaged condition to a productive state, and increase yields of high-quality water. Within the framework of these categories, one can look at watershed management opportunities and practices from a global perspective and then more specifically in terms of watersheds in dryland regions.

A Global Perspective

Management practices on watershed lands that are prevalent throughout the world are associated with the social and economic patterns that endanger the environment. With the present 5 billion people and an estimated daily addition of 200,000 individuals, the population of the world is likely to increase to 6 billion people by the year 2000 (Worldwatch Institute 1991). The amount of cultivated agricultural land per capita is less than one-half a hectare in many countries. Only a few decades ago, food production was increased in these countries by cultivating additional hectares and extending livestock grazing areas. However, that option is no longer available in many regions of the world.

As the population of the world increases, more pressure is being exerted on remote watersheds and the resources found on these watersheds, which already may be utilized beyond "acceptable" limits. It is not feasible to simply preserve or set aside these watershed lands to allow them to recover. Most rural inhabitants are dependent for their livelihood upon watersheds and the resources found on these lands. In addition, many countries are aspiring to better economic and social standards, requiring some utilization of these resources. The problem confronting watershed managers is to develop management practices that will provide the desirable levels of products and uses from these watershed lands without adversely impacting basic soil and water resources.

Between 50 and 80 percent of the populations of developing countries live on lands that are "marginal" in terms of agricultural crop production. For the millions of people who live on these areas, it is a fact of life that the harder they work, the poorer they become. Their land is too steep or too dry, or the soil is too poor to support no more than a subsistence level of existence. In the more temperate and moist tropical regions of the world, forested slopes of watersheds are cleared for fuelwood, fodder, or agricultural cultivation. Fires started to clear forests, woodlands, or crop residues often escape from agricultural fields and, as a result, forests are burned indiscriminately. Overgrazing by livestock can prevent the natural reproduction of forests and woodlands. Networks of roads and trails are established with little concern for the hazards of erosion they create. In the dryland regions of the world, where agricultural cultivation or the harvesting of wood frequently is not feasible, overgrazing by livestock has resulted in desertification of more than 4 million square kilometers in the past 50 years. Misuse of watershed lands has accelerated soil loss, loss in productivity, land deterioration, general environmental degradation, and further impoverishment of the rural inhabitants themselves.

On many watersheds, the protective vegetative cover of the soil has been removed, resulting in substantial soil erosion. Soil loss reduces soil water storage capacities, which leads to more runoff of water over the soil surface and even greater erosion rates. The results of these actions have been increased flash flooding and shifting of stream channels, causing water and silt to invade agricultural lands, irrigation structures, reservoirs, and floodplains. Streamflow during "dry periods" becomes unreliable and insufficient for the prevention of disease, maintenance of irrigations works, and urban and industrial needs. When infiltration rates of water into the soil are reduced on large enough areas, groundwater levels often decline, resulting in the failure of springs and wells.

Dryland Regions

Water relationships in dryland regions are likely more critical to a greater number of people than those of the more temperate and humid regions. Water is always in critical balance in dryland environments, and this balance is being upset by people and their land use practices at alarming rates over large areas.

It was mentioned in Chapter 1 that dryland regions extend over more than one-third of the Earth's land surface. Slightly more than one-half of this land is inhabited by people. The remainder of the land is so dry and unproductive that it cannot support human life on a sustained basis. Furthermore, the continued degradation of land and water resources by human activities is turning potentially productive drylands into desert wastes.

Aridity in the southwestern United States is legendary. The shortage of water conditions and circumscribes all of the behavior in the region. Much of the water being demanded in this rapidly growing area is pumped from underground aquifers, resulting in a steady decline in water tables. This decline, in turn, has affected local economies by prohibitively increasing costs of pumping in many situations. People are searching for ways by which new water sources can be tapped to cope with the possibility of a future shortfall. Vegetative modifications on upland watersheds is one approach.

Catchment experiments in the southwestern United States have demonstrated that water yields for some areas can be increased by changing structures and compositions of vegetation (Bosch and Hewlett 1982, Ffolliott and Thorud 1977, Hibbert 1983). The additional water is attributed to less water being evaporated or transpired and more water contributing to streamflow. It appears that vegetative modifications on upland watersheds can be designed to increase water yields and still provide the wood, forage, wildlife, and amenity values required by people in some optimal combination. However, careful planning and the coupling with economic and social considerations are prerequisite to the formulation of operational water augmentation programs with multiple benefits.

It has been estimated that a collective area larger than Brazil, with precipitation above the level to be classified as "semiarid," has been transformed into desertlike conditions (Brooks et al. 1991). About 60 million people in developing countries live in these "semiarid" zones, located between deserts and the more productive temperate areas. Desert encroachment in the Sahelian region of West Africa has received the greatest international attention recently. Reliable reports from the Sahara estimate that 650,000 km^2 of land suitable for agriculture or intensive grazing have been lost to desertification over the past 50 years.

The drylands of the Near East and North Africa are experiencing degradation due largely to excessive human populations. The increasing population in Morocco, for example, is shifting people onto watershed lands that are steep and relatively unproductive. These watersheds are being overgrazed and farmed to such an extent that acute erosion and sedimentation exist. Watersheds in the Rif mountains provide water for downstream multipurpose reservoirs, which, in turn, supply water for irrigation, hydroelectric power generation, and municipal demands. However, if present land use practices continue, most reservoir and irrigation systems will be filled with sediment and, therefore, unable to provide irrigation water and water for hydroelectric power.

In one Morocco study, the benefits of watershed management activities have been estimated to exceed the direct economic losses or costs due to poor land use practices (Brooks et al. 1982). A variety of erosion control practices, including gully plugs, terracing, and revegetation, have been implemented. Unfortunately, these physical and biological solutions must be considered only temporary, unless land use practices on watersheds are modified to control the cultivation of steep uplands and overgrazing by livestock that presently exist. These changes in land use can take place only when the watershed inhabitants are convinced that such practices are worthwhile and their livelihood is improved.

Present land use patterns also must change, so that the delicate water relations are not "pushed" beyond their limits. As the numbers of people and animals in dryland regions increase and productivities of the land on which they live decline, people will suffer unless adequate solutions are found. Loss of soil and inherent productivity of watershed areas on these lands constitutes long-term losses that cannot be recovered in a matter of a few years, or even a few decades.

To better appreciate watershed management practices and their role in water resource development, an understanding of the hydrologic cycle is necessary.

HYDROLOGIC CYCLE

Managers of watershed lands must address specific questions in relation to land use. These questions include—What land use activities can take place without causing undesirable hydrologic effects, such as flash flooding, erosion and sedimentation, and water quality degradation? What land use alternatives can be implemented to change a hydrologic response for a beneficial purpose, such as increasing water yield, improving water quality by reducing sedimentation, and reducing flood damages? To answer questions such as these, relationships between watershed management practices and resulting hydrologic responses can be analyzed by studying the hydrologic cycle. Importantly, hydrologic processes of the biosphere and the effects of vegetation and soil on these processes must be understood. The hydrologic cycle is complex, but it can be simplified as a series of storage and flow components as illustrated in Figure 4.1.

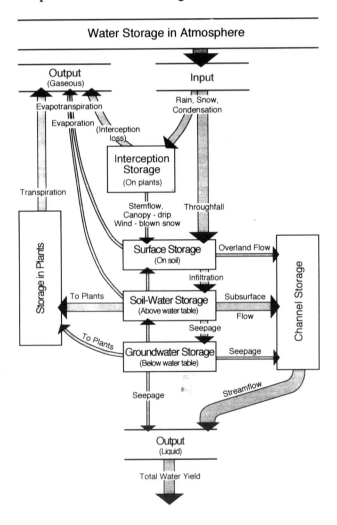

Figure 4.1. The hydrologic cycle is a series of storage components and the solid, liquid, or gaseous flows of water with and between the storage points (adapted from Anderson et al. 1976)

Water Budget Concept

The water budget is a concept in which components of the hydrologic cycle are categorized into input, output, and storage components. To illustrate this concept, for a watershed and specified time interval:

$$I - O = \Delta S \qquad (4.1)$$

where I = Inflow of water to the watershed
   O = Outflow of water from the watershed
   ΔS = Change in storage of the volume of water in the watershed, that is, storage at the end of a period (S_2) minus storage at the beginning of a period (S_1)

The water budget represents an application of the "conservation of mass" principle to the hydrologic cycle, which provides a useful tool to study the hydrologic behavior of watersheds. It is essentially an accounting procedure that quantifies and balances these hydrologic components for a watershed. Coupled with energy, *precipitation* is the primary input to a watershed system. A portion of this precipitation input is *intercepted* and *evaporated*, which represents a loss from the soil-moisture reserve or the water-flow process. *Infiltration* is the process of water entering the soil surface. *Evapotranspiration*, which represents the sum of all of the water evaporated and transpired from a watershed, is the most difficult of all to quantify. However, the evapotranspiration component and its linkage to soil water storage and the movement of water off of a watershed is one of the hydrologic processes most affected by vegetative manipulations. Relationships of precipitation, infiltration, and soil water storage affect volumes and rates of water movement downstream.

The part of the precipitation input that runs off a land surface and the part that drains from the soil and, as a consequence, is not consumed through evapotranspiration is the *water-flow* component of the hydrologic cycle. Some water flows quickly to produce streamflow, while other water flows (e.g., through groundwater aquifers) can take weeks or months to become streamflow, as illustrated in Figure 4.2. The streamflow response of a watershed is the integrated response of the various *pathways* by which "excess precipitation" moves.

The most direct pathway from precipitation to streamflow is that part of the precipitation that falls into stream channels, called *channel interception*, shown as pathway *A* in Figure 4.2. Channel interception causes the initial rise in a streamflow hydrograph, after which the hydrograph recedes soon after the precipitation stops. *Surface runoff*, also referred to as *overland flow*, occurs from impervious areas or areas on which the rate of precipitation exceeds the infiltration capacity of the soil, illustrated by pathway *B* in Figure 4.2. Some of the surface runoff is detained by the roughness of the soil surface, but, nevertheless, it represents a "quick" flow response to a precipitation input. *Subsurface flow*, also called *interflow*, is that part of the precipitation that infiltrates the soil, but it arrives in the

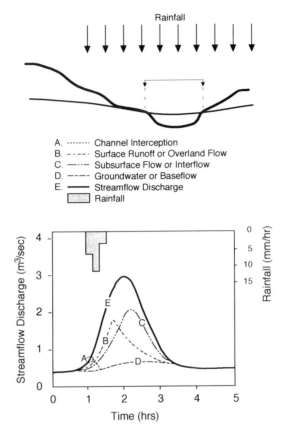

Figure 4.2. Relationships between pathways of water flow on a watershed and the resultant streamflow hydrograph (adapted from Brooks et al. 1991)

stream channel over a short enough time period to be considered part of the "stormflow" hydrograph, pathway C in Figure 4.2.

In contrast to more humid regions, watersheds in dryland environments frequently exhibit lower infiltration capacities and shallow soils with lower soil moisture storage capacities. Surface runoff, therefore, is an important pathway of flow from watershed lands in dryland regions. These watersheds generally respond more quickly, with relatively higher peak streamflows for a given amount of rainfall excess than watersheds in other regions. Furthermore, because of a lack of soil moisture storage, deep groundwater, and relatively low and frequently sporadic precipitation input, the streamflow often is ephemeral or intermittent.

A perennial stream, that is, a stream that flows throughout the year, is likely to be sustained by *groundwater*, shown by pathway D in Figure 4.2. This component sustains streamflow between periods of precipitation. Because of the long pathways involved and the slow movement of subsurface flow, groundwater flow does not respond quickly to rainfall.

One characteristic of stream channels in dryland regions is high *transmission losses* within the channels. When stream channels are dry most of the year, much of the water moving through the systems in a runoff event can infiltrate into the channel. This water is lost from surface streams and ends up as bank storage or percolates into lower soil storage or groundwater systems. As water moves farther downstream, the volumes of water in the channel can diminish until there no longer is flow in the channel at some point downstream.

The Water Budget as a Hydrologic Method

Analysis of a water budget allows unknown or unmeasured components of the hydrologic cycle to be estimated. Substituting with the components of the hydrologic cycle, equation (4.1) becomes:

$$P - (Q + ET) \pm L = \Delta S \qquad (4.2)$$

where P = Precipitation
Q = Streamflow, including groundwater flow
ET = Evaporation and transpiration losses
L = Leakage out of the watershed system by deep seepage (−) or leakage into the watershed system from an adjacent watershed (+)

Quantification of the components in the hydrologic cycle facilitate use of a water budget in studying the hydrologic behavior of a watershed (Ffolliott 1990, Freitchen and Gay 1979). It is important, therefore, to understand the instrumentation and measurement techniques for this purpose.

Precipitation   Rainfall is collected and measured in rain gauges. Most rain gauges consist of a cylinder of a known cross-sectional area. A *standard nonrecording* rain gauge is read at specified time intervals, at either the termination of a rainfall event or, for example, every 24 hours. A *storage* rain gauge, also a *nonrecording* rain gauge, has a greater storage capacity than a standard nonrecording rain gauge but is read weekly, monthly, or seasonally. A recording rain gauge allows for continuous measurements of rainfall amounts, which then are used to describe the duration, intensity, and amount of rainfall for each storm event.

A rain gauge must be far enough away from trees, shrubs, and other obstructions so that these objects do not affect the collection of rainfall. A rain gauge should be located on a flat area, with the opening oriented so that the rainfall is measured in terms of the depth that accumulates on the flat surface. The orifice of the gauge should be situated 1 m above the ground surface. A number of rain gauges frequently are located in a network throughout a watershed so that spatial and elevational differences in rainfall can be measured accurately.

Unfortunately, the number and distributions of rain gauges often are inadequate in the dryland regions of the world, largely because of the spatial and temporal variabilities in rainfall events. On the Walnut Gulch watershed in southeastern Arizona, for example, convective rainfall events that accompany summer thunderstorms are so variable that rain gauges must be placed at intervals of 0.5 km or less to obtain "reliable" estimates of rainfall amounts on the watershed (Hershfield 1968).

The importance of long-term measurements of rainfall must be emphasized, not only in terms of understanding the hydrology of watersheds, but also in the context of planning for the grazing of livestock, agricultural cultivation, and forestry practices. Long-term averages of precipitation have little value because of the extreme variability that is associated with year-to-year measurements (Example 4.1). Precipitation patterns need to be understood better, so that contingency planning can take place to deal with the severe effects of drought.

Example 4.1

Rainfall Variability of Selected African Locations   The variability of precipitation in dryland regions point to occurrences of few high and numerous low values. In analyzing data sets, therefore, average values of annual rainfall can be misleading. To illustrate this point, Jackson (1989) reported the following annual rainfall data from Griffiths (1972):

	Maximum	Mean (*mm*)	Minimum
Mogadishu, Somali	997	339	57
Harbell, Liberia	1,203	461	123

Variability occurs not only from year to year but also within a year. Much of the annual rainfall in dryland environments often comes in a few months, with long periods with little or no rainfall.

Interception   Interception is determined by measuring rainfall either above tree or shrub canopies or in a large clearing within a forest, woodland, or plantation and then subtracting the amount of rainfall that reaches the soil surface as *throughfall* and *stemflow*. A rain gauge located above the canopy is mounted on a tower above the height of the tallest trees or shrubs. When in a large clearing, once again, the rain gauge is situated far enough away from obstructions so that these objects do not affect the collection of rainfall.

Throughfall is measured by placing a number of rain gauges in a random pattern beneath the tree or shrub canopy in sample plots. The heterogeneity of tree and shrub canopies affects the amount, intensity, and spatial distribution of throughfall and, therefore, the number of rain gauges needed and size of the sample plot. Troughs also are used to measure throughfall, although spatial variations in throughfall are difficult to estimate with the measurements obtained in troughs.

Stemflow is measured by placing metal "collars" in notches in the bark around stems of sample trees or shrubs and then collecting and measuring the flow from these collars. Sample plots are established to place the streamflow measurements on an area basis. The size and number of the sample plots and the number of trees to measure on a sample plot are determined from the variations in the tree and shrub canopies and desired accuracy in measurement.

Infiltration *Infiltration capacity*, the maximum rate at which water enters the soil surface, is measured with *infiltrometers*. Two commonly used infiltrometers are the *flooding type* and *rainfall-runoff* plot type. Entry of water into the soil is measured on a small plot for both instruments. The flooding-type infiltrometer is a cylinder that is driven into the soil surface. Water is added and maintained at a constant depth in the cylinder, with the amount of water needed to maintain the depth recorded at specified times. A double-ring infiltrometer commonly is used, in which one cylinder is placed inside another. Water is added to both cylinders or rings, but the measurements are made only in the inner ring. The outer ring is a buffer that reduces boundary effects.

In using a rainfall-runoff plot type infiltrometer, water is applied either to the soil surface with sprinklers to simulate rainfall or in a system for which natural rainfall events can be evaluated. The plot has a boundary strip that forces surface runoff to flow through a measuring device. Rainfall simulators can be adjusted to represent a range of drop sizes and rainfall intensities. The rainfall simulator approach is more difficult to apply and costly on sites with dense trees or shrubs that interfere with the sprinkler rainfall simulation.

Evapotranspiration Evapotranspiration losses from a watershed cannot be measured directly by practical field methods. The best estimates of evapotranspiration come from a water budget analysis, where all but this component of a water system is measured and evapotranspiration obtained by subtraction, or through *paired watershed* experiments. With this latter method, two watersheds are selected on the basis of similar features. Streamflow is measured at the outlet of both watersheds for a sufficient time so that the streamflow from one can be predicted from streamflow measurements at the other. After this relationship has been established, vegetation on one watershed is modified, for example, by a clearing or thinning treatment. Streamflow measurements then continue on both watersheds. Unless the soils are compacted or otherwise altered physically, the change in the relationship established before the treatment, if one occurs, is attributed primarily to changes in evapotranspiration.

The absence of practical methods of measuring evapotranspiration requires knowledge of evapotranspiration processes of plant and soil systems in which they are working. One approach is to employ the concept of *potential evapotranspiration*, which is the maximum amount of water that can be evaporated and transpired from an area where water is not limited. Potential evapotranspiration, therefore, is related to the available water in the watershed system. This approach requires knowledge of soil-water characteristics and plant response to soil-water changes (Brooks et al. 1991, Lee 1980).

Soil Moisture   Changes in storage that are needed for a water budget analysis can be estimated from periodical measurements of the soil water content on relatively small watersheds. Soil moisture can be measured by either removal of a sample from the soil or measuring the moisture of soil in place. One widely used method of determining soil moisture is the *gravimetric method*, in which a soil sample is removed and weighed as soon as possible to obtain the wet weight value. The sample then is dried to a constant weight in an oven at 105°C. The difference in weights represents soil moisture, expressed as a percentage of the dry weight. This percentage is multiplied by the bulk density of the soil sample to convert the value to percentage by volume.

Methods of measuring the moisture of soil in place include the use of neutron probes, tensiometers, and measurements of electrical resistance from electrodes embedded in a block of plaster of paris placed in the soil at specified depths. Details of these methods are presented in references on the measurement of soil moisture.

Streamflow   The most common method of measuring streamflow requires a measurement of the height of the water in the stream, referred to as the *stage*, at some point along a stream with a *staff gauge* or a *continuous water-level* recorder. A staff gauge is used for periodical observations on streams where continuous water-level recorders are not needed or are not feasible. Continuous water-level recorders measure the stage on a scale that can be read accurately. A requirement of continuous water-level recorders is an open time-scale strip-chart system on which the rise and fall of the water levels can be reproduced accurately. Protection for a continuous water-level recorder is provided in the form of a stilling well for the float and a shelter for the recording mechanism. When a stilling well is used, it is located to one side of the stream channel so it will not interfere with the normal pattern of streamflow.

The stage of a stream is converted to streamflow discharge by measuring the streamflow velocity at a control section, installing a precalibrated structure, or solving one of several empirical equations available to estimate streamflow discharge values. The measurement of streamflow velocity at a control section involves the use of a floating object or a *current meter*. One of the simplest methods of measuring streamflow discharge is to observe the time required for a floating object that is tossed into the stream to travel a specified distance on the surface of the water. This observation, which is a measure of streamflow velocity at the surface, is multiplied by the cross-sectional area of the stream to estimate streamflow discharge. Although this method of streamflow is relatively simple, it is not necessarily the most accurate, because the velocity of water at the surface of the stream is greater than the average velocity of the stream.

The cross-sectional area of the stream is divided into a number of vertical sections in measuring streamflow discharge with a current meter. The streamflow velocity is estimated by measuring the average velocity of each section with the current meter.

A critical aspect of measuring streamflow velocity is selection of the control section. The control section is that section of the stream for which a *rating curve*, a graph of the stage and streamflow discharge, is established. Only a few measurements of the stage and streamflow discharge are necessary to establish a rating curve for a staff gauge site. However, a complete rating curve for a control section with a continuous water-level recorder can require months or years to establish, as measurements must be taken to represent the range of streamflow discharge conditions. The control section must be stable and have a sufficient depth of water for velocity measurements at the lowest streamflow.

On small watersheds less than 1,000 ha in size, precalibrated structures often are used to measure streamflow discharge because of their accuracy and convenience. Weirs are preferred in those situations where streamflows become quite low. When sediment-laden streamflows are common, flumes are more convenient. Weirs and flumes are constructed from concrete-treated wood, concrete blocks, and metals. The notch of a weir generally is a steel blade set into concrete. Flumes can be lined with steel for permanence. Precalibrated structures may not be large enough to measure the high rates of streamflow observed for larger watersheds. In these cases, it can be necessary to use a standard current meter to measure high streamflows and a precalibrated structure to measure lower streamflows.

Application of a Water Budget

Application of a water budget to study the hydrologic behavior of a watershed is relatively simple. As mentioned above, if all but one component of the hydrologic cycle is measured or estimated accurately, it then is possible to solve directly for the unknown component.

An annual water budget for a watershed often is used in an analysis because of the simplifying assumption that changes in storage in the watershed system in a year generally are small. Water budget computations can be made, beginning and ending with "wet" months (A to A') or "dry" months (B to B') on the watershed, as illustrated in Figure 4.3. In either case, the difference in storage between the beginning and end of the year's period is relatively small and, as a result, can be ignored in the calculations. By measuring the precipitation input and streamflow for a year, annual evapotranspiration (ET) can be estimated from:

$$ET = P - Q \tag{4.3}$$

Provided that an "acceptable" measurement of precipitation is obtained, a second assumption made is that the total outflow of water from the watershed has been measured. In general, it is assumed that there is no loss of water by deep seepage to underground geological strata and that all of the groundwater flow from

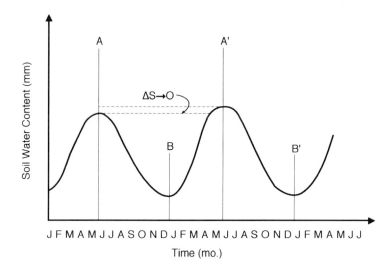

Figure 4.3. Hypothetical fluctuation of soil moisture on an annual basis (adapted from Brooks et al. 1991)

the watershed is measured at a gauging station. However, transmission losses can be relatively high and, furthermore, when geologic strata such as limestone underlie a watershed, the surface boundaries might not coincide with the boundaries governing the flow of groundwater. In such instances, there are two unknowns in the water budget, ET and groundwater seepage (L), which result in:

$$ET + L = P - Q \qquad (4.4)$$

When it is not appropriate to assume that the change in storage is small, the change must be estimated. This task is difficult, although changes in storage often can be estimated by periodical measurements of the soil water content on relatively small watersheds. Such measurements can be made gravimetrically, with neutron attenuation probes, or through the use of other methods (Ffolliott 1990, Freitchen and Gay 1979).

A Water Budget Example

Application of the water budget as a hydrologic method is illustrated with a hypothetical but realistic water budget for a watershed in the southwestern United States, as shown in Table 4.1. In this example, average annual precipitation and evapotranspiration before a vegetative treatment were 635 and 560 mm, respectively, leaving 75 mm for surface runoff. After the vegetative treatment, a partial cutting of the forest overstory in the timber management operation in this example, the annual streamflow runoff was increased by 25 mm, attributed to a reduction in evapotranspiration of 25 mm. The annual precipitation input of 635 mm remained

TABLE 4.1. Average Annual Precipitation, Evapotranspiration, and Surface Runoff for Hypothetical Watershed in the Southwestern United States in Untreated and Treated Conditions

Water Budget Component	Untreated	Treated
	(mm)	
Precipitation	635	635
Evapotranspiration	560	535
Surface Runoff	75	100

Source: Adapted from Ffolliott and Thorud (1977).

the same, as precipitation patterns generally are not affected by modifications in the structure and composition of vegetative cover on watershed lands.

Annual surface runoff yield increased by 33 percent in this example, while annual evapotranspiration decreased by 5 percent. It should be noted that no matter what vegetative treatment is imposed on a watershed, in general, the annual evapotranspiration will change but little. However, as demonstrated above, a small reduction in evapotranspiration can cause a substantial increase in streamflow runoff.

Surface runoff from some watersheds can be increased by vegetative management without denuding the watershed of vegetative cover and unacceptable changes in erosion and sedimentation (Bosch and Hewlett 1982). Available evidence also suggests that vegetative treatments designed for water yield improvement can be developed in a manner that is compatible with other watershed uses and multiple use values.

A water budget also can be used to analyze proportions of the water excess that are allocated to different pathways of flow. Example 4.2. indicates such a water budget for a brushland watershed in southeastern Arizona and points to magnitudes of transmission losses that can occur in ephemeral stream channels.

Example 4.2

Water Budget Components for a Brushland Covered Watershed in Southeastern Arizona, Indicating Different Pathways of Flow (Renard 1970) A precipitation input of 305 mm on the Walnut Gulch Watershed resulted in 51 mm of runoff and 254 mm of evapotranspiration. Of the 51 mm of on-site runoff, 44 mm was lost from the alluvial channel through transmission losses, with only 7 mm of runoff leaving the watershed. As indicated by Branson et al. (1981), ephemeral runoff per unit of area in dryland regions can decrease with watershed size. Furthermore, these authors pointed out that on watersheds similar to Walnut Gulch, for example, in the Rio Grande Basin in New Mexico, at least 250 mm of precipitation is needed before appreciable runoff occurs.

WATER RESOURCE MANAGEMENT

Water limits much of what people can do. Stability of water supplies is critical to programs of development. Emphasis in water resource management in dryland regions generally is placed on developing or conserving water supplies. The usefulness of water supplies to people also depends largely upon its physical, chemical, and biological characteristics. It is important, therefore, that both quantity and quality be considered in the management of water resources.

Developing Water Supplies

Numerous methods have been used in developing water supplies in the dryland regions of the world (Brooks et al. 1991, NAS 1974). Water harvesting is one example of note. Water-harvesting systems were used by people in the Negev Desert over 4,000 years ago, with interest in this technology continuing to the present (Armitage 1987, Thames 1989). Not all of the systems have been successful, although some form of water harvesting has been necessary to sustain livestock and agricultural crop production, and forestry, in many instances.

Water-harvesting methods involve the collection and, in many instances, storage of rainfall until the water can be used beneficially. The components of water harvesting systems include:

- A catchment area, which often is treated to improve runoff efficiency.
- A storage facility for collected water, unless the water is to be utilized immediately, in which case a water-spreading system is necessary.
- A distribution system when the stored water is to be used later for irrigation purposes.

A discussion of water-harvesting methodologies is presented in Chapter 13 in reference to applications of water harvesting in irrigated forest plantations.

Other methods of developing water supplies have little to do with the management of watershed lands directly. However, their applications in increasing the amounts of water available for irrigation, livestock production, or human use provide a means of increasing land productivity that, in turn, reduces the pressures of overgrazing by livestock, improper agricultural cultivation, and deforestation. Irrigation with saline water, reuse of irrigation and wastewater, and construction of wells and development of springs are some of these methods (NAS 1974). Other, more imaginative proposals, including cloud seeding, desalinization of sea and other saltwater, and transfers of water from water-rich areas to water-poor areas, have applications only under special conditions.

Conserving Water Supplies

Water conservation, where available water supplies are conserved for use at a later date, involves a variety of methods to reduce evaporation, transpiration, and seepage losses. Some of these methods pertain to treatments of water, soil, and plant surfaces, while others consist of manipulations of vegetative surfaces.

Reducing evaporation can lead to significant savings of water. Among the methods of reducing evaporation from small ponds and livestock tanks are covering these water bodies with blocks of wax, plastic, or rubber sheeting and floating blocks of concrete, polystyrene, or other materials. Liquid chemicals that form monomolecular layers on a water surface (e.g., aliphatic alcohols) have been used on larger bodies of water, although their effectiveness often can be limited because of wind and deterioration in the sun. The use of evaporative retardants can be restricted by adverse environmental effects of aquatic organisms in natural lakes or reservoirs.

Transpiration losses from plants can be reduced in many ways, including:

- Replacing plant species that have high transpiration rates with species that have lower transpiration rates.
- Removing *phreatophytes*, plants with deep rooting systems that can extract water from shallow water tables, from stream banks.
- Planting windbreaks of trees or shrubs to reduce wind velocities.
- Applying antitranspirant compounds that either close stomata or form a film on leaf surfaces.

The first two methods also can increase water yields from watershed lands, as discussed later in this chapter. Planting of windbreaks and the related environmental effects are discussed in Chapter 17. Antitranspirants, although effective in experimental investigations, have not been used widely on a large scale in natural vegetative communities.

Earthen canals and reservoirs that are constructed in pervious soils can lose considerable amounts of water through seepage. Methods of reducing seepage losses from these structures include the compaction of the soil, treatment of the soil surfaces with sodium salts to break up aggregates, and lining canals and bottoms of small reservoirs with various impervious materials. This latter method is expensive for large reservoirs, although it usually is effective for a long period of time.

Water Quality

Quality of water can present as much of a limitation on available water supplies as deficient quantities. In many instances, there can be an abundance of water, but its quality is such that it cannot be used safely for irrigation, domestic consumption, or other uses. Therefore, water supplies must be considered in the context of usable water, or water that is suitable for a specified use.

The quality of water in dryland regions, as elsewhere, is affected by natural geological-soil-plant-atmospheric systems and land uses (Brooks et al. 1991). Water quality characteristics of concern to people can be grouped into physical, dissolved chemical, and biological characteristics.

Physical Characteristics Physical characteristics that determine water quality include suspended sediments, turbidity, thermal pollution, dissolved oxygen, biochemical oxygen demand, pH, acidity, and alkalinity. Rainfall events in dryland regions frequently produce large amounts of runoff in short periods of time. These events can promote erosion and transportation of sediments. Streams in the drylands commonly transport high levels of suspended sediment and exhibit high *turbidity*, the latter indicating that light penetration into water is reduced severely.

Dissolved oxygen and biochemical oxygen demands are a concern in perennial streams, lakes, and reservoirs where biodegradable materials enter these bodies of water. The temperatures of water in dryland environments usually are high. In upland areas with cooler water temperatures, care is needed to prevent temperatures from increasing in water bodies where cold-water fish are found. In general, surface water and groundwater resources in dryland regions tend to be alkaline with high pH, due largely to the typically high levels of calcium and salts in the water.

Chemical Characteristics Dissolved chemical constituents in surface water and groundwater systems reflect the characteristics of the drainage area. Processes such as the weathering of rock, physical-biological processes occurring on watershed lands, and atmospheric deposition all affect chemical compositions of water. Because it is an excellent solvent, when water comes into contact with rock surfaces and other soil materials, its chemical composition changes. The longer the contact is, the greater the change, such as the case with groundwater. Rock and soil substrates generally control ion concentrations, including calcium, magnesium, potassium, and sodium, on watersheds with little human disturbance. Nitrogen and phosphorus concentrations are affected by biological activities, although much of the nitrate, chloride, and sulfate anions are added through atmospheric inputs.

Concentrations of selected constituents in streamflows from the pinyon-juniper woodlands are presented in Table 4.2 to illustrate the concentrations of dissolved chemical constituents in water samples from dryland regions of the southwestern United States. These concentrations are indicative of the relative low concentrations of dissolved chemical characteristics in streamflows from undisturbed watershed lands in these natural ecosystems (Clary et al. 1974). When pinyon-juniper woodlands were converted to grasslands to increase forage production, many of these chemical constituents increased in concentrations.

High concentrations of dissolved solids (salts) present some of the greatest limitations for the use of water. Salts tend to concentrate because of high evaporative rates and limited amounts of water in dryland environments. As a result, salinity frequently exceeds 100 ppm. People can tolerate salinity levels of 2,500 to 4,000 ppm, at least temporarily (Heathcote 1983). Livestock can tolerate 3,000 ppm. Irrigation, when feasible, often is restricted to salt tolerant plants, and it is necessary to flush salts through the soils so that levels of salt accumulations do not become toxic.

TABLE 4.2. Dissolved Chemical Constituents of Water Samples from Streamflow in the Pinyon-Juniper Woodlands of the Southwestern United States

Constituents	Utah Juniper Subtype	Alligator Juniper Subtype
	(*mg/l*)	
Ca	17.5	7.3
Mg	3.7	2.4
K	2.5	1.8
Na	3.4	3.7
NO_3	0.7	0.2
Cl	1.7	0.4
SO_4	6.6	5.8

Source: Adapted from Clary et al. (1974).

Biological Characteristics Biological characteristics are determined largely by the organisms that affect water use for drinking and other forms of human contact. Disease organisms are associated with situations in which human and other animal wastes are treated improperly, or the deposition of these wastes has been in close proximity to bodies of water. Many dryland areas in developing countries suffer from waterborne disease because of water supplies for domestic use becoming contaminated with human and animal wastes.

EFFECTS OF WATERSHED MANAGEMENT PRACTICES ON WATER RESOURCES

Manipulations of vegetation that accompany management of forests, woodlands, plantations, and grazing lands can affect long-term productivities of watershed lands. Of particular concern in this chapter are impacts on quantities and qualities of water that originates from upland watersheds. It is important, therefore, to recognize the environmental effects that watershed management practices frequently have on the hydrology of watershed lands.

Environmental Effects

Many watershed lands are subjected to grazing by livestock and wild ungulates, agricultural cultivation, harvesting of trees and shrubs for fuel and other wood products, and other forms of human interventions. The harvesting of trees or shrubs or converting from one vegetative type to another can enhance water supplies if the watersheds are managed properly. However, when managed improperly, these manipulations also can lead to (Brooks et al. 1991):

• Excessive surface runoff.
• Increased soil compaction and surface erosion.

- Increased gully erosion and mass soil movement.
- Increased sedimentation in downstream channels.
- Increased export of nutrients from upland watersheds.
- Increased temperature of stream waters.

If surface runoff and downstream sedimentation increase as a result of improper land practices, the prospects for downstream flooding also are increased. Soil erosion and the export of nutrients reduces the nutrient capital and, hence, the subsequent productivities of these watersheds. Stream water temperatures and increases in nitrate, phosphorus, and other nutrients affect aquatic organisms adversely. Introduction of residues from the harvesting of trees and shrubs into stream systems can lead to higher levels of biochemical oxygen demands and reduce dissolved oxygen, also adversely affecting aquatic ecosystems.

With properly planned and implemented watershed management practices, detrimental impacts on watershed lands should be minimized. Revegetation of deforested areas, for example, might return watershed lands to their former conditions, although the time for recovery is longer in dryland environments than in more humid ecosystems. In the United States and a number of other countries, "best management practices" have been established as guidelines for watershed management practices that help to avoid environmental problems.

Water Yield Increase

Water yields often are increased through manipulations of vegetative cover on watersheds when one or more of the following actions are taken (Bosch and Hewlett 1982):

- Plant species with high consumptive use are replaced with species with lower consumptive use.
- Forests or woodlands are clearcut or thinned.
- Species with high interception capacities are replaced with species with lower interception capacities.

Opportunities for water yield improvement from upland areas in most dryland regions are best when deep-rooted plant species are replaced with shallow-rooted species. Clear-cutting or thinning of trees and shrubs, often prescribed as part of wood harvesting operations, also can increase yields of water, although the effects of these silvicultural treatments diminishes as the trees and shrubs regenerate (Example 4.3). Reductions in interceptive losses of vegetative cover alone normally do not result in significant changes in water yields, unless these changes are accompanied by reductions in transpiration rates. These reductions are attributed to the fact that soil moisture tends to be at a level below field capacity of the soil

Example 4.3

Increases in Water Yields in the Southwestern United States (Hibbert 1983) Conversions of chaparral and similar shrub species to grasses has increased annual water yields from 5 to 100 mm in Arizona and California. Likewise, clearcutting aspen (*Populus tremuloides*) and ponderosa pine (*Pinus ponderosa*) forests on upland watersheds can increase water yields in excess of 100 mm annually. These increases might be maintained if the cleared sites are converted to grasses and forbs, although there can be some loss in other watershed management attributes of trees and shrubs, such as increased surface runoff, reduced slope stability, and the possibility of higher erosion rates.

much of the time. For the most part, differences in interception and, therefore, net rainfall simply are added to the soil and transpired at a later time.

The opportunities to increase water yield in upland areas through manipulations of vegetation are related directly to annual precipitation amounts. Hibbert (1983) and Ffolliott and Brooks (1988) suggest that the potentials for increasing water yield in the southwestern United States are realized only on sites with annual precipitation in excess of 450 mm. The greatest increases are observed in regions of higher precipitation and where precipitation is concentrated in the cool season of the year.

Increases in water yield on upland watersheds represent on-site effects. However, the net increases in water yield diminish as distance increases between upland areas and downstream reservoirs and other areas where the water is used. These reductions in streamflow result from transmission losses in channels, evaporation of water in route, and transpiration by vegetation along the stream bank. To illustrate the magnitude of these losses, Brown and Fogel (1987) indicate that increases in water yield attributed to vegetative changes on upland watersheds in the Verde River Basin of central Arizona (ranging from 25 to nearly 100 mm annually, depending largely upon the vegetative type and seasonal precipitation regimes) are reduced to less than one-half by the time water has traveled 150 km to downstream points of use.

In lowland areas, the consumptive use of water by phreatophytes can be substantial, as shown in Table 4.3. Opportunities for salvaging groundwater through eradication of phreatophytes has been attempted in parts of the western United States. One problem with such eradication is that these riparian systems also have values as wildlife habitats and a source of fuelwood, which can be higher than the value of groundwater that is salvaged (Horton and Campbell 1974). However, where dense plant communities have developed, such as saltcedar (*Tamarix* spp.) stands in the southwestern United States, there can be opportunities to salvage groundwater to a limited extent and, at the same time, maintain a sufficient riparian ecosystem for wildlife habitats and other purposes.

TABLE 4.3. Annual Consumptive Use of Water by Selected Phreatophytes in the Western United States

Species	Annual Consumptive Use	Depth to Water Table	Locality
	(*m*)	(*m*)	
Cottonwood	1.6–2.3	0.9–1.2	California
Mesquite	1.1	3.0	Arizona
Saltcedar	2.2–2.8	1.2–2.1	Arizona
Willow	1.3	0.6	California

Source: Adapted from van der Leeden et al. (1990).

Riparian Ecosystems

Riparian ecosystems are valuable components of dryland environments. *Riparian ecosystems* are found in the transition between aquatic and adjacent terrestrial ecosystems, and identified largely by soil characteristics and unique vegetative communities that require free or unbounded water (DeBano and Schmidt 1989, 1990, Johnson et al. 1985). Standing-water and running-water habitats are found in riparian ecosystems (Figure 4.4). As relatively small areas, riparian ecosystems are diverse and unique systems that are subjected to a number of uses and, as a frequent consequence, detrimental pressures.

Riparian ecosystems are often the only sites on a landscape that have trees and shrubs. They represent areas of relatively high levels of forage production and, as a result, are attractive to livestock. Riparian ecosystems are important wildlife habitats because of their abundance of food and cover, extensive edges between different forms of vegetation, and proximity to water. These ecosystems frequently are corridors of migration for animals. In terms of watershed management, riparian plant communities stabilize stream banks, and reduce soil erosion and delivery of sediments to aquatic ecosystems (DeBano and Schmidt 1989, 1990).

Special care is necessary to protect riparian ecosystems from environmental degradation because of their frequent high use by people and their livestock. Cuttings of trees and shrubs, and grazing by livestock must be controlled to maintain protective vegetative covers (Figure 4.5). Riparian sites can be fenced where excessive livestock grazing occurs. Water can be piped to tanks located outside of the enclosure to move livestock away from sites susceptible to compaction, erosion, or concentrations of animal wastes that can degrade water quality. When fencing is not feasible, the construction of water developments elsewhere, salting, and herding of livestock help in protection. Activities such as road construction and intensive, unplanned recreational use should be minimized in riparian ecosystems.

Degraded riparian ecosystems can be returned to a more productive status by improving the conditions on upland watersheds. One objective of these improvements is to increase streamflow, although these flows should be more stable and

| Lakes | Ponds | Seeps, Bogs, Meadows |

Standing Water Habitats

| Rivers | Streams | Springs |

Running Water Habitats

Figure 4.4. Riparian ecosystems include standing-water and running-water habitats (adapted from Thomas et al. 1979)

less variable than when the systems are degraded. Increased streamflow often is accomplished by encouraging subsurface flow rather than overland flow (DeBano and Schmidt 1989, 1990). Measures that increase durations of flows in stream channels also promote re-establishment and maintenance of riparian vegetation.

Gully plugs, check dams, and other small engineering structures constructed in stream channels can be used to increase durations of flows and stabilize the channels to help in the re-establishment of riparian vegetation. These structures trap and store sediments, providing water retention systems. The stored sediments become saturated following storm events and, as drainage continues, the water is released more slowly and sustained for longer periods of time than in unobstructed channels.

Optimum management of riparian ecosystems requires consideration of both the environmental factors and economic needs of the area. It is seldom that riparian

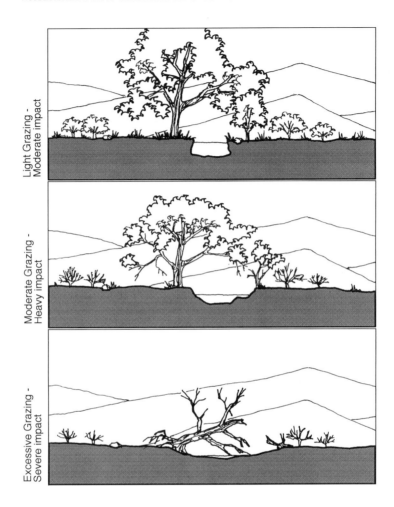

Figure 4.5. Impacts of livestock grazing intensity on vegetation, soil, and streams (adapted from Thomas et al. 1979)

ecosystems are managed best for only a single use, as, for example, in livestock production (Horton 1972, Horton and Campbell 1974). A compromise form of management usually results in the greatest value to people. In some instances, riparian ecosystems might have to be set aside as natural areas.

DEVELOPMENT OF MANAGEMENT PROGRAMS FOR WATERSHED LANDS

There is clear evidence that a potential exists on Earth to feed a much larger population than currently lives here. Despite this encouragement, it also must be remembered that the resources of individual countries vary widely. Development of the resources on watershed lands also takes a long period of time before it yields benefits. Conversely, once degraded, watershed restoration also takes a long period of time. Unfortunately, political leaders often have short-term goals. They focus on immediate and popular concerns. Yet, the production and conservation of the resources on watershed lands are dependent upon long-term and extensive commitments. Both rich and poor countries must be ready to make this commitment to the development of the watershed lands if future land degradation and desertification are to be avoided.

It is important to recognize that the problems of managing resources on watershed lands do not arise necessarily from physical limitations nor from lack of technical knowledge. Wood harvesting practices, reforestation programs, and methods of livestock grazing have been developed to largely prevent adverse impacts on soil and water resources. Likewise, the technology to solve many watershed problems is at hand. However, methods are needed to effectively demonstrate the benefits of instituting environmentally sound watershed management programs. The social and economic benefits from watershed management programs must be quantified and compared to the costs of not implementing these programs. Inhabitants of watersheds and their livelihoods must be considered as an integral part of any watershed management program, requiring integration of social, economic, and political factors in addition to biological and physical considerations.

SUMMARY

Watershed management involves the manipulation of natural, agricultural, and human resources to achieve specified objectives on watershed lands, taking into account the social, economic, and institutional factors operating within a river basin and other relevant regions. This chapter has introduced the subject of watershed management and has provided sufficient information so that you should be able to:

1. Understand the importance of the hydrologic cycle in studying the relationship of watershed management to the resulting hydrologic processes.
2. Discuss the instrumentation and measurement techniques that are used to quantify the components of the hydrologic cycle.
3. Apply a water budget to study the hydrologic behavior of a watershed that is subjected to a vegetative manipulation, such as a partial cutting of the forest overstory in a fuelwood-harvesting operation.

It is important that both quantity and quality be considered in the management of water resources in dryland regions. When you have completed this chapter, therefore, you should understand:

1. The ways of developing or conserving water supplies in dryland regions, including the use of water-harvesting methods and methods of reducing evaporation, transpiration, and seepage losses.
2. The general nature of the physical, dissolved chemical, and biological characteristics of water in relation to the usefulness of water to people.
3. How the grazing by livestock and wild ungulates, agricultural cultivations, harvesting of trees for fuelwood, and other forms of human interventions affect the availability of water sources.

REFERENCES

Anderson, H. W., M. D. Hoover, and K. G. Reinhart. 1976. Forests and water: Effects of forest management on floods, sedimentation, and water quality. *USDA Forest Service, General Technical Report* PSW-18.

Armitage, F. B. 1987. *Irrigated forestry in arid and semi-arid lands: A synthesis.* International Development Research Center, Ottawa, Canada.

Bosch, J. M., and J. D. Hewlett. 1982. A review of catchment experiments to determine the effect of vegetation changes on water yield and evapotranspiration. *Journal of Hydrology* 55:3–23.

Branson, F. A., G. F. Gifford, K. G. Renard, and R. F. Hadley. 1981. *Rangeland hydrology.* Kendall-Hunt Publishing Company, Dubuque, Iowa.

Brooks, K. N., P. F. Ffolliott, H. M. Gregersen, and J. L. Thames. 1991. *Hydrology and the management of watersheds.* Iowa State University Press, Ames, Iowa.

Brooks, K. N., H. M. Gregersen, E. R. Berglund, and M. Tayaa. 1982. Economic evaluation of watershed management projects—an overview of methodology and application. *Water Resources Bulletin* 18:245–50.

Brown, T. C., and M. M. Fogel. 1987. Use of streamflow increases from vegetation management in the Verde River Basin. *Water Resources Bulletin* 23:1149–60.

Clary, W. P., M. B. Baker, Jr., P. F. O'Connell, T. N. Johnsen, Jr., and R. E. Campbell. 1974. Effects of pinyon-juniper removal on natural resources products and uses in Arizona. *USDA Forest Service, Research Paper* RM-128.

DeBano, L. P., and L. J. Schmidt. 1989. Improvement in southwestern riparian areas through watershed management. *USDA Forest Service, General Technical Report* RM-182.

DeBano, L. P., and L. J. Schmidt. 1990. Potential for enhancing riparian habitats in the southwestern United States with watershed practices. *Forest Ecology and Management* 33-34:385–403.

Easter, K. W., and M. M. Hufschmidt. 1985. *Integrated watershed management research in developing countries.* Environment and Policy Institute, East-West Center, Honolulu, Hawaii.

Ffolliott, P. F. 1990. *Manual on watershed instrumentation and measurements.* ASEAN-US Watershed Project, College, Laguna, Philippines.

Ffolliott, P. F., and K. N. Brooks. 1988. Opportunities for enhancing water yield, quality, and distribution in the Mountain West. In Schmidt, W. C. (compiler). 1988. Proceedings —future forests of the Mountain West: A stand culture symposium. *USDA Forest Service, General Technical Report* INT-243, pp. 55–60.

Ffolliott, P. F., and D. B. Thorud. 1977. Water yield improvement by vegetation management. *Water Resources Bulletin* 13:563–71.

Freitchen, L. J., and L. W. Gay. 1979. *Environmental instrumentation*. Springer-Verglag, New York.

Griffiths, K. L. 1972. *Climates of Africa*. Elsevier Publishers, Amsterdam, Netherlands.

Heathcote, R. L. 1983. *The arid lands: Their use and abuse*. Longman, London.

Hershfield, D. M. 1968. Rainfall input for hydrologic models. *International Association of Scientific Hydrology Publication* 78:177–88.

Hibbert, A. R. 1983. Water yield improvement potential by vegetation management on western rangelands. *Water Resources Bulletin* 19:375–81.

Horton, J. S. 1972. Management problems in phreatophyte and riparian zones. *Journal of Soil and Water Conservation* 27:57–61.

Horton, J. S., and C. J. Campbell. 1974. Management of phreatophyte and riparian vegetation for maximum multiple use values. *USDA Forest Service, Research Paper* RM-117.

Jackson, I. J. 1989. *Climate, water and agriculture in the tropics*. Longman Scientific and Technical, New York.

Johnson, R. R., C. D. Ziebell, D. R. Patton, P. F. Ffolliott, and R. H. Hamre. (eds.). 1985. Riparian ecosystems and their management: Reconciling conflicting uses. *USDA Forest Service, General Technical Report* RM-120.

Lee, R. 1980. *Forest hydrology*. Columbia University Press, New York.

NAS. 1974. *More water for arid lands*. National Academy of Sciences, Washington, D.C.

Renard, K. G. 1970. The hydrology of semiarid rangeland watersheds. *USDA ARS* 41–162:26.

Thames, J. L. 1989. Water harvesting. In FAO. 1989. Role of forestry in combating desertification, *FAO Conservation Guide* 21, Rome, Italy, pp. 234–52.

Thomas, J. W., C. Maser, and J. E. Rodiek. 1979. Wildlife habitats in managed rangelands—The Great Basin of southeastern Oregon. *USDA Forest Service, General Technical Report* PNW-80.

van der Leeden, F., F. L. Troise, and D. K. Todd. 1990. *The water encyclopedia*. Lewis Publishers, Chelsea, Michigan.

Worldwatch Institute. 1991. *State of the world*. Norton and Company, New York.

5 Wildlife, Recreation and Tourism, Amenity Plantations

Wildlife, recreation and tourism, and amenity plantations are important components in many programs for sustainable development of dryland regions. Although it is not always possible to place monetary values on these components, they are important to the developmental activities of these regions and to the general well-being of people. The purpose of this chapter is to discuss the varied roles that wildlife, recreation and tourism, and amenity plantations have in these regions.

WILDLIFE

Indigenous and, in some instances, introduced wildlife species are vital to the well-being of many people in dryland regions because they provide meat, skins, and other values. Some of these wildlife species are "superior" to domesticated livestock in terms of their adaptive physiologies, disease resistances, and general capacities to survive on marginal diets. In addition, many wildlife species are exploited commercially in a variety of ways. It also is true, however, that some wildlife species contribute relatively little to human subsistence. Furthermore, wildlife often compete adversely with livestock for the limited forage and water resources. To the extent that is possible, therefore, it is necessary to reconcile conflicting values of wildlife in the development and implementation of land management practices.

Characteristics of Wildlife in Dryland Regions

Species of wildlife that are found in dryland regions often have physiological and ecological advantages in relation to livestock. Among the most significant of their relative advantages are abilities to thrive without an abundance of surface water by tactical movements in time and space, make optimal use of sparse vegetative resources for food and cover, and exert only minimal impacts on the environment when their populations are balanced properly with environments (Child 1989). Many of these wildlife species also possess attributes of disease, heat, and drought tolerance, and reproductive and meat production characteristics that generally are more efficient than livestock (Dasman 1964, Pratt and Gwynne 1977).

Examples of wild *ungulates*, hoofed wild animals with high values to people and their economies, which thrive in dryland environments in the various regions of the world, include:

- *Western United States*—antelope (*Antilocapra americana*), mountain sheep (*Ovis canadensis*), buffalo (*Bison bison*), deer (*Odocoileus hemionus, O. virginianus couesi*), and elk (*Cervus canadensis*).

- *Western Africa*—scimitar-horned oryx (*Oryx dammah*), addax (*Addix nasomaculatus*), and gazelle (*Gazalla dorcas, G. dama, G. leptoceros*).

- *Eastern Africa*—east African oryx (*Oryx gazella*), gazelle (*Gazella granti, G. soemmeningi*), buffalo (*Syncerus caffer*), wildebeest (*Connochaeter taurinus*), impala (*Aepyceros metampus*), and zebra (*Equus burchelli*).

- *Southern Africa*—gemsbok (*Oryx gazella*), springbok (*Antidorcas marsupialis*), wildebeest, impala, and zebra.

- *Western Asia*—white oryx (*Oryx leucoryx*), gazelle (*Gazella gazelia, G. subgutturosa, G. dorcas*).

- *Central Asia*—gazelle (*Gazella gutturosa, G. subgutturosa*), wild ass (*Equus hemionus*), nilgai antelope (*Boselaphus tragocamelus*), and spotted deer (*Axis axis*).

Use of Wildlife Resources

The principal ways in which wildlife resources are used by people in dryland regions include cropping for meat, skins, trophies, and other consumptive products and viewing and photography by tourists. Cropping of wildlife is a form of use on open lands that are not sanctuaries, while tourism is more prevalent in national parks and reserves where concentrations of wildlife can be seen. Among the reasons for the utilization of wildlife resources, both consumptively and nonconsumptively, are to increase local, regional, and national economies; make wildlife available for the enjoyment of people; and, when management requires, assist in long-term conservation efforts for the resource itself.

Cropping for Meat   The meat from wildlife species is important food for pastoralists and agricultural cultivators of marginal drylands, particularly in times of drought. Most of the documented examples on the use of wild meat for human consumption are found in Africa, where a variety of species play important dietary roles for many people (Table 5.1). It is likely that the importance of wildlife for meat will increase in many countries in the future as the carrying capacities for livestock continue to decline because of overgrazing.

Meat that is acquired by subsistence hunters is eaten fresh or preserved by drying or smoking for subsequent consumption. When large ungulates are killed, the reduction in weight of the meat by drying is a consideration in transportation back to villages or homes (Child 1989). After evisceration, smaller animals often are dried and smoked whole, while larger animals are cut into strips to facilitate dry-

TABLE 5.1. Wildlife as a Source of Food in Africa

Country	Food Consumption and Species Involved
Botswana	Game meat comprised 60 percent of the annual consumption of animal protein by people.
	Estimated annual consumption of game meat in the Kalahari area is 16.4 kg per person.
	Over 50 species of wildlife, including elephants, other ungulates, rodents, bats, and small birds, provide animal protein in excess of 90 kg per person annually in some areas of the country and contribute 40 percent of their diet.
	Over 3 million kg of meat from springhares is obtained by Botswana hunters.
Ethiopia	Large but unknown quantities of mice and giant rats are consumed in tropical western border areas.
Ghana	About 75 percent of the population depends largely upon traditional sources of protein supplied by fish, insects, caterpillars, maggots, and snails.
	In a 17-month period in 1968–1970, almost 160,000 kg of bushmeat from 13 species of wildlife were sold in one Accra market alone.
Ivory Coast	In the northern part of the country, nearly 30 gm of bushmeat are consumed daily per person.
Morocco	Squirrels and porcupines commonly are eaten.
Nigeria	Nearly 20 percent of locally produced food in 1965–66 was game species consumed largely in rural areas.
	The Isoko tribe in the Niger delta obtain 20 g of animal protein daily, mainly from game species.
	Game meat constitutes about 20 percent of the mean annual consumption of animal protein by people in rural areas of the country.
Senegal	A minimal consumption rate for the country's human population of almost 300,000 is 375,000 metric tons of animal protein from wildlife species.
Zimbabwe	Game species yield up to 10 percent more animal protein that livestock, a conservative estimate being 2.5 million kg.
	The Shoma people hunt and consume mice widely throughout the country.

Source: Adapted from the Food and Agriculture Organization of the United Nations (1985).

ing. Smoking also is employed to reduce wastage from decomposition. Meat can be preserved by the addition of salt, when affordable.

Subsistence and commercial hunters shoot with bows and guns and trap, snare, or spear their quarry. In some countries, fire is used to drive larger animals from protective cover and smoke is used to eject smaller animals from holes and other hiding places. Trapping and snaring enables animals to be caught alive so that slaughter can be delayed until meat is needed. Some of these harvesting methods cause relatively little disturbance to wildlife populations as a whole, provided that the methods used remain "traditional" and undue commercialization is not permitted (Child 1989).

Organized large-scale cropping activities for subsistence or commercial purposes are part of wildlife utilization practices in many dryland countries (Child 1989, Heady and Heady 1982, Pratt and Gwynne 1977). The techniques that are employed in these activities vary greatly with the species to be harvested, the terrain confronted, and the time available for cropping. Importantly, the slaughter of large numbers of animals at one time should be considered carefully in terms of impacts on inherent population dynamics, habitat limitations, and economic benefits derived, if any accrue.

It also should be noted that the importance of wildlife for meat is minimal in some countries, although there can be abundant and diverse wildlife populations. For example, culture and religion greatly influence the use of wildlife and domesticated livestock in India.

Skins and Trophies Skins and trophies, which can command high prices in national and international marketplaces, also generate incomes for local people and increases in regional economies. However, for optimal returns, the skins and trophies must be prepared suitably, free from damage, and stored properly before they are offered for sale. Hunters and skinners employed for the purposes of obtaining skins and trophies frequently benefit from training programs offered on the proper handling of these wildlife products (Child 1989). The harvesting of wildlife species solely for skins and trophies is driven mainly by needs for increased incomes in many African countries, and, as a consequence, populations can be decimated without regard to other, more sustainable wildlife values.

Wildlife Management Practices

It is important to know something about wildlife population dynamics, appropriate habitat management practices, and relationships between wildlife and livestock production in order to achieve sustainable use of wildlife resources in dryland regions.

Wildlife Population Dynamics Wildlife numbers rarely remain constant but fluctuate seasonally and annually. The primary causes for fluctuations in wildlife numbers are changes in the amount of available food and water. Grazing ungulates (e.g., gazelle, oryx, and elk) depend largely upon perennial grasses, while browsing animals such as deer use small trees and shrubs for food. In times of drought, grasses usually become scarce, but woody plants survive droughts better than grasses and, as a consequence, are a food source after grasses have disappeared.

However, when a drought continues with no lessening in wildlife numbers, trees and shrubs can be damaged and even destroyed through their increased use by wildlife. When grazing lands are subject to periods of drought, some wildlife species migrate, following the rains to areas where green forage is available. Many of these wildlife species move on a regular, seasonal basis according to annual precipitation patterns.

The effects of predation on fluctuations of prey populations must be considered in studying wildlife population dynamics, although these effects are difficult to determine. In general, predator species do not reduce or eliminate their food supplies and still survive. Therefore, there usually is a balance between predator and prey numbers, although not necessarily of equal numbers (Example 5.1). Parasites and diseases also affect wildlife numbers. Incidences of parasites and diseases require wildlife to use up energy reserves, sometimes causing death. Animals weakened by parasites and diseases frequently become more vulnerable to predators.

Wildlife populations are restricted by the available habitat resources. When all of the necessary food, cover, and water in the habitats are available and decimating factors are reduced, wildlife populations can experience rapid growth. Good habitat conditions in dryland regions generally improve in the rainy seasons, when forage quality is excellent. However, in time, an increasing wildlife population can begin to place stresses on the available forage resources. Prolonged periods of less-than-normal rainfall amounts diminish the forage supplies still further. When there no longer is enough forage, wildlife turn to remaining plants species with often less nutritional values (Holechek et al. 1989, Pratt and Gwynne 1977). Eventually, starvation and other decimating factors occur and, as a result, population numbers decline. This situation is compounded when populations of more than one species

---

Example 5.1

Predator and Prey Numbers on the Kaibab Plateau in Arizona (Caughley 1970, Patton 1992, Rasmussen 1941)   One study of predator control often cited as the reason for an increase in deer populations is that on the Kaibab Plateau. Before predator control was begun in 1906, the North Kaibab had an estimated 4,000 deer. Mountain lions, wolves, coyotes, and bobcats were removed by paid hunters and trappers from 1906 to 1923. Twenty years later, just before a major die-off because of the imbalance between predator and prey numbers, the deer population was estimated to be 100,000, although the accuracy of this estimate was questionable. The results of this study also were confounded by the fact that 200,000 sheep and 20,000 cattle were removed from the plateau in the same period.

compete for diminishing forage resources. Therefore, it is important to understand the natural cycles of wildlife populations so that extreme fluctuations might be avoided.

Knowledge of population numbers present, increments in populations in terms of birth and immigration, and losses from predators, poachers, parasites, and diseases are required to manage wildlife properly. However, one count in one area at one point in time likely will not be sufficient to characterize wildlife populations. Wildlife population measurements should be repeated in different seasons and years to determine the kinds of changes taking place. A number of methods to census wildlife populations have been developed, including aerial surveys, animal counts in a sample area, and fecal and track counts (Caughley 1977, Davis 1982, Hawkes et al. 1983, Schemnitz 1980). Animal movements are monitored with mark and recapture methods, and, in recent years, through radio tracking. Capturing, weighing, and measuring individual animals of different sexes and ages provide information about the total biomass present. Correlations of wildlife populations with the presence of specified vegetative communities are helpful in management planning.

Habitat Management Practices Wildlife populations require adequate food, proper cover, and opportunities to reproduce and to nurture the young. A principal route to the management of wildlife populations lies in habitat management. *Habitats* supply space, food, cover, and special items needed by every wildlife species. Importantly, these aspects of habitats are altered more readily than actual populations of wildlife species. It is here that forestry can play a role by altering the nature of woody plant communities to benefit wildlife species through habitat improvements, in addition to meeting goals of wood production, erosion control, and recreation and other amenities. The planting of trees and shrubs, the removal of trees and shrubs for fuelwood or other wood products, and the conversion of woody communities to grasslands or other herbaceous covers, regardless of the reasons, enhance habitat qualities for some wildlife species when properly planned. However, vegetative alterations also can affect the habitats of other species adversely.

Some wildlife species in particular habitat situations have a considerable impact on other species present. A first concern, therefore, can be to promote improvement of habitats for the *dominant* species. One wildlife species often will use more than one habitat. Large ungulates, for example, can graze in a number of habitats in their normal home ranges. Migratory animals frequently move across various habitat types in their life cycles and, in many instances, across national boundaries. When this is the case, the manager has to consider a complex of habitats jointly, making management difficult.

Wildlife species should be studied throughout their lifetimes, not just for a season or two, to determine habitat requirements. Species with relatively long life spans frequently have a greater effect on their environment than species whose individuals only live for one or a few years. Older animals can have different habitat requirements than younger animals, and females of a species also can differ from males in their habitat requirements. Therefore, knowledge of habitat requirements for wildlife populations of differing age and sex structures throughout their life spans is a key to sustainable wildlife management.

The removal of excess wildlife from an area becomes necessary when populations are larger than the carrying capacities of the habitat. Animals can be live-trapped or taken with drugs and then moved in crates or cages to areas where populations of that particular wildlife species are relatively low. Wildlife also can be harvested for meat or through hunting for sport. When the latter is practiced, however, it becomes necessary to prescribe the kinds and numbers of animals to be hunted to regain a balance between the animals and the habitats.

Habitat loss poses significant managerial problems that must be resolved in a number of countries. Fragile habitats are lost for a variety of reasons, including overgrazing by livestock, agricultural cultivation on marginal lands, and the cutting of trees and shrubs for fuel and other wood products. Unfortunately, the effects of habitat loss on wildlife are difficult to evaluate. The notion of critical habitat loss suggests that once forest, woodland, or grassland ecosystems are impacted detrimentally in terms of habitat qualities, wildlife species living there cease to exist.

Mapping of potential habitat loss is not easily accomplished. One approach to mapping is to initially determine the extent of vegetative formations (communities) that would exist if it were not for human or other disturbances and then estimate how much of the formations are left after disturbances. This estimate is about as close as one can get to broad estimates of habitat loss in many instances (World Resources Institute 1990). Such work has been done on a regional basis for dryland environments in sub-Saharan Africa, as shown in Table 5.2. While these broadly defined vegetative formations do not correlate directly with habitats for wildlife species, the extent of these formations include habitats for many wildlife species.

Wildlife and Livestock Production Natural fluctuations in wildlife numbers affect the ability of lands to support animals in much the same way as do fluctua-

TABLE 5.2. Vegetative Formation Loss in Sub-Saharan Africa, 1986

Vegetative Formation	Original Area	Percent Remaining	Percent Protected
	km²		
Dry forest	8,216,808	41.6	15.0
Upland montane	790,712	37.2	7.3
Woodland	5,896,200	42.4	17.2
Other	1,556,896	41.0	11.3
Savanna-Grassland	6,954,875	40.8	10.5
Scrub-Desert	176,600	97.8	10.1

Source: Adapted from World Resources Institute (1990).

tions in livestock numbers. It is necessary, consequently, for the managers of wildlife and livestock to constantly evaluate conditions of animals, their numbers, and the rangelands.

When a rangeland deteriorates because there are too many wild ungulates, wildlife numbers often are reduced, although the reverse also can be prescribed, depending largely upon the relative economic values placed on each. The managers of wildlife populations generally aim to prevent excessive buildups in population numbers in wet years when food is abundant and catastrophic mortality in dry years when food is scarce.

To integrate management of wildlife species with production of livestock, the extent to which wildlife and livestock species interact with each other and the combined effects that they have on the environment must be recognized. Specific requirements of each species must be known if wildlife and livestock are to simultaneously thrive. Food preferences, yearly reproductive cycles, migratory patterns, and the biology of the species involved must be known (Example 5.2). A primary question to answer is *How do wildlife and livestock species fit into holistic management programs for the ecosystem?*

Social interactions, especially competition, between wildlife and livestock are difficult to evaluate, as forage availability, distribution of water, and the terrain of the habitats in question confound the analyses (Holechek et al. 1989, Peek 1986). Most of the work concerning interactions with livestock involves wild ungulates. In the western United States, deer, mountain sheep, and elk appear to have social aversions to livestock, although this seems to be minor in importance if livestock stocking rates are low. There are little data showing aversions of other mammals and birds to livestock.

The transmission of diseases between wild ungulates and livestock, which can effect production of either or both seriously, is not well understood. However, it appears that a lack of forage through overgrazing often results in nutritional stresses in animals, causing greater susceptibilities to diseases (Mackie 1978). In these critical situations, diseases also spread more quickly than occur otherwise, because animals often concentrate in areas in which forage remains and, because of their nutritional stresses, they are in weakened physiological conditions.

Example 5.2

Dietary Overlap Between Deer and Cattle on La Michilia Biosphere Reserve, Mexico (Ezcurra et al. 1980) Little dietary overlap between deer and cattle exists in the dry pine-oak forests in northern Mexico. Furthermore, these animals have opposite preferences for grasses, forbs, shrubs, and trees in their respective diets. Competition between the two animals, therefore, is minimal. Increases in deer populations on rangelands that are similar to La Michilia should have little effect on the availability of forage for cattle.

Introductions of Wildlife Species

At times, exotic wildlife species have been introduced in dryland areas. This practice has met with mixed success, however, and must be considered with caution and only after monitoring and evaluation of small-scale introductions (Example 5.3). As a general rule, extensive, large-scale introductions of wildlife species should not be adopted as a management practice. There are numerous examples of ecological disasters that have resulted from these actions (Child 1989). Introductions of wildlife also have had detrimental impacts on sustainable livestock and agricultural crop production.

In situations in which the ecological conditions have been disturbed severely, introductions of wildlife to augment depleted populations of indigenous species might be justified. Stocking for these and other purposes must be monitored carefully, however, to minimize potential conflicts in habitat selection with the indigenous animals. Such conflicts are pronounced when indigenous species are attempting to re-establish themselves after depletion.

Reintroductions of wildlife differ from introductions. In the case of reintroductions, a species that has become absent in an area in historical times is established from part of its known or former home range. Reintroductions can be acceptable wildlife management options in dryland regions. A classical example of ongoing, successful reintroductions is that of Arabian oryx into parts of its former natural range (Filter 1982, Jungius 1978, Nielsen and Brown 1988). General guidelines for the successful reintroductions of wildlife are provided by Child (1989):

- Appropriate release areas for reintroduction should be established, considering habitat requirements for the species involved.

Example 5.3

History and Recent Trends of Introductions of Exotic Wildlife Species in Texas (Nelle 1992) Introduction of wild exotic ungulates on Texas rangelands began in 1930, when ranchers released nilgai antelope in southern Texas. Four more species of antelope and deer were introduced by 1932. During the 1950s, four more species of deer and sheep were released. By the time of the first statewide survey of exotic wildlife species in 1963, there were 13 species totaling about 13,000 animals on 178 ranches. Twenty-five years later, in 1988, 68 species and 164,000 animals were present on 468 ranches.

With seven species of indigenous ungulates and three major kinds of domesticated livestock, ranchers have introduced 68 other species of exotic ungulates into rangeland ecosystems in the state. However, three of the seven indigenous species no longer have viable populations. Furthermore, the increasing numbers of exotic ungulates depending upon the range resources of Texas require application of innovative range management techniques to survive.

- Holding pens and breeding paddocks should be constructed if needed.
- Proper releasings should be scheduled in terms of time, space, and number of animals released at one time.
- Local people should be informed of locations of release areas and numbers of animals released.
- Released animals should be marked for subsequent identification in monitoring efforts to evaluate successes.

Wildlife Ranching

Wildlife ranching has become a profitable enterprise in many dryland regions of the world (Dasman 1964, Holechek et al. 1989, Pratt and Gwynne 1977). Furthermore, when properly planned, wildlife ranching can be a tool in combating desertification processes. In the past, deterioration and destruction of many grasslands used for grazing followed the substitution of livestock for indigenous wildlife species, which then were killed or otherwise reduced to reduce competition with livestock for forage resources (Hopcraft 1990). Through appropriate wildlife ranching operations, this destructive process often is reversed by returning to the use of indigenous animals.

Wildlife ranching typically involves fee hunting for sport or raising indigenous wildlife for the production of meat and other products (Example 5.4). Economic returns from fee hunting can exceed those from solely livestock production in some localities, for example, in southern Africa (Child 1990) and Texas. Mixed

---

Example 5.4

Wildlife Ranching in Kenya: An Example (Hopcraft 1990) In a variety of forms, the practice of wildlife ranching has gained momentum steadily worldwide over the past 25 years. Successful harvesting operations are ongoing in New Zealand, South Africa, the former Soviet Union, and elsewhere. The focus of these activities is generally on sport hunting or meat production exclusively, however. In contrast, wildlife ranching on a cattle ranch on the Athi River in Kenya is more relevant to the specific needs of areas where both economic development and resource production are essential.

The selective harvesting of game animals has been a notable success from a commercial standpoint. Net returns per hectare are ten times those of the average "traditional" cattle ranch in the area, although the stocking of wildlife is one-sixth that of normal cattle numbers. A new industry has evolved in Kenya as a result of this effort, with demands for game products in local and foreign markets developing rapidly. At the same time, there has been a re-establishment of natural species diversity, enabling the land to return to a condition "favoring" the entire range of native animals, plants, birds, insects, and soil organisms.

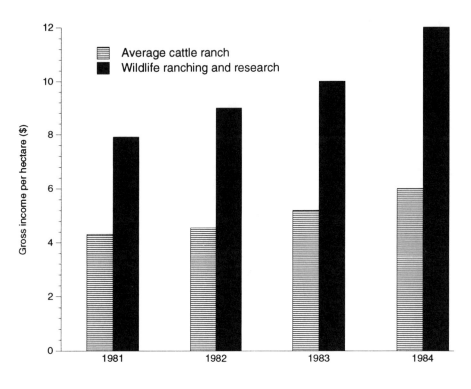

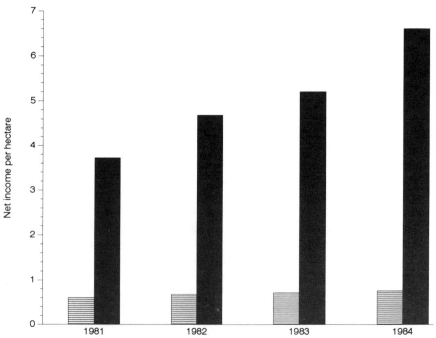

wildlife and livestock ranching also have been profitable in Kenya (Figure 5.1). Fee-hunting operations are successful where the following criteria are satisfied (Holechek et al. 1989):

- Opportunities to hunt on open public lands are limited.
- Sport hunting is a recreational pursuit that is acceptable culturally.
- A relatively affluent human population is located in close proximity to lands capable of producing high populations of game animals that can be hunted.
- Wildlife and livestock are complementary in their use of forage resources.

The husbandry of wildlife species as a source of meat and other products has been practiced on a limited scale in the United States (White 1987), but it has been developing with success in parts of Africa (Child 1990, Holechek et al. 1989, Pratt and Gwynne 1977). A fundamental idea behind this type of wildlife ranching is that the indigenous animals are adapted better to local conditions than are domesticated livestock. Another factor in support of this form of wildlife management is that the demands for wild meat have increased in recent years, largely because of its low fat content in comparison to that of livestock (White 1987). Also, wild ungulates and other native wildlife species in many dryland environments are adapted much better to stresses of heat, diseases, low forage qualities, and limited water sources than are most livestock.

RECREATION AND TOURISM

Recreation and tourism collectively can be large income generators in dryland regions. The importance of wildlife to recreation and tourism, for hunting for sport, and for viewing and photography is paramount to local and national economies in many countries. Other on-site, generally dispersed recreational opportunities include hiking, camping, sightseeing, and picnicking. Unfortunately, comprehensive statistics on levels of these nonconsumptive uses are incomplete. For whatever reasons, however, growing numbers of people are spending increasing amounts of time and money enjoying the unique resources of these dryland environments.

Importance of Wildlife

One of the more widely pursued recreational activities in the dryland regions of the world is the hunting of game animals for sport. Hunting for sport generally takes

---

Figure 5.1. Comparisons of gross and net returns from average "traditional" cattle ranching and mixed wildlife (ungulates) and cattle ranching in Kenya. Operations involve raising animals for meat and other products (adapted from Hopcraft 1990).

place on open public lands, outside of parks and other preserves, and on wildlife ranches. Hunting for sport earns comparatively little revenues directly, with most of the money obtained from licenses, permits, and fees for permission to hunt in designated areas.

In some countries, like the United States, significant proportions of revenues from licenses and permits are channeled back to the local wildlife manager to improve habitats and hunting conditions. However, in other countries, for example, in Kenya (Pratt and Gwynne 1977), most of these revenues go to the central governments and little money is returned to the wildlife manager for conservation purposes. Sustainability of hunting for sport often is impossible without this monetary incentive.

Hunting for sport attracts people who then contribute to economies in other ways. The purchases of guns and ammunition, clothing, and lodging or camping equipment and meals, and wages paid to hunting guides are examples of revenues generated indirectly through experiences of hunting for sport. This money also has *multiplier effects* in local, regional, and country-wide economies.

Viewing and photography of wildlife occur largely in parks, preserves, and other sanctuaries in which the numbers of visitors are controlled to limit disturbances of wildlife populations. Such parks and preserves can be important tourist attractions. Most of the money obtained from this nonconsumptive form of wildlife utilization are *hidden revenues* obtained from hotels, travel, and retail economies, although it is wildlife that attracts people.

Other Recreational Uses

Recreational use of drylands has increased greatly in the past few decades, due largely to their spectacular scenic beauty, diverse wildlife populations, relatively clean air, and other amenities, such as open space (Example 5.5). Much of this increase in recreational use is attributed to the rapidly increasing human populations and, in the case of some countries, the increased affluency and leisure time of these people.

Recreation is becoming a more important industry than livestock production (Holechek et al. 1989) and, in some instances, the harvesting of wood on many of the drylands of the western United States. If the current trends continue, recreational values may become greater than those for forage or wood on most of these lands in the future.

Recreational activities are varied, as indicated in Table 5.3. The values of many of these activities (e.g., hunting and fishing) can be quantified economically, at least in part, through the expenditures for licenses, permits, and equipment purchased for these purposes. However, values of activities such as camping, hiking, and picnicking are difficult to determine and, as a result, imputed indirectly in most cases. Nevertheless, there is no question that these recreational activities contribute directly or indirectly to tourism revenues.

Some of these recreational activities have relatively minor environmental impact. Others, with off-road vehicle travel being a prime example, are destructive

Example 5.5

National Parks, Wilderness Areas, and Biosphere Reserves in the Southwestern United States and Northern Mexico   In the southwestern United States, the National Park Service administers 16 national parks, national monuments, and recreational areas, many of which are noted for their scenic beauty, wildlife populations, and open space. Forests, woodlands, and other resources on 14 of these sites have been protected for 50 years or more. Relatively high concentrations of archaeological sites also are found on these areas. Wilderness areas have been and continue to be designated in the region in response to the public's interest in protection of these areas. National parks and other reserves in northern Mexico also contribute to conservation of woodland ecosystems. Currently, there are five biosphere reserves, components of Unesco's Man and the Biosphere (MAB) Program, in the southwestern United States and northern Mexico that also help to protect unique recreational resources.

to the environment and, if uncontrolled, can lead to severe land and resource degradation.

AMENITY PLANTATIONS

Amenity plantations are comprised of trees and shrubs planted in home gardens and parks, buffer strips along streets and sidewalks, roadside plantations, and greenbelts around cities and villages, largely for beautification and protective purposes. The phrase *beautifying the landscape* is used often in the dryland regions of the world in reference to the changing of countrysides from their normal brown color to green (FAO 1989a). Amenity plantations help to affect this change.

TABLE 5.3. Types of Recreational Uses of Drylands

Activities with Major Impacts	Activities with Minor Impacts
Hunting	Hiking
Horseback riding	Camping
Off-road vehicle travel	Fishing
Home building	Boating
	Rock hounding
	Mountain climbing
	Relic hunting
	Bird watching
	Picnicking

Source: Adapted from Holechek, J. L., R. D. Pieper, and C. H. Herbel, *Range Management: Principles and Practices*, © 1989, p. 420. Reprinted by permission of Prentice-Hall, Englewood Cliffs, New Jersey.

Home Gardens and Parks

Planting of trees and shrubs in home gardens, in addition to its possible agro-forestry function (as discussed in Chapter 16), is undertaken to beautify the home environments and, in many instances, effect psychological attitudes of people toward their lives (Field 1992). A house located in a barren setting without trees or shrubs can lack appeal, and, therefore, there frequently is a different psychological attitude toward a house in a setting like this compared to a house that is beautified by trees and shrubs planted in home gardens.

The following general characteristics are important in selecting trees or shrubs to plant in home gardens (FAO 1989a):

- Trees and shrubs have a number of functions to play in home gardens—for example, providing shade, shelter, ornament, fruit, or habitats for birds and other wildlife species. The first point to consider, consequently, is the purpose for which a planting is to be done. Some tree or shrub species only fill one or two roles, while others can satisfy more.
- Species selected should be adaptable to local climate and soil conditions.
- Degrees to which species tolerate pruning can be an important consideration for planting around homesteads.
- Many tree and shrub species for dryland forestry are evergreen, although deciduous species also are used in plantings in home gardens. In temperate regions, one advantage of deciduous trees and shrubs is their ability to provide shade and shelter in the summer but allow sunlight to penetrate in the winter. A disadvantage is that their leaves must be gathered after their fall.

When the main purpose of an amenity plantation is to provide protective shade, desirable characteristics of trees and shrubs include (FAO 1989a, Sanchez et al. 1990):

- Broad, round forms that cast wide shadows.
- Dense foliage canopies that block most, but not necessarily all, of the sun.
- Fast-growing species with rapid regeneration of leaves. Ideally, trees and shrubs with a moderate growth rate and a long life span should be planted for shade. One option is to consider a mixture of fast- and slow-growing trees and shrubs, with faster growing species removed as the slower growing plants reach an "effective" size.

Plantings in parks furnish shade and shelter from the sun and blowing dust, and the beauty of the parks is enhanced by planting species of varying size, shape, and color. Selection of species for these plantings is based more on these characteristics than on their value for wood products (FAO 1989a). Planting in small clumps or individually dispersed trees and shrubs usually is more desirable than plantings in long, straight rows not conforming to the landscape. Plantings in parks, therefore, should be consistent with environmental perspectives that people possess.

Buffer Strips

Buffer strips are planted along streets and sidewalks in cities and villages for beautification purposes, and to furnish shade and shelter, control noise and traffic pollution, and moderate microclimates. As suggested by McPherson (1988), the term *buffer strip* is used more appropriately for this type of amenity plantation in lieu of *windbreak*, because the primary function of a windbreak is implicit in its term, while the word *buffer* is more general. Seldom are buffer strips planted solely to reduce wind velocities in urban areas, but rather they perform more than one function.

For use in plantings of buffer strips, the trees and shrubs should be (FAO 1989a):

- Easily established, have abilities to be transplanted as advanced planting stock, and grow quickly to the stage at which they provide the function specified.
- Adaptable to the environment in which they are planted, be long-lived, and not be subject to damage from wind.
- Maintenance free.
- Suitable, in terms of growth form, for the width of adjacent streets or sidewalks.

In meeting these criteria, either a single species or a mixture of tree and shrub species can be planted. The decision is often a matter of taste. A variety of species can be selected to increase scenic beauty and biological diversity of a setting that might otherwise be monotonous or sterile.

Roadside Plantations

Roadside plantations are established to increase the comfort and pleasure of travelers by providing shade, shelter, and attractive surroundings; to act as windbreaks for adjacent agricultural fields and pastures; to protect the roads themselves against moving sand dunes; and, in some instances, to help in alleviating the shortages in wood, food for people, fodder for livestock, and habitats for birds and other wildlife species (FAO 1989a). Trees and shrubs to be planted in roadside plantations should be selected carefully. The more important factors to consider in the selection process include:

- Hardiness, longevity, a minimum of windthrow and breakage, attractiveness, and minimal maintenance requirements.

- Suitability to the climate, topography, and soils.
- Providability of needed wood and nonwood products when this is included as an objective of a roadside plantation.

The location of a roadside plantation in relation to the layout of a road is paramount in importance. For example, trees and shrubs should not be planted close to the inside of curves or near road intersections, where plantings could obscure vision and, in doing so, create a driving hazard. In planning planting operations, considerations also should be given to the possibilities of future modifications in the design of a road, such as its widening or the development of two traffic lanes.

Greenbelts

Many large cities, for example, Cairo, Egypt (Mahoney 1991), and villages in dryland regions have established greenbelts in their municipal areas to enhance the beauty of these areas, provide recreational sites for urban dwellers (Example 5.6), reduce the detrimental effects of dry winds and dust storms and control encroachment of sand dunes onto urban lands. A number of trees and shrubs are suitable for greenbelt plantings, with selection of specific species based largely upon many of the factors considered for other types of amenity plantations. A listing of species for greenbelt plantings, and for amenity plantations in general, is found in Appendix II and other references on dryland forestry (FAO 1989a).

Greenbelt plantings should be well designed in advance, planned for a number of years, and implemented with care to be effective. One example of such a planting program is the Greenbelt Movement of the National Council of Women in Kenya, initiated in 1977 (Harrison 1987). This program helps communities to establish greenbelts of 1,000 or more trees and shrubs in open areas, on school grounds, and along roads. Through the program, the planting of trees and shrubs by

---

Example 5.6

A Greenbelt Planting Renews a Town in Arizona (Woodruff 1992) Pinal Creek meanders around and through Globe, an Arizona town in the midst of the Tonto National Forest in the eastern part of the state. Renewing the riparian ecosystem along the creek by the Globe Greenbelt is planned to rejuvenate the town and perhaps the entire area. The emerging idea of the Globe Greenbelt is to serve the populations of Globe—roughly 6,000 people, with another 4,000 nearby—with an environmental recreational area, a wildlife habitat, a means for alternative travel by bicycle or foot, and increased economic possibilities. The Greenbelt, when completed, will be along the nearly 4 km Pinal Creek that moves through the middle of town.

---

women, children, and political leaders has become well publicized. Currently, there are in excess of 1,000 greenbelts in urban areas and 20,000 "mini-greenbelts" on lands of individual families, and the movement is continuing to grow.

SUMMARY

Wildlife, recreation and tourism, and amenity plantations can be important components of programs for conservation and the sustainable development of dryland regions. Unfortunately, however, it is not always possible to place monetary values on these components. Nevertheless, after having read this chapter, you should be able to:

1. Appreciate the ways in which wildlife resources are used by people in dryland regions.
2. Understand the dynamics of wildlife populations, importance of habitat management to the sustained use of wildlife resources, and how to achieve proper use of wildlife and livestock populations.
3. Know the situations in which the introductions and reintroductions of wildlife species can be considered and when wildlife ranching can be a profitable enterprise.
4. Recognize the importance and unique roles of recreation and tourism in dryland environments.
5. Discuss the varied ways by which amenity plantations "beautify the landscapes" of dryland regions.

REFERENCES

Caughley, G. 1970. Eruption of ungulate populations with emphasis on Himalayan Thar in New Zealand. *Ecology* 51:53–72.

Caughley G. 1977. *Analysis of vertebrate populations*. John Wiley & Sons, Inc., New York.

Child, B. 1990. Wildlife as a tool for sustainable economic development in southern African savannas. IUFRO, *XIX World Congress Report B*:238–51.

Child, G. S. 1989. Utilization of wildlife. In FAO 1989b. Role of forestry in combating desertification. *FAO Conservation Guide* 21, Rome, pp. 173–82.

Dasman, R. F. 1964. *African game ranching*. Pergamon Press, New York.

Davis, D. E. 1982. *Census methods for terrestrial vertebrates*. CRC Press, Inc., Boca Raton, Florida.

Ezcurra, E., S. Gallina, y P. F. Ffolliott. 1980. Manejo combinado del venado y el ganado en el norte de Mexico. *Rangelands* 2:208–9.

FAO. 1985. *Arid zone forestry programmes: State of knowledge and experience: An overview*. FAO, Rome.

FAO. 1989a. Arid zone forestry: A guide for field technicians. *FAO Conservation Guide* 20, Rome.

Field, R. T. 1992. Kenya's green challenge. *Urban Forests* 12(1):20–21.

Filter, R. 1982. Arabian oryx returns to the wild. *Oryx* 16:406–10.

Harrison, P. 1987. *The greening of Africa: Breaking through in the battle for land and food.* Penguin Books, New York.

Hawkes, C. L., D. E. Chalk, T. W. Hoekstra, and C. H. Flater. 1983. Prediction of wildlife and fish resources for national assessments and appraisal. *USDA Forest Service, General Technical Report* RM-100.

Heady, H. F., and E. B. Heady. 1982. *Range and wildlife management in the tropics.* Longman Group Limited, Essex, UK.

Holechek, J. L., R. D. Pieper, and C. H. Herbel. 1989. *Range management: Principles and practices.* Prentice Hall, Englewood Cliffs, New Jersey.

Hopcraft, D. 1990. Wildlife land use at the Athi River, Kenya. In NAS. 1990. *The improvement of tropical and subtropical rangelands.* National Academy of Sciences, Washington, D. C., pp. 332–40.

Jungius, H. 1978. Plan to restore Arabian oryx in Oman. *Oryx* 16:329–36.

Mackie, R. J. 1978. Impacts of livestock grazing on wild ungulates. *Transactions of the North American Wildlife and Natural Resources Conference* 43:462–76.

McPherson, E. G. 1988. Functions of buffer plantings in urban environments. In Brandle, J. R., D. L. Hintz, and J. W. Sturrock (eds.). 1988. *Windbreak technology.* Elsevier, New York, pp. 281–98.

Mahoney, M. 1991. The green streets of Cairo. *Urban Forests* 11(2):20–21.

Nelle, S. 1992. Exotics—at home on the range in Texas. *Rangelands* 14:77–80.

Nielsen, L., and R. D. Brown (eds.). 1988. *Translocation of wildlife animals.* The Wisconsin Humane Society, Inc., Milwaukee, Wisconsin, and The Caesar Kleberg Wildlife Research Institute, Kingsville, Texas.

Patton, D. R. 1992. *Wildlife habitat relationships in forested ecosystems.* Timber Press, Portland, Oregon.

Peek, J. M. 1986. *A review of wildlife management.* Prentice Hall, Englewood Cliffs, New Jersey.

Pratt, D. J., and M. D. Gwynne. 1977. *Rangeland management and ecology in East Africa.* Robert E. Krieger Publishing Company, Huntington, New York.

Rasmussen, D. I. 1941. Biotic communities of the Kaibab Plateau. *Ecological Monographs* 3:229–75.

Sanchez, D. K., R. Borel, A. Bonnemann, and J. Beer. 1990. Shade trees in plantation culture. In Moore, E. (ed.). 1990. *Agroforestry land-use systems.* Nitrogen Fixing Tree Association, Waimanalo, Hawaii, pp. 75–83.

Schemnitz, S. D. (ed.). 1980. *Wildlife management techniques.* The Wildlife Society, Washington, D.C.

White, R. J. 1987. *Big game ranching in the United States.* Wild Sheep and Goat International, Mesilla, New Mexico.

Woodruff, D. 1992. Globe Greenbelt renews a town. *Arizona Land and People* 42(1):26–27.

World Resources Institute. 1990. *World resources 1990–91.* Oxford University Press, New York.

6 Forestry

Trees and shrubs play vital roles in maintaining the ecological balance of dryland ecosystems, improving the livelihoods of people in the dryland regions of the world (FAO 1989a) and helping to combat the devastating effects of desertification (FAO 1989b, Salem 1988). It is important, therefore, that the various functions and places of trees and shrubs in dryland landscapes be understood in a general context for these roles to be developed further.

This chapter also serves as an introduction to the remaining parts of this book, in which *forestry* in the dryland regions of the world, as defined broadly in Chapter 1, is discussed in detail and in relation to planning and management for multiple benefits.

FUNCTIONS OF TREES AND SHRUBS

Trees and shrubs play vital roles in maintaining an ecological balance and improving the livelihood of people in dryland regions. Woody vegetation serves a variety of purposes. Trees and shrubs act to hold soil in place and prevent water and soil erosion. The roots of woody vegetation help to stabilize steep slopes, and the shade that the vegetation provides is important to people and their animals.

Trees and shrubs can be an important source of fodder for livestock and browse for wildlife at times when other herbaceous forage is not available. Multipurpose trees and shrubs are ideal for protecting and improving the soil, while providing high fodder and browse yields in the dry months without impairing agricultural crop production in the rainy season. Trees and shrubs are also a source of wood products, including fuelwood, poles, and timber for construction purposes. Trees and shrubs can be a source of food for people. Many fruits, leaves, young shoots, and roots provide valuable food in the dry season and, therefore, comprise an important reserve for emergencies.

Trees and shrubs are a frequent source of nonwood products. Many tree and shrub species are characterized by a high content of tannin in their bark or fruit, which can be utilized by the leather industry. Other trees and shrubs yield fibers, dyes, and pharmaceuticals. Flowers of many trees and shrubs are used for honey production.

Due to unrestricted cutting of wood, overgrazing by livestock, and cultivation of unsuitable lands, many dryland regions have inadequate forest and woodland cover and, as a result, inadequate fuelwood, timber, and fodder and browse resources.

Attempts to develop dryland regions for increased sustainable use by people, therefore, should include a forestry component, which can benefit local people and contribute considerably to a more balanced environment. In this sense, forestry must be integrated with agriculture and animal husbandry to optimize land use. A look at the functions of trees and shrubs in providing fuelwood, fodder and browse and in improving agricultural crop production illustrates the importance of this point.

Fuelwood

Many natural forests and woodlands, and forest plantations are used for the production of fuelwood in the dryland regions of the world. The production of fuelwood can be crucial to people. Over 50 percent of the wood removed from the world's forests, woodlands, and plantations is used for fuel, and 90 percent of the inhabitants of developing countries rely on it for their domestic needs (Example 6.1). These people simply cannot afford other sources of energy.

Fuelwood is a marketable commodity that, in many situations, is transported over long distances. The demands for fuelwood are increasing, and wood is likely to continue to be an important source of fuel for small-scale industrial uses in rural and urban areas. Much of the fuelwood in the world still comes from natural forests and woodlands that are being cut down and destroyed at alarming rates. However, fuelwood also can be grown on an intensive and sustained scale in forest plantations.

Example 6.1

Importance of Fuelwood in Nigeria (Cline-Cole 1990) The importance of fuelwood to people in developing countries is illustrated in the Kano region of Nigeria, an area of ever increasing fuelwood demands. Here, two-thirds of the households rely upon wood as the sole source of energy for cooking and heating. Annual consumption of fuelwood is approximately 0.5 m^3 per person, a level that is less than estimates in other tropical African countries but still a significant amount in comparison to available supplies. Many of the people in the region obtain their fuelwood in a marketplace, spending up to one-fifth of their monthly wages on this necessity. Due to a continually increasing population, the aggregate demand for fuelwood has increased by a factor of five since the early 1950s. There is a serious question as to whether the primary sources of fuelwood in Kano, which include natural forests and woodlands, forest plantations, farmed parks, and shrublands, will be sufficient to meet these demands in the future. A transition to alternative sources of energy is anticipated, although fuelwood presumably provides more energy at less cost than the alternatives. The situation in the Kano region also holds significance for the broader Nigerian setting and other areas of the African savanna.

A scarcity of fuelwood can create further problems. People frequently turn to agricultural residues and animal droppings in times of fuelwood scarcity instead of using these materials to maintain soil fertility on agricultural land. Furthermore, a change in the availability of fuelwood often affects the health and nutrition of a whole family, which then might be forced to use more fast cooking and less nutritious foods and have less money for food as fuelwood prices increase. Fuelwood scarcities affect several aspects of family life, as more time must be spent in gathering fuel at the expense of more productive work.

Land must be set aside to secure a production base, either as intensively managed natural stands or forest plantations to meet increasing demands for fuelwood. Large-scale fuelwood plantations can be required to supply urban areas, including industrial operations within these areas. Small-scale forestry activities may be sufficient to meet demands for fuelwood in rural areas, which are under less population pressure. When land is used for this purpose, one talks about village woodlots or forestry at the farm level. In principle, it is only the size of the operation that differs from a large-scale system. However, a major obstacle to forestry at this level is making land available for fuelwood production. Concerned local people must be convinced that to obtain fuelwood, some land must be set aside.

Fodder and Browse

Another significant role of trees and shrubs in dryland regions can be to provide fodder and browse (Example 6.2). The protein obtained from woody vegetation during the dry season constitutes an essential element in an animal's diet. Among the various sources of feed (e.g., concentrates, cereals, and annual fodder crops) woody vegetation is often the cheapest and the one on which the majority of livestock rely. In addition, trees and shrubs are important food for many wildlife species.

The importance of trees and shrubs in fodder and browse production can be illustrated in three situations—normal scarcity, prolonged drought, and intensive fodder production. In normal scarcity situations, that is, during the dry season when grasses and other herbaceous plants are not available, it is likely that only trees and shrubs are available to provide the necessary feed for livestock and wildlife species. When such vegetation is not available, the production of livestock and health of wildlife can be affected seriously, as people normally do not have the resources to acquire other types of feed for these animals. The creation of fodder and browse resources for situations of normal scarcity, therefore, is a vital activity for maintaining the production of animals. Overall resources can be enhanced by managing existing woody vegetation for increased fodder and browse production or by creating additional resources through tree and shrub plantations.

Not only is rainfall in dryland regions variable during a year, but, as pointed out earlier, there is considerable variation in rainfall from year to year. Prolonged periods of drought frequently occur. Under these emergency situations, trees and shrubs assume even greater importance in the form of fodder and browse reserves.

Example 6.2

Some Tree and Shrub Species for Fodder and Browse (Child et al. 1987) Trees and shrubs that provide fodder and browse can be selected from among hundreds of species. One well-known example is *Acacia albida*, a tree that can attain 20 m in height while growing along streams in savannas and grasslands of Africa and eastward into India. Its leaves begin to grow at the start of the dry season, creating a fodder resource at this critical time, and are shed at the beginning of the rainy season. A mature tree yields up to 100 kg of pods annually. *Acacia senegal*, a smaller tree or shrub, produces gum arabic, a valued product often for export. It also is a fodder plant, providing both leaves and pods that are palatable and nutritious.

Species of *Prosopis*, many of which have value as fuelwood and in nitrogen enhancement of the soil, furnish fodder and browse resources from northern Africa to southern Asia and in the dry regions of the Americas. *Prosopis juliflora* is one example.

Atriplex spp. are grown as fodder shrubs in areas receiving annual rainfall amounts of 200 mm and less. Several species are highly palatable and, as a consequence, care must be taken to prevent overgrazing that kills younger, more succulent plants. It seems logical to encourage the planting of trees and shrubs for fodder and browse, if only on a small scale. Unfortunately, silvical characteristics of these woody plants are little understood and planting stock is difficult to obtain in sufficient numbers for management.

Woody vegetation is better able to survive extended periods of drought than annual and perennial forage species.

The most intensive method of fodder and browse production is the establishment of fodder plantations. Fodder and browse species can be grown in pure stands, harvested in a controlled way, and then fed to livestock and wildlife when needed. Where grasses are grown, animals can be moved between the different areas of production to enable optimal use of both types of forage. Another possibility is to establish two-storied pastures, with suitable fodder and browse species over an understory of grasses and legumes.

Improvement in Agricultural Crop Production

Productivity of agricultural land in dryland regions is inherently low and the risk of failure is high. This situation is due not only to low and unreliable rainfall but also to the effects of wind and water erosion and low soil fertility.

Wind erosion is a serious problem in most of the dryland regions of the world. Destruction of vegetative cover exposes soil to the desiccative effects of hot, dry wind, resulting in dust storms, formation of sand dunes, and other forms of severe wind erosion. Wind is not only responsible for the transport of soil particles and loss of soil nutrients, but through its desiccating effect, wind often reduces growth and development of food crops and livestock production. Wind assumes a larger role in irrigated agriculture than it does in rainfed agriculture. By increasing evaporation, wind facilitates the upward movement of salts and their subsequent concentration in the rooting zones of agricultural crops. The particles of dust and sand carried by wind can be deposited in irrigation channels and drainage ditches, increasing maintenance costs of irrigation. Such damages can be diminished by the establishment of *windbreaks*. Windbreaks are barriers established to protect a site from damaging wind flows. Windbreak plantings consisting of woody plants, a particularly effective type of windbreak (Example 6.3), are a topic of Chapter 17.

Erosion by water also is an important phenomenon in most of the dryland regions. This type of erosion is the result of the susceptibility of the soil to erosion, high rainfall intensities, and frequent destruction of the vegetative cover. When these conditions occur, considerable amounts of soil are washed down from upland catchment areas. Roads are damaged, lowlands are flooded, and streams and wadis are filled with muddy water. Some of this sediment-laden water accumulates in reservoirs or is transported to lakes or the ocean. The loss of water through runoff

---

Example 6.3

Windbreak Plantings in the Sahelian Region of West Africa: A Case Study (Harrison 1987) Improvement in agricultural crop production as a result of windbreak plantings has been observed in the Majjia Valley in central Niger, West Africa. A program of windbreak plantings was initiated in 1975 in response to local villagers asking the local forestry officer if anything could be done to help them in controlling the destructive wind erosion in the valley. For the next 10 years or so, locally grown neem (*Azadirachta indica*), a deep-rooted evergreen tree from Asia, was planted in locations selected by the local forestry officer and protected from grazing by livestock by local farmers and paid guards.

The results after 10 years suggested that benefits of the plantings far out-weighed the costs. Although the windbreaks took up to 15 in every 100 m^2 of land, yields of millet, sorghum, and cowpeas increased by about 25 percent, in comparison to that on similar lands unprotected by windbreaks. This increase in yields of agricultural crops was attributed to a reduction in soil erosion, smothering of crops by sand, and evaporation losses and an increase in the level of soil moisture for crop production.

People in the Majjia are well aware of the benefits of the windbreak plantings. Nearly 75 percent of the local farmers have indicated that the windbreak plantings were the reason that food production increased significantly. Farmers from outside of the valley also have expressed a desire to be included in windbreak planting programs.

---

and the ensuing soil erosion can be controlled by adopting preventive soil conservation measures. The role of trees and shrubs in an overall strategy for the management of vegetation can reduce siltation of reservoirs, affect stream flow, and reduce flash floods and soil erosion.

Agricultural crop production in dryland regions frequently is hindered by poor soil fertility. However, the importance of soil fertility often is overlooked. Water shortage is considered the principal constraint. Whereas a conventional and relatively expensive method to improve soil fertility commonly consists of repeated application of mineral fertilizers, this problem also can be solved through systematic use of soil-improving, salt-tolerant species of trees and shrubs.

PLACEMENT OF TREES AND SHRUBS IN DRYLAND LANDSCAPES

To grow trees or shrubs in any form or for any purpose is a forestry practice. Forestry, in turn, is a land use practice. Pressure on land for agriculture is high in dryland regions, so high that land unsuitable for agriculture often is used in a desperate effort to grow crops. As a result, forestry can be relegated to lands which are too poor for crop growth. Unfortunately, there is often a general misconception that forestry is best allocated to poor sites, which largely is incorrect. It must be realized, however, that forestry, like agriculture, places demands on land to reach satisfying production levels. Two basic requirements are needed to achieve these levels in terms of forestry interventions in dryland regions—trees and shrubs should not be confined to areas designated as "marginal," and forestry must be integrated into overall land use strategies (FAO 1989a).

There are numerous ways to place, grow, and manage trees and shrubs in dryland landscapes, including:

- Windbreak plantings to protect agricultural crops and pastures against wind desiccation, as mentioned above.
- Intermixtures with agricultural crops to protect the crops and to reconstitute and enrich the soil.
- Scattered plantings in agricultural fields during fallow periods to enrich the soil and to provide fuelwood, timber, fodder and browse, and nonwood products.
- Linear plantations along roads and waterways to protect infrastructures and adjacent fields and to provide shade and contribute to the production of fuelwood, timber, fodder and browse, and nonwood products.
- Forest plantations and woodlots established under rainfed or irrigated conditions to make the best use of often unused land and to contribute to needed wood supplies.
- Intensive management of natural forests and woodlands to maintain a stable environment and yield essential products traditionally used by local populations.
- Plantations in areas threatened by sand dune encroachment.

Within the above options, the most appropriate combination of land uses is selected to improve agricultural and livestock production, stabilize and enrich the environment, and meet essential needs for fuelwood, timber, and nonwood products. In general, the proper introduction of trees and shrubs into the landscapes of dryland regions through properly planned forestry projects can improve the living conditions for people and the rural economies of the inhabitants of dryland regions and, in so doing, contribute to sustainable development (FAO 1989a, 1989b, Salem 1988).

ACHIEVING SUSTAINABLE DEVELOPMENT IN FORESTRY

Sustainable development is a broad term that is difficult to define. Furthermore, it often is difficult to determine if and when sustainable development has been attained. From the perspective of forestry and other natural resources projects, there are some characteristics of the results obtained from a project that generally point toward sustainability (Gregersen and Lundgren 1990). Once a project has met its immediate objectives and, therefore, is "successful" by definition, the question of sustainability requires that the characteristics of *continuity, diffusion,* and *externalities* be considered.

Continuity refers to continuation of forestry project activities and effects after the formal end of the intervention. If the activities and effects initiated by the project stop after the project ends, it cannot be considered sustainable. *Diffusion* refers to the spread of good ideas, practices, and technologies developed by the project to areas outside of the boundaries of the project. Most projects address only a small part of a much larger problem area, so diffusion of project concepts and practices to a much wider area is essential for sustainable development. *Externalities* refers to both biophysical and human-institutional impacts and effects that occur outside of the project area as a result of project activities. For example, downstream benefits or costs that result from forestry projects that are implemented on upstream watershed lands are externalities that should be considered in the planning, implementing, and evaluating these upstream projects, because they do effect sustainability.

Biophysical Barriers

Planning and implementation of forestry projects and the achievement of sustainability requires that *biophysical* and *human-institutional* barriers be overcome. Biophysical barriers include climate, soils, topography, and water—conditions that impose restrictions on the development of forestry and natural resource projects. Each tree or shrub species and forest or woodland type has specific requirements for establishment, growth, and reproduction. Dryland regions impose rather harsh physical and environmental barriers to sustainable forest resource management.

The variability of dryland environments requires special attention when planning forestry and natural resource projects. Planning for forestry, livestock, or agricultural practices must recognize and account for the uncertainty that is associated with low and erratic amounts of rainfall. Many dryland regions have sufficient annual precipitation to develop productive forestry, livestock, and agricultural systems. However, the rain often falls all at once with considerable runoff and results in little replenishment of soil moisture. Furthermore, dryland regions typically experience annual dry periods, often of several months, with little or no rainfall. Tree and shrub species must be able to become established, grow, survive, and, in natural systems, reproduce under conditions of limited soil moisture. These species also must be able to survive droughts that, although they are certain to occur, are nonetheless unpredictable. Tree and shrub species must be selected that are adapted to dryland environments and, at the same time, produce goods, services, and amenities needed by people.

Human-Institutional Barriers

Human-institutional barriers include all of the social, economic, technological, cultural, legal, and political factors that might affect sustainability of a forestry project. The particular characteristics of a social-economic-cultural system in one part of the world can provide certain barriers and opportunities that may not be found elsewhere. Land tenure institutions, problems of the homeless, landless, or refugees can all affect sustainability of forest resource development and sustainability. Other barriers might include institutional deficiencies such as a lack of adequate knowledge or technology, a lack of adequate human and capital resources, inadequate institutions and institutional support (including infrastructures and organizations), and inadequate incentives among different groups of people involved with or affected by forestry and natural resource projects.

Methods of overcoming biophysical and human-institutional barriers to sustainable development include changing and improving institutions, developing and disseminating appropriate technologies, and providing education, training, and extension. In large part, the remaining chapters of this book consider the barriers to sustainable development and the opportunities to overcome these barriers in terms of forestry-related interventions in the dryland regions of the world. However, for these barriers to be overcome also requires opportunities for investment, employment, and income generation, as discussed in the following chapter.

SUMMARY

The roles of trees and shrubs in helping to achieve the sustainable development of dryland regions have been stressed in this chapter, which also serves as an introduction to the remainder of the book. At this point in the text, you should be able to:

1. Describe the role of trees and shrubs in providing fuelwood, fodder and browse, and improvement in agricultural crop production.

2. Describe ways to place, grow, and manage trees and shrubs in a dryland landscape.

3. Define *continuity*, *diffusion*, and *externalities* in relation to the activities of a forestry project.

4. Explain and present examples of the biophysical and socioeconomic barriers to achieving the sustainability of forestry projects and how these barriers can be overcome.

REFERENCES

Child, R. D., H. F. Heady, R. A. Petersen, R. D. Pieper, and C. E. Poulton. 1987. *Arid and semiarid rangelands: Guidelines for development*. Winrock International, Morrilton, Arkansas.

Cline-Cole, R. A., J. A. Falola, H. A. C. Main, M. J. Mortimore, J. E. Nichol, and F. D. O'Reilly. 1990. *Wood fuel in Kano*. United Nations Press, Tokyo, Japan.

FAO. 1989a. Arid zone forestry: A guide for field technicians. *FAO Conservation Guide* 20, Rome.

FAO. 1989b. The role of forestry in combating desertification. *FAO Conservation Guide* 21, Rome.

Gregersen, H. M., and A. L. Lundgren. 1990. *Forestry for sustainable development: Concepts and a framework for action*. Forestry for Sustainable Development (FFSD) Program, Working Paper 1, University of Minnesota, St. Paul, Minnesota.

Harrison, P. 1987. *The greening of Africa: Breaking through in the battle for land and food*. Penguin Books, New York.

Salem, B. B. 1988. A strategy on the role of forestry in combating desertification. In Whitehead, E. E., C. F. Hutchinson, B. N. Timmermann, and R. G. Varady (eds.). 1988. *Arid lands: Today and tomorrow*. Westview Press, Boulder, Colorado, pp. 841–69.

7 Investment, Employment, Income Generation

Sustainable forestry is dependent upon the availability of profitable investment opportunities and, as a result of this investment, employment and income generation. Much of the investment in forestry in the dryland regions of the world is public investment, especially in the southwestern United States. Investment by the private sector also occurs in some situations.

Public investment in the multiple use management of forests and woodlands in the southwestern United States is relatively large, because these ecosystems are mostly in the public domain. The level of this investment is reflected by the operational budgets of the governmental agencies responsible for the management of these forests and woodlands. Some private investment is made in livestock and agricultural crop production, water resources development, enhancement of recreational facilities, and harvesting of wood, where permitted. The level of this investment frequently is constrained by perceived high risks and low returns anticipated.

Investment in forestry activities in dryland regions elsewhere in the world often is tied to projects in developing countries. Much of this investment is made by governmental and nongovernmental organizations (NGOs) through financial support from external public and private donors. It is largely this form of investment that is considered in this chapter. A "farmer's perspective" has been taken in many instances, because it is investment at this level that is required to encourage development or expansion of forestry-based enterprises.

This chapter consists largely of a series of "case studies" that illustrate these opportunities for investment, employment, and income. The general conclusions drawn from these studies suggest opportunities for investment, employment, and income generation in terms of forestry interventions in dryland regions.

INVESTMENT OPPORTUNITIES

Opportunities for profitable investment in the sustainable use of a renewable natural resource base are more limited in dryland regions than other regions because of the harsh environmental conditions that exist, particularly the limited availability of water. However, the need for increased levels of investment, employment, and income generation is great in dryland regions. In most of these regions, there is rapid population growth, coupled with rapid growth of food and other renewable natural resource based imports. The mounting imports are causing severe economic impacts in some areas.

In the West Asia-North Africa region, for example, the population is expected to triple between 1990 and 2030, reaching about 1.5 billion people. Yet, even now, this region has become the developing world's largest food importing region, with over 40 percent of the value of all food imports by developing countries (ICARDA 1992). Agricultural imports account for over 25 percent of the region's total import bill. Investments to reduce the dependence on agricultural imports are being made. However, the problem being confronted is one of scarcity of arable land and water to support large-scale irrigation. Only an estimated 128 million ha, or 8 percent of the region's 1.7 billion ha, is thought to be arable. Another 22 percent is permanent pasture. Only small areas are covered with forest, woodland, or other perennial vegetation. Some 70 percent of this region, therefore, is "desertlike" in character.

Investment opportunities to sustain agriculture and to produce forest products are linked closely in the economic development of dryland regions. It is important that one recognizes the "characteristics" of these investment opportunities, from both pro and con viewpoints.

Investment to Sustain Agriculture

A key to profitable investment in renewable natural resource activities, including agriculture, is water. Water always is a scarce commodity in dryland regions. Yet, it is not always treated as such, as illustrated by the pricing of water for agricultural and industrial uses. Investment in irrigated agriculture is substantial, often at the expense of investment in more water-saving agricultural technologies. Overinvestment in irrigated agriculture can occur because of water-pricing policies that encourage overuse of water. There is mounting evidence that irrigated agriculture investments can not be sustainable in most dryland areas, despite the high levels of investment that have taken place. Among other things, drawdown of water tables is proceeding at rates of 1 m or more annually in many irrigated agriculture areas. In some regions, this "mining" of water might lead to disaster in only a few years. In some countries, irrigation systems already have dried up and the benefits from such investment are long gone in many cases.

More investment is needed to increase food production and reduce the unsustainable, water-consuming practices that are so widespread. Since the option of agricultural expansion generally implies expansion of irrigation and water use, this option likely could lead to increased pressure on already insufficient water supplies in many dryland regions. Rather, it is appropriate that investment be oriented toward intensification of agriculture through, for example, seed improvement and development of alternative technologies. This intensification includes technologies that involve the better use of trees and shrubs in agroforestry practices and windbreak plantings. Investment in forestry-related research also is needed to better understand the role of forestry in improving and sustaining food self-reliance in dryland environments.

Investment to Produce Forest Products

When it occurs, investment in forestry takes place in dryland regions for the same reasons as investment in other parts of the world. Scarcity of forest outputs increases, and with this increased scarcity come higher values and higher prices for those outputs. As returns on investment become more attractive, capital enters the market to produce the various outputs in demand. In some cases, wood becomes scarce rather rapidly, and adequate investment response by either the public or private sector is not forthcoming quickly enough. The fact is that it takes time to grow wood in dryland regions. Therefore, investment and expanded growing of wood need to anticipate scarcities, commercialization, and rising prices.

If early investment does not take place, the problems faced can be more than rising prices. Periods of limited supply can occur, and, as experience has shown, local shortages of wood can cause loss of employment, hardships, and environmental degradation (Example 7.1). These impacts are intensifying in many countries. A key policy question is how to help people anticipate future shortages and take actions to avoid them. In most cases, direct government investment and

---

Example 7.1

Wood Scarcity and Loss of Employment: Two Case Studies (Centre for Science and Environment 1985; Hoskins 1980)

India. A distressing story comes from Nirmal, 200 km from Hyderabad in Andhra Pradesh, known for its handcrafted wooden toys which are exported in substantial quantities. The art of toy making, believed to go back a thousand years, is based upon the use of a light wood called *ponki*, purchased from local or nearby forest sales depots. Local fisherfolk also use ponki for their catamarans, and the toy makers even borrow wood from them when supplies run short. Ponki is today in short supply. One "unit" of the wood cost *Rs* [rupees] 0.25 in 1967, while it cost *Rs* 17.50 in the middle 1980s. In a desperate bid to survive, the toy makers' cooperative is trying to get 40 ha reserved for a local ponki plantation.

Africa. A lobi potter reported that her husband had left home in search of work because his blacksmith trade had become uneconomical due to a scarcity of fuelwood. She had given up making large pots and, as a consequence, was wondering how much longer she would be able to support her family as a potter, because it had become difficult to get fuelwood to fire even the smaller pots. Many women in developing countries throughout the world depend largely upon wood fuel not only to cook for their families, but also to earn money by processing foods such as "snacks" that are sold in the markets. Many of these women work in small industries that depend upon wood for energy, for example, in smoking fish.

incentive programs for the private sector are needed to stimulate adequate investment at an early enough stage.

A relatively large amount of public investment has gone into forestry in the
drylands of many countries in the world. Unfortunately, much of this investment
has not borne fruit because of bureaucratic problems or because the investments
were not "thought out" well enough in terms of their likely total impacts, including
their impacts on water consumption. There are many examples of relatively large
investments in fuelwood plantations that never survived to produce fuelwood,
fodder production programs that did not meet anticipated needs, and water and soil
protection practices that ended up being disasters because it was forgotten that
trees and shrubs also use scarce water.

EMPLOYMENT AND INCOME GENERATION[1]

Effects of commercialization on income generally are considered to be positive in
a developmental context. Jobs are created and increased income is earned. However, some caution must be exercised in planning forestry programs in dryland
areas that promote large-scale commercial activity. When a natural forest or
woodland, or forest plantation output moves from the free or subsistence category
of use to the market or commercial category, users who do not produce it have to
pay a price in either money or kind. This cost can cause a hardship for the poor if
they are not the producers. A prime example of this is the frequent commercialization of fuelwood, which results in families in some parts of the world having to pay
as much as a third of their income to meet their essential fuelwood needs.

There are indications that some market-oriented forestry projects can detract
greatly from the *social forestry objective* of helping to meet the needs of the poorest rural people. Criticism has been leveled against several otherwise successful
programs because they mainly helped better-off farmers and, in many instances,
hurt landless laborers by taking away previous sources of employment (Shiva et al.
1982). Policies associated with employment creation and commercialization of
social forestry outputs need to be considered carefully and planned in advance.

There can be a close link between forestry, income and employment, and food
security (Arnold and Falconer 1987). The gathering and processing of fuelwood,
fruits, resins, nuts, and various fibers can provide income that in turn can be used
to purchase food. These opportunities often are seasonal and fit into work schedules during slack times in agriculture. Trees and shrubs also can be looked at as a
form of investment that creates savings in some cases (Chambers and Leach 1987).
Seen from the point of view of the rural poor, trees and shrubs are like bank
deposits with low initial deposits, low managerial costs, and high rates of appreciation.

---

[1]Adapted from Gregersen et al. (1989).

Local forestry activities can provide employment opportunities for farm families and the landless. These income-earning opportunities are not only in seedling production and the planting, tending, and harvesting of trees and shrubs. Income-earning opportunities also are found in complementary activities such as the processing and sale of wood, other parts of trees and shrubs (such as fruits, bark, resin, branches, and leaves), and other forest products grown among trees (fodder, berries, roots, mushrooms, and tubers). These activities, in turn, can stimulate service employment in transportation and maintenance. In situations of high unemployment, this aspect of forestry can be critical in a strategy for sustainable development (FAO 1987).

A major portion of off-farm employment in some rural areas is found in forestry-related activities, often using wood produced by local farmers or communities. Small-scale investment opportunities in these activities and farm forestry itself can be attractive for rural families in terms of generating employment, income, and savings. Off-farm employment in small-scale enterprises (SSEs) in the forestry-based sector is significant in many parts of the world. For example, in one country, Sierra Leone, which has been studied in some detail, forestry-based SSEs account for more than one-fifth of the total employment in the nonagricultural, small-scale enterprise sector, representing the major employer of rural labor (FAO 1985). The typical forestry-based SSE is small. The mean number of employees per firm in Sierra Leone was about two, and enterprises employing one person (the owner) accounted for about 70 percent of the total in Egypt.

Activities undertaken by wood-based SSEs are diverse and often labor intensive (Example 7.2). At the same time, however, these SSEs appear to be as efficient in the use of capital as their more modern, larger-scale counterparts (FAO 1985). The diversity of activity in the SSEs ranges from oak and pine mushroom production and marketing by village forestry associations in the Republic of Korea (Gregersen 1982) to women's groups producing tree seedlings for sale in Senegal.

Page (1978), in analyzing employment in small industries in selected African countries, found that carpentry-furniture making was the second largest industrial sector (after the manufacturing of clothing), employing between 8 and 20 percent of the labor force in the "intermediate sector" of the countries studied. There have

---

Example 7.2

Village Carpenters in Pakistan (Khattak and Amjad 1981) It has been estimated that Pakistan has about 98,000 village carpenters. This estimate excludes furniture producers (another 41,000) and carpenters employed in the urban building industry. These village carpenters use significant amounts of wood annually. About 249,000 m^3 of wood were utilized in 1981, in comparison to the estimated 506,000 m^3 of wood used in the building industry. Village carpentry is the largest single category of employment and represents about one-third of a total employment of 320,000 in the forestry sector.

been only a few estimates of total employment in such activities for most countries, however. Recognizing this, the FAO financed a number of activities in this area. These activities included small-scale industries in Bangladesh, Egypt, Sierra Leone, and Zambia (FAO 1985, 1987). The SSEs found in these countries produce a variety of outputs for both local and export markets, as shown in Table 7.1.

Some studies have shown that the numbers of people employed in the forestry-based SSEs sector are much greater than indicated in official statistics. In selected areas of Bangladesh and Sierra Leone, for example, employment in SSEs was underestimated in official censuses by 59 and 44 percent, respectively (FAO 1985).

SSEs get their wood supplies either from nearby forests, woodlands, and plantations or from local farmers and other private sources. However, the competition for wood is mounting and, as a consequence, SSEs are experiencing severe wood supply problems in many parts of the world (FAO 1985, 1987). These problems appear to be long-term and, therefore, critical to future planning for the sector. Shortages and large price increases have a severe impact, since raw material represents a significant portion of total costs in many forestry-based SSEs.

Forestry links to wood supplies and SSE activities go far beyond the enterprises that produce wood-based products. Enterprises that produce tobacco, pottery, coffee, bread, and salt are major consumers of wood for fuel and energy in many parts of the world. On the one hand, these enterprises create direct competition with villagers seeking wood for their own use. On the other hand, they create markets for small holder-grown wood and employment for local people in wood harvesting and transport.

Many forestry-based SSEs could not operate without a reliable source of relatively inexpensive fuelwood. Therefore, wood-growing activities that increase fuelwood supplies in wood-poor areas can help save jobs, which is just as important as creating employment opportunities in forestry-based SSEs. Wood supply and market concerns need to be considered in plans for forestry projects that have

TABLE 7.1. Small-scale Enterprises (SSEs) with Forestry-based Activities

Activity	Bangladesh	Egypt	Sierra Leone	Zambia
		—%—		
Sawmilling	0.9		0.1	5.6
Carpentry/furniture	27.3	23.8	66.8	14.3
Wood carving	11.6		5.9	11.9
Basket/mat/hat making	32.4	70.4	23.8	60.3
Others[a]	27.9	5.8	3.4	7.9
Total	100.0	100.0	100.0	100.0

[a]*Others* includes activities such as making containers and agricultural tools in Bangladesh, making agricultural tools in Egypt, and collecting fuelwood in Zambia.

Many SSEs do not specialize in the production of one item, so classification sometimes depends upon the most dominant or most important activity.

commercial components, particularly in situations where fuelwood use is growing and unemployment is high.

A significant proportion of the proprietors and workers in the forestry-based SSEs have other sources of income. This proportion in Sierra Leone, for example, is 83 percent, much of it in income from farming (FAO 1985). Whether this farming activity includes the growing of wood is unknown, however. It has been found that significant proportions of small farmers also have off-farm incomes in the People's Republic of China, the Republic of Korea, and northern Nigeria. In these countries, about 50 percent of the managers or owners of forestry-based SSEs listed "farming" as the occupation of their fathers. It is apparent, therefore, that the forestry-based SSE sector has close economic ties to agriculture.

INVESTMENT RETURNS AND INCOME FLOWS

There are three main questions of major interest in considering investment returns and income flows from forestry:

- Can commercial farm or community forestry activity be profitable for the participants?
- What is the nature of the cash flows involved?
- How does a farmer's cash flow pattern change as the growing of trees or shrubs is expanded?

There are no *general* answers to these questions because investments in farm or community forestry and the results of those investments vary widely from situation to situation. Reports from India, for example, indicate that a program in Gujarat, involving farmers planting *Eucalyptus* for sale in cities, produced relatively high rates of return for individual farmers in the early days of the program (Eckholm 1979, Wood et al. 1980). This finding is probably a main reason why farmer participation has expanded so rapidly. Rates of return are low or negative, largely because of inherently slow tree or shrub growth, poor markets, or the need for expensive inputs to make trees and shrubs survive and grow in other parts of the dryland world.

Between these extremes, there are many projects that provide reasonable rates of return to farmers. Evaluations of tree-farming projects that were financed by The World Bank in countries with at least portions of their areas in dryland environments indicated *financial* rates of return to farmers ranging from 15 to 18 percent, as shown in Table 7.2. More intensive types of farm forestry can produce even higher rates of return, rates which often exceed those from other uses of the land. To illustrate this point, Srivastava and Pant (1979) provided data for a farm forestry project at Vatava, Ahmedabad, in Gujarat State of India, which showed a 89 percent rate of return to farmers. These authors also summarized two other

TABLE 7.2. Financial Rates of Return for Selected Tree-farming Projects

Country	Average Farm Size (ha)	Species	Rotation (yr)	Product	Initial Investment Cost[a] ($/ha)	Financial Rate of Return to Farmer (%)
Brazil	20	*Eucalyptus*	22	Pulpwood, fence posts, fuelwood, sawlogs	350	18
Republic of Korea	11	*Robinia, Alnus, Lespediza*	5	Fuelwood	250	18
Sudan	25	*Acacia*	5	Gum arabic	30	15

[a]*Initial investment cost* represents cost of establishment, including farm labor costs, during initial three years, in 1977 prices.

In the Sudan, gum arabic is grown as an integral part of a rotation that includes millet and groundnuts as the principal crops. It accounts for about 20 percent of the total cropped area and 25 percent of the net farm income. The financial rate of return would drop to approximately 10 percent if the gum arabic component was excluded from the rotation.

Source: Adapted from Spears (1978).

studies with similar rates of return, based on work of Rowe (1980) (Table 7.3). In the case of roadside plantings and village plantations, the calculated financial rates of return varied widely, from 7 percent for several village plantations on poorer soils to 32 percent for a roadside planting in Haryana State, where tree seedlings were protected and watered.

TABLE 7.3. Financial Rates of Returns for Two Forest Plantations in India

Type of Plantation	Net Present Value (12%) (Rupees)	Benefit-Cost Ratio (12%) (Rupees)	Financial Rate of Return (%)	Total Employment (days)
Private farm: hybrid *Eucalyptus* planted in five-year rotation; hybrid castor intercropped between *Eucalyptus* rows; irrigated and fertilized.	11,123	3.18	17	1,781
Private farm: hybrid *Eucalyptus* planted in five-year rotation; intercropping pattern: year 1, cotton; year 2, *Bajra* and wheat; year 3, jowar and tobacco; year 4, napier grass; irrigated and fertilized.	9,567	1.85	75	4,752

Source: Adapted from Srivastava and Pant (1979).

An analysis for Madhya Pradesh State, India, showed similar rates of return for village fuelwood plantations when outputs not intended for sale were valued using existing market prices (Bromley 1983). Even the least profitable fuelwood plantation had an internal rate of return of 13 percent. A plantation with 20 percent fruit trees included had an internal rate of return of 33 percent. More typical plantations had internal rates of return in the neighborhood of 20 percent.

Spears (1987) reported that investment in agroforestry practices increased internal rates of return to farmers in northern Nigeria when soil conservation and benefits of increased agricultural crop yields derived from windbreak plantings were taken into account (Table 7.4).

It is becoming increasingly apparent that income generation, in addition to food production for their families' use, has a prominent place in farmers' production objectives. This is especially the case for the poorest farmers. Land-use strategies involving the growing of wood often fit in well with the income generation objective, and the high cost of capital and the high opportunity cost for labor when a farmer does not own enough land to make a living from it. Therefore, when the size of a holding is small, a farmer frequently is forced to find outside employment and, as a consequence, shifts to land use practices that involve less labor than production of agricultural crops. Many forestry and agroforestry practices accommodate this need and, at the same time, provide attractive income opportunities (Arnold 1986, 1987; The World Bank 1986).

Different *forestry activity models* indicate different returns to investment (capital), land and labor, as shown by the illustration from Malawi presented in Table 7.5. Discount rates of 25 and 50 percent reflect what farmers actually perceive to be the discounting of future earnings (The World Bank 1984). With such great differences in returns, it matters greatly how farmers perceive relative input scarcities. Farmers with more land than their families can handle have to hire labor to undertake additional activity. In this case, labor productivity would be of con-

TABLE 7.4. Appraisal of Economic Benefits of an Agroforestry Investment in Northern Nigeria

Component	Internal Rate of Return (%)
Agroforestry	
Wood-fruit benefits alone	7.4
Wood-fruit benefits plus positive impacts of trees on soil conservation and agricultural crop yield	16.9
Windbreaks	
Wood benefits alone (fuelwood, fence posts)	4.7
Wood benefits plus positive benefits of windbreaks on soil conservation and agricultural crop yield	21.8

Source: Adapted from Spears (1987), based upon Anderson (1987).

TABLE 7.5. Forestry Activity Models in Malawi

Activity	Returns to Investment (Internal Rate of Return, %)	Returns to Land (Net Present Value, MK[a]/ha)		Return to Labor (Net Present Value, MK/Discounted Labor Day)	
		Discounted at 25%	Discounted at 50%	Discounted at 25%	Discounted at 50%
Growing poles	185	858	256	8.9	4.0
Growing fuelwood	65	84	13	1.0	0.2
Collecting fuelwood	> 1,000	(does not require land)		0.3	0.3
Improved maize plus fertilizer	240	198	146	1.4	1.0
Local maize, no fertilizer	> 3,000	69	57	0.7	0.5

[a]MK = U.S.$0.75.

If a full harvesting of fuelwood was undertaken in year 4 and, thereafter, at 4-year intervals, as with poles, the returns to land for growing fuelwood would increase from 84 to a net present value of 104 at the 24 percent discount rate.

Source: Adapted from The World Bank (1984).

cern. For the small farmer, labor might or might not be considered a scarce resource, depending largely upon whether off-farm employment is in the picture or not. If not, fuelwood collecting might be the rational choice of activity, since labor is abundant and capital and land scarce. Arnold (1987) provides an example from Kenya that sums up several points regarding farmer investment decisions in relation to perceptions of scarcities and risk (Example 7.3).

Example 7.3

Farmers Investment Decisions in Relation to Perceptions of Scarcities and Risk: A Case Study (Arnold 1987, Gelder and Kerkhof 1984, The World Bank 1986) Tree growing in Kenya tends to be practiced by poor farmers who are unable to meet their food needs and for whom it is a principal source of farm income. In the Vihiga location in Kakamega District, for example, average farm size is about 0.6 ha, of which some 25 percent is represented by *Eucalyptus* woodlots. Gross income per hectare in this area is considerably lower from tree growing than from other agricultural crops. A study by the World Bank suggests that farmer preference for tree crops in these circumstances is conditioned by the availability of capital and labor, and their attitudes to risk management. Alternative crops often require investments at levels beyond small farmers' access to capital. By contrast, growing of trees requires relatively little expenditure. Tree growing also is attractive in an area where there is a shortage of labor, which is the case here, because of widespread out-migration of male members of farm households to seek off-farm employment. Where markets for tree products are strong, returns to labor from wood product production have been estimated to be 50 percent greater than from maize production. Consequently, tree growing is a rational use of resources for poor farmers needing to devote a substantial part of their labor to nonfarm employment.

This decision to grow trees has been influenced by two factors. One is the high cost of labor and capital and the advantages that tree cultivation offer in this respect because of its low input requirements. The other is the prominent part that income generation, as distinct from food production, plays in the farmers' production objectives.

BENEFITS LOST THROUGH COMMERCIALIZATION

In many instances, adoption of an intensely "commercial attitude" has resulted in the loss of broader social forestry benefits, particularly to the poorer members of a community. Pursuing opportunities to foster commercial markets is often a central theme of development, which is appropriate in many cases. What is at issue, however, is the matter of objectives and priorities. Over time, an economically healthy commercial agricultural sector is a necessity for development, including the development of benefits for the landless and the poorest people in communities. It is through taxing the profits of "strong" sectors and producers that financial resources are raised to support programs for the poor who cannot escape the circle of poverty without help.

It often is possible to combine commercially oriented development plans and socially oriented programs at the same time. For example, in addition to emphasizing commercialization, India's social forestry program includes such objectives as allocating degraded forest and agricultural wasteland to landless families, who will be assisted in becoming cash crop tree farmers (Bromley 1983).

Issues associated with commercialization need to be addressed and not suppressed as the process of commercializing previously subsistence forest products continues to reach further into rural areas. Arnold (1986) has stated that the growing of trees and shrubs in response to market forces is becoming an increasingly important component of forestry for local community development programs. Therefore, sound market development and commercialization should be encouraged, although these actions also should be given increasingly critical attention in planning efforts and project implementation.

Some commercial wood-growing activities undertaken by farmers can provide attractive economic returns and stable employment. However, much of this attraction depends upon local market situations and transportation infrastructures available to move wood or other forest products to marketplaces. Significantly, the rate

Example 7.4

Bargaining Power Needed to Ensure a Fair Share of Returns: An Example from Tanzania (Mnzava 1983) In Dodoma, Tanzania, some villagers carry bags of their home-produced charcoal to sell in towns from distances up to 15 km. Observations reveal that the buyers of the charcoal, who normally are merchants who resell the charcoal, make between 120 and 300 percent return or profit. Rural charcoal producers usually do not have an alternative, however. They have to sell their merchandise quickly to return home in time to do other tasks. One way to circumvent this difficulty is to encourage the village charcoal producers to form informal groups to increase their bargaining power. These producers also should use their village organizations to help them get regular customers, once they themselves have become organized.

of return to the tree grower can erode rapidly if the farmer has to depend largely upon middlemen who hold "strong" bargaining positions (Example 7.4).

Citing work done for The World Bank (Baah-Dwomoh 1983), Arnold (1987) pointed out that the price of standing wood in two West African situations was only 1 to 1.5 percent of the retail price of the wood in the market. Even if the wood was cut and stacked at the farm gate, the cost would be only between 11 and 13 percent of retail market price. The rest of the return went to those people who transported and marketed the wood. Low returns generally caused farmers to lose interest in tree growing as a commercial venture. If rural people develop some form of organization that can influence pricing and provide distribution services, their returns likely can be increased.

The "cooperative" approach is sensitive to cultural and economic environments within which it must operate. Cooperatives in forestry have failed miserably in some countries, while they have thrived in others (Gregersen and McGaughey 1985). Each case, therefore, must be considered on its own merit. In developing any program to encourage commercialization of wood or other forest-related products, markets and organization need to be considered seriously. Failures or disappointments in cooperatives hit hard in poor, rural communities. It frequently will take a long time to get a community involved in new ventures if failure is still fresh in mind.

A MULTIPLE USE APPROACH

Much of this chapter has focused on investment, employment, and income generation solely in the forestry sector. However, it should be mentioned that investment in multiple use management also can allow people to increase and, in many cases, diversify their levels of employment and income in many instances (Ffolliott and Brooks 1986). The primary purpose of multiple use management is to take advantage of the interrelationships among natural resources, and the products and uses derived therefrom, so that from planned manipulations of one or a few of the natural resources, additional benefits are obtained from the many related resources involved. Through multiple use management, therefore, attempts are made to optimize benefits of livestock and agricultural crop production, wildlife, recreation and tourism, and forestry, providing a wide array of benefits to people in many sectors in addition to forestry.

It was stated earlier that a relatively large investment is made in multiple use management of forests and woodlands in the southwestern United States. It is suggested here that the multiple use management approach to investment, employment, and income generation throughout the dryland regions of the world likely will become increasingly relevant in the future, as rural and urban developments take place on the more fragile lands. A discussion of multiple use management is presented in Chapter 10.

SUMMARY

Sustainable forestry requires investment opportunities that generate employment and income, while maintaining the resource base. Much of this investment comes through the public sector in the drylands of the southwestern United States, largely through the operational budgets of the governmental agencies responsible for the management of trees and shrubs in the public domain. However, investment elsewhere, and especially in developing countries, is made by governmental and nongovernmental organizations through the financial support of external public and private donors. It is this latter form of investment that has been considered in this chapter. At this point, you should appreciate:

1. What kinds of investment opportunities are related to the sustainable use of natural resources in dryland regions.
2. In general, the linkages between forestry, income and employment, and food security.
3. How off-farm employment is used in forestry-related activities and, particularly, traditional small-scale enterprises.
4. Why the loss of broader social forestry benefits can occur through the commercialization of forestry projects.
5. How investments in multiple use management might allow people to increase and diversify their levels of employment and income.

REFERENCES

Anderson, D. 1987. *The economics of afforestation: A case study in Africa.* The World Bank, Occasional Paper 1, The Johns Hopkins Press, Baltimore.

Arnold, J. E. M. 1986. Forestry for local community development and integrated forest management. In FAO. 1986. Strategies, approaches, and systems in integrated watershed management. *FAO Conservation Guide* 14, Rome, pp. 361–88.

Arnold, J. E. M. 1987. Economic considerations in agroforestry. In Steppler, H. A., and P. K. R. Nair (eds.). 1987. *Agroforestry: A decade of development.* International Council for Research in Agroforestry, Nairobi.

Arnold, J. E. M., and J. Falconer. 1987. *Income and employment, forestry and food security.* FAO, Rome.

Baah-Dwomoh, J. 1983. *Estimating stumpage value of wood in the Sahel.* The World Bank, Washington, D.C.

Bromley, D. 1983. The economics of social forestry: An analysis of a proposed program in Madhya Pradesh, India. In Braatz, S. M., and K. McNamara (eds.). 1983. *Forestry and development in Asia: Opportunities and constraints.* USAID/The Asia Society, Washington, D.C., pp. 258–86.

Centre for Science and Environment. 1985. *The state of India's environment 1984–85—The second citizens' report.* Centre for Science and Environment, New Dehli.

Chambers, R., and M. Leach. 1987. *Trees to meet contingencies: Savings and security for the rural poor.* Overseas Development Institute, Social Forestry Network Paper 5a, London.

Eckholm, E. 1979. Planting for the future: Forestry for human needs. *Worldwatch Paper* 26, Washington, D.C.

FAO. 1985. *The contribution of small-scale forest-based processing enterprises to rural non-farm employment and income in selected developing countries.* FAO, Rome.

FAO. 1987. Small-scale forest-based processing enterprises. *FAO Forestry Paper* 79, Rome.

Ffolliott, P. F., and K. N. Brooks. 1986. Multiple use: Achieving diversified and increased income with a watershed management framework. In FAO. 1986. Strategies, approaches and systems in integrated watershed management. *FAO Conservation Guide* 14, Rome, pp. 114–23.

Fisseha, Y. 1987. Basic features of rural small-scale forest based processing enterprises in developing countries. In FAO. 1987. Small-scale forest-based processing enterprises. *FAO Forestry Paper* 79, Rome, pp. 31–60.

Gelder, B. van, and P. Kerkhof. 1984. *The agroforestry survey in Kakamega District: Final report.* Kenya Woodfuel Development Programme, Working Paper 6, Beijer Institute, Nairobi.

Gregersen, H. M. 1982. *Village forestry development in the Republic of Korea—a case study.* FAO Forestry for Local Community Development Programme Series, Rome.

Gregersen, H. M., and S. E. McGaughey. 1985. *Improving policies and financing mechanisms for forestry development.* Economic and Social Department, Inter-American Development Bank, Washington, D.C.

Gregersen, H. M., D. Elz, and S. Draper (eds.). 1989. *People and trees: The role of social forestry in sustainable development.* The World Bank, Washington, D.C.

Hoskins, M. W. 1980. Community participation in African fuelwood production, transformation, and utilization. In French, D., and P. Larson (eds.). 1980. *Energy for Africa: Selected readings.* USAID, Washington, D.C., pp. 155–88.

ICARDA. 1992. Australia and ICARDA. *Ties That Bind*, No. 3, ICARDA, Aleppo, Syria.

Khattak, G. M., and M. Amjad. 1981. *A survey of socio-economic conditions for manpower engaged in forestry and wood-based industries in Pakistan.* Pakistan Forest Institute, Peshawar.

Mnzava, E. 1983. *Tree planting in Tanzania: A voice from villagers*. Forestry Division, Dar es Salaam, Tanzania.

Page, J., Jr. 1978. Economics of scale, income distribution, and small enterprise promotion in Ghana's timber industry. *Food Research Institute Studies* 16:159–82.

Rowe, R. D. H. 1980. *India: Himalayan integrated watershed development project brief*. The World Bank, Washington, D.C.

Shiva, V., H. C. Sharatchandra, and J. Bandyopadhyay. 1982. Social forestry—no solution within the market. *The Ecologist* 12:158–68.

Spears, J. S. 1978. *The changing emphasis in World Bank forestry lending: A summary of recent experiences and problem areas of relevance to the Eighth World Forestry Congress sessions concerned with "Forestry for rural communities."* The World Bank, Washington, D.C.

Spears, J. 1987. Agroforestry: A development bank perspective. In Steppler, H. A., and P. K. R. Nair (eds.). 1987. *Agroforestry: A decade of development*. International Council for Research in Agroforestry, Nairobi, pp. 53–68.

Srivastava, P. V., and M. M. Pant. 1979. Social forestry is a cost? Benefit analysis framework. *Indian Forester*, January 1979.

The World Bank. 1984. *Malawi forestry sub-sector study (A review of selected issues)*. Report 4927-MAI, The World Bank, Washington, D.C.

The World Bank. 1986. *Economics issues and farm forestry*. Working Paper prepared for the Kenya Forestry Sector Study. The World Bank, Washington, D.C.

Wood, D. H., D. Brokensha, A. P. Castro, B. A. Jackson, B. W. Riley, and D. M. Schraft. 1980. *The socio-economic context of fuelwood use in small rural communities*. U.S. Agency for International Development, Evaluation Special Study 1, Washington, D.C.

PART II

Planning and Assessing Forestry Projects, Multiple Use Management

8 Planning

The purpose of management is to make resources productive in satisfying the needs of people. Planning is one of the most important functions of management (Stuth 1991). The applications of human, capital, and natural resources to carry out the necessary tasks can require relatively little structured planning in small forest management organizations with simple goals and a short time frame. However, more formal planning is necessary in larger organizations with diverse human, capital, and natural resources and with multiple goals and objectives to be achieved in a long period of time. As organizations, tasks, and responsibilities become increasingly complex, it becomes necessary to carefully consider the different ways in which these goals might be achieved to assure that any use of resources is effective and efficient.

Planning can be done at various levels of administrative responsibility within a forest management organization, such as:

- Top level of management that provides strategic directions for the organization.
- Administrative units within the organization.
- Functions within the organization.
- Units that are responsible for budgets, scheduling, and assigning individual jobs.

It is not possible to discuss all of the planning that may be carried out within large organizations dealing with forestry projects in dryland regions. Instead, this chapter will focus on the more general issues, concepts, and principles related to the planning processes that apply to the different types of plans that an organization may develop.

FUNCTION OF PLANNING

The function of planning within a forest management organization can:

- Provide formal and systematic consideration and evaluation of available resources, organizational capabilities, and alternative courses of action and their consequences.
- Provide guidance and direction to individuals within the organization.

- Assure continuity of operations as personnel assignments change.
- Clarify the goals and objectives of specified activities.
- Provide a justification to higher administrative levels for proposed operations.
- Fulfill legal requirements and assure compliance with laws and regulations.
- Provide a record of decisions and the analyses that lead up to the decisions.
- Provide a mechanism for obtaining external comments and suggestions about planned activities.

The dynamic nature of larger forest management organizations, involving many people with diverse job assignments and responsibilities, can lead to frequent changes in job assignments as people retire or are hired or promoted. Plans furnish a form of continuity of purpose and action for the organization in such a situation. This continuity is particularly true in forest management organizations because these organizations typically plan in long time horizons that frequently involve many decades.

It is important to distinguish between two types of planning carried out within a forest management organization. *Strategic planning* is concerned with providing the general direction for the organization or activities of the organization. Strategic planning is more concerned with identifying *what* should be done. *Operational planning*, in contrast, is more concerned with *how* something should be done—that is, the mechanics for carrying out the strategic plan. Operational planning provides a plan of action to be followed by particular personnel within the organization.

Organizations need both strategic and operational planning to ensure that they make effective and efficient use of their resources to achieve their goals. Strategic planning by itself provides the sense of direction, but it is not a plan for getting there. Operational planning by itself furnishes a plan for carrying out project activities. Each of these types of planning is discussed in more detail below.

STRATEGIC PLANNING

Strategic planning is concerned with developing the mission and direction of a forest management organization and with strategies for accomplishing the mission. Strategic planning must confront difficult choices, set broad priorities, envision the organization's future, and develop procedures to successfully achieve that future (Pfeiffer et al. 1989). The time frame is 5 to 10 years or longer. Strategic planning is the responsibility of senior management.

Strategic planning should not be thought of as simply long-term planning, because it focuses more on identifying, managing, and resolving issues and emphasizes the assessment of the environment outside and inside of the organization to a much greater extent. Furthermore, it is concerned more with the "vision of success" of the organization and how to achieve it, and anticipates and prepares the organization for future but unknown changes. Long-term planning usually is based upon historical projections and does not work well when external conditions are changing rapidly. Long-term planning also tends to overlook the managers' potential roles in creating the future (Hanna 1985).

Importance

Forest management organizations need to respond quickly and effectively to changing circumstances. The external environment within which forest management organizations operate often is characterized by uncertainty. This uncertainty is pronounced in dryland environments. Strategic planning helps to define an overall sense of direction and purpose for these organizations and, thereby, helps managers respond to change in a consistent fashion. Hanna (1985) and Barry (1986) identified potential contributions of strategic planning, including:

- Providing direction, coherence, and unity to organizational efforts.
- Improving organizational performance.
- Introducing a discipline for long-term thinking.
- Raising awareness about external environments.
- Enhancing the dialogue among managers about strategy.
- Building teamwork and planning expertise.
- Stimulating forward thinking in the organization, especially among top levels of management.

This last point is perhaps the most important. Strategic planning is not an end in itself, but it should be used to help forest managers think and act strategically. Successful forest management organizations are guided by strategic thought and action, and a strategic planning process can aid in developing this perspective.

Limitations

Strategic planning can be a tool in managing any organization, but it should not be oversold. The limitations of strategic planning must be recognized clearly before undertaking the development of formal strategic planning for a forest management organization. Barry (1986) and Rocheteau (1989) discussed the following limitations:

- *Costs can outweigh benefits*—Depending upon the scope of the planning effort, strategic planning can be costly in money and human resources, especially the time and efforts of top-level managers, administrators, and policymakers. The potential of strategic planning should be weighed against these costs. If the planning effort ultimately is unsuccessful, or if the resulting plan is not likely to be used, then the resources devoted to planning would be used more productively in other areas.

- *Strategic planning can be unnecessary*—Some forest management organizations operate effectively by responding quickly to new opportunities as they emerge, or they "muddle along" without formal planning. A formal strategic plan can be unnecessary for small organizations that operate effectively in this manner. In addition, some organizations have leaders who instinctively manage strategically. Although such leadership is rare, organizations with unusually insightful leaders may not need to develop a strategic plan.
- *Planning can become a bureaucratic exercise*—One of the main goals of strategic planning is to help forest managers think and act strategically. But, formal strategic planning sometimes becomes an exercise in bureaucracy that actually lowers initiative, creativity, and risk-taking.

Preparing Strategic Plans

Before strategic planning is started, it is necessary to agree on the purpose of strategic planning, how it is to be done, and who is involved. A strategic planning team should be formed within the forest management organizations to address the following questions:

- Who should be involved in the efforts?
- Who will be on the planning team?
- Who will oversee the effort?
- What are the potential benefits to the organization?
- What are the desired outcomes?
- What steps should be followed?
- What should be the form and timing of reporting?

Key decision makers should be included on the strategic planning team, perhaps with some representatives of possible *stakeholders*, the latter being individuals likely involved in and affected by the proposed forestry project (or program). In some instances, the managers may decide not to involve stakeholders until they become more comfortable with the concepts of strategic planning, since outside involvement often complicates the planning process. The planning team might consist of only a few individuals in small forest management organizations. Two groups can be required to help ensure an effective planning effort in large organizations: a relatively large group to provide broad representations and legitimization of the planning process and a smaller group to act as an executive committee that does most of the actual work and makes recommendations to the larger group.

The process of developing a strategic plan begins once the planning procedures, purposes, and expected outcomes have been defined. The process of preparing a strategic plan involves the following steps:

- Assessing the external environment to identify key issues.

- Describing the current situations in terms of where we are now and our strengths, weaknesses, and capabilities.
- Formulating goals and objectives and setting priorities.
- Outlining program and implementation strategies.

Assessing External Environment A major purpose of strategic planning is to assess the external challenges and opportunities that may demand a response in the foreseeable future. The idea here is to prepare an organization to respond effectively, before a crisis arises or an opportunity is lost, by anticipating future events and thinking about potential responses before they occur. Assessing trends in the external environment is, therefore, an important part of strategic planning. An effort is made to identify factors in the organization's environment that might have an impact on its planned program in the future. Emerging trends that may affect the organization need to be determined. These trends could include political, economic, social, technological, and environmental trends and issues that can be local, regional, national, or worldwide in scope.

An essential step in preparing a strategic plan for a forest management organization is identifying the emerging issues that are related to the future management and use of natural resources. By doing so, organizations can be prepared to deal with the effects of emerging and unanticipated problems. This preparation is critical in dryland environments, where natural resources are susceptible to the climatological extremes that affect productivity and resource management options. Bryson (1988) defined a strategic issue as a fundamental policy choice facing an organization. Strategic issues affect an organization's mandates; missions and values; and kind, level, and mix of outputs provided. These issues arise when:

- External events beyond the control of the organization make it difficult to accomplish objectives with the resources available.
- Choices for achieving organizational objectives change (such as changes in technology, financing, staffing, or management).
- New threats or opportunities arise.

Particular attention should be given to potential discontinuities that might have a major impact on the organizations (Hanna 1985). Strategic issues that a forest management organization might face include increasing rates of deforestation; changing demands for the uses of forest, woodland, or plantation resources; increasing conflicts among stakeholders who utilize these resources; or long-term declines in budgets or civil service salaries (Bengston 1989).

The process of identifying strategic issues involves reviewing the mandates, mission, external threats and opportunities, and internal strengths and weaknesses of the organization. One way to do this is to ask each member of the planning team to individually identify emerging issues that are likely to affect the capabilities and plans of the organization. Members of the planning team then are asked to answer the following questions for each issue that they identified:

- *What is the issue?*—The issue should be described clearly and thoroughly and framed as a question that the organization can address.
- *What factors make the issue a fundamental policy question?*—It is important to know how the issue affects the mandates, mission, and internal strengths and weaknesses of the organization.
- *What are the consequences for not addressing the issue?*—If there are no consequences, it is not a strategic issue. However, if the organization will be affected significantly by a failure to address an issue or miss an opportunity, the issue should receive high priority as a strategic issue.

Some large organizations use formal, institutionalized, external scanning procedures to identify important issues in an external environment (Pflaum and Delmont 1987). But, elaborate and demanding procedures generally are less desirable than simple and practical approaches. Many forest management organizations rely on the knowledge of members of the strategic planning team and use group discussions to identify external challenges and opportunities, and to assess their significance to the organization. Other approaches might include workshops involving stakeholder representatives to identify major issues or various survey techniques (Milne 1988, Jakes et al. 1989).

One can never be sure what forestry-related problems are likely to emerge. The future essentially is unknowable. However, it is possible to pool that general knowledge and information in the minds of experienced people who are familiar with past and current situations in order to obtain estimates of possible future issues that are likely to emerge as events unfold. One process for eliciting the opinions of informed people about future events is the *Delphi technique*. This technique can be used to identify emerging issues far enough in advance to prepare plans to address these problems (Example 8.1). The technique is useful when quantitative information is lacking and, as a result, one must rely upon collective expert judgment.

It is well to keep the advice of Pfeiffer et al. (1989) in mind, regardless of the approach that is used to assess the external environment. They recommend that scanning and assessing the external (and internal) environments should be a continual activity so that the relevant information always is available to key decision makers.

Describing Current Situations   In addition to describing the external environment within which a forest management organization operates, it is important to clearly describe the current status of the organization, that is, its internal environment. This, too, should be an ongoing activity, so that information about the organization is available to decision makers as they implement operational plans.

An assessment of the internal environment seeks to identify and justify the organization's capabilities, strengths, and weaknesses that help or hinder the organization in carrying out its missions. This assessment generally describes the:

Example 8.1

Application of the Delphi Technique (Gregersen et al. 1989)   The Delphi technique was used to identify the emerging issues in the management and use of the natural forests in the United States as a tool for research planning. A series of three questionnaires were used in a countrywide survey of forest supervisors and rangers of the USDA Forest Service and selected researchers to determine their views on which issues in management and use will be most important in the next 10 to 15 years and possible barriers to resolving these issues. The study found that there was widespread agreement among forest managers at all levels in identifying and setting priorities on 11 emerging issues to be faced in the near future. Only a few of these key issues related to the lack of technical knowledge. Most related to "people problems," including perceived conflicts among various user groups.

- Current state of the organization, including its internal structure.
- Past and current missions and objectives of the organization.
- Resources available to the organization, including professional, technical, and support personnel, equipment, facilities, supplies, information resources, computers, and funding.
- Current types of activities conducted by the organization.
- Organization's accomplishments in recent years.

It also is important to identify an organization's stakeholders and their relevant concerns as part of an assessment of the current situation. It should be recognized that within each broad stakeholder category, different groups of people can have different concerns in the organization's activities and the outcomes of those activities (Example 8.2). In considering the dwellers and users of forests, woodlands, and plantations, for example, it can be important to recognize the differing perceptions and concerns of women and children as compared to men. In the past, the role of women and children in many countries often has been treated in a perfunctory manner.

A key to the success of a forest management organization and its ability to generate financial and political support is the satisfaction of the stakeholders. It is necessary, therefore, for an organization to answer the following questions:

- Who are the organization's stakeholders?
- What do the stakeholders want from the organization?
- What criteria do the stakeholders use to evaluate the organization?
- How is the organization performing against those criteria?

Example 8.2

Categories of Potential Stakeholders in Dryland Forestry Projects (Gregersen et al. forthcoming) Categories of stakeholders that can have a claim on an organization's attention, resources, or outputs include:

- *Dwellers and users of forests, woodlands, and plantations*—These stakeholders include people who largely depend upon forests, woodlands, and plantations for their existence. Sedentary agriculturalists and shifting cultivators, pastoralists, and hunters and gatherers are included.
- *Other consumers of goods and services derived from forests, woodlands, and plantations*—Members of this group include those people who consume the wide variety of goods and services obtained from forests, woodlands, and plantations. It also includes future generations of people who will use future forests, woodlands, and plantations to meet their needs.
- *Small-scale converters*—Members of this group generally are land-poor people who convert forests, woodlands, plantations, and other wildlands to lands used for agricultural crop production or the grazing of livestock. These people sometimes are given lands for their personal use in resettlement schemes, and sometimes they are illegal encroachers who have little security and, therefore, limited incentive to think in the long term.
- *Environmental-advocacy groups*—This group is concerned with the local, regional, country-wide, or global environmental consequences of forest, woodland, or plantation use and, as a consequence, seeks to improve the protection and preservation of threatened ecosystems. These people also have concerns about the loss of biological diversity, preservation of endangered species and ecosystems, water and air pollution, and global warming. This group can possess substantial "power," as they often are linked to international organizations with lobbying power in many countries.
- *Social-development groups*—These stakeholders include groups, nongovernmental organizations (NGOs), governmental agencies, and others who are concerned with improving the economic and social well-being of the rural and urban poor and other disadvantaged peoples. These people can have an interest in forests, woodlands, plantations, water, and land use policies as a means of improving the lives of poor people.
- *Bilateral, multilateral, and nongovernmental organizations (NGOs)*—This group includes a variety of local, national, and international organizations with wide-ranging interests in economic and social development and sustainable resource use. They become stakeholders for a number of political, social, cultural, and religious reasons and, in recent years, have assumed a larger role in national and international policies related to the environment.
- *Governmental agencies*—Governmental agencies ideally should not be stakeholders, but the reality is that they or individuals within them often

behave as stakeholders. Government organizations or employees can establish a stake in the resources that they deal with by purchasing land or becoming involved in the industries with which they deal as a means to supplement their incomes or provide security for the future. Though these investments may not be illegal or unethical, these actions give those people who make them a stake in the outcomes of policy decisions and implemented projects.

Once the strategic planning team has completed the stakeholder analysis by answering these questions, the analysis should serve as a basis for a discussion of how the various stakeholders influence the organization. It can be useful to order the stakeholders according to their perceived importance to the organization. The more important stakeholders, therefore, will be identified.

Formulating Goals and Objectives and Setting Priorities Forest management organizations are administered in response to externally imposed mandates. It is important to identify these mandates and understand how they affect the organization before formulating goals and objectives and setting priorities. Mandates can be *formal*, such as legal mandates, and governmental policies and regulations, in which case the following questions should be addressed:

- What is the organization required to do under the laws and regulations formulated by legislative bodies, the executive branch of the government, or the higher administrative levels of the organization under which it operates?
- What is the organization *allowed* to do?
- What is the organization *not permitted* to do?

Consideration also should be given to *informal mandates*, such as customs, interest group reports, and agreements and understandings with other organizations and individuals. These mandates can be no less binding and can act as constraints to proposed forestry projects. The boundaries within which an organization can operate become clearer when the mandates that rule out certain activities are identified. In addition, this clarification gives others outside of the organization structure a picture of the external factors that govern and influence the organization and its work.

Identifying organizational mandates is straightforward. The strategic planning team can compile a list of formal and informal mandates affecting the organization. This list then is reviewed and modified to understand what the various mandates imply for the organization's mission.

Because the mission statement provides a guideline for the future directions of an organization, it should determine the organization's future activities and provide a vision of the organization's goals and guiding principles. The stakeholder analysis is useful in developing the mission statement by identifying the clients and their concerns, needs, and values. A description of the constraints within which the organization operates also is helpful. However, additional information is needed in most instances. The mission statement should evolve from responses to the following questions:

- Who are we as an organization?
- What social needs do we exist to fill?
- What should our organization do to recognize or anticipate and respond to these needs?
- How should we respond to our stakeholders and their concerns?
- What are our philosophy and our "core" values?
- What are our organization's comparative advantages over other organizations in achieving goals?

Thoughtfully addressing these questions and developing a mission statement that accurately incorporates a vision based upon the values of the organization is a demanding process (Peters 1987). The strategic planning team should answer these questions individually first and then come together as a group for a subsequent discussion. A draft mission statement should be developed following the group discussion. This draft should be modified as needed throughout the remainder of the strategic planning process.

Because a mission statement provides a guidepost for the forest management organization, it is not enough to look only at what the organization is currently doing. It is even more important to establish a vision of what the organization should attempt to be in the future (Drucker 1986). If it is to be useful, the mission statement should be a relatively brief, clear statement that can be read quickly and easily.

A mission statement should be reviewed periodically to determine if it still is appropriate for the organization. One indication that a mission statement is inappropriate is when managers make decisions that have little relevance to the statement. If this occurs frequently, employees and other stakeholders will begin to assume that the mission statement is no longer relevant and, therefore, can be disregarded.

With the mission statement serving as a basis, strategic plans are prepared to achieve goals and objectives. Setting and defining the goals and objectives, therefore, becomes one of the most important parts of strategic planning. In common practice, the terms *goals* and *objectives* are used interchangeably. However, there is a distinction between the two terms. The term *goal* refers to a desired condition, while the term *objective* refers to something toward which an effort is directed.

Goals for a forest management organization emerge from the organization's mandates and mission, a consideration for the natural resource base and other resources (people, funding, and facilities) it has to work with, and the demands of its various stakeholders. In turn, the objectives of the organization should be indicated for a specified planning period and within the more immediate constraints under which it must operate.

In setting goals and objectives, care must be taken not to define them too broadly. If one wishes to state a goal or an objective, it is well to ask the question, *How will we know when we get there?* A goal or objective has little use if we cannot know whether it has been achieved. Therefore, goals and objectives must be stated clearly, with measurable criteria established to judge the degree to which they have been achieved (Mager 1972). This need is particularly true when an organization has multiple goals that can conflict with one another. For example, a goal of increasing the productivity of a forest, woodland, or plantation to meet the expanding needs of the local people for fuelwood can conflict with a goal of increasing the level of habitat protection for endangered wildlife species. Both goals can be desired, but, in some instances, it may not be possible to attain both at the same time. It can be necessary to quantify trade-offs between the two goals and then set specific target levels for each to be achieved.

There is nothing more discouraging than to be faced with goals and objectives that cannot be achieved with the time and resources available. Personnel of an organization who must operate under these conditions become accustomed to failure. It is better to set goals and objectives that can be achieved so that people become accustomed to success and gain confidence in their ability to accomplish their assigned tasks.

In setting goals and objectives, it is necessary to maintain flexibility to meet the diverse needs of different regions, socioeconomic conditions, and cultural or other differences encompassed by the organization. There can be a diversity of biophysical and socioeconomic conditions, needs, and wants faced by the forest management organization. Importantly, the goals and objectives should not be so rigidly interpreted that they serve to constrain the organization from meeting local needs that are at variance with more general conditions. Goals and objectives also should reflect a balance between "centralized" and "decentralized" authority and responsibility.

It is rarely possible to satisfy all of the goals and objectives that an organization might believe is desirable. Constraints imposed by legislative and administrative policies, the resources and institutional support available, and the often conflicting aims, goals, and objectives of stakeholder groups require that an organization weigh alternatives and establish priorities among competing goals and objectives. Setting priorities requires assessments of the:

- Critical factors in the organization's external environment that affect the organization's activities.
- Organization's internal capabilities, strengths, and weaknesses,
- Organization's mission and formulated goals and objectives.
- Conflicting interests, concerns, and values of key stakeholder groups.

Managers should seek inputs from a variety of sources, including the key stakeholder groups, in the process of setting priorities. A number of formal or informal quantitative and qualitative techniques have been used in attempting to set priorities. However this is done, there is a danger in relying too greatly upon quantitative methods for setting priorities, because these methods can exclude important items that cannot be measured easily. It is important not to exclude factors on the grounds that they cannot be measured easily. The first step is to identify *all* of the important factors and then decide later how they are to be taken into account in the process of setting priorities.

Outlining Program and Implementation Strategies   Once the goals and objectives have been established and priorities have been set, there still remains the task of formulating strategies for implementing the activities in order to achieve the desired goals and objectives. Strategies that are developed serve to link the forest management organization and its clients to the organization's external environment. However, the development of strategies to address high-priority issues inevitably results in a compromise between what the organization would like to do and what the organization can do. Disagreements about priorities often involve top-level administrators and policymakers, those who are closely linked in the day-to-day operations of the organization, and the organization's clients.

Those people who are involved in the political process and top-level administrative officials usually are informed about the general desired needs of their constituencies and, therefore, are in a position to set goals and priorities among competing areas of development. However, many of these people lack the information needed to develop strategies as to how best to accomplish the goals they would like to achieve and about the needs of the varied clients for the use of the resources involved. As a consequence, direction from the top down can point only to the general direction in which these people believe the organization should be headed. Unfortunately, suggestions that come from the top legislative or administrative levels may not be feasible, given the limitations of the human, physical, and financial resources available, the current state of knowledge, and the knowledge of what can be done within the constraints of the time and resources available.

In contrast, those who carry out the operations of the organization often are aware of what the organization will be able to accomplish. These people know the on-the-ground strengths and weaknesses of the facilities, equipment, and personnel within the organization, which can be at variance with the information that is available to top-level managers and administrators. However, operational suggestions that come from lower levels in the organization might not take into consideration the broader aims and goals of the organization, the funding limitations, and the particular needs of the organization's clients.

Clients of the organization can be aware of many of their needs, but they may be less informed about the capabilities of the organization to meet those needs. In developing strategies for addressing high-priority issues, therefore, it is essential that a way be found to address these competing views of the organization—top-down, as opposed to the bottom-up development of courses of action—that involve both those within the organization and the organization's clients. Feasible strategies that address high-priority issues will emerge from the interactions of upper-level policymakers and administrators, middle-level managers, lower-level operational personnel, and the organization's clients.

OPERATIONAL PLANNING

The preparation of a strategic plan for a forest management organization should not be viewed as an end in itself. Strategic plans are only a necessary first step in preparing plans that will guide the ongoing work of the organization. However, these plans typically contain little information about how the organization will carry out its mission and achieve its goals. To meet these purposes, two types of operational planning often are used:

- Project (or program) plans, which describe and justify a proposed project to achieve specified goals and objectives of the organization.
- Annual work plans, which specify the specific activities that are planned for a particular year, what resources will be required, and what accomplishments are expected by the administrative units and individuals of the organization.

Types of Operational Planning

The two types of operational planning provide a framework to guide the operations of a forest management organization in implementing their strategic plans (Figure 8.1). A combination of both types of planning will ensure that the organization has a comprehensive view to guide its long- and short-term activities. However, these types of planning must be linked to each other and the organization's strategic plan to be effective.

Project plans outline how the goals identified in the strategic plan are to be achieved and the mission accomplished, usually for a period of several years.

Figure 8.1. Project plans and annual work plans are used to implement strategic plans

These plans are useful to managers because they provide a framework for guiding the activities of the organization. Such plans not only help managers to systematically organize activities of forestry projects, but they also justify the requests for resources. These plans cover work to be scheduled for several years or a few months, weeks, or days.

Annual work plans help in managing resources by specifying the activities that will be undertaken during the current or upcoming year to implement the project plan.

Annual work plans provide a means of coordinating the activities that often are carried out by an organization unit or individual. Annual work plans identify the tasks to be accomplished in a specified period of time and the resources (people, funds, and equipment) that will be required to accomplish these tasks.

Operational planning should not be an isolated activity. It should be both a top-down and bottom-up process. However, some guidance must be provided by top administrators to those preparing the plan on the level of expected funding, personnel restrictions, and other factors that are likely to affect the planned activities. Senior management becomes involved in operational planning, especially the manager of the unit for which the plan is being prepared. Others in the organizational unit and key stakeholder groups also have roles to play. These people collectively can provide a realistic appraisal of the organizational unit's capacity to carry out the specified activities. A project plan based upon unrealistic expectations will lack relevance and be of little use to the organization.

Project Planning Principles

Project planning is more of an art than a science. Blindly following a planning procedure in designing a forestry project is likely to lead to disaster. A project planning team must have the initiative and flexibility to use the planning process agreed upon as a guide, not necessarily as a rigid template. Principles that can be helpful in preparing project plans are listed in (Example 8.3).

With and Without Principle   One of the approaches to planning is comparing alternative scenarios of what is likely to happen *with* and *without* the project. A listing of the project activities, project inputs and outputs, and project results that would occur if the project were to be implemented is compared with the activities, inputs and outputs, and results that would occur if the project were not to be implemented. The project planners are faced with imagining what the future would be like under the two sets of conditions.

One can visualize what changes are likely to happen if the project is implemented. However, it often is more difficult to visualize what is likely to happen if the project is not implemented. The absence of the project does not necessarily mean that changes will not take place. The lack of a fuelwood production project can mean an increasing deterioration of vegetative cover, the increasing use of dung for fertilizer, and a resulting decline in agricultural crop production due to declining soil fertility. It is important to identify all of the biophysical and socio-

Example 8.3

Some Practical Planning Principles (Gregersen 1982) A number of factors that were responsible for the successful implementation of the Village Forestry Program in the Republic of Korea can be used to develop some practical planning principles:

- Use a broad-based approach to achieve improvements in conditions influencing rural welfare.
- Use an incremental approach that emphasizes results rather than ideals.
- Blend top-down with bottom-up planning, emphasizing cooperation between the government and people.
- Emphasize short-term gains in income and welfare to gain the participation of rural people as a first step in achieving long-term goals.
- Emphasize the development of appropriate technology.
- Use thorough logistical planning to assure the timely delivery of technical services and materials.
- Provide rural people with appropriate and timely financial incentives and access to resources, linking this assistance to a "self-help" attitude to prevent problems of increased dependence on external support.
- Require rural people to reinvest some of their "gains" from the projects to encourage their personal interest in having the project succeed.
- Develop the necessary laws and regulations to define the appropriate responsibilities needed to achieve the desired results, recognizing that the results can be achieved only if the rural people themselves participate in "policing" the activities.
- Use existing social traditions and organizations to conduct the project activities wherever possible to gain acceptance by the people with a minimum disruption of local customs.

economic elements that might be affected for each of the possible alternative courses of action in comparing the with and without project scenarios.

Multiple Alternatives Rarely is a project design so constrained that there is only one option to consider. There usually are a number of possible ways to achieve the project's goals and objectives and several possible technologies that could be used to this end. One of the most important tasks facing a planning team is identifying a set of feasible alternatives. It is important that the planning team consider a wide range of possible alternatives and not lock themselves into too narrow a choice too early in the planning process.

There is no simple way of choosing possible alternatives for evaluation. This task is best done as an iterative process among the members of the planning team—those who are aware of the technical possibilities for achieving the desired goals and objectives and those personnel from the operations staff who will be implementing the plan in the field. Options that fail to meet a minimum criteria for acceptance should be rejected early in the planning process.

Preparing Project Plans

The iterative process of project planning requires that one defines the problem, specifies the goals and objectives, develops a model of the situation, establishes criteria to be used in judging alternatives, formulates alternatives, selects the best course of action, implements the planned activity, and then monitors, evaluates, and reports the results (Figure 8.2).

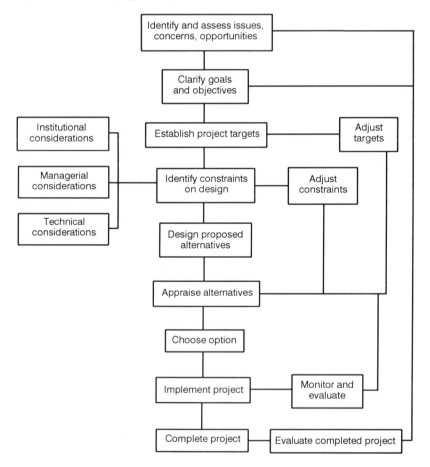

Figure 8.2. The iterative process of project planning (adapted from FFSD Program 1989)

These steps are elaborated upon below:

- The first step in project planning is to identify and assess the issues, concerns, and opportunities that can affect the proposed forestry project. Experience gained from evaluations of previous projects can help to clarify the issues, concerns, goals and objectives, and opportunities for subsequent interventions.

- Once agreement on goals and objectives is achieved, the next step is to determine how the project will set about achieving these goals and objectives by establishing targets. These targets, in turn, help identify constraints that can be imposed on the project design by institutional, managerial, and technical considerations. The targets and constraints influence the design of the possible alternative courses of action.

- After alternatives have been developed, each is appraised against the criteria and methodologies that have been agreed upon by the planning team. This appraisal can suggest the need to reconsider the constraints imposed or how these constraints can be overcome. Or, the appraisal can indicate a need to reconsider the project targets that were originally set. The altered constraints or targets then can suggest additional alternatives for the project that, in turn, are subjected to appraisal.

- The results of the appraisal of alternatives then are presented to the appropriate decision makers, and one of the courses of action is chosen for implementation. While it is possible that the decision makers will reject all of the alternatives and request that the planning team prepare and appraise a new set of alternatives, such a wholesale rejection is unlikely if the planning team has been working with the operations staff in developing the original set of alternatives. The operations staff should be informed about the alternatives to be appraised before the appraisal is undertaken.

- After the alternative is implemented, monitoring of the project activities provides information that can be used to modify the design as the project unfolds. New constraints may emerge or new targets may be established that can force a redesign of the project. Monitoring and the subsequent evaluation provides valuable feedback to the project's managers, as discussed in Chapter 21.

- Once completed, an *ex-post* evaluation of the project can furnish useful information for future projects with similar goals and objectives.

Seldom does a planning team have all of the information needed for the project planning on hand at the beginning of the planning process. Rarely is the planning effort completed before any decisions are made. Instead, decisions and choices are made throughout the planning process. Options are evaluated initially and, if necessary, discarded before conducting a thorough evaluation, saving time in gathering detailed information about an option that is not appropriate (Rose et al. 1982).

In practice, therefore, project planning involves a process of successive approximations.

Project planning often is viewed as a one-time task, that is, something that is done every few years and then put aside. However, forestry projects can change in time, as priorities and informational needs change. A project planning process that is built into the operating procedures of the organization and subject to review and updating as conditions change is likely to provide a more useful guide to the operations of the organization. Interactions with all stakeholders can help identify changing issues and ensure that strategies remain relevant as conditions change.

UNCERTAINTY

Because of the uncertainties about our knowledge and estimates of the future, project planners must recognize the problems of uncertainty and devise strategies for coping with those uncertainties.

Uncertainties in Planning

There are two forms of uncertainties that must be considered in planning. The first form is associated with the information currently known about past operations, technical relationships, past or present economic and social conditions, and all of the other information that is used in developing the estimates upon which plans are based. Information needed for planning often may not be available, can be outdated, or not relevant to a particular situation.

The second form of uncertainty is concerned with the problem of estimating future conditions. Planners always are planning for situations that will take place in the future. But the future cannot be observed or measured. It must be estimated from past or current information (with its own uncertainties) or imagined by other means. Information about future inputs and outputs, prices and other values, social and political conditions, and the value systems themselves can be estimated only for the purposes of planning. There is no way of estimating the reliability of these estimates of the future until they have occurred.

Planners of forestry projects face a number of uncertainties that they must cope with in the planning process. These uncertainties include:

- *Climatological uncertainties*—Climate plays a key role in the planning of forestry projects to be implemented in dryland regions, where the survival and growth of plants is often near the critical level. Irregularities in the climate make forecasts of future climatological events uncertain. One cannot prepare a plan for a forestry project based upon the average climatological conditions. It is the extremes that challenge foresters and the managers of other natural resources in dryland regions. Often the occurrence of the more extreme conditions determine whether a forestry project is likely to succeed.

- *Technical uncertainties*—A lack of knowledge about cause-and-effect relationships can lead to uncertainty in planning. Alternative technologies that can be used in a forestry project might not be well understood. For example, reliable information about the effects of different plant covers on soil erosion may not be available. Information about the yield of a particular tree or shrub species may be incomplete. Information about tree and shrub growth for most species in the dryland regions of the world is inadequate. In many cases, therefore, a planning team can only guess at what the outputs will be, leading to uncertainty about the estimates.

- *Socioeconomic uncertainties*—There generally is more uncertainty about socioeconomic variables than technical variables. Information needed for planning on the current status of people's welfare, such as income, wealth, and education, can be difficult to obtain for local areas. Estimates of the people's welfare in the future are far more uncertain. Socioeconomic conditions can change rapidly in developing countries. Populations are increasing, urbanization is expanding, and the economies are evolving. Estimates of future levels of supplies and demands for specified products are uncertain in the face of these rapid socioeconomic changes.

Coping with Uncertainty

Planners of forestry projects, who typically deal with longer time periods than the planners of many other developments, must be aware that there are strategies for coping with uncertainty that can be incorporated into their planning effort. These strategies include:

- *Increase understanding*—Suggestions include postponing the decision to acquire more information, conducting a sensitivity analysis to determine how changes in our assumptions affect the results, and imagining alternative futures that reduce future surprises.

- *Increase flexibility*—Suggestions include planning initially only for small incremental changes and monitoring the results, contingency planning for the likelihood that things might go wrong, diversification to reduce the risks, and planned obsolescence by building temporary structures and facilities with a short life to reduce the costs of building permanent structures and facilities.

- *Encourage innovations*—In many instances, relying upon a team of innovative people with considerable autonomy for action has been a more successful strategy in coping with uncertainty than preparing detailed long-range plans.

Plans are prepared to cope with future events, and, therefore, they are based upon the expectations of the planning team. Even when we have the "best information" available in preparing the plans necessary for forestry, the resulting plans still are based upon a perception of the world in which the plans will be implemented. In view of the uncertainties found in the "real world," therefore, it is well to use the results obtained from a planning process with caution.

SUMMARY

Planning is needed to deal systematically with the interrelated aspects of dryland forestry projects. Since forest management practices have interrelated impacts, both spatially and temporally, the planning of these activities and their coordination is a productive undertaking. Planning involves a number of steps—specifying goals and objectives for overcoming the problems; identifying constraints; defining possible alternatives to achieve the goals and objectives; evaluating likely environmental, social, and economic impacts of the alternative courses of action; and ranking the alternatives and formulating recommendations. At the end of this chapter, you should be able to answer the following questions:

1.   What is involved in the planning of forestry projects?
2.   What is the meaning of strategic and operational planning, and why are these two types of planning important to a forest management organization?
3.   Who should become involved in the planning process?
4.   How can one go about implementing the plans for forestry projects?
5.   How can uncertainties be dealt with in a planning process?

REFERENCES

Barry, B. W. 1986. *Strategic planning workbook for nonprofit organizations.* Amherst H. Wilder Foundation, St. Paul, Minnesota.

Bengston, D. N. 1989. Price indexes for deflating public forestry research expenditures. *Forest Science* 35:756–74.

Bryson, J. M. 1988. *Strategic planning for public and nonprofit organizations: A guide to strengthening and sustaining organizational achievement.* Jossey-Bass Publishers, San Francisco.

Drucker, P. F. 1986. *The practice of management.* Harper & Row, Publishers, New York.

FFSD Program. 1989. *The role of forestry in sustainable development of dryland regions: Training manual,* Amman, Jordan, May 13–25, 1989. Forestry for Sustainable Development Program, College of Natural Resources, University of Minnesota, St. Paul, Minnesota.

Gregersen, H. M. (compiler). 1982. *Village forestry development in the Republic of Korea: A case study.* GCP/INT/347/SWE, FAO/SIDA Forestry for Local Community Development Programme, FAO, Rome.

Gregersen, H. M., A. L. Lundgren, P. J. Jakes, and D. N. Bengston. 1989. Identifying emerging issues in forestry as a tool for research planning. *USDA Forest Service, General Technical Report* NC-137.

Gregersen, H., K. Brooks, P. Ffolliott, A. Lundgren, B. Belcher, K. Eckman, R. Quinn, D. Ward, and T. White (forthcoming). *Natural resource policy issues: Guidelines for developing options.* College of Natural Resources, University of Minnesota, St. Paul, Minnesota.

Hanna, N. 1985. *Strategic planning and management: A review of recent experience.* World Bank Staff Working Paper No. 751, The World Bank, Washington, D.C.

Jakes, P. J., H. M. Gregersen, and A. L. Lundgren. 1989. Research needs, assessment and evaluation: Identifying emerging issues as a key to forestry research planning. In Lundgren, A. L. (ed.). 1989. The management of large-scale forestry research programs and projects. *USDA Forest Service, General Technical Report* NE-130, pp. 107–13.

Mager, R. F. 1972. *Goal analysis.* Lear Siegler, Inc./Fearon Publishers, Belmont, California.

Milne, G. R. 1988. *Strategic forest sector issues in Newfoundland and potential CFS program initiatives.* Information Report N-X-267, Newfoundland Forestry Centre, St. John's, Newfoundland, Canada.

Peters, T. 1987. *Thriving on chaos: Handbook for a management revolution.* Harper & Row Publishers, New York.

Pfeiffer, J. W., L. D. Goodstein, and T. M. Nolan. 1989. *Shaping strategic planning.* Scott, Foresman and Company, Glenview, Illinois.

Pflaum, A., and T. Delmont. 1987. External scanning, a tool for planners. *Journal of the American Planning Association* 53:56–67.

Rocheteau, G. 1989. *Planification strategique d'un systeme national de recherche agricole.* ISNAR Document de Travail No. 20, International Service for National Agricultural Research, The Hague.

Rose, D. W., H. M. Gregersen, A. R. Ek, and H. Hofanson. 1982. Planning with minimum data and technology. In Vodak, M. C., W. A. Leuschner, and D. I. Navon (eds.). 1982. *Symposium on forest management planning: Present practice and future decisions.* FWS-1-81, School of Forestry, Virginia Polytechnic Institute and State University, Blacksburg, Virginia, pp. 188–97.

Stuth, J. W., J. R. Conner and R. K. Heitschmidt. 1991. The decision-making environment and planning paradigm. In Heitschmidt, R. K., and J. W. Stuth (eds.). 1991. *Grazing management: An ecological perspective.* Timber Press, Portland, Oregon, pp. 201–23.

9 Assessing Forestry Projects[1]

The purpose of this chapter is to present a framework to follow in assessing forestry projects. Assessments are made throughout the developmental process. Assessments that occur before a project has been implemented are called *appraisals*, while assessments that look at a past, implemented project are referred to as *evaluations*. One also talks about *feasibility* assessments, *performance* assessments, and *impact* assessments. The first refers to appraisal of whether a project is feasible to undertake, the second to monitoring and evaluating project performance, and the third to impacts, both actual and likely in the future. Most of this book deals with issues related to feasibility and performance. In this chapter, therefore, we focus on impacts in terms of both appraising likely future impacts and evaluating past impacts.

The main objective of impact assessments is to identify and analyze changes that take place in the welfare of *stakeholders*, or those people affecting or affected by a forestry project. To move toward satisfying this objective, one needs to identify:

- The project stakeholders.
- The nature of the project impacts on stakeholder welfare.
- The dimensions of welfare to associate with impacts.

The scope of these questions is determined largely by the nature of the forestry project being considered.

IDENTIFYING PROJECT STAKEHOLDERS

Individuals involved in and affected by a forestry project are the stakeholders. Some stakeholders have access to the resources necessary to carry out the project, while other stakeholders have resources that can be mobilized to prevent the project from being performed (Honadle and Cooper 1989). Therefore, it is common that different stakeholders attempt to achieve different and, sometimes, contradictory ends.

Decisions made by different stakeholders concerning their participation in a project depend largely upon their interests, personal objectives, and understanding

---

[1]This chapter is adapted from Gregersen et al. (forthcoming).

of how the project might impact upon them. For example, governmental agencies decide about timing and allocation of resources to the project. Private landowners, who may be expected to participate in the project, decide whether or not they are willing to become involved. Buyers decide which project outputs to buy and how much they are willing to pay. Internal and external donor organizations decide how much of their resources and technical assistance should be allocated to the project.

To obtain desired impacts and reduce future conflicts in a project, it is important that stakeholders who have different viewpoints and agendas be identified and that their interests be considered in the project's outcome. One must recognize that different agendas often create problems that can divert a project from its stated objectives. Attaining this recognition, particularly a recognition that many forestry activities have political implications at both macro- and micro-levels, is a major achievement.

Efforts should be made to involve representatives of stakeholder groups in the design of assessments. Only by involving these groups will results of the assessment likely be used effectively (Patton 1986, Weiss and Bucuvalas 1980). This involvement is a key to the *new generation* of forestry projects that are emphasized in this book. These projects differ from "traditional" large-scale industrial projects in that they require the participation of local stakeholders (including indigenous people and the rural poor) in the project and the inclusion of *indirect* stakeholders (or those who can be affected negatively or positively through environmental impacts) in the assessment process. Decision makers must be sensitive to a range of potential environmental, social, financial, economic, and institutional impacts on stakeholders because of the project considered.

IDENTIFYING IMPACTS ON STAKEHOLDER WELFARE

Forestry projects change the character of natural forests and woodlands, establish forest plantations, increase productivity, change erosion rates, or change farming systems through introduction of agroforestry practices. When these changes cause changes in the environment, they are called *environmental* impacts. These environmental impacts, in turn, lead to *social* and *economic* impacts on people.

It is critical that environmental impacts be translated into social and economic terms—that is, impacts on the welfare of people—for the environmental changes to have meaning to most decision makers. When decision makers compare alternative uses of scarce resources, they compare the impacts of resource use on people or increases in the welfare of target groups than can be achieved with alternative investments of resources. Decision makers have to see environmental impacts in terms of impacts on people (Example 9.1). Answers to questions about environmental impacts need to be generated before assessing people impacts, because the latter are a direct result of the former in most cases involving forest management practices.

Welfare impacts are associated with human values. Therefore, these impacts are assessed in terms of values attached to them. These values vary from direct mone-

---

Example 9.1

Translating Environmental Impacts into Social and Economic Impacts: A Hypothetical Example (Gregersen et al. forthcoming)   A forester suggests to a regional governor that afforestation and related control measures might reduce the annual rates of soil erosion on abandoned agricultural lands on the slopes of a river valley by 7 t/ha. It is agreed that reducing soil erosion is a positive *environmental impact*. However, the reduced soil loss in and of itself is not necessarily a benefit to people, which is a concern to the governor. Therefore, the governor asks how this environmental impact will affect the people in his jurisdiction, that is, what are the *social* and *economic* impacts?

The social and economic benefits involved depend largely upon where the environmental impacts occur. At one extreme, benefits from reduced erosion are likely to be small in terms of short-term social and economic benefits if the river valley is populated sparsely and the river flows into the ocean with little planned use by the people. In this case, the regional governor likely will not be interested in the proposal, which takes scarce resources from other projects.

At the other extreme, however, assume that the river flows into a reservoir for use in generating hydropower and domestic and irrigation water for hundreds of thousands of people in the governor's territory. The reduced soil loss here could reduce sediment accumulations and the associated loss of needed reservoir capacity and, therefore, avoidance of losses below the dam that could have direct social and economic impacts on the people. Social and economic benefits from the afforestation leading to reduced sedimentation could be significant in this instance, even though the environmental impact is the same. The point made is that a positive environmental impact due to a reduction in erosion will mean relatively little to most decision makers unless it is translated into social and economic terms in relation to impacts on people, in this case, through the avoidance of loss of on-site production values, reduction in loss of life because of flooding, and reductions in loss of hydropower, drinking water, and irrigated agricultural crops.

---

tary measures of financial values associated with direct uses of forests, woodlands, or plantations to qualitative, psychological, nonuse values associated with the mere existence of these ecosystems (Example 9.2). In the world of academic economists, a distinction frequently is made between the different types of values, with economic values being all of those values that can be expressed in monetary terms. In the real world, however, this distinction is not clear. Psychological, social, and economic values all need to be considered together in most instances.

Example 9.2

Direct, Indirect, and Nonuse Values Associated with Forests, Woodlands, and Plantations (Gregersen et al. forthcoming)

Direct use values associated with:

Consumptive use:
- Commercial-industrial market goods, for example, fuelwood, poles, fodder, animal products, fruits and nuts, and medicines.
- Indigenous nonmarket goods and service, including fuelwood, poles, animal products, and fruits and nuts.

Nonconsumptive Use:
- Recreational opportunities.
- Educational opportunities and study.

Indirect values associated with:

- Protection of downstream areas through watershed management (Example 9.1).
- Protection of soil resources.
- Improvement of soil fertility.
- Protection of habitats and biological diversities.
- Improvement of air quality through reduction of "greenhouse" gases.

Nonuse values:

- People can value a forest, woodland, or plantation purely for its existence, without any intention to use the ecosystem resources in the future. That is, these people value these ecosystems for their existence and, therefore, wish to perpetuate their existence. Many people are willing to contribute money, time, and other resources in preserving endangered species and threatened ecosystem communities. These economically manifested existence values are based largely upon cultural, religious, spiritual, or other values held by individuals or groups within a society. Although these values are difficult to measure, they should be recognized in valuing the contributions of forests, woodlands, and plantations to human welfare.

IDENTIFYING DIMENSIONS AND MEASURES OF WELFARE

Decision makers generally focus on the following dimensions of welfare when assessing forestry projects:

- *Distribution of benefits and costs*—that is, who gains and who loses, and how is local participation in decisions and distribution of benefits increased. Included are impacts on the different stakeholders, classified by income classes; on regions or locations; on different points in time; on gender, age, type of occupation; and so forth. These classifications that are used depend largely upon the project situation and institutional environment in which it exists.

- *Sustainability of positive impacts*—that is, whether the positive changes in welfare can be sustained through time. Included here is the concept of *livelihood security*. The Brundtland Commission's Panel on Food, Agriculture, Forestry, and the Environment (The Brundtland Commission 1987) proposed livelihood security as an integrating concept, defining it as the combination of adequate stocks to meet basic needs, secure access to productive resources, and maintain resource productivity on a long-term basis.

- *Economic efficiency*—that is, the relationships between benefits and costs with and without the project involved or the relationships between incremental benefits and costs, which translates into economic efficiency measures.

Both monetary and nonmonetary measures are used to assess the magnitudes and significance of these three dimensions of impacts on welfare. Nearly any type of environmental change that is attributed to the implementation of a forestry project can be associated with all three of these dimensions. For example, if the project creates employment opportunities:

- There will be distributional consequences, that is, previously unemployed people obtain jobs and income. As a result, these people gain "new status" and psychological benefits from being employed and providing support for their families. Goods and services not produced previously will affect different groups of people in different ways, depending upon what is being produced.

- The changes in employment can contribute to increased sustainability of development, or these changes can lead to more nonsustainable development, for example, increased pollution and loss of valuable habitats.

- There can be economic efficiency gains, that is, benefits exceeding costs. As a consequence, a country's overall wealth can increase.

Types of environmental impacts associated with forestry projects and questions about them are endless. These impacts and questions occur as hierarchies. To illustrate this point, a change (an increase) in fuelwood supplies (the output) can impact employment, which in turn, impacts health, food supplies, and so forth, ultimately ending with a change in human welfare or satisfaction for one or more groups of stakeholders.

Impacts and questions about them that will be prioritized in an assessment situation depends largely upon the circumstances surrounding a project and the interest groups associated with it. To some, employment can be top priority; to others, it can be foreign exchanges; while to still others, it can be expansion of local empowerment, health improvement, or political stability. The choice of impacts will be made ultimately by those who make decisions, with the hope that consideration will be given to the interests of the different stakeholders involved.

The focus of forestry projects, therefore, is largely upon the following points:

- Distribution of benefits to poor and other disadvantaged groups, including the distribution of power or empowerment of local participants in the project.
- Environmental stability and contributions to people's livelihood security by the projects beyond their scheduled lives.
- Economical efficiency associated with use of resources in the project, which is the "traditional" dimension of interest to decision makers and remains important in an overall assessment of impacts.

QUESTIONS CONCERNING IMPACTS

Relevant questions that should be considered in impact assessments will be examined in terms of distributional impacts, sustainability and livelihood security impacts, and economic efficiency impacts.

Distributional Impacts

One of the underlying objectives of forestry projects is to ensure equity in access to developmental resources and in the distribution of the ensuing benefits. Therefore, distributional impacts of forestry interventions should be studied to ascertain who is benefiting and also how those people are benefiting. Care must be taken to distinguish between the different stakeholder groups and their different agendas and needs. This distinction is true particularly in the case of men and women in relation to their interests in and access to available resources (FAO 1989c). Women are often in a distinctive tenure position regarding rights to land, trees, and shrubs. They may not have the same rights as do men and may not be allowed to grow specific species or grow trees and shrubs in certain tenure niches within family landholdings (Bruce 1989).

Women and men use trees and shrubs for different purposes. In the case of fuelwood, for example, women are concerned primarily with its availability for domestic use, while men often are interested more in wood as a cash crop. In the case of secondary products, women frequently are involved in collecting food for people or fodder for animals. In contrast, men may have little interest in collecting food products or fodder. Hence, a decision to restrict access to these resources will have a more negative, direct impact on women and, indirectly, on the family as a whole (Hoskins 1983). This distributional concern also holds for minority groups whose interests may have been ignored. Forestry projects, therefore, must ensure that the rights of minorities and the "voiceless" are respected and their interests integrated into the proposed activities (Ingersoll 1990). Failure to do so can cause severe social and political problems.

Different groups of people are dependent upon forests, woodlands, and plantations in a variety of ways, such as subsistence, surplus production, and income generation for subsistence. The level of dependence varies, though often the poorest are the most dependent and vulnerable to changes made in the nature of the tree and shrub base. What is required is a specification of these groups, and what goods and services these groups obtain from the forests, woodlands, and plantation (Peluso 1991).

Questions commonly asked in assessments of distributional impacts of forestry projects include the following:

- *How are project benefits and costs distributed among different stakeholders?* This is a question of who pays and who gains. Monetary and nonmonetary benefits and costs are considered. Countries and regions often are concerned with income redistributional effects of public investments, that is, the *equity issue.* Concern centers on different income classes, regional groups, or cultural groups. Intergenerational equity issues also might be of concern when looking at the sustainability dimension.
- *How has the project helped disadvantaged people, such as women, the landless, and minorities?* Forestry projects are positioned uniquely to benefit the disadvantaged because of the roles that trees and shrubs play in a household economy in which the woman's position is crucial, the rehabilitation of degraded lands can benefit the landless, and the livelihood security of people can be dependent upon trees and shrubs and their products. These roles are reinforced by a growing awareness of the relationships between environmental degradation and poverty alleviation. Answering this question calls for awareness of the different stakeholder groups living and working in the project area.

This question is stated more easily than it is answered, since disadvantaged people often remain *invisible* and "voiceless" unless the analyst makes a deliberate effort to talk with them. Those analysts who make brief visits to the countryside have been termed *development tourists,* since they generally focus their attention on elites, men, the healthy, users of services, and adopters of technologies (Chambers 1983). Others excluded are the poor, the women, the sick, and the old.

- *Who has lost as a result of the project and how have they lost?* There are people who lose as a result of certain types of forestry projects. In the past, this often has been the case with land settlement projects. It also happens on a smaller scale when new ways of structuring marketing activities displace "traditional" traders or middlemen. In some instances, segments of a population can be excluded by the conditions introduced by the project. For example, where women play important management and production roles, a project directed toward men can place women and their children at risk (Partridge 1984). In cases in which people have lost as a result of planned interventions, it is important to know what forms of assistance the project has provided for project victims to mitigate their losses. These eventualities should be taken into consideration in a project's design, but often they have not.

- *In what way has the project encouraged equitable distributions of benefits and costs among local people?* Given human nature and the "track record" of many forestry projects, equitable distributions of project benefits and costs rarely happen on their own, especially when there are different stakeholder groups and interested parties competing for scarce development resources. Equitable distributions of benefits and costs require the introduction of mechanisms to establish consensus about what is equitable, to monitor progress, and, where necessary, to enforce agreed-upon standards of benefit distribution. This introduction can be accomplished in various ways, including the establishment of a representative body (such as a committee, task force, or working group), the devolution of authority to a local body, or some form of central mandate. The focus here is on the extent to which a project has taken this concern into consideration, what it has done about it, and how successful the proposed solutions have been.

- *How has the project affected local empowerment and participation in development?* Despite agreement on the need for people's participation in forestry projects if the projects are to succeed, most projects still are not planned from the beginning with a "strong" participatory approach. Rural organizations are a key element in participatory planning and the sustainability and continuity of the project once implementation begins. However, these organizations often are regarded with apprehension by decision makers, who often view them as a nuisance or as a threat to their power. Yet, these organizations play a key role in sustainability. As such, it is important to know what role they will play in the project and what impact the project has on them.

The fact that people take advantage of the resources and services offered by the project does not necessarily mean that they are *actively* involved in determining what happens. The focus, therefore, is on ways in which local people are involved in project design, implementation, and monitoring and evaluation and the extent to which they are to be empowered to sustain project benefits.

What is required is an assessment of capabilities and willingness of local organizations and institutions to undertake the project, together with identification of principal constraints in fulfilling their present mandates. With a view toward sustainability, this assessment also should identify possible mechanisms for local management of project activities. Equally important are the linkages with other organizations and institutions involved with the project. Linkages at all levels are important for the provision of political support and obtaining access to information and resources.

- *In cases in which project success depends upon stakeholders being involved in commercial aspects of the project, is that involvement financially acceptable (profitable) for them?* The questions here include:
- Do key stakeholders (particularly private investors) have sufficient financial incentives to participate?
- What will be the benefit and cost flows for private investors or participating farmers and landowners?

If the different groups of stakeholders do not find the project attractive enough, it may be necessary to consider providing incentives to give the key stakeholders motivation to participate.

- *What are the budget impacts of the project for different agencies and groups?* The questions of importance here include:
- Does the project stay within budget limitations?
- What funds will be needed to cover operating expenses?
- When will funds be required to support the project (outflows), and when can receipts (inflows) be expected?
- What are the recurrent cost requirements in the future, that is, costs for road maintenance, forest management practices, and so forth?

The issue of cash flow and ability to maintain it also is relevant here.

- *How does the project affect foreign trade and exchange balances? How does the project impact other sectors and financial stability in the country or region?* These questions relate to foreign exchange impacts and the distributional question of how the project affects such other sectors as agriculture and transportation. In countries with a large *negative* foreign exchange balance, this question can be critical, and how it is answered can influence decisions on foreign exchange expenditures in the project and the levels of subsidies and tariffs. Other impacts of interest are those related to the stability of regional income and jobs. For example, a nature tourism project can be seasonal in terms of benefits and, therefore, involve a great deal of instability in terms of annual income flows in that sector.

Sustainability and Livelihood Impacts

Account seldom is taken of assets and their role in maintaining households at acceptable standards. Nor has much attention been paid to what people do with their assets when the opportunities to earn income diminish. Yet, those who are falling *below* the poverty line often develop *adaptive strategies* for survival. Even in conditions of "moderate" poverty, many households invest off-farm. (*Poverty*, often a synonym for *deprivation*, is measured in terms of income or consumptive flows.) If this investment is insufficient, the households often seek support from their extended kin. Should this prove insufficient, people will begin to dispose of their productive assets, such as livestock. Increasingly, trees and shrubs are regarded as productive assets in the same way as livestock.

A common priority expressed by rural people is a desire for an adequate, secure, and decent livelihood that provides for physical and social well-being. However, once survival is secured, there appears to be a propensity in many societies to save when the opportunity arises and to take the long view. Examples of this propensity to save are the sacrifices that parents make to invest in their children's education or the tenacity with which farmers will struggle to retain rights to land, even if these sacrifices are not needed for their immediate survival. Providing people with a base upon which to build and create for the future is a prerequisite for good stewardship (Chambers 1989).

Forestry interventions should concentrate on assisting local people to develop their productive resources and, in cases where these resources are limited or insufficient, assisting them to create new resources. Possibilities for achieving this goal include:

- Securing rights of ownership of assets, including sale and inheritance.
- Transforming small-scale tenancy and sharecropping into inheritable rights to land.
- Allocating degraded land to poor households for growing trees and shrubs or growing agricultural crops or raising livestock, where appropriate.
- Reinforcing livelihood strategies by supporting diversification, including nonagricultural activities.

These findings are corroborated in a study of natural resource management in the Sahelian region of West Africa (Shaikh et al. 1988). This study focused on on-farm crop production practices that showed promise for sustainable agricultural growth in Gambia, Mali, Niger, and Senegal. Emphasis was placed upon determining what works. It was found that the interventions with the greatest impact were those that resolved the problems of the local people rather than those of the environment *per se*. Because environmental degradation threatens local production systems and their capacity to survive, farmers have turned to natural resource management practices to protect soil and water resources upon which their production depends or to provide opportunities for income, such as pole production, orchards, gardens, fuelwood, and fodder sales.

Questions commonly addressed in assessments of sustainability and livelihood security impacts include:

- *What are the impacts on sustainability and livelihood security, with a primary focus on resource control and income generation?* The focus here is on the positive effects of forestry interventions on the lives of local people, with an emphasis on the more productive aspects. From a social perspective, these interventions should concentrate on assisting local people to develop their productive resources and assisting them to create additional resources in cases in which these resources are insufficient, providing a more "favorable" context for improved stewardship of the natural resource base. What is required is a specification of *how* benefits have contributed to sustainability and livelihood security, and vice versa.

If forests, woodlands, and plantations are to be managed on a sustainable basis, the key often is local participation in management through some system of communal management. There is increasing interest in the role of *common property resources* in the form of forests, woodlands, and plantations and in the extent to which these ecosystems satisfy local needs for wood products, fodder, food, and amenity values. There is also an acceptance that the common management of local resources is currently in a state of crisis, thanks largely to privatization, encroachment, and government appropriation (Arnold 1991). One solution to this crisis has been the introduction of *communal* management systems, where responsibilities are shared between local people and governmental forestry agencies (Poffenberger 1990). The sociological principle here is to create a link between groups of people and a tract of land that is to be managed, with the active support and involvement of the governmental forest agencies, particularly in protecting boundaries of the tract of land against outside use and encroachment. Members of the group need to perceive a correlation between their contributions and their returns (Cernea 1985).

Where increased control over local resources is not possible, the emphasis should be placed upon employment generation as a result of the planned interventions. *Commercial* forests, woodlands, and plantations can provide employment opportunities for rural families who depend upon the money earned from gathering, selling, and processing forest products to buy food and other necessities. Forest products are often a key source of cash income for the poor and women. The forest products obtained vary from region to region, depending largely upon markets, local traditions, alternative means of employment, and types of forest resources available (FAO 1989b). Many of the small-scale enterprises (SSEs) produce furniture, construction materials, agricultural implements, vehicle parts, and a variety of nonwood products (such as baskets, hats, and mats made from canes, reeds, vines, grasses, and similar materials), as mentioned in Chapter 7. The demands for most of these products are local. In contrast, handicraft goods, the other sizable group of products, have their main markets outside rural areas.

- *Are benefits sustainable over time?* In an analysis of benefits, it is important to specify which benefits are to be sustained once the external assistance of formal project ends. This analysis can include all the benefit flows or, more likely, specific benefits. Ways in which sustainability will be pursued should be outlined. Importantly, the analyst should include information about measures undertaken in the project to provide the necessary economic and political security for both individuals and institutions to pursue sustainability and livelihood security. Information also should be included on the obligations and responsibilities of each of the respective parties for achieving sustainability. Finally, the analysis should identify the financial, institutional, economic, environmental, technical, and political constraints to achieving this.

- *What are budget and financial sustainability (recurrent cost) implications of the project?* A common cause of nonsustainability of project benefits is a lack of ability of local entities to sustain costs that are needed to keep project activities going, for example, road maintenance costs. During the life of the project, the budgetary capacity of local organizations needs to be built up and developed so that it will be in place when the project is terminated.

Economic Efficiency Impacts[2]

The third dimension of welfare deals with overall relationships between the benefits and costs associated with the project. Similar to answering the financial questions asked in relation to the distributional dimension of welfare impacts, analysis of economic efficiency uses monetary units as the measure of impact. The question of financial efficiency, including the consideration of profits, has been dealt with earlier, in reference to questions concerning distributional impacts. Here, we consider economic efficiency. There are two significant differences between economic and financial efficiency measures. They relate to:

- *What benefits and costs (positive and negative impacts) are included in the assessment?* Only direct market-traded returns and costs are considered in a financial analysis, while as many as possible of the nonmarket benefits and costs (positive and negative impacts) also are included in an economic analysis.

- *How are those benefits and costs (impacts) valued?* Market prices always are used in a financial analysis. However, an economic efficiency analysis uses the best estimates of people's willingness to pay for goods and services. In an economic efficiency analysis, market prices may be adjusted to more accurately reflect a willingness to pay. These values are referred to as *shadow prices*. For example, if a project employs otherwise unemployed laborers, one might apply a labor shadow price lower than the ongoing

---

[2]This section is adapted from Gregersen and Contreras (1992).

wage in an economic analysis to reflect a lower opportunity cost for labor than otherwise would be unemployed.

A *financial analysis* is concerned only with actual monetary flows from (cost) and to (return) individuals or groups of individuals within a society. A financial analysis, therefore, deals only with those goods and services for which people pay or are paid, such as land, labor, and capital. Financial analyses always are undertaken from a specific stakeholder's point of view, for example, a governmental agency, cooperative, private firm, or individual.

Economic efficiency analysis is concerned with the benefits and costs to society as a whole, regardless of who pays and who gains. It looks at benefits measured in terms of what society actually is willing to pay for goods and services and the value of the opportunity costs involved, that is, the values of the opportunities foregone when a resource is used for one purpose rather than its next best use. These concepts are valid whether or not money is actually paid for a good or service.

Relationships between the steps in a financial and economic efficiency analysis are summarized in Table 9.1. The procedures for conducting these analyses are found in the literature (Dixon and Hufschmidt 1986, Gittinger 1982, Gregersen and Contreras 1992, Gregersen et al. 1987, Hufschmidt et al. 1983, Schuster 1980).

In most cases, only one question is asked in the assessment of economic efficiency impacts:

- *Does the project involve an economically efficient use of the country's or region's resources?*

In other words, do the benefits to the country or region exceed the costs of the project when both are appropriately valued? If there is some way of making more efficient use of the country's or region's resources, then the answer is *no*. In this case, one has to ask:

- Could we eliminate any of the separable components of the project and get higher net benefits?
- Could we obtain the same benefits with lower cost or with less use of resources?

When an objective of a forestry project is to increase the aggregate economic benefits (goods and services) derived from the use of limited resources, the economic efficiency question becomes a central one of concern to decision makers.

If both financial and economic efficiency questions are being asked, they are dealt with together, since both have much in common in terms of information requirements and procedure. However, steps in a financial analysis are clearer in concept and more straightforward to carry out. Therefore, impact assessments generally start by answering the financial questions related to financial profitability

TABLE 9.1. Relationship Between Steps in a Financial and Economic Efficiency Analysis

Financial Analysis	Economic Efficiency Analysis
1. Identifying and Quantifying Inputs and Outputs	
Direct inputs provided by the financial entity and outputs for which the entity is paid are included.	In addition to direct inputs and outputs, indirect effects are included, i.e., effects that are not included in the financial analysis since they are not bought or sold within a project context. These inputs and outputs are effects on others in society.
2. Valuing Inputs and Outputs	
Market prices are used. Future markets are estimated for inputs and outputs that occur in the future.	Consumer willingness to pay (wtp) is used as the primary measure of value. In cases in which market prices adequately reflect wtp, these prices are used. In other instances, *shadow prices* are estimated to provide a measure of wtp.
Inputs and outputs are multiplied by market prices to obtain total benefits and costs, which are entered in a *cash flow table*. Transfer payments (for example, taxes, subsidies, and loan transactions) are added to the cash flow table.	Inputs and outputs are multiplied by economic values to obtain total economic benefits and costs, which are entered in a *total value flow table*. Transfer payments are not treated separately but included as part of the economic costs or benefits, as appropriate.
3. Comparing Costs with Benefits	
Calculate selected measures of project worth or commercial profitability, using the information in the cash flow table.	Calculate selected measures of economic efficiency or economic worth, using the information in the total value flow table.

Source: Adapted from Gregersen and Contreras (1992), by permission of the Food and Agriculture Organization of the United Nations.

for different shareholder groups, and then the results of this step are used as a starting point for the economic efficiency analysis.

DESIGN OF IMPACT ASSESSMENTS

It is important to design an overall approach to impact assessments of forestry projects before deciding on the methods and techniques to use in answering each of the questions asked above. This design must consider the following points:

- Need for the adequate specification of questions.
- Stage in the project at which the question is asked.
- Technical and institutional constraints on the overall assessment.

The first consideration is needed so that the impact assessment is framed to answer the right questions. Too often, an assessment is started without specifying in detail what the end product should look like, that is, what type of answer is wanted. Without adequate specification, wasted effort can result. The second consideration is necessary for two reasons. First, the same questions are relevant at each stage in a project's evolution, but approaches to answering them will be different. Therefore, the same questions are asked *ex ante* at the early stages and *ex post* at latter stages, after the project is being implemented. The second reason to consider the project stages is that duplication in effort might be avoided in latter stages if one consciously remembers that the same questions need to be addressed throughout the life of the project. The third consideration is important so that limited resources can be allocated properly to answering each of the questions, timing and intensity of efforts can be adjusted to reflect needs and resource constraints, and concerns of the decision maker for credibility and reliability can be taken into account.

Specification of Questions

Decision makers may ask a question without specifying it in enough detail to answer it. In that case, the analyst will have to elicit specification. For example, if the decision maker asks, *What is the financial worth of the project?*, the analyst will have to find out whose point of view should be taken for determination of financial worth and what the measure of financial worth is that the decision maker wants. Similarly, an economic efficiency analysis can be carried out from either the country, regional, or local viewpoint. Therefore, the point of view needs to be specified, since the information required and the results generated will be different for different points of view.

There is a need to be explicit about which groups of stakeholders should be considered in the case of income distribution questions. The analyst must determine, for example, what is meant when asked to address the following question:

- What are the benefits to low-income project stakeholders?

In answering this question, it is necessary for the analyst to define *low income* in the assessment. Interactions between the decision maker and analyst are necessary to reach agreement on the answers to these types of questions early on.

When proposing that an impact assessment be conducted, decision makers sometimes neglect to consider the perspectives of all stakeholders involved. Stakeholders control resources and, consequently, must decide whether to commit these resources to a forestry project. The analyst has to keep this in mind when defining the array of questions to be considered. A project can be attractive from a countrywide economic efficiency point of view, but if it is not also financially attractive to private entities that have to commit resources to it, then it will not be undertaken as planned.

A financially unattractive project can be made financially attractive if the government (the public) provides subsidies (incentives). Whether such subsidies are justifiable in a socioeconomic context depends largely upon their required magnitude in relation to the economic surplus associated with the project (economic benefits minus costs, appropriately adjusted to take time into account). Similarly, an assessment that shows that a project appears to be more attractive financially than economically can provide some indication of the desirability to "tax" the beneficiaries involved.

Introduction of forestry interventions implies that changes will occur and benefits will result that can have an effect at various levels, including household, community, national, regional, and international (FAO 1989a). An impact assessment should propose ways to monitor the planned benefits of these interventions. This means moving beyond questions related to outcomes (for example, volume of wood harvested, number of nurseries established, or number of technicians trained), and on to questions regarding impacts they will have—specifically, what benefits will result in relation to the chosen dimensions of welfare. This calls for identifying simple, key indicators of impacts that can be used in answering the questions (Example 9.3).

Example 9.3

Household Types: An Indicator of Social Status   One of the "favored" indicators of social status in the rural areas of developing countries is house type. In its crudest form, the number of tin roofs can be used as a measure of the relative affluence of families or villages, at either one time or over time (Chambers 1985). But this has its limitations.

Two sets of indicators compiled to measure the relative prosperity of beneficiaries in central Java, Indonesia (Soetoro 1979), have applicability elsewhere. The first set focuses on the standard items of material wealth that could be observed about the household compound, including the type of materials used in the construction of the walls, windows, floor, and roof. The second set concentrates on the perceptions of a particular group of villagers about who was and was not prosperous. The first set is more amenable to quick "checks" by an outsider, while the second set draws more heavily on the knowledge and values of the local people. Furthermore, an approach based upon this second set of indicators has the following advantages (Honadle 1982):

• It has a higher probability of being continued as a "yardstick" after external project assistance is withdrawn because it is rooted in the local context.

- It improves the likelihood that locally defined social categories will not be overlooked by a technical staff.
- It mobilizes local knowledge, articulates it, and begins a process of basing analytical categories on rural perceptions.

Phases of Assessment

Decision makers and stakeholders need answers to the questions asked at different phases of a forestry project's life. This process involves the four main phases of *identification, preparation, implementation*, and *follow-up*. Figure 9.1 illustrates these phases. The kinds of questions asked depend largely upon whether they are being asked about a proposed project, an existing ongoing project, or a completed project.

As already stated, impact assessments are made at all phases in the project development and implementation process. An assessment at one phase of a project can differ in some particulars from assessments at other phases, because assessments are designed to answer specific kinds of questions. Although questions can vary with the project phase, there are similarities in the questions that need to be answered at the different phases. Furthermore, similar methods of assessment are used at each phase of the project and require similar kinds of information. However, the means for obtaining information and the level of detail required frequently varies from one phase to another. Some of these differences can be illustrated by looking at the process of financial assessment.

At the project identification phase, estimates of benefits and costs often are sufficient to determine whether proposed forestry projects are acceptable for further consideration. More detail and precision may be needed to evaluate alternative project designs at the project's preparation phase. At both phases, however, data on benefits and costs are estimates of future events. There likely is a degree of uncertainty associated with these estimates, therefore, and it must be recognized that the results of assessments at these phases are based on estimates of future events, which are never known with certainty.

At the project implementation phase, attempts should be made to measure the benefits and costs that have occurred, monitor ongoing expenditures and receipts, and estimate those that are likely to occur. Here, time and funds may not allow adequate observations to determine "true" benefits and costs. It can be difficult to obtain information about past costs and benefits from existing records, which may not be available, complete, and accurate. Since the project is not complete at this phase, only estimates of future benefits and costs can be made, with all of their associated uncertainties.

After project completion, benefits and costs must be estimated from evidence existing in records, if they are available, or observations of current conditions. The longer the period of time since project completion, the less the likelihood that the records of project activities and results will be available.

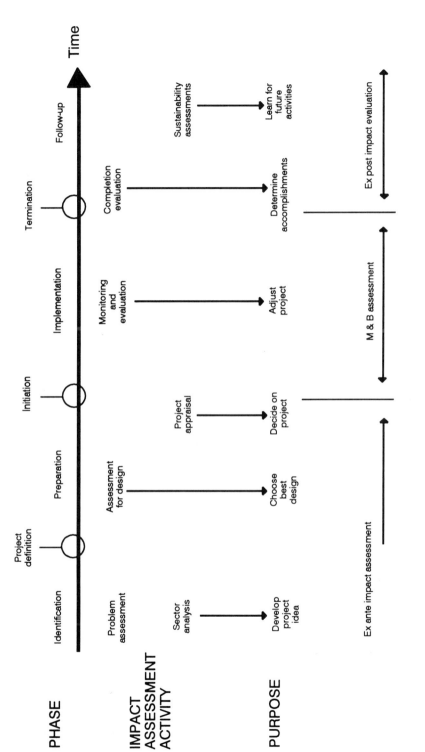

Figure 9.1. Phases of a project development process (adapted from Gregersen and Contreras 1992), by permission of the Food and Agriculture Organization of the United Nations

175

One of the difficulties in obtaining information at various phases of the project is that the assessment at each phase frequently is isolated from assessments at other phases. Therefore, at a later date, an analyst may have little information available from assessments of the same project at earlier phases. Information is costly to obtain, and, as a consequence, efforts should be made to use it effectively and efficiently. Impact assessments should be viewed in a *systems context* within the project development process. Plans should be made to closely link assessment activities throughout the project process, but without compromising the independence and verification functions of some types of assessments.

Regardless of the phase in the project, designing an impact assessment should be an iterative process, as suggested in Figure 9.2. Decision makers pose questions they want answered and suggest funding and time constraints for the proposed assessment. Technical personnel determine which assessment methods might be used to answer the questions and whether data and information required by the methods are available or, if they are unavailable, could be obtained within the funding and time constraints specified. It may not be possible to answer all of the posed questions in the detail desired with the funds and time available. If this is so, the decision maker then may have to change the questions and constraints, or it might be necessary to change the assessment methodology to arrive at a feasible compromise.

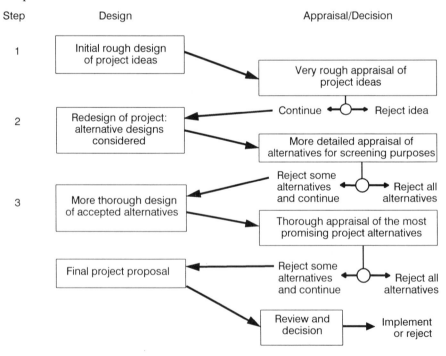

Figure 9.2. Iterative process in the design of impact assessments (adapted from Gregersen et al., forthcoming), by permission of the Food and Agriculture Organization of the United Nations

Technical and Institutional Constraints

The previous paragraphs have laid out the fundamental factors to consider in designing an assessment strategy and approach. In choosing a particular empirical approach to assessing the various impact questions asked, not only the technical merits of different approaches should be considered but also the objectives involved and criteria used in judging the usefulness and credibility of the assessment (Figure 9.3). It helps little to choose the most technically defensible assessment approach if it produces results that do not meet the needs of the decision maker or are too late to be used, or the costs are too high to be acceptable.

In choosing the approach to be used in an impact assessment, one must weigh carefully the technical factors, the purpose and primary use of the assessment, its usefulness in terms of timeliness and relevance, and the likely credibility of the results. This latter point is sometimes overlooked. If the assessment results are to be used in justifying future or past project activities to others, then one must be concerned with how these other people will view the results of the assessment. The assessment, no matter how well it is conducted from a technical standpoint, is likely to be useless in achieving that stated objectives if the:

- Reputation of the analysts is suspect.

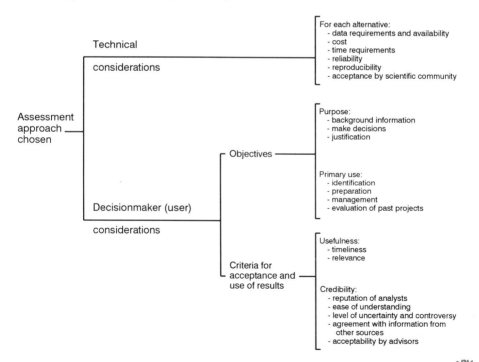

Figure 9.3. Factors affecting the approach to impact assessments of forestry projects (adapted from Gregersen et al., forthcoming), by permission of the Food and Agriculture Organization of the United Nations

- Results are not understood easily.
- Quality of data and information used by the analysis has a high level of uncertainty.
- Results are not in agreement with information available from other sources.
- Results are not acceptable to the project advisors.

In deciding upon an approach and how the impact assessment is going to be carried out, decision makers and planners should recognize the limitations imposed on the assessment by the:

- Questions to be answered about the project.
- Funding and time constraints imposed on the assessment process.
- Capabilities of those making the assessments and the constraints under which they must work.
- Availability of data and information required by the proposed assessment methodologies.

Practical steps can be taken to help make the approach as straightforward as possible. The first such step is to establish priorities and identify information needs. The questions that must be borne in mind are, *Who is going to use this information?* and *For what purpose?* Answering these two questions should determine what to ask and how to present the results.

Depending on the type of forestry project and the phase it has reached in its evolution, those directly involved must specify what information is needed, why it is needed, and who will use it. Also relevant is how much it will cost to collect, process, analyze, and present this information. To make this process easier, Chambers (1981) has defined the two concepts of *optimal ignorance* and *appropriate imprecision*. Optimal ignorance refers to the minimum information required to make reasonable decisions. The ability to determine what this level is comes with experience. Appropriate imprecision refers to the fact that, while imprecision is not a virtue, saving time and money is. The degree of "precision" depends largely upon the nature of the questions asked. In a forestry project to promote multiple use management, for example, more precision might be desirable on information about individual incentives than, say, information about available technologies.

SUMMARY

The main objective of impact assessments, the primary focus of this chapter, is identifying and analyzing the changes that can take place in the welfare of the stakeholders affected directly or indirectly by a forestry project. Questions concerning distributional, sustainability, and livelihood security, and economic efficiency impacts must be answered in conducting these assessments. With this in mind, at this point in the book, you should be able to:

1. Identify the stakeholders who might be involved in and affected by the types of forestry projects emphasized in this book and the impacts that these forestry projects can have on the stakeholders' welfare.

2. Explain the meaning and importance of the distributional, sustainability, and economic efficiency dimensions of welfare.

3. Answer the relevant questions that should be considered in impact assessments and, specifically, those concerned with distributional, sustainability, and livelihood security, and economic efficiency impacts.

4. Design a general approach to impact assessments of forestry projects, in which the need for adequate specifications of the questions, the phases in the project at which the questions are asked, and the technical and institutional constraints to the overall assessments are considered.

REFERENCES

Arnold, J. E. M. 1991. Community forestry: Ten years in review. *FAO Community Forestry Note* 7, Rome.

Bruce, J. W. 1989. Community forestry: Rapid appraisal of trees and land tenure. *FAO Community Forestry Note* 5, Rome.

The Brundtland Commission. 1987. *Food 2000: Global policies for sustainable agriculture; a report of the Advisory Panel on Food Security, Agriculture, Forestry and Environment to the World Commission on Environment and Development.* Zed Books, London.

Cernea, M. M. 1985. Alternative units of social organization sustaining afforestation strategies. In Cernea, M. M. (ed.). 1985. *Putting people first: Sociological variables in rural development.* Oxford University Press, New York, pp. 267–93.

Chambers, R. 1981. Rapid rural appraisal: Rationale and repertoire. *Public Administration and Development* 1:95–106.

Chambers, R. 1983. *Rural development: Putting the last first.* Longman, New York.

Chambers, R. 1985. Shortcut methods for gathering social information for rural development projects. In Cernea, M. M. (ed.). 1985. *Putting people first: Sociological variables in rural development.* Oxford University Press, New York, pp. 399–415.

Chambers, R. 1989. Sustainable rural livelihoods: A key strategy for people, environment and development. In Conroy, C., and M. Litvinoff (eds.). 1989. *The greening of aid: Sustainable livelihoods in practice.* Earthscan Publication, London, pp. 5–48.

Dixon, J. A., and M. M. Hufschmidt (eds.). 1986. *Economic valuation techniques for the environment: A case study workbook.* The Johns Hopkins University Press, Baltimore.

FAO. 1989a. *The state of food and agriculture.* FAO, Rome.

FAO. 1989b. Forestry and food security. *FAO Forestry Paper* 90, Rome.

FAO. 1989c. *Women in community forestry: A field guide for project design and implementation.* FAO, Rome.

Gittinger, J. P. 1982. *Economic analysis of agricultural projects.* The Johns Hopkins University Press, Baltimore.

Gregersen, H. M., and A. Contreras. 1992. Economic assessment of forestry projects impacts. *FAO Forestry Paper* 106, Rome.

Gregersen, H. M., J. E. M. Arnold, A. Lundgren, D. Gow, A. Contreras, and M. de Montalembert. (forthcoming). *Assessing forestry project impacts: Issues and strategies.* FAO, Rome.

Gregersen, H. M., K. N. Brooks, J. A. Dixon, and L. S. Hamilton. 1987. Guidelines for economic appraisal of watershed management projects. *FAO Conservation Guide* 16, Rome.

Honadle, G. 1982. Rapid reconnaissance for development administration: Mapping and moulding organizational landscapes. *World Development* 10:633–45.

Honadle, G., and L. Cooper. 1989. Beyond coordination and control: An interorganizational approach to structural adjustment, service delivery, and natural resource management. *World Development* 17:1531–41.

Hoskins, M. W. 1983. *Rural women, forest outputs, and forestry products.* FAO, Rome.

Hufschmidt, M. M., D. E. James, A. D. Meister, B. T. Bower, and J. A. Dixon. 1983. *Environment, natural systems and development—an economic valuation guide.* The Johns Hopkins University Press, Baltimore.

Ingersoll, J. 1990. Social analysis in AID and The World Bank. In Finsterbuch, K., J. Ingersoll, and L. Llewellyn (eds.). 1990. *Methods for social analysis in developing countries.* Westview Press, Boulder, Colorado.

Partridge, W. L. 1984. Planning and design stage. In Partridge, W. L. (ed.). 1984. *Training manual in development anthropology.* American Anthropological Association, Washington, D.C., pp. 18–30.

Patton, M. Q. 1986. *Utilization-focused evaluation.* Sage Publications, Newbury Park, California.

Peluso, N. L. 1991. *Studying household dependence on forests and trees: A method and a trial study.* FAO, Rome.

Poffenberger, M. (ed.). 1990. *Forest management partnerships: Regenerating India's forests.* Workshop on Sustainable Forestry, The Ford Foundation, New Delhi.

Schuster, E. 1980. *Economic impact analysis for forestry projects: A guide to evaluation of distributional consequences.* FAO, Rome.

Shaikh, A., E. Arnould, K. Christopherson, R. Hagen, J. Tabor, and D. Warshall. 1988. *Opportunities for sustained development: Successful natural resources management in the Sahel.* U.S. Agency for International Development, Washington, D.C.

Soetoro, A. 1979. *Prosperity indicators for Java.* Development Alternatives, Washington, D.C.

Weiss, C. H., and M. J. Bucuvalas. 1980. *Social science research and decision-making.* Columbia University Press, New York.

10 Multiple Use Management

Multiple use is cited as a guiding principle in almost any discussion of natural resources management. At times, one gets the impression that multiple use is a "cure-all" for all the problems of natural resource management. However, while there has been little difficulty in gaining a general acceptance of the multiple use concept, it has had much less success as a working tool for natural resource management. Most people might concede that wood or forage production is not necessarily the sole production function of management and that water, wildlife, and recreation also should be considered in managerial decisions. But, how much managerial effort should be allocated to each natural resource is not easy to resolve. The reconciliation of conflicting interests continues to be important to the organizations responsible for the management of natural resources.

MEANING OF MULTIPLE USE

The term *multiple use* can be applied to either areas of land or particular natural resources. When applied to land areas, *multiple use* refers to the management of various natural resource products and uses or product and use combinations on a particular land area. A relationship of natural resource products and uses to one another can be complementary, supplementary, or competitive.

Products or uses increase together in a *complementary relation*. A *supplementary relation* is a relation in which changes in one product or use will have no influence on another. A *competitive relation* exists between products or uses when one must be sacrificed to gain more of another. Conceivably, the relationships of several products or uses to one another on a particular land management area can be complementary, supplementary, and competitive, depending upon the range of the production functions being considered (Example 10.1). In this situation, it is important for managers to know what range of "management concerns" is being confronted.

When applied to a particular natural resource, *multiple use* refers to utilization of the resource for various purposes. Wood can be utilized for fuel, poles, or timber in the construction of houses. Forage can have value as food for livestock or wildlife species. Water can be used for irrigation, industrial operations, or fisheries. Here again, the utilization of the natural resource can be complementary, supplementary, or competitive. In practice, the multiple use concept involves both multiple use of the land and of particular natural resources. Demands on particular

Example 10.1

Functions for the Production of Wood, Herbage, and Water in Northern Arizona (O'Connell and Brown 1972)   Production functions have been identified by the USDA Forest Service for alternative forest management practices in northern Arizona. One set of production functions, shown below, illustrate effects of different levels of strip cutting in ponderosa pine (*Pinus ponderosa*) forests on wood, herbage, and water. It can be seen that the relationships between natural resource products vary from complementary to supplementary to competitive stages depending upon the levels of strip cutting.

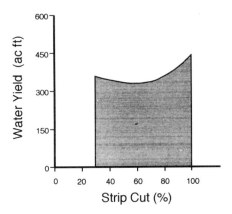

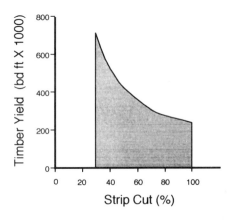

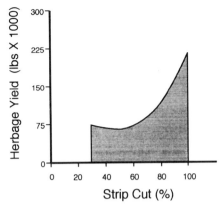

Effects of different levels of strip cutting in ponderosa pine forests on natural resource products in northern Arizona (adapted from O'Connell and Brown 1972)

natural resources (wood) for specific uses (fuel), in turn, place demands on lands on which natural resources are produced or used.

OBJECTIVE OF MULTIPLE USE MANAGEMENT

The objective of multiple use management is to manage a natural resource base for the most beneficial combination of present and future uses. The idea of maximizing benefits from a given natural resource base is not necessarily new, but it becomes more important as competition for limited natural resource products increases, which is the case in many dryland regions throughout the world. Every unit of land does not necessarily have to be managed for all of the possible natural resource products and uses simultaneously, however. Instead, most lands are utilized to varying degrees for a wide array of natural resource products and uses, as determined by the inherent potentials of the lands and dictated by the relative levels of available supplies and people's demands. In fact, multiple use can be accomplished by any one of the following options or by combinations of the them:

- Concurrent and continuous use of several natural resource products obtainable on a particular land area, requiring production of several goods and services from the same area.
- Alternating or rotating uses of the various natural resource products or combinations thereof on the land.
- Geographic separation of uses or use combinations, so that multiple use is accomplished across land management areas, with any particular unit of land being put to the single use to which it is most suited.

All of these options are legitimate multiple use management practices and, therefore, should be applied in the most appropriate combinations. From society's point of view, multiple use involves a broader set of parameters than those that concern a single person. Societies are likely to be more interested in preserving the benefits from natural resources for future generations, requiring investments beyond the dictates of relatively limited business economies and financial situations. On the other hand, one person typically makes decisions based largely upon relatively short-term profit motives. In practice, therefore, effective multiple use management should accommodate the full spectrum of today's needs while, at the same time, providing for tomorrow's requirements.

TYPES OF MULTIPLE USE MANAGEMENT

There are two general types of multiple use management, that which is *resource-oriented* and that which is *area-oriented* (Brooks et al. 1991, Ffolliott and Gallina 1981, Ridd 1965). Resource-oriented multiple use management is largely dependent upon knowledge of the interrelationships that describe how the management of one natural resource affects the use of others or how one use of a particular natural resource affects other uses of the same resource. Substitutions between and among natural resource products and uses and associated benefit-cost comparisons of alternative production or use combinations are taken into account. Resource-oriented multiple use management deals with a single natural resource with alternative uses or two or more natural resources with alternative uses for each.

Natural resources must not only be related to each other to accomplish effective and efficient multiple use, but also to the needs and wants of people. Area-oriented multiple use management meets this objective through considerations of the physical, biological, economic, and social factors that relate to the development of natural resources in a particular area. This type of multiple use provides a framework in which information concerning the management of land management areas can be arranged, analyzed, and evaluated for the purposes of making sound management decisions. Area-oriented multiple use draws that information needed to describe the potentials for the development of natural resources from resource-oriented multiple use management and then relates this information to the dynamics of local, regional, and national supplies and demands. Area-oriented multiple use management is not necessarily intended to replace other forms of land management, but rather to complement them. Hopefully, the gap between natural resource management and "on-the-ground" problems will be closed by doing so.

An application of multiple use management in rehabilitating and improving the conditions on a watershed in the southwestern United States is presented in Example 10.2. The underlying theme of this application is integrated natural resource management, a key to effectiveness and to sustainable multiple use management.

Example 10.2

Multiple Use Management in Northern New Mexico (Montoya et al. 1990) The 3,481 ha Leguino Wash watershed, located on the Santa Fe National

Forest, supports a pinyon-juniper woodland community with a short-grass understory that was overgrazed seriously by livestock in the 1930s. The USDA Forest Service assumed management of the area in 1947, with the responsibility of improving the range condition and reducing soil erosion. Fencing, water developments, and the removal of pinyon-juniper overstories were begun on selected sites to improve range condition. Gully erosion control activities, including the construction of check dams and soil ripping, also were initiated. Grazing management practices, including the introduction of deferred and rotation grazing systems, were implemented. However, the livestock producers who had permits to graze these lands were not convinced that these rangelands could be improved.

An integrated natural resource management approach began in 1987 to provide a multiple use managerial strategy for the area. An interdisciplinary team consisting of range, wildlife, watershed, and recreational specialists prepared a preliminary management plan for the area. Information solicited through public hearings involving the Livestock Grazing Association, New Mexico Game and Fish Department, USDA Soil Conservation Service, and others were incorporated into the approved management plan for the area. This plan consisted of the following components:

- Improving management of "sensitive" soils subjected to grazing pressures and off-road vehicle use.
- Enhancing the production of forage for livestock and wildlife and improving habitats for wildlife and fish.
- Creating opportunities to improve fuelwood production and availability.
- Protecting threatened and endangered plant species.
- Enlarging recreational opportunities.
- Providing a natural area for research and educational purposes.

The interdisciplinary team formulated a strategy for multiple use management of the Leguino Wash watershed that included the production and use of natural resources, environmental objectives, and a set of benefit-cost analyses of the alternatives. This strategy included rangeland improvements, water developments, improved animal control, gully erosion reduction, a travel management plan for the area, and the maintenance of watershed structures. Although the results are not known completely at this time, the point is that there is a process in place at this time that considers the relationships and trade-offs that must be understood before the goals of multiple use management are realized. Flexibility has been a key to the success of this program, so that appropriate changes can be made in response to changes in inputs and outputs and to people's needs over time.

INTEGRATING FORESTRY INTO THE MULTIPLE USE CONCEPT

The problems of integrating forestry into the multiple use concept are not always fully realized by planners, managers, and decision makers. While these problems can be structured in terms of resource-oriented multiple use management objectives, people also must be aware of area-oriented multiple use management implications. This awareness especially is important when multiple use management plans are developed for implementation on large areas.

Forestry involves the development, application, and evaluation of forest management practices designed for a specified purpose, for example, to increase wood production. Using this managerial goal as an illustration, the impacts of a forest management practice on a natural forest, woodland, or forest plantation are likely to extend beyond attempts to increase the flow of wood to users. Other natural resource products and uses that are obtained from the forest, woodland, or plantation in addition to wood also can be demanded by people. It is for this reason that a forest management practice that increases wood production or, more generally, any natural resource product or use should be planned in the broader multiple use concept.

It is important to note that multiple use is occurring in the dryland regions of the world whether one does or does not plan and manage in the multiple use context. This fact cannot be ignored. Therefore, it is to the benefit of all concerned that forest management practices are planned and implemented in reference to multiple use management.

There often are alternative forest management practices to consider, regardless of the management goal. One should think in terms of alternatives in the planning of interventions, as there usually are a number of ways to achieve a goal. One alternative is to allow things to remain as they are. Other alternatives, therefore, will reflect some form of managerial change. In selecting the best course of action, it is necessary to determine the advantages and disadvantages of alternative forest management practices in terms of multiple use management before a practice is implemented and becomes operational. In this regard, it becomes necessary to:

- Estimate flows of natural resource products and uses for the alternative forest management practices being considered.
- Determine the benefits and costs associated with the implementation of these alternatives.
- Select from the alternatives the most appropriate forest management practice to implement.

Estimation of Natural Resource Products and Uses

Estimation of the flows of all of the natural resource products and uses, either directly through on-site measurements or indirectly through simulation techniques, is necessary to determine their responses to the alternative forest management practices being considered. In essence, estimates of what the levels of production or use will be before and after the forest management practices are implemented are needed. For multiple use management, these estimates often include:

- Wood production and quality for wood products.
- Forage production, which subsequently can be translated into livestock gains.
- Wildlife habitat potentials.
- Water yields and quality.
- Information about hunter use to indicate, in part, recreational values.
- Aesthetic values associated with recreational opportunities.

Estimation of the flows of natural resource products and uses can be summarized in a *product mix table*. In essence, this table describes multiple use options by quantitatively presenting all of the natural resource products and uses obtainable from a particular area. Values before a forestry practice is implemented form a reference for comparison with the values that predict conditions after implementation. These comparisons, therefore, provide a basis to estimate what is gained and lost in multiple use terms for the alternative forest management practices being considered.

In the product table mix presented in Table 10.1 for a pinyon-juniper woodland on 1 ha in the southwestern United States, if things remain as they are, T_0, annual outputs will be 0.133 m^3 of fuelwood, 33.6 kg of livestock forage, 1.85 cm of water, and 0.674 kg of sediment. Wildlife habitat quality, evaluated in terms of a ranking from A (the highest quality) to E (the lowest quality), is A. With a conversion of a pinyon-juniper woodland to grassland through uprooting of the woodland overstory by cabling, T_1, annual outputs are estimated to be 0 for fuelwood (as the woodland overstory will be removed by cabling), 248 kg of livestock forage, 2.00 cm of water, and 1.74 kg of sediment. Wildlife habitat quality will be ranked as D. Column T_2 displays the estimated responses to a conversion of a pinyon-juniper woodland to grassland by the application of herbicides. It is important to note that the existing land management practice, T_0, should be retained if it is the "best" as judged by an assessment of the gains and losses in natural resource products and uses.

TABLE 10.1. A Product Mix Table for a Pinyon-Juniper Woodland in the Southwestern United States

Item	T_0 As Is	T_1 Cabling	T_2 Herbicides
Fuelwood production (m^3/ha)	0.133	0	0
Livestock forage (kg/ha)	33.6	248	91.9
Wildlife habitat (ranking)	A	D	C
Streamflow (cm/ha)	1.85	2.00	2.90
Sediment (kg/ha)	0.674	1.74	0.739

The values presented in a product mix table, such as those shown in Table 10.1, represent *average* responses of natural resources to forest management practices. In addition to average values, however, it is helpful to have information about related variabilities. As stressed earlier in this book, there are large variations in seasonal and yearly rainfall in dryland regions, with these large variations frequently contributing to large variabilities in the values presented in a product mix table. The amount of forage that is produced in a particular year, for example, is linked directly to the rainfall patterns in that year. Therefore, the greater the variability in seasonal and yearly rainfall, the greater the variability in the estimated *average* forage production.

Benefits and Costs

Determining the benefits that are associated with multiple use management and the costs of implementing and maintaining a forest management practice as a multiple use management system are prerequisite to management of natural resources in a multiple use context. These benefits and costs must be identified at a common point in the economic "stream" of activities. Valuing benefits at one point and costs at another point leads to incorrect evaluations of worth and, as a result, incorrect selection of the forest management practice for implementation.

Benefits   The benefits of multiple use management can be recognized easily in some instances. The value of wood that is removed in the initial establishment of a forest management practice often can be quantified in a marketplace if the wood has commercial benefit. However, calculations based on a market for only one wood product (e.g. fuelwood) become obsolete if markets for other wood products become available. The presence of these additional market outlets can alter expected monetary returns by making previously unmerchantable wood salable. Because market conditions can change quickly and because they affect benefits so significantly, wood resources should be described in terms of "multiple-product" potentials, if possible, providing the necessary growth and yield information for making management and product utilization decisions on a continuing basis.

The benefits obtained from other natural resource products and uses, including forage for livestock and wildlife species, water, and recreation, can be determined by comparable objective analyses at times, although the "markets" for many of these other natural resources are defined more poorly than markets for primary wood products. Values of forage for livestock consumption often are derived from information about the economic returns of weight gains in the animals. In some instances, wildlife values are estimated from the money that people will spend in hunting or viewing wildlife resources. Values for water and many forms of recreation are difficult to derive, largely because of a lack of marketplaces in which these "commodities" are traded. The benefits from tourism can be determined by knowing the levels of expenditures for identified activities.

In spite of the difficulties in estimating the benefits of changes in many natural resource products and uses, it is important that rigorous attempts be made to do so.

Otherwise, economic analyses of alternative forest management practices can be jeopardized.

Costs A large body of information about the costs of implementing and maintaining forest management practices is available in the literature. Unfortunately, this information usually reflects a particular economic situation and point in time and, consequently, cannot easily be adjusted to local conditions. Costs expressed in terms of physical input-output variables that characterize a management system and land area can help in overcoming this problem (Worley et al. 1965).

Inputs collected include supervision time, labor time, equipment time, and materials. Outputs specify total work completed, for example, as hectares thinned, cleared, or were otherwise treated. Costs are determined by multiplying inputs by current wage rates, machine rates, and material costs. The summation of all costs divided by the number of work units accomplished is an estimate of average unit-costs for a forest management practice.

Flexibility derived from collection of time-independent benefit-cost data allows multiple use management to be re-evaluated as the economic conditions change through time (Example 10.3). A forest management practice that initially was considered impractical economically could become operational with increased market outlets for natural resource products, a change in wage or machine cost rates, or combinations thereof.

Example 10.3

A Benefit-Cost Analysis of Manipulations of Pinyon-Juniper Woodlands in the Southwestern United States (Clary 1975) Pinyon-juniper woodlands have been converted to herbaceous cover in attempting to increase the production of forage plants and water on a set of experimental watersheds in northern Arizona. Conversion treatments to remove overstory trees included the use of mechanical methods and herbicides. Response of natural resource products and uses to these treatments have been quantified and subjected to a benefit-cost analysis in evaluating their potentials for operational applications. It was found that:

- Herbage production increases significantly after removals of pinyon-juniper overstories, but livestock carrying capacities varied greatly due to differences in plant compositions.
- Mechanical methods of pinyon-juniper overstory removal are not likely to increase water yields from upland watersheds. However, under certain situations, removal of the overstories by applications of herbicides has potentials for water yield improvement.
- Costs of conversion treatments at the time of the treatments (1963–1968) were low in comparison to current costs. The principal reasons for the

original low costs appeared to be that only the more favorable sites were treated at the time, follow-up work on smaller trees often was ignored, and labor and equipment costs were much lower.

More successful treatments in converting pinyon-juniper woodlands to a "good" stand of forage plants nearly break even from a benefit-cost standpoint, in terms of benefits and costs at the time of the treatments. If fuelwood sales accompanied a conversion project, however, costs of conversion likely would be reduced, improving net economic benefits.

Economic Evaluations

To make a multiple use evaluation of a forestry practice designed, for example, to increase wood production, economic objectives can be selected to form a basis of choice. Among these objectives are to maximize benefits, to maximize returns on an investment, or to achieve a specified production or use goal at the least cost. Information to satisfy the first two objectives includes estimates of values for natural resource products and uses, physical responses in natural resource products and uses that result from alternative forest management practices, and costs of implementing and maintaining the forestry practices considered. Production goals for various levels of costs are derived generally through political decision-making processes to satisfy the third objective.

Economic evaluations of multiple use management consist largely of an array of pertinent economic analyses, each of which is designed to help people to make a better decision. An individual economic analysis can yield a "one-answer solution" to the problem of selecting a forest management practice that will maximize collective benefits to an area. However, a group of economic analyses, based on different criteria, will result in an array of items for decision makers. Such an array might include:

- Estimates of multiple use production and use associated with alternative forest management practices.
- Estimates of costs for the alternative of forest management practices.
- Least-cost solutions for different goals of multiple use production and use.
- Benefits, both gross and net, associated with the range of alternative forest management practices.
- Investment returns and benefit-cost ratios associated with the alternative forest management practices.

POLICY FORMULATIONS AND INSTITUTIONAL CONFLICTS

With an array of economic relations, people should be able to choose the "best course of action" in terms of implementing a forest management practice that is designed to achieve a specified purpose. However, there likely are policy issues and institutional conflicts that also must be resolved before management becomes operational within the multiple use concept.

The question of who will pay for the implementation of a forest management practice designed, for example, to increase fuelwood production must be answered. In many instances, the group of local people or management organization that executes the practice may not derive benefits from all of the natural resource products and uses affected. In the United States, it is questionable that the USDA Forest Service, which is responsible for forest management programs on many of the public lands in the United States, receives benefits that are commensurate with their costs. Therefore, the role of local groups benefiting from increased fuelwood production on forests, woodlands, or plantations affected by the forest management practices has to be established regarding the sharing of costs. Similar situations are found elsewhere in the world, particularly where central governments are charged with managing forests, woodlands, or plantations for society's benefits.

The benefits and costs of a forest management practice designed to increase the production of fuelwood must be ascertained in respect to the needs of society as a whole. Different viewpoints must be adopted so that people can determine how the forest management practice is going to affect them individually and collectively. Local groups on or near the area that are affected directly by the forest management practice want to know how the program can affect them personally. Their viewpoint often is determined by an evaluation of "raw" natural resource products and uses on-site or the value added through "manufacturing stages" in economic streams from areas affected by management to consumers within the local area. A single economic solution may not be suitable, but broader analyses that reflect different viewpoints might furnish the required answer.

Regional interests, such as a "state" government, can bear a large portion of the investment for a forest management practice. A determination of the effects of the management practice on the economy of a state seems appropriate to this viewpoint. A "nationwide" viewpoint also is the basis for some evaluation in many countries, because many of the lands that are subjected to forest management practices are managed by the central government. Therefore, the central government may make at least a portion of the investment.

It is likely that the greatest problem that faces a manager pursuing the multiple use concept is developing an efficient institutional framework through which lands subjected to multiple use management can be managed. To be effective, a realistic multiple use land management plan must be executed within an existing institution or, if necessary, a modified institutional framework. An assessment of political and social organizations through which natural resources are currently managed can suggest a necessity for institutional reform.

SUMMARY

Multiple use management takes advantage of the interrelationships between and among natural resources, so that by manipulating one or more of the natural resources, additional benefits are derived from the related natural resources. More efficient use can be made of the natural resource base in recognizing these multiple use potentials. The emphasis on integrating forestry into the multiple use concept will become increasingly important in the dryland regions of the world in the future, as people demand more benefits from the natural resources in these fragile environments. After completing this chapter, you should be able to:

1. Explain the meaning, objective, and types of multiple use management.
2. Discuss how dryland forestry can be integrated into the multiple use concept by considering the estimation of natural resource products and uses, associated benefits and costs, and the economic evaluations of multiple use management.
3. Discuss the major constraints to the implementation of multiple use management from the standpoints of policy formulations and institutional conflicts.

REFERENCES

Brooks, K. N., P. F. Ffolliott, H. M. Gregersen, and J. L. Thames. 1991. *Hydrology and the management of watersheds.* Iowa State University Press, Ames, Iowa.

Clary, W. P. 1975. Multiple use effects of manipulating pinyon-juniper. In *Watershed management symposium.* 1975. American Society of Civil Engineers, Logan, Utah, pp. 469–77.

Ffolliott, P. F., and S. Gallina. 1981. *Deer biology, habitat requirements, and management in western North America.* Publication No. 9, Instituto de Ecologia, Mexico, D. F.

Montoya, J., B. Sims, D. Monte, P. Tatschi, and T. Roybal. 1990. Integrated resource management: Leguino watershed project, El Pueblo allotment. In Gonzales-Vicente, C. E., J. W. Russell, A. B. Villa-Salas, and R. H. Hamre (technical coordinators). 1990. International symposium: Integrated management of watersheds for multiple use. *USDA Forest Service, General Technical Report* RM-198, pp. 151–55.

O'Connell, P. F., and H. E. Brown. 1972. Use of production functions to evaluate multiple treatments on forested watersheds. *Water Resources Research* 8:1188–98.

Ridd, M. K. 1965. Area-oriented multiple use analysis. *USDA Forest Service, Research Paper* INT-21.

Worley, D. P., G. L. Mundell, and R. M. Williamson. 1965. Gross job time studies—an efficient method for analyzing forestry costs. *USDA Forest Service, Research Note* RM-54.

PART III
Technical Considerations

11 Nursery Operations and Improvement of Planting Stock

Nurseries are sites on which planting stock is raised for the establishment of forest plantations. Planting stock is nurtured in nurseries, starting at the time of inception, to enable their endurance of severe planting conditions. Whether indigenous or introduced tree or shrub species are considered, planting stock from nurseries has a better chance of survival than other kinds of plantation establishment.

The production of planting stock is a major expense in forestry programs and, consequently, efforts should be made to produce the highest quality planting material at least cost. Nursery operations must be well planned to achieve this goal (Landis et al. 1989a). The purpose of this chapter is to describe, in sequential order, general nursery operations that are followed in the production of seedlings and other types of planting stock for establishment of forest plantations in dryland regions.

CHOICE OF NURSERY SITE

The production of a required amount of planting stock of the desired size and quality at the appropriate time is a prerequisite to the success of planting programs. A properly sited, well-designed nursery, therefore, is necessary (FAO 1989, Schubert and Adams 1971, Weber and Stoney 1986). A nursery must be situated where an adequate supply of suitable water is available. A source of soil for the planting mixture, if it is part of the mixture, should be close to the site. A nursery site must be on well-drained and level or slightly sloping ground when irrigation is planned. Valley bottoms, where cold air could stagnate, should be avoided. Shelter against prevailing winds also is important. The availability of labor and road access must be taken into consideration for the choice of a nursery site.

When a planting program is large scale, a decision must be made as to whether the program is best served by a large, permanent, central nursery or several small, temporary, scattered nurseries. A choice of "big" or "small" is made after considering the technical aspects and relative economies of the two options. Large nurseries often are more efficient in their operations than small nurseries. However, the transportation of planting stock over long distances from a central nursery to the planting site can be harmful to young plants, especially if delayed in route. When transport facilities are not available, the nursery should be close to the planting site. Where plantations for rural communities are planned, it often is best to establish small nurseries in each community to better involve the members of the community in the planting program.

Layout

The layout of a nursery should minimize activities such as handling of soil, planting containers, and other materials. Vehicle access and movement within the nursery also must receive careful attention. In nurseries where soil is to be mixed with a fertilizer, a sterilized section must be set aside for that purpose. When a soil mixture is to be placed into containers, an area immediately adjacent for mixing and sterilizing should be set aside for the filling operation.

Size

The size of a nursery is determined largely by whether it is a *bare-rooted* or a *containerized* facility. Many of the nurseries in dryland regions produce containerized planting stock. The term *containers*, as used here, includes *pots*, *tubes* and, more generally, anything that contains growing media in which the planting stock is grown.

The production area in a container facility varies with the diameter of the containers. A relationship between the diameter of containers (from 5 to 15 cm) and the production area of a nursery area for 100,000 containerized seedlings is illustrated in Figure 11.1. One can see that 240 m^2 of production surface is required for containers with a diameter of 5 cm.

A general "rule of thumb" developed by FAO (1989) can be used to estimate the total nursery area, shown in Figure 11.1. The production surface is multiplied by 2.5 to include service areas, and 100 m^2 are added for pathways, based upon a production of 2,000 seedlings per m^2 of production area. Therefore, in general:

$$\text{Total Nursery Area} = (2.5 \times \text{Production Surface}) + 100 \text{ m}^2 \qquad (11.1)$$

and, for Figure 11.1:

$$\text{Total Nursery Area} = (2.5 \times 240) + 100 + 700 \text{ m}^2 \qquad (11.2)$$

Where bare-rooted planting stock is produced, the size of a nursery facility depends largely upon the average size of the planting stock and the amount of planting stock to be produced.

Shading Requirements

Seeds of most tree and shrub species germinate more readily under "light" shade than in full sunlight. It is easier to maintain suitable moisture conditions for germination under shade. As a consequence, seedbeds and freshly sown containers are shaded throughout the germinative period, and for a short time thereafter, until the seedlings are large enough to withstand gradual exposure.

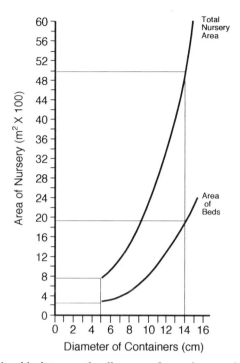

Figure 11.1. Relationship between the diameter of containers and production area of a nursery for the production of 100,000 seedlings (adapted from the Food and Agriculture Organization of the United Nations, 1989)

Transplanting bare-rooted seedlings is a task in many nurseries. Precautions must be taken to avoid damage to the seedlings from heat and direct sunlight in the transplanting operation. Shading of transplant beds, therefore, is necessary, although, normally, shade can be removed within 3 weeks following transplanting.

Different types of materials, including sorghum stalks tied together, bamboo splits, sacking, or white cotton material, can be used in creating artificial shade. Shade and windbreak cloth manufactured from high-density polyethylene filament and tape, extruded with carbon black or an inhibitor to limit ultraviolet degradation, provides an alternative shading material in areas where natural materials are not available.

Shelter and Protection

When a nursery site is exposed to winds, a shelter around the nursery is desirable. Hedges of closely planted trees or shrubs can provide this shelter. Mats, screens, or windbreak cloth also can be used. The presence of a shelter generally improves growth rates and reduces the time required for stock to reach a size suitable for planting.

Protection of a nursery from grazing and browsing by livestock and wildlife is necessary and requires fences to be built. The planting of live fences is feasible in some cases. Ditching also has been used for this purpose.

Watering Requirements

Water is one of the limiting factors in selecting nursery sites. Water used in producing planting stock should have a pH of 7 or less, be relatively free of particles and debris, and have a low total salt content. It is mandatory that water be available in adequate quantities throughout the production period. The amount of water applied at any one time varies with the weather conditions, soil infiltration rate, and size of the plantlets. Frequent "light" waterings are necessary to keep seedbeds moist but not saturated during the period of initial growth. As seedlings become larger, the total quantity of water applied is increased and frequency of application often is reduced.

As a guide to estimate the amount of water to apply to a seedbed in 1 month, the following calculation is made (FAO 1989):

$$\text{Amount of Water} = \text{Water Loss Factor} \times E \times \text{Area of Seedbed} \qquad (11.3)$$

where

$$\text{Water Loss Factor} = \text{Values Between 1.2 and 1.4, Averaging 1.3}$$

$$E = \text{Monthly Evapotranspiration}$$

Assuming a water loss factor of 1.3 for a monthly evapotranspiration (E) of 0.2 m and a seedbed area of 10,000 m^2, the watering requirement for 1 month is:

$$\text{Amount of Water} = 1.3 \times 0.2 \times 10,000 = 2,600 \ m^3 \qquad (11.4)$$

Water can be applied by hand or through irrigation. Watering cans, hoses with spray nozzles, or knapsack mist sprayers are used in small nurseries. A fine droplet size is essential for watering containers or seedbeds in which seeds have been sown. Otherwise, the seeds can be washed out of the ground or the materials covering the seeds will be washed away and the soil surface consolidated.

Irrigation in one form or another is often the adopted method of watering in large nurseries. A general discussion of irrigation systems, with the pros and cons of each pointed out, is presented in Chapter 13.

PLANNING OF NURSERY OPERATIONS

Nursery operations are scheduled in relation to the planting season that coincides with the rainy season in most dryland situations (FAO 1989, Landis et al. 1989a,

Weber and Stoney 1986). When the rainy season begins, therefore, a nursery must be able to deliver the required planting stock. Nursery operations in areas with summer rainfall likely will follow a different schedule of operations than that of a nursery in an area with winter rains.

COLLECTION AND STORAGE OF SEEDS

Collection and, if necessary, storage of seeds are critical when the planting stock produced is seedlings. The tasks that frequently are undertaken in the collection and storage of seeds are shown sequentially in Figure 11.2. Adequate quantities of high-quality seeds required for a planting program must be obtained. Seeds should be of known origin. When large quantities of seed are required, availability can become a controlling factor. The establishment of orchards or knowledge of the location of other sources of seed to ensure a constant local supply of high-quality seeds can be necessary. Seeds also can be collected from indigenous or introduced trees and shrubs that grow within the specified environmental limits of proposed planting sites and meet desired characteristics.

Information about the time of year when various tree and shrub species flower and their yield of seed is required to plan the collection (Goor and Barney 1976, Weber and Stoney 1986). The suitable time of seed collections changes frequently from species to species and from location to location. Therefore, knowledge of local seeding characteristics is needed. A number of species indigenous to dryland regions produce good seed crops at intervals of only 2, 3, or 4 years (Doran et al.

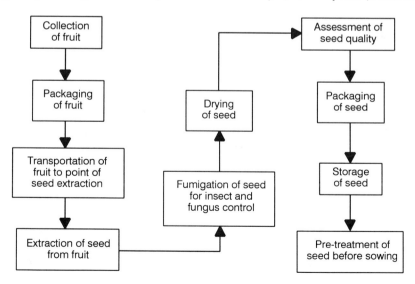

Figure 11.2. Tasks in collection, handling, storage, and pretreatment of seeds (adapted from Ffolliott and Thames 1983, the Food and Agriculture Organization of the United Nations)

1983, Ffolliott and Thames 1983, Weber and Stoney 1986). As a consequence, it is necessary to harvest a large supply of seeds during "good" seed years. Arrangements for the collection, transport, extraction, processing, and storing of seeds must be considered carefully.

The proper storage of seeds is essential to ensure a continuous supply and meet the needs of plantation establishment between seed years. Seeds also must be stored when they have been ordered from elsewhere and received before the date of sowing. The storage facilities must ensure that seeds maintain a potentially high germinative capacity. In general, seeds should be kept in airtight containers and stored at a temperature that is near or slightly below the freezing point.

Insects and fungi that seriously harm seeds and, as a result, reduce germination must be destroyed completely before the seeds are stored. Insecticidal dusts, for example, carbon bisulfide or methylbromide, can be used for treating seeds (Johnson 1983, Landis et al. 1989e, Southgate 1983). Insecticide and seeds frequently are placed together in a sealed container for 24 hours, after which the seeds are aerated quickly and stored.

TESTING OF SEEDS

There are a number of tests to determine the capacity of seeds to germinate and grow into seedlings. Tests to verify the identity of tree or shrub species and races, moisture content, and degree of maturity also are made when required.

Direct Inspection of Seeds

People working with seeds learn to distinguish one species from another and observe differences in appearance of certain geographical races. When there are questions about seed source or whether the seeds are from a "correct" species, reference seed collections should be consulted or identification made by seedlings raised from seeds.

Seeds should be bright in color and clean in appearance. A moldy appearance or a rancid odor often indicates old or improperly stored seeds. Old seeds that have been "brightened" up to appear healthy by applying oil to improve their luster can be detected by shaking in hot water.

Purity Analysis

Seeds need not be completely free from dirt and impurities to be high in germinative quality. However, it is important to know the proportion of good seeds, since this influences the density of sowing in seedbeds and costs to produce seedlings. While some impurities may not injure seeds, insect eggs, dirt, or material containing fungus spores damage seeds in storage or when they are sown. The risks of introducing insects and diseases must be minimized. Insistence on high standards of purity in seeds is justified on this point alone.

Of concern in purity analyses is the recleaning and the interior conditions of the seeds. Seeds that are mixed with a large amount of chaff should be recleaned before an accurate purity test is made. Interior conditions of seeds can be assessed when cut or crushed. Seeds that are empty, that have partially formed or dried and shriveled embryos, that have endosperms that are full of sawdust-like matter, or that contain fungi or insects generally are worthless for seedling production. Healthy seeds have firm, white, yellow, or green contents, depending upon the species, and they frequently are sweet-smelling. The cutting test is most useful as a quick method of checking the value of a seed lot.

When a quantitative test of apparent viability is to be made, a representative sample of seeds should be drawn from the lot. The seeds then are spread out on a smooth board or sheet of paper, cut in two with a knife, and the condition of each seed tallied. Small seeds can be crushed with the flat side of a knife. A hand lens or a reading glass is helpful in examining the seeds. Hard seeds might have to be broken with a hammer, an anvil, or a block of wood.

Since empty or poorly developed seeds of some species float in water and good seeds sink, placing a sample of seeds in water often can be used to determine quality. This test should be restricted to freshly collected seeds that have not become dry. However, the cutting test is more reliable.

Tests of Viability

To what extent a seed sample is capable of germination is harder to determine than whether or not it contains impurities. The relative expense of tests of viability is small in comparison with their value, when large quantities of seeds are involved. Seeds that have been in storage a long time should be retested before shipment or use.

Reasons that the testing of seeds is not undertaken more universally are not always because of the expense but rather because of the time required for germinative tests of some species, a lack of testing facilities with trained personnel, and the absence of laws or regulations requiring this test. The procedural details of tests of viability are found in standard references on the subject (ISTA 1976).

Limitations of Viability Tests

Viability tests of seeds that undergo a prolonged dormancy can be impractical because of the time required. When viability tests are made, they often must be either cutting tests or one of the "quick" methods (e.g., excised embryo tests or staining tests), provided facilities are available for carrying out these tests. Even with improved techniques, viability tests are not always reliable indications of seed quality.

KINDS OF PLANTING STOCK

The kind of planting stock to be used has direct bearing on the planting method employed. The main types of planting stock are *bare-rooted*, *ball-rooted*, and *containerized* seedlings and stumps, cuttings, and sets (Chapman and Allan 1978, FAO 1989). Characteristics of bare-rooted, ball-rooted, and containerized seedlings are described below. Stumps, cuttings, and sets are discussed under the heading of "Vegetative Propagation" later in this chapter.

Bare-Rooted Seedlings

Bare-rooted seedlings are dispatched from a nursery after shaking excess soil from the roots, leaving only a thin layer for protection. These seedlings are tied in bundles and protected from drying in transit by covering the roots with wet moss or leaves or by dipping them into clay slurries or other specially prepared mixtures. Bundles are placed in paper or plastic sacks or cardboard cartons for transport. Plastic or paper sacks lined with plastic film are permeable to carbon dioxide but impermeable to water, minimizing risks of drying.

Bare-rooted seedlings are susceptible to losses in viability when the roots are exposed to sun or wind. Therefore, the roots should be kept covered on delivery to the planting site until the time of planting. Whenever there is a possibility of more than only a few hours delay between delivery and planting, the bundle should be *heeled in*, that is, placed in dug trenches and the roots covered with moist sand, peat, or light soil. Bare-rooted seedlings that have been heeled in carefully and then watered can survive several days without damage.

Ball-Rooted Seedlings

Seedlings are dispatched from a nursery with their roots surrounded by soil for protection in ball-rooted planting. One method of obtaining ball-rooted seedlings is to carve up a nursery bed into sections and place the sections into shallow-sided boxes. Another method is to grow seedlings directly in the boxes. Individual seedlings with small blocks of soil are cut from the box for planting.

One problem with ball-rooted planting is preventing the soil from being shaken loose from the roots during transit from the nursery. A number of techniques can be used to overcome this problem, including enclosure of the bare roots of nursery stock in balls or blocks of compressed soil (consisting of clay, sandy loam, and peat or humus in equal parts), or in earth-filled containers. Planting stock treated in this manner is called *balled plants*.

Containerized Seedlings

The frequent problem of root exposure often is overcome by use of seedlings raised in containers. Containers can be either *pots*, which have a closed bottom, preferably with drainage holes, or *tubes*, which have no bottom but require a soil medium that is adhesive so it will not fall out when handled (Tinus and McDonald 1979). Containerized seedlings have a capacity to withstand extended dry periods after planting, and, therefore, their use can prolong the planting seasons in harsh environments.

A major emphasis has been placed on use of containerized seedlings in this chapter because of their widespread use in the dryland regions of the world. This emphasis does not necessarily mean that bare-rooted or ball-rooted plants are unimportant, however. To the contrary, when grown in prescribed growing conditions and transported to planting sites as soon as possible after their removal from a nursery, forest plantations can be established successfully by carefully planting bare-rooted and ball-rooted seedlings. Nevertheless, containerized seedlings generally withstand dry periods prior to planting for a longer time than other kinds of planting stock, which increases the flexibility in planting schedules and the probability of achieving an even more successful plantation.

TYPES OF CONTAINERS

Various types of containers are available (FAO 1989, Landis et al. 1989b, Tinus and McDonald 1979). A common practice is to raise plants either in polyethylene pots (also called *polypots*) or tubes. Other types of containers include pressed earth blocks, peat pots, paper pots, banana leaf pots, bamboo, and tubes of metal, cardboard, veneer, and waterproof paper. These types of containers are less convenient or more expensive than polyethylene pots or tubes, especially when a large number is required.

The polyethylene used for pots or tubes is usually from 150 to 250 gauge (a thickness of from 37.5 to 62.5 microns) and is black or transparent. Black polyethylene often is preferred, as it allows less growth of algae in the container. Polyethylene pots have a closed bottom and drainage holes, while polyethylene tubes have no bottom. Choice between the two depends largely upon whether the available soil is cohesive enough for tubes and, when this is so, will not fall out of the bottom when handled. Polyethylene pots have an advantage over other types of containers because they are inexpensive, light, and easy to handle.

The size of polyethylene pots or tubes to use varies with the species to be produced and the time required to raise the seedlings to planting size. Savings in costs can be achieved by using smaller sizes. In general, it is accepted that the minimum diameter should be 5 cm and the height 15 cm (FAO 1989). Transplanting becomes difficult when the diameter is less than 5 cm.

GROWING MEDIA

The need to establish nurseries on sites with fertile soils all but disappears with the use of polyethylene pots, tubes, and other kinds of containers, as the growing media frequently used are in the form of imported mixtures. While proper soil

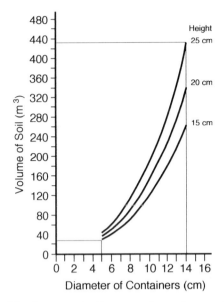

Figure 11.3. Relationships between the diameter of containers and their heights and the volume of growing media needed (adapted from the Food and Agriculture Organization of the United Nations, 1989)

mixture remains important in bare-rooted nursery facilities, emphasis has been placed here on imported growing media placed into containers.

The growing medium should be light and cohesive, have a good water retentive capacity, and possess a high organic and mineral content (Landis et al. 1989b, Tinus and McDonald 1979). It also should contain required nutrients, which can be supplied in the form of artificial fertilizers. Most of these fertilizers contain nitrogen, phosphorus, and potassium in varying proportions. The proportions of the constituents vary from one successful operation to another.

The quantity of growing media needed in a containerized nursery operation is related to the size of the containers used. The relationships between the diameter of containers (ranging from 5 to 15 cm) and their heights (15, 20, and 25 cm) and the growing media volume (in m³) are shown in Figure 11.3. The comparison between the smallest containers (diameter 5 cm, height 15 cm) and the largest (diameter 15 cm, height 25 cm) is striking. To fill 100,000 small containers, 28 m³ of growing medium is needed, while 442 m³ of growing medium is needed for filling 100,000 of the largest containers. Figure 11.3 can be used as a basis for estimating the amount of growing medium needed to fill containers of the sizes shown.

PRETREATMENT OF SEEDS

Seeds of some tree and shrubs species are ready for sowing as soon as they are collected. Others pass through periods of dormancy, during which time their embryos complete development. For these latter species, a pretreatment of the seeds often is used to hasten or improve the rates of germination. Methods of pre-treatment vary with different types of dormancy. The main types of dormancy include (FAO 1989):

- Exogenous dormancy associated with mechanical, physical, or chemical properties of the pericarp or seed coat.
- Endogenous dormancy, which is determined by morphological or physiological properties of the embryo or endosperm.
- Combined exogenous and endogenous dormancy.

The most frequently encountered type of dormancy in dryland regions is exogenous (Goor and Barney 1976, Weber and Stoney 1986). Some of the commonly used methods to attempt overcoming this type of dormancy are described below.

Small numbers of seeds can be scarified by scratching them with sandpaper, cutting each seed with a knife, or sandpapering the end of the seed that is opposite to the radicle until the cotyledon is seen. With large numbers of seeds, mechanical scarification can be achieved by pounding with sand or rubbing the seeds over an abrasive slab.

The soaking of seeds in cold water from 1 to several days is sufficient to ensure germination for some tree and shrub species. Improvement in germination is caused by a softening of the seed coats and then the insurance of adequate water absorption by living tissues. Water should be changed at intervals when long soaking periods are required. It is important to sow the seeds immediately after soaking because drying reduces the viability of seeds.

Seeds of many trees and shrubs that are indigenous to dryland regions (e.g., *Acacia* and *Prosopis*) have tough outer coats that can delay germination after sowing unless the seeds are pretreated by immersion in hot or boiling water (Example 11.1). To improve germination, these seeds are immersed in 2–3 times

---

Example 11.1

Pretreatment of **Dadeneae** *Seeds by Soaking in Boiling Water Improves Germination Rates.* *Dadeneae* is one of the tree species recommended for planting in the Near East. However, it often is necessary to pretreat the seeds to attain high enough germination rates for operational planting programs. In looking for a relatively inexpensive but effective way to improve germination, samples of seeds from *Dadeneae* were immersed in boiling water for 1, 5, and 10 minutes and then planted in containers filled with vermiculite and soil. Germination of the pretreated seeds was compared to that of untreated seeds also planted in containers. All of the seeds immersed in boiling water germinated at the end of a 3-week test, regardless of the period of immersion. None of the untreated seeds had germinated by this time, or even several weeks thereafter. Therefore, the soaking of *Dadeneae* seeds in boiling water can be an effective way to overcome dormancy and produce planting stock in a nursery.

---

their volume of boiling water and allowed to soak 1–10 minutes or until the water is cold. Gummy mucilaginous exudations from the seed coats are washed off by stirring the seeds in several lots of clean water.

Soaking in solutions of acid frequently is done in the case of seeds with hard coats. Concentrated sulfuric acid (98 percent) is the chemical used most generally (FAO 1989). Soaking times vary from 15 to 30 minutes. After soaking, the seeds must be washed immediately in clean water. Tests should be made to determine optimum periods of treatment for each tree or shrub species, since overexposure to solutions of acid can damage seeds.

In special cases, seeds can be scarified by placing them in revolving drums to crack or pierce the outer seed coats (Doran et al. 1983, Flynt and Morton 1969). Sometimes, the seeds have to be cracked or cut open or partially cut by hand to obtain good germination. In some countries, seeds of *Acacia* and *Prosopis* species are fed to goats and later collected from their droppings. Partial digestion enhances germination.

SOWING OF SEEDS

Most of the nursery operations described up to this point are undertaken to permit sowing of seeds into either seedbeds or containers at the ideal time. In order to determine the prescribed sowing time, one counts backward from the beginning of the planting season to identify the number of months required to raise the required amount of high-quality seedlings. The time to raise plantable seedlings varies with the tree or shrub species, climatic conditions, and the way the nursery is managed (Landis et al. 1989c, 1989d, 1989f). Each planting project should prepare sowing schedules for locally important tree or shrub species, taking into account the above considerations (Example 11.2). With large amounts of seeds, not all of them should be sown at the same time. It is better to spread out sowing dates in 1-week intervals.

A common method of raising seedlings is to sow the seeds in seedbeds or trays and then to transplant into containers as soon as the seedling are sufficiently large to handle. The seedbeds can be either broadcast sown or sown at intervals along lines. Small seeds often are mixed with some kind of inert fine material to facilitate even distribution. Seedling trays or boxes commonly are used for production of seedlings that are transplanted into containers. Trays can be made from kerosene or gas tins by cutting them lengthwise into halves. The bottoms of the trays should be perforated to allow drainage or irrigation by absorption. The bottoms can be filled with a 2-cm layer of gravel or charcoal to facilitate drainage. Afterward, the trays can be used for packing and transporting container seedlings.

After the seeds are sown in seedbeds or seedling trays, they must be covered adequately with soil, which is pressed down to establish a good contact between seeds and soil. Depth of sowing depends upon the size of the seeds. The normal depth of sowing is 1–3 times the diameter of the seeds, but, in many instances, it can be desirable to sow slightly deeper to avoid the washing of seeds out of the soil by irrigation or by rains.

Example 11.2

Planting Schedule for **Acacia Albida** *in Sub-Saharan Africa (Weber and Stoney 1986)* Planting schedules for *Acacia albida* in sub-Saharan Africa are set so that seedlings will be well-developed for planting at their permanent site immediately after the onset of the rainy season, which also is the beginning of the planting season. Foresters determine the time that the species must be grown in a nursery to schedule planting correctly. They then calculate the date for sowing by subtracting the estimated time required for production in the nursery from the number of weeks left before the predicted start of the rains. If the seeds are to be sown in containers, it is estimated that up to 14 weeks of growth in a nursery is necessary. If the rains are predicted to start in 24 weeks, the containers must be sown in about 10 weeks.

It is important that the conditions for growth in the nursery be controlled to meet the target date. Otherwise, more time in the nursery is scheduled, moving up the date of sowing.

TRANSPLANTING OF SEEDLINGS INTO CONTAINERS

A seedling that is growing in or has been lifted from a seedbed or tray in which it was originally sown is technically a *seedling*. When a seedling is lifted and replanted in another bed or container, it is termed a *transplant* thereafter. Transplanting of seedlings, also referred to as *pricking*, is undertaken to induce a better development of root systems by increasing the number of absorbing rootlets that develop profusely near the severed root ends. Transplanting is carried out before the seedlings have acquired large, heavy root systems, but after they have developed strong stems. This stage normally occurs after the complete unfolding of the cotyledons and during the unfolding of the first true leaves.

A sharp object is inserted into the soil and the seedling is loosened to remove it from a seedbed or tray. The seedling then is pulled out and placed immediately into a planting hole that has been made in the growing medium within the container by a sharp pointed instrument. Roots of the seedling should not be exposed to direct sunlight. When necessary, roots can be pruned to fit the depth of the prepared hole.

Once in place, the sides of the hole are pressed firmly against the roots of the seedling along its whole length. A key point here is a minimum of handling and exposure but adequate firming of the seedling in the container. Transplanting is a delicate, time-consuming operation. Therefore, when possible, there is a tendency to sow directly into the containers. This procedure has an advantage of saving time and labor, and reducing losses of seedlings and retardation in plant growth caused by transplanting.

DAMPING-OFF

Soil used in either seedbeds or growing media for containers should be acidic. The pH should not be higher than 6.0 for the growth of most planting stock. On more alkaline soils, growth often is poor, with symptoms of chlorosis and iron deficiency, and the planting stock is prone to *damping-off* and other fungal diseases (Landis et al. 1989e).

Damping-off is a common disease in many nurseries. It can occur in either seedbeds or containers after transplanting. Damping-off is a preemergent and seedling disease caused by various fungi. Some of these fungi attack seeds as germination starts and others infect newly germinated seedlings. Affected seedlings topple over, as though broken at the ground line, or remain erect and dry up. A watery-appearing constriction of the stem at the ground line is visible evidence of the disease. Damping-off is favored by high humidity, a damp soil surface, heavy soil, cloudy weather, an excess of shade, a dense stand of seedlings, and alkaline conditions.

Preventative measures for damping-off include maintaining a dry soil surface through repeated cultivation, reducing the sowing density, and thinning seedlings to create better aeration at the ground line (FAO 1989). A need for soil fumigation is minimized when fresh soil mixtures are used. When damping-off occurs, there are three types of control—soil acidification, soil sterilization, and use of fungicides.

Soil acidification is beneficial because of the frequently encountered soil alkalinity in dryland environments. Sulfuric acid is a satisfactory chemical for acidifying the soil. In general, the equivalent of 200–400 m^3 of concentrated sulfuric acid is applied in dilute solution (2 percent by volume) per m^2 of soil surface.

In soil sterilization, formaldehyde and methyl bromide frequently are used. Commercial (40 percent) formaldehyde can be used in a water solution. The effective dosage, 80 cm^3 in 5 L of water per m^2 of soil surface should be applied 7–10 days before sowing. One of the better methods of soil sterilization is fumigation with methyl bromide gas. An approach to fumigation with methyl bromide is to evenly distribute the gas throughout the soil by releasing it under a plastic sheet stretched over a soil clamp. The gas then slowly diffuses through the soil. Methyl bromide is available in cans that contain its liquid form under pressure. The liquid becomes gaseous when pressure is released.

Fungicides are chemicals that are toxic to fungi but harmless to plantlets in the specified amounts used. These chemicals are applied to either the soil or the seed before sowing. Fungicides are available under a variety of trade names. Some that have been used successfully in dryland regions, such as thiram and captan, can be applied as a dust or in a water suspension directly to the soil before or after seeding.

ROOT PRUNING

When raised in containers, if the taproots of seedlings are not pruned, they can emerge from the bottom of a container and grow into the soil of the bed beneath. The purposes of root pruning are to prevent development of a long taproot and to encourage growth of a fibrous lateral root system in the container (FAO 1989, Landis et al. 1989f). Root pruning can be achieved by drawing a thin wire between the base of a container and bed surface in order to cut through descending roots. Root pruning also can be accomplished by lifting the container and snapping off the roots. Timing and frequency of pruning are adjusted to the rate at which roots grow and emerge from the bottom of the containers.

HARDENING

Hardening is one of the most overlooked phases of nursery operations, but it also can be one of the most critical in the production cycle of seedlings and other kinds of planting stock (Landis et al. 1989f, 1989g). It is relatively easy to produce acceptable planting stock in a nursery, but these plants often have relatively low rates of successful establishment unless they are properly conditioned to survive and grow on the planting site. Hardening is the process in which growth is reduced, stored carbohydrates accumulate, and the seedling becomes better able to withstand harsh conditions (Penrose and Hansen 1981). The objectives of hardening include:

- Minimize the physical damage to planting stock during handling, transport to the planting site, and planting.
- Acclimatize the planting stock to the environment in which it will be planted and to the internal dormancy requirements of some species.

The hardening process includes the leaching of excess nutrients out of the growing medium, reducing amounts of water given to the plantlets, and placing the plants in locations to be exposed to the sun, all of which help to condition the planting stock for planting. Hardening should be induced in stages, with the process usually taking about 6 to 8 weeks. Seedlings becoming hardened will appear healthier in the open than under nursery shade.

VEGETATIVE PROPAGATION

Tree and shrub species whose propagation by seed is difficult often can be reproduced by vegetative propagation. Planting stock that is obtained by vegetative propagation includes *stumps*, *cuttings*, and *sets* (Chapman and Allan 1978, FAO 1989, Rao 1963).

Stump is a term applied to planting stock of broad-leaved tree or shrub species that have been subjected to pruning of both the shoot and the roots. The shoot generally is cut back to 2 cm and the roots to about 22 cm. Stump planting is suitable for "taproot-dominated" species. Stumps normally are covered with wet sacks or layers of large leaves during transit to the planting site. Stumped plants frequently are used in sand dune stabilization plantations.

A cutting is a short-length section cut from a young living stem or branch for propagating. A cutting produces a whole plant when planted in the field. A rooted cutting is one that has been rooted in the nursery prior to field planting. Sets are long, relatively thin, stem cuttings or whole branches.

SIZE AND QUALITY OF PLANTING STOCK

The desired sizes of planting stock can vary, regardless of the kind, for the establishment of forest plantations. Optimum sizes depend largely upon the tree or shrub species to be planted, whether the seedlings are bare-rooted or containerized, and the characteristics of the planting site.

Plants with well-proportioned root-to-shoot ratios generally represent good stock. But, it is difficult to define an "optimum" root-to-shoot ratio for all species. A root-to-shoot ratio based on weight can be a more accurate measure of balance. Stem diameter and height are examples of other criteria for setting of minimum acceptable limits. Past experience indicates that medium-size stock, between 15 and 40 cm in height, with a woody root collar has a better survival rate than do smaller plants (FAO 1989).

The maximum sizes for planting containerized seedlings are determined largely by the size of a container. The larger the container, the larger the seedling that can be grown in it, although the growth is limited by root restriction. Excessively tall plants can be loosened in the ground and blown over, as their root development might be restricted or inadequate to cope with the high transpiration demands of a large top. Large seedlings in big containers also are difficult to handle.

Grading of planting stock is based upon local experience and the establishment of local standards. The main objectives of a grading system are to eliminate seedlings that have damaged or diseased tops or roots and those seedlings below minimum standards of size and root development, and to segregate seedlings that exceed minimum standards into two or more quality classes (Weber and Stoney 1986).

TRANSPORT OF PLANTING STOCK TO PLANTING SITE

The packing of planting stock for transport to a planting site presents comparatively few problems, although speed of transport is essential (NAS 1990). The planting stock simply can be put in trays and loaded into vehicles. Tins that have been used as seedling trays often are used for transporting container plants. Sometimes, wooden trays are used, but these often are heavy.

Planting stock can be damaged during transport to the planting site. Therefore, care must be taken to avoid mishandling during their loading and unloading from vehicles. Something often forgotten is that the planting stock requires protection during transportation because the air flows encountered can cause drying (Landis et al. 1989g). It also is important that the stock is packed tightly so that it cannot move. Shelves for stacking trays can be added to a vehicle platform, with one shelf about 50 cm above the other. When possible, the planting stock should be transported on cool, cloudy, or even rainy days to prevent desiccation during transport.

It is important that shipping schedules be planned to avoid delays and allow for the proper disposition of planting stock immediately upon arrival. Normally, the stock should arrive one day ahead of planting. The planting stock can be brought in several days in advance when shade and watering facilities are available. As soon as the planting stock arrives at the planting site, it should be watered and, if not planted immediately, stored in a cool, moist, shaded place until they are needed for planting.

IMPROVEMENT OF PLANTING STOCK

Before moving on to considerations of the establishment and management of forest plantations, it is appropriate to consider the ways of obtaining higher quality planting stock. It is important that the productivities of forest plantations be maximized in many dryland regions. More intensive silvicultural treatments and forest management practices can result in increased productivities. The improvement of planting stock also has potentials in many situations (FAO 1985, Rao 1963, Zobel and Talbert 1984), although efforts to improve the planting stock for dryland environments has not received as much attention as found in other regions.

Objectives

Improvement methods are undertaken to satisfy one or more of the following objectives (Zobel and Talbert 1984):

- To improve the yields and qualities of wood products by improving growth rates or modifying the specific gravity of the wood.
- To develop disease and insect resistance in susceptible tree and shrub species.
- To develop trees and shrubs capable of suitable performance on undesirable sites in adverse environmental conditions. For example, salt-tolerant and drought-resistant varieties are beneficial in many dryland regions.
- To develop trees and shrubs for special uses, such as windbreak plantings, agroforestry purposes, or production of gums, oils, and other biochemicals.

- To develop trees and shrubs for multiple benefits, for example, fuelwood production, fodder or browse, and enhancement of nitrogen in soil.

There are three requirements that need to be considered in planning for the improvement of planting stock (Zobel and Talbert 1984). If one or more of these requirements is lacking, the potential gains obtained through improvement may not justify the expenses involved. These requirements are:

- A planned large-scale tree or shrub planting program.
- Sufficient variations in the tree or shrub characteristics to be improved.
- Sufficient "genetic control" of these tree or shrub characteristics.

Improvement Methods

Methods for the improvement of planting stock include *species selection, provenance testing, seed production areas* and *seed orchards, progeny testing, hybridization, clonal forestry,* and *gene conservation* (FAO 1985, Rao 1963, Zobel and Talbert 1984). General considerations for species selection are presented in Chapter 12 and elsewhere in this book. No further mention of this improvement method will be presented here other than to mention that provenance testing should be considered when dealing with exotics. Variations in the survival and growth of exotics from different provenances can be dramatic. Potentially valuable tree and shrub species might be overlooked because the species trials consisted of inappropriate or incomplete provenance testing. Therefore, a number of provenances should be included in any species trial.

Provenance Testing   A *provenance* is the original geographical area from which seeds or vegetatively propagated planting stock of a tree or shrub species has been obtained. A *source* is the actual area in a provenance from which the planting stock was obtained. These two terms can be, but are not necessarily, synonymous. Seeds of *Prosopis juliflora* trees collected near Tucson, Arizona, would be both a "Pima County" provenance and "Pima County" seed source. If some seedlings from this collection were grown in northern Chile and subsequent seed collections were made from those trees, the seed source would be "Chile," and the provenance still would be "Pima County." In this latter situation, both seed source and provenance should be recorded.

A provenance test is an experiment that compares the performances of trees or shrubs that are grown from seeds or propagated vegetatively plant sections that are collected in many parts of the natural range of a species (Burley and Wood 1976, Zobel and Talbert 1984). When properly designed, a provenance test provides information on the amounts and patterns of genetic variation that are present in a tree or shrub species and an indication of patterns of genetic variation. With this information, the best provenances in which to collect seeds or plant parts to propagate vegetatively can be identified. The greatest, cheapest, and quickest gains in improvement frequently are made through the use of proper species and seed sources for that species.

Provenance testing usually is conducted in three phases:

- A rangewide trial that includes many provenances and utilizes relatively small study plots. Because of its scale, this phase is not conducted efficiently on an international basis.
- A restricted trial which includes more complete sampling within the best provenances identified in the first phase and utilizes larger plots.
- Provenance testing that includes sampling of tree or shrub stands within the best provenances and utilizes still larger plots that are maintained for at least one-half of the expected rotation age.

One or more of these phases can be eliminated because of time or financial constraints. However, the safest course of action, especially in the case of exotics, is to employ all of the phases. Provenance tests must be well designed, randomized, and replicated. These tests should be repeated on locations that are representative of the areas to be planted. Tests can be made in the nursery, when desired. If properly designed and evaluated, provenance tests facilitate separation of genotypic differences from environmental variation.

Seedlots and planting beds must be kept separate and adequately identified throughout the collection, shipping, storage, treatment, sowing, lifting, and outplanting tasks. If necessary, the planting sites should be prepared before planting. Maps of provenance tests should be prepared. Records of seed collection and handling, planting dates, and nursery and field layouts are necessary. These records should include information about the climatological and soil factors, latitude and longitude, elevation, slope and aspect, associated plant species, and descriptions of the sample trees or shrubs.

Seed Production Areas and Seed Orchards   Seed production areas are locations of phenotypically superior stands of native species or plantations of indigenous species, which are managed within better provenances to produce large quantities of seed. When properly selected and managed, these areas represent sources of readily available, inexpensive, and high-quality seed. Although there is no guarantee of genetic superiority from these areas, the probability of this being the case is greater than in random collections of seed. Seed production areas can serve as an interim seed source until seed becomes available from seed orchards. If nothing else, seed production areas are a reliable source of seed of known origin.

Isolation zones should be established around seed protection areas to prevent undesirable pollen from reaching the trees or shrubs. Trees or shrubs in the areas often are thinned to encourage large crown development. Fertilization might be required to promote seed production. The removal of noxious vegetation can be necessary to eliminate competition and facilitate seed collection. Sometimes, seed production is encouraged by girdling or root pruning, although these practices should be evaluated initially on a small scale.

Seed orchards, which are natural stands or plantations of superior trees or shrubs, are established and managed for production of seed of proven genetic quality. Superior individuals or families, as determined from progeny tests, should be included in seed orchards. Progeny tests are converted subsequently into seed orchards, in some instances.

The site for a seed orchard should be accessible and close to nursery facilities. Fertilization and the control of weeds, diseases, and insects are practiced as required. Because a seed orchard represents a major investment, it should be maintained and managed carefully.

Progeny Testing   *Progeny* are the offspring from the mating of two individuals. Progeny tests are experiments that compare the performances of both offspring and parents. These tests provide baseline data for calculation of heritable traits and selection of genetically superior individual trees or shrubs, stands, or plantations. If progeny resemble their parents in the specific trait considered, that trait can be assumed to be under "strong" genetic control and, therefore, heritability for it will be high. The selection of such a trait should result in genetic gains. Information gained from progeny tests also indicate amounts and patterns of variation within a population of trees or shrubs. This knowledge provides a basis for determining the best selection and breeding methods to use for the species in question.

Progeny tests must be well designed, randomized, and replicated experiments made on representative sites. Care should be taken to maintain progeny identification and to keep complete and accurate records. Records of parental information are essential if progeny tests are to provide useful information.

Hybridization   *Hybrids* are the offspring of crosses between two different species. These offspring frequently display hybrid vigor, called *heterosis*, a phenomenon in which hybrids are superior in certain traits or qualities than either parent. Heterosis, which can be expressed in terms of growth rates, form, or adaptation to the environment, is the quality that makes many hybrids more desirable than "pure" species. Not all hybrids necessarily will display heterosis, so adequate testing of a range of sites or growing conditions is necessary before a large-scale planting program with hybrids is undertaken. The hybrids of tree or shrub species are propagated vegetatively to maintain the desirable genotype.

Clonal Forestry   A *clone* is all of the vegetatively reproduced individuals from a single parent. Individuals in a clone have the identical genotype of the parent, with a potential for the same phenotypical development. Tree and shrub species are cloned by using rooted cuttings, root cuttings, grafting, air layering, or tissue and shoot culture. The practice of clonal forestry often can lead to quick genetic gains when parents of proven superior genotypes for highly heritable traits are used. The resultant tree or shrub stands are usually more uniform than stands originating for seed. Many tree and shrub species cannot be propagated vegetatively, however, restricting the applications of clonal forestry.

Because a limited number of clones normally are used in a planting program, there is an increased danger of disease or insect epidemics with clonal forestry. Furthermore, the increased costs of producing planting stock can be prohibitive.

Gene Conservation   There often is a concern that improper forest management practices can result in losses of irreplaceable genetic material. It is becoming important, therefore, to conserve existing gene pools. Even for tree and shrub species in which this loss is not occurring currently, it is important to maintain a broad genetic base when long-term improvement programs are planned.

Gene conservation can be accomplished in various ways. Forest and woodland preserves have been established in some countries. Arboreta also can be established to preserve rare or endangered tree or shrub species. *Clone banks*, which are plantings of representative individuals of a species, often are established in early phases of improvement programs. Seed and pollen storage, efficient usually on only a short-term basis, can serve to maintain geotypes until arboreta or clone banks are established. The techniques of tissue and shoot culture also are becoming useful in gene conservation, as these techniques are developed further (McKeand and Weir 1984).

Preventing Genetic Decline

The use of natural forests and woodlands, and forest plantations by people with little consideration for proper forest management practices can result in a loss of desirable genotypes or a decline in genetic quality. Fortunately, there are managerial practices that a forester can employ to alleviate this situation. While these practices will not necessarily result in an improvement of genetic quality, their implementation can enable the maintenance of the genetic quality that is present in the population.

One opportunity to restrict genetic decline and, in some instances, attain genetic gains occurs when planning seed collections. Proper supervision and control of seed collections are important. When collecting seeds from exotics, only provenances that have proven themselves in the long term and the general area to be planted should be considered. It should be verified that the seeds collected are the proper species and obtained from a guaranteed source. Collections should be made only from vigorous, well-formed, disease- and insect-resistant trees. These precautions can require an additional expense, although the costs of seed collection is only a small fraction of the total costs of obtaining the necessary planting stock. The resultant increase in the success and productivity of a planting program likely will more than offset these costs.

SUMMARY

The production of planting stock can be a major expense of forestry programs, but it is one of the more important aspects of forestry involving the establishment of forest plantations. It is necessary, therefore, that one understands the sequence of nursery operations that are followed in the production of tree and shrub seedlings or other types of planting stock. Planting stock can be improved through provenance testing, seed production areas and seed orchards, progeny testing, and other methods. After you have read this chapter, you should be able to:

1. Describe the criteria used in making a choice of a nursery site.
2. Describe the sequence of tasks that are undertaken in the collection and storage of seeds.
3. Explain how seeds are sown into seedbeds or containers and why seedlings might be transplanted subsequently.
4. Explain how planting stock is obtained by vegetative propagation.
5. Describe how the planting stock is transported to a planting site.
6. Understand the methods of improving the quality of planting stock.

REFERENCES

Burley, J., and P. J. Wood. 1976. A manual on species and provenance research, with particular reference to the tropics. *Commonwealth Forestry Institute, Tropical Paper* 10, Oxford.

Chapman, G. W., and T. F. Allan. 1978. Establishment techniques for forest plantations. *FAO Forestry Paper* 8, Rome.

Doran, J. C., J. W. Turnbull, D. J. Boland, and B. V. Gunn. 1983. *Handbook of seeds of dry zone acacias.* FAO, Rome.

FAO. 1985. Forest tree improvement. *FAO Forestry Paper* 20, Rome.

FAO. 1989. Arid zone forestry: A guide for field technicians. *FAO Conservation Guide* 20, Rome.

Ffolliott, P. F., and J. L. Thames. 1983. *Collection, handling, storage and pre-treatment of* Prosopis *seeds in Latin America.* FAO, Rome.

Flynt, T. O., and H. L. Morton. 1969. A device for threshing mesquite seed. *Weed Science* 17:302–03.

Goor, A. Y., and C. W. Barney. 1976. *Forest tree planting in arid zones.* The Ronald Press Co., New York.

Johnson, C. D. 1983. *Handbook on seed insects of* Prosopis *species.* FAO, Rome.

ISTA. 1976. International rules for seed testing. *Seed Science and Technology* 4:49–177.

Landis, T. D., R. W. Tinus, S. E. McDonald, and J. P. Bartlett. 1989a. The container tree nursery manual—Volume one: Container nursery planning, development, and management. USDA Forest Service, *Agricultural Handbook* 674.

Landis, T. D., R. W. Tinus, S. E. McDonald, and J. P. Bartlett. 1989b. The container tree nursery manual—Volume two: Containers and growing media. USDA Forest Service, *Agricultural Handbook* 674.

Landis, T. D., R. W. Tinus, S. E. McDonald, and J. P. Bartlett. 1989c. The container tree nursery manual—Volume three: Container nursery environment. USDA Forest Service, *Agricultural Handbook* 674.

Landis, T. D., R. W. Tinus, S. E. McDonald, and J. P. Bartlett. 1989d. The container tree nursery manual—Volume four: Seedling nutrition and irrigation. USDA Forest Service, *Agricultural Handbook* 674.

Landis, T. D., R. W. Tinus, S. E. McDonald, and J. P. Bartlett. 1989e. The container tree nursery manual—Volume five: The biological component: Nursery pests and mycorrhizae. USDA Forest Service, *Agricultural Handbook* 674.

Landis, T. D., R. W. Tinus, S. E. McDonald, and J. P. Bartlett. 1989f. The container tree nursery manual—Volume six: Seedling propagation. USDA Forest Service, *Agricultural Handbook* 674.

Landis, T. D., R. W. Tinus, S. E. McDonald, and J. P. Bartlett. 1989g. The container tree nursery manual—Volume seven: Seedling processing, storage, and outplanting. USDA Forest Service, *Agricultural Handbook* 674.

McKeand, S. E., and R. J. Weir. 1984. Tissue culture and forest productivity. *Journal of Forestry* 82:212–18.

NAS. 1990. *The improvement of tropical and subtropical rangelands*. National Academy Press, Washington, D.C.

Penrose, R. D., and D. I. Hansen. 1981. Planting techniques for establishment of container-grown or bareroot plants. In Stelter, L. H., E. J. DePuit, and S. A. Mikol (technical coordinators). 1981. *Shrub establishment on disturbed arid and semi-arid lands*. Wyoming Game and Fish Department, Laramie, Wyoming, pp. 37–46.

Rao, H. S. 1963. Vegetative propagation and forest tree improvement. *Indian Forester* 79:176–83.

Schubert, G. H., and R. S. Adams. 1971. *Reforestation practices for conifers in California*. Division of Forestry, Department of Conservation, State of California, Sacramento, California.

Southgate, B. J. 1983. *Handbook on seed insects of Acacia species*. FAO, Rome.

Tinus, R. W., and S. E. McDonald. 1979. How to grow tree seedlings in containers in greenhouses. *USDA Forest Service, General Technical Report* RM-60.

Weber, F. R., and C. Stoney. 1986. *Reforestation in arid lands*. VITA Publications, Arlington, Virginia.

Zobel, B. J., and J. T. Talbert. 1984. *Applied forest tree improvement*. John Wiley & Sons, Inc., New York.

12 Establishment and Management of Rainfed Forest Plantations

The role, or roles, of forest plantations should be clear before they are established. There can be a number of roles that can be combined through careful planning to obtain multiple benefits. Among these roles are the production of fuelwood, poles, building materials, and other wood products, protection of fragile sites from erosion, and amenity purposes (FAO 1989). Forest plantations, regardless of their role, are established to furnish benefits in areas in which natural forests or woodlands are inadequate to meet local needs on a sustainable basis.

The topic of this chapter is the establishment and management of rainfed forest plantations. Only general considerations are presented here, because the details about establishing and managing plantations for fuelwood production, agroforestry practices, and windbreak plantings are presented in other chapters. Irrigated forest plantations are discussed in the following chapter.

SELECTION OF A PLANTING SITE

An initial task in selecting a site for the establishment of a forest plantation is to make a reconnaissance of the area being considered for planting. Specific planting sites in the area can be selected from information obtained in this reconnaissance.

Site Reconnaissance

Site conditions in the area need to be well known, so that tree and shrub species are selected that are best suited to the area. The following lists information most commonly included in site reconnaissance (FAO 1989, Goor and Barney 1976, NAS 1990, Weber and Stoney 1986):

- *Climate*—temperature, the amount and patterns of rainfall, relative humidity, and seasonal wind patterns.
- *Soil*—depth of soil and its capacity to retain moisture, texture and structure classes, parent material, pH, degree of compaction, and drainage.
- *Topography*—elevation, slope percent, and orientation.
- *Vegetation*—composition and ecological characteristics of vegetation. (On areas that have not been degraded, vegetation can provide an indication of

site quality. Unfortunately, vegetation has been so disturbed in many of the dryland regions of the world that it is not a reliable indicator of potential planting sites. Site selection can be based upon soil surveys in these situations.)

- *Other biotic factors*—past history and present land use influences on the site, including fire, livestock and wildlife, and insects and diseases.
- *Water table levels*—a knowledge of depths and variations of water tables in wet and dry seasons can be crucial in selecting tree and shrub species. (Water table levels are estimated from observations in wells or by test borings made for this purpose.)
- *Availability of supplemental water sources*—ponds, lakes, streams, and other waterways.
- Distance from nursery.

Apart from biophysical information, socioeconomic factors also play an important role in the selection of the planting site. Included among these factors are:

- Availability of labor.
- Distance from proposed forest plantations to the marketplaces and other consumptive centers.
- Land tenure considerations.

Site Selection

Where to plant the trees or shrubs in the general area is a collective decision made by policymakers, foresters, and planting crews, based upon information obtained in the site reconnaissance. They should be sites that will lead to the establishment of "successful" forest plantations in the shortest possible time. The choice of planting sites frequently is limited to "marginal" lands that are not suited for livestock or agricultural crop production (NAS 1990). When this is the case, the site reconnaissance information gains in importance.

The boundaries of the planting site should be marked. A boundary fence should be established when there is a danger of trespassing and damage by grazing or browsing animals. However, fencing is costly and therefore should only be built when other means of protection are not effective. When roads and other passageways traverse the site, they also should be contained with fences. Once the forest plantation is established, fences can be removed.

In many instances, the planting of trees or shrubs is undertaken to protect fragile sites from degradation. In some cases, however, sites are too fragile to be planted. Where gullies have been degraded severely by erosion, protective measures other than the planting of vegetation, such as building small check dams, can be necessary.

SPECIES SELECTION

When the best information possible has been collected about the characteristics of the site to be planted, one can select the tree or shrub species to plant. The aim here is to choose species that are suited to the site and will remain healthy throughout the anticipated life of the plantation, attain acceptable growth rates and yield, and meet the objectives of the forest plantation (Falker 1987, FAO 1989, Weber and Stoney 1986).

In some instances, species are selected before the site is selected, in which case the planting stock of the species is produced in a nursery specifically for the establishment of a forest plantation in the area. It is important that the species is matched to the site in question, regardless of whether the species or site is selected initially. Important and commonly used tree and shrub species in the dryland regions of the world are listed in Appendix II.

Performance Data

In planning for the planting of trees or shrubs, performance data may have to be extrapolated from one locality to another. The results from a locality in which a selected tree or shrub species is growing naturally strictly apply only to that locality. Their application in another locality involves the assumption of site comparability, an assumption that may not be justified. When information shows a close similarity between the site to be planted and that on which the species already is growing successfully, it generally is possible to proceed to large-scale planting programs.

Performance data for many tree and shrub species are unavailable. When this is the case, planting becomes somewhat "experimental" and, therefore, should proceed initially on a small-scale basis. In these instances, detailed performance records should be maintained throughout initial planting periods to evaluate the planting success.

Analogous Climates

The selection of tree or shrub species to plant through use of analogous climates is important as a first step. Importantly, this step also needs to be amplified by an evaluation of local factors, such as soil, slope and aspect, and biotic factors, which collectively can be more important than climatological similarities. However, the ability to match closely a planting site and a natural habitat for a tree or shrub species should not preclude species trials, since climatological or ecological matching might not reveal the adaptability of a particular species to a site. Without species trials, the choice of tree or shrub species to plant is risky. Since planting in dryland regions is frequently an expensive undertaking, large-scale failures resulting from the wrong choice of species or failure to evaluate performance of the species can prove costly.

Planting Guides

The question of which tree or shrub species to plant often is addressed best at the local level. The selection of specific species to be planted in specific conditions requires *planting guides*. Planting guides indicate which tree or shrub species are adaptable to the local soils, exposures, and weather patterns, and how these species should be planted and maintained. In many instances, planting guides for specific species are not available for the area in question, in which case a forester must consider general criteria and, if available, local experience as a basis for species selection. General criteria for species selection include (FAO 1989, Ffolliott and Thames 1983, Goor and Barney 1976):

- Choosing indigenous tree or shrub species for which biological and silvicultural knowledge is available.
- Introducing exotic tree or shrub species only if their suitability for the area has been demonstrated by testing.
- Selecting seeds or plant parts of known genetic superiority for vegetative propagation, whenever possible, to produce planting stock.
- Selecting either indigenous or introduced tree or shrub species in reference to the following requirements: ease of obtaining planting stock, ease of establishment, immunity to insects and disease, fast growth, required wood products if the plantation is established for production, and social acceptability.
- Understanding the seasonal rainfall patterns that are critical for the tree or shrub species to survive and grow. Tree and shrub species native to winter rainfall areas usually will not thrive in summer rainfall areas, although tree and shrub species native to summer rainfall areas are more likely to succeed in winter rainfall areas.
- As a general rule, a tree or shrub species can be moved successfully from its home range to other areas of the same latitude because of the similarity in climate. However, some tree and shrub species are so exacting in their requirements that even small variations in rainfall patterns or other site factors can cause failure.
- Making sure that the tree or shrub species to be planted meets the purpose of the plantation, whether it be fuelwood, windbreaks, or watershed protection.
- Considering the following necessities to ensure successful results: site preparation, when to plant, how to plant, the spacing and arrangement of the plantings, and care after planting.

In addition to planting guides, other criteria frequently must be considered when selecting a tree or shrub species for specific purposes. Chapters in this book listed under "Special Topics" should be consulted for these criteria.

PREPARATION OF PLANTING SITE

Once the planting stock arrives from a nursery, the site should have been prepared so that the planting operation can proceed without delay. The conditions in dryland regions can demand more intensive and thorough site preparation than is necessary for planting programs in moister climates. The objectives of site preparation include (FAO 1989, Schubert and Adams 1971, Weber and Stoney 1986):

- Remove competing vegetation.
- Prepare soil to optimize conditions for growth of planted stock.
- Create conditions in which dangers from fire and pests are minimized.

Site preparation should assure rapid early growth of planted stock. The methods of site preparation vary with the type of competing vegetation, the amount and distribution of rainfall, the presence or absence of impermeable layers in the soil, the need for protection from desiccating winds, fire, and pests, and the scale of the planting operations. The value of trees or shrubs to be grown also is important in determining the amount of money that can be justified in plantation establishment.

Elimination of Competing Vegetation

The drier the site, the more important it is to eliminate competing vegetation. Uprooting of competing vegetation often is necessary, something that can be accomplished manually on some sites. Herbicides can eliminate competing vegetation in some instances (Example 12.1). However, before herbicides are applied, they should be evaluated in terms of their suitability, safety in handling, and potential environmental damage.

Example 12.1

Herbicide Use for Preparing Planting Sites in the Southwestern United States (Heidmann 1967) Competing vegetation is detrimental to establishment of ponderosa pine (*Pinus ponderosa*) trees in dryland regions of the southwestern United States. Survival of bare-rooted seedlings is low without removal of Arizona fescue (*Festuca arizonica*), a perennial grass that grows actively in the spring drought periods of May and June, by applications of herbicides. The USDA Forest Service, in testing a number of herbicides, found that dalapon, a sodium salt, when applied in a water carrier in July after the Arizona fescue was growing vigorously, killed in excess of 80 percent of the grass. In addition, soils retained higher levels of moisture under a mulch of grasses killed by the herbicides than where the grasses were removed by scalping.

There was no subsequent damage to ponderosa pine seedlings at the levels of application tested, approximately 10 kg/ha. Residual toxicities of all herbicides must be known before operational applications are undertaken, however.

Planting usually is necessary immediately following the removal of competing vegetation to obtain the highest survival of trees or shrubs (Schubert 1974, Schubert and Adams 1971). Plantings delayed for 2 or more years usually fail and, as a result, costly replanting must be undertaken to establish the plantation.

Soil Preparation

Preparation of the soil can be necessary to create conditions optimal for growth of planting stock. Infiltration and soil moisture conditions are improved by breaking up impermeable soil surfaces. In addition, roots can penetrate more easily into the soil. Soil can be prepared manually or by mechanical means. It might be necessary to use tractors equipped with a deep working ripper to break up the soil if there is a hardpan.

The preparation of soil by hand tools is possible and economic only for relatively small-scale planting projects in which the clearing of competing vegetation and working the soil is not too time-consuming. Under certain conditions, animal-drawn ploughs and harrows also can be economical for small-scale operations. Mechanized soil preparation is a common practice in many areas, because the time available for preparation is too limited to permit large-scale projects to be undertaken by hand.

Soil preparation can be undertaken in patches or strips, or by complete cultivation. Complete cultivation is necessary for the planting of tree and shrub species that are intolerant of competition from other plants, such as most *Eucalyptus* species (FAO 1989). Sometimes, spot preparation is sufficient, but the spots should be at least 1–1.5 m in diameter. Other methods of soil preparation by hand include the *ash-bed method, tie-ridging, trenching* and *terracing*, and *"steppe" method* (Goor and Barney 1976, FAO 1985, Weber and Stoney 1986)

The ash-bed method of site preparation consists of piling debris left from the harvesting or clearing of the land into long lines or stacks. After drying, the debris is burned and vegetation is planted in ash patches. Lines or stacks of debris can be covered with "clods" to obtain more intense heat when burning. The advantages of this method are that burning kills the competing vegetation, the area remains free of this vegetation for a period of time, and the ash provides a useful fertilizer for the planted trees or shrubs.

Tie-ridging involves cultivation of the entire area and formation of ridges at specified intervals by hoeing. The main ridges, aligned along the contours, are joined by smaller ridges at right angles to create a series of more-or-less square basins that retain rainwater and prevent erosion. The ridges generally are 3 m apart. Trees and shrubs are planted on the ridges. Tie-ridging is suitable for flat or gently sloping ground and, if desired, can be combined with agricultural crops in agroforestry schemes in the initial stages of plantation establishment.

Trenching techniques can be used in the site preparation of hilly country. The trenches can be continuous, divided by cross banks, or consist of short discontinuous lengths, so arranged that gaps between the trenches in one row are opposite those in the next row. Runoff from rainfall is caught in this latter instance.

Trenches usually are formed manually. The *herring-bone* technique can be used on gently sloping terrain (Figure 12.1).

Terraces, which are wider and flatter than trenches, are formed manually or mechanically on the side of a hill by digging the soil from the uphill side and depositing it on the downhill side. The bottom of the terrace usually is made to slope into the hillside. The purpose of terracing is to retard and collect water runoff between successively aligned terraces. Conditions for plant growth are improved because of improved soil moisture conditions. The trees or shrubs are planted on the ridge of soil, at the base of the ridge, or in patches at the bottom of the trench, according to moisture conditions. Terraces, used widely on moderate to severe slopes, can be 2 to 3 m or several hundred meters in length (Figure 12.2). Shorter terraces can be staggered on the hillside, wherever convenient. Crescent-shaped

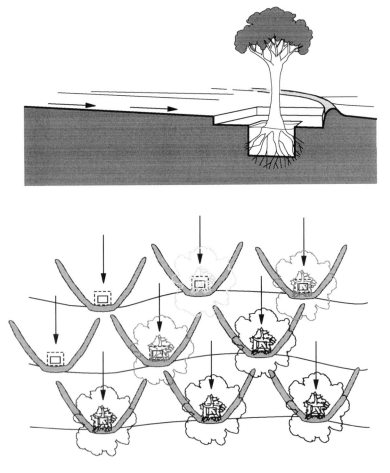

Figure 12.1. Herring-bone technique of soil preparation (adapted from the Food and Agriculture Organization of the United Nations, 1989)

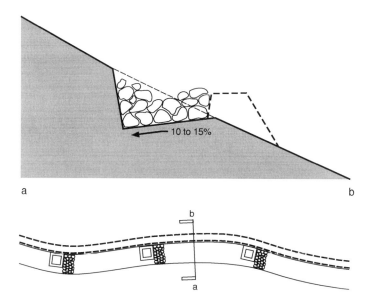

Figure 12.2. Construction of terraces on steep slopes (adapted from the Food and Agriculture Organization of the United Nations, 1989)

terraces sometimes are constructed, with the two tips of the crescent pointing uphill.

The "steppe" method of site preparation is designed to promote the growth of trees and shrubs in extremely dry areas. The surface soil is modified by breaking up and stirring the deep layers with rooters, rippers, or large discs and building widely spaced, parallel ridges with topsoil along the contour. The trees or shrubs are planted on the lower half of the ridges facing the slope, where the depth of moist soil is greatest because of the accumulation of water after rain. A purpose of the "steppe" method is to maintain a reserve of moisture in the deep layers of the soil. Spacing between ridges generally is greater with lower rainfall, as the catchment area between the ridges is increased.

All of these soil preparation methods can have an added benefit of controlling soil erosion. However, if not properly designed and constructed, the methods can fail and, in doing so, cause soil erosion to accelerate.

Elimination of Conditions for Fire and Pests

The threat of fire is highest where there are excessive buildups of fuels. The elimination of these conditions is achieved largely through the removal of these fuels. Removal by hand is feasible if the materials are small and light, and if a labor force is available. Controlled burning of the fuels also is possible on some sites, although well-developed burning prescriptions are necessary.

The habitats of pests must be destroyed on sites where the pests present problems to survival of planted stock. Grass-covered areas are habitats for grasshop-
pers, mice, and ground squirrels, while brushlands are favored habitats for hares
and rabbits. The habitats for these pests are destroyed while removing these vegetative covers by site preparation, and, as a result, the pests are displaced.

TIMING OF PLANTING

The timing of planting in many dryland regions coincides with the onset of the
rainy season. Planting usually starts as soon as a specified amount of rain has
fallen, an amount best determined on the basis of local experience. Planting also
can be initiated when the soil profile has been wetted to a specified depth, for
example, a depth of 20 cm (FAO 1989).

A common mistake is to begin planting too soon. On the other hand, if planting
is started too late, it can be difficult to complete a large planting program in the
scheduled time. In this latter case, plants will lose the maximum benefits of rains
after planting, a serious matter in areas where the rainfall is low and erratic.

PLANTING

Planting of trees or shrubs must follow specified procedures and techniques if forest plantations are to be established successfully. Efforts to obtain high-quality,
vigorous planting stock from a nursery and carefully transport this stock to the
planting site are lost if proper planting methods are not followed. It is important,
therefore, that the planting crews be trained in use of the planting methods prescribed (Chapman and Allan 1978, Goor and Barney 1976, Weber and Stoney
1986).

Planting of Bare-Rooted or Ball-Rooted Stock

Hand planting with shovels, planting bars, or other appropriate tools is one of the
easiest and cheapest methods of planting bare-root or ball-rooted stock. Attention
to details is likely more important than the method itself, however. The depth of
planting and proper closure of the planting pit has a greater effect on the survival
of the trees or shrubs than all of the other "errors" in planting that cause mortality.
The following is the general procedure for hand planting of bare-rooted or
ball-rooted stock (Schubert et al. 1969, Schubert and Adams 1971):

- Prepare the planting spot by clearing away litter and dry soil from the spot
  of planting.
- Dig the planting pit with the back side of the pit at the upper edge of the
  cleared space. Make the pit deep enough to plant the stock without coiling

up the roots at the base, and dig the rear of the pit vertically, or nearly so. (Coiling of roots in planting is more of a problem with bare-rooted than with ball-rooted stock.)

- Set the stock in the planting pit so its roots are against the vertical rear wall of the pit. Hold the stock so it will be set at about the same depth as it grew in the nursery. Shallow planting often results in plantation failures, while planting 2–3 cm deeper than the original ground line normally will not lower survival.

- Fill the planting pit by holding the stock in position with one hand, filling one-half of the pit with *moist* soil, and packing with the other hand. Complete filling of the pit with moist soil and pack firmly in place. Use of one's hand is recommended for packing of the soil in the lower one-half of the pit. The upper one-half of the pit can be packed with the feet or a planting tool, although care must be taken not to damage the stock.

- Once the stock is planted, loose dry soil and litter should be pushed around the stock to reduce evaporation of soil moisture.

Other methods of planting bare-root stock or ball-rooted stock include the use of tractor-powered planting pit diggers or one of many types of planting machines. However, these "mechanical" methods have limited applications on dryland sites with extensive rock covers. Planting machines are difficult to operate on steep slopes. Another drawback can be the high costs of operation.

Planting of Containerized Stock

Containerized stock is planted with or without the container, depending upon the type of container used in the nursery. In either case, the stock is planted in pits that are large enough to take the container or planting plug. It is essential that the surrounding soil is packed down around the plants once they have been planted to avoid formation of air gaps, which can lead to root desiccation.

A common practice in the preparation of a planting pit for containerized stock is to surround it with a small ridge of soil, 15–20 cm high, to obtain a small basin about 80 cm in diameter (Chapman and Allan 1978, FAO 1989). This practice is helped when the stock is watered individually after planting. The small basin formed also can be covered with a plastic sheet that is held in place on the ground with stones or earth, as illustrated in Figure 12.3. An opening in the center of the sheet facilitates growth of the plant. The plastic sheet impedes evaporation of groundwater from the planting pit. Rainwater also collects on its surface and runs to the central opening of the sheet to irrigate the roots. Plastic films facilitate early establishment and initial growth of tree and shrubs through the conservation of soil moisture. Another benefit of opaque plastic films is that they inhibit the growth of noxious plants by reducing light penetration. Labor also can be saved with the suppression of weeds in the immediate vicinity of the plants.

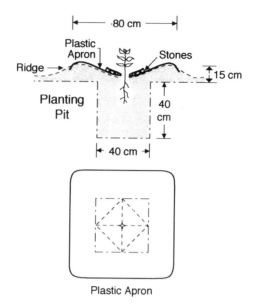

Figure 12.3. A planting pit with plastic apron to impede evaporation of groundwater (adapted from the Food and Agriculture Organization of the United Nations, 1989)

A serious threat to newly planted trees and shrubs in dryland environments is the high rate of transpiration. Unless the plants can establish themselves quickly and compensate for transpiration by taking in water through their root systems, they will wilt soon after planting. This is why even a single watering immediately after planting can be helpful. In general, containerized seedlings have a distinct advantage over bare-rooted seedlings in that the earthball surrounding the roots provides protection during transport to the planting site and enables the plant to establish itself quickly and easily.

A restriction of lateral root extension, a frequent result of using containers, can cause root malformation and coiling. To reduce the problem of root malformation, a common practice is to remove the container from the soil cylinder before planting and make two or three vertical incisions in the rootball to a depth of 1 cm with a knife to cut "strangler" roots. The bottom 0.5–1 cm of the soil cylinder can be sliced off as a further precaution. Care must be exercised to ensure that the soil does not disintegrate and expose roots to desiccation.

Coiling of roots can kill the plant in extreme cases. In other situations, coiling can reduce wind firmness or lead to stunted growth. Unfortunately, the symptoms of coiling may not become apparent until a number of years after planting.

SPACING AND ARRANGEMENT OF PLANTINGS

The amount of water available to a tree or shrub in a forest plantation is proportional to the density of these plants in the plantation (FAO 1989, Goor and Barney

TABLE 12.1. Number of Trees or Shrubs per Hectare According to Spacing

Spacing Between Lines	Spacing of Plants in the Lines								
	0.50 m	0.60	0.70	0.80	0.90	1.00	1.20	1.40	1.50
0.50 m	40,000	33,333	28,569	25,000	22,222	20,000	16,666	14,285	13,333
0.60	33,333	27,777	23,809	20,833	18,518	16,666	13,888	11,904	11,111
0.70	28,569	23,809	20,408	17,857	15,873	14,285	11,904	10,204	9,523
0.80	25,000	20,833	17,857	15,625	13,888	12,500	10,416	8,928	8,333
0.90	22,222	18,518	15,873	13,888	12,345	11,111	9,259	7,936	7,407
1.00	20,000	16,666	14,285	12,500	11,111	10,000	8,333	7,142	6,666
1.20	16,666	13,888	11,904	10,416	9,259	8,333	6,944	5,952	5,555
1.40	14,285	11,904	10,204	8,928	7,936	7,142	5,952	5,102	4,762
1.50	13,333	11,111	9,523	8,333	7,407	6,666	5,555	4,762	4,444
1.60	12,500	10,416	8,928	7,812	6,944	6,250	5,208	4,464	4,167
1.80	11,111	9,259	7,936	6,944	6,172	5,555	4,630	3,968	3,704
2.00	10,000	8,333	7,142	6,250	5,555	5,000	4,166	3,571	3,333
2.50	—	—	—	—	—	4,000	3,333	2,857	2,667
3.00	—	—	—	—	—	3,333	2,778	2,381	2,222
3.50	—	—	—	—	—	—	—	—	—
4.00	—	—	—	—	—	—	—	—	—
4.50	—	—	—	—	—	—	—	—	—
5.00	—	—	—	—	—	—	—	—	—
5.50	—	—	—	—	—	—	—	—	—
6.00	—	—	—	—	—	—	—	—	—
6.50	—	—	—	—	—	—	—	—	—
7.00	—	—	—	—	—	—	—	—	—
8.00	—	—	—	—	—	—	—	—	—
9.00	—	—	—	—	—	—	—	—	—
10.00	—	—	—	—	—	—	—	—	—

1976). On drier sites, it is necessary to plant widely apart and remove all competing ground vegetation. When mechanical cultivation is practiced, it is common for plants to be placed in straight rows and to adjust spacings to the width of the machinery used. The actual spacing of plantings varies with the species, site, and purpose of the forest plantation. Where maximum production of total biomass is important (e.g., in fuelwood plantations), one might prescribe closer spacings than employed in other kinds of forest plantations. Seldom can a spacing of less than 3 × 3 m be applied, however (FAO 1989).

Once the appropriate spacing of plantings has been determined, the density of the plantings can be specified. The number of trees or shrubs per hectare, in terms of the spacing between the lines in a plantation and spacing of plants within a line, is given in Table 12.1. To illustrate the use of this table, a planting density of 1,111 trees per ha will be required with a spacing between lines of 3 m and a spacing of plants within a line of 3 m.

TABLE 12.1. *(Continued)*

Spacing Between Lines	Spacing of Plants in the Lines								
	1.60 m	1.80	2.00	2.50	3.00	3.50	4.00	4.50	5.00
0.50 m	12,500	11,111	10,000						
0.60	10,416	9,259	8,333						
0.70	8,928	7,936	7,142						
0.80	7,812	6,944	6,250						
0.90	6,944	6,172	5,555						
1.00	6,250	5,555	5,000	4,000	3,333				
1.20	5,208	4,630	4,166	3,333	2,778				
1.40	4,464	3,968	3,571	2,857	2,381				
1.50	4,167	3,704	3,333	2,667	2,222				
1.60	3,906	3,472	3,125	2,500	2,083				
1.80	3,472	3,086	2,778	2,222	1,852				
2.00	3,125	2,778	2,500	2,000	1,666	1,428	1,250	1,111	1,000
2.50	2,500	2,222	2,000	1,600	1,300	1,142	1,000	888	800
3.00	2,083	1,852	1,666	1,300	1,111	952	833	747	666
3.50	—	—	1,428	1,142	952	816	714	635	571
4.00	—	—	1,250	1,000	833	714	625	555	500
4.50	—	—	1,111	888	747	635	555	493	444
5.00	—	—	1,000	800	666	571	500	444	400
5.50	—	—	909	727	606	548	454	404	363
6.00	—	—	833	666	555	476	416	370	333
6.50	—	—	—	—	—	—	384	341	307
7.00	—	—	—	—	—	—	357	317	285
8.00	—	—	—	—	—	—	312	277	250
9.00	—	—	—	—	—	—	277	247	222
10.00	—	—	—	—	—	—	250	222	200

The spatial arrangements of trees or shrubs in a forest plantation can be rectangular, triangular, or other geometric patterns. Often, the spatial arrangements of trees and shrubs in windbreaks, especially those comprised of only a few lines of plantings, are triangular to provide a more efficient barrier to wind (Example 12.2).

MAINTENANCE OF A FOREST PLANTATION

The work of a forester is not finished once a forest plantation has been established. It is necessary to protect the plantation against weather and from fire and pests once establishment is achieved. In addition, a variety of cultural treatments can be required to attain and then maintain the conditions desired for optimal development and to meet the purpose of the plantation.

TABLE 12.1. *(Continued)*

Spacing Between Lines	Spacing of Plants in the Lines								
	1.60 m	1.80	2.00	2.50	3.00	3.50	4.00	4.50	5.00
0.50 m									
0.60									
0.70									
0.80									
0.90									
1.00									
1.20									
1.40									
1.50									
1.60									
1.80									
2.00	909	833							
2.50	727	666							
3.00	606	555							
3.50	548	476							
4.00	454	416	384	357	312	277	250		
4.50	404	370	341	317	277	247	222		
5.00	363	333	307	285	250	222	200		
5.50	330	303	279	259	227	202	181		
6.00	303	277	256	238	208	185	166		
6.50	279	256	236	219	192	170	154		
7.00	259	238	219	204	178	158	142		
8.00	227	208	192	178	156	138	125		
9.00	202	185	170	158	138	123	111		
10.00	181	166	154	142	125	111	100		

Source: By permission of the Food and Agriculture Organization of the United Nations.

Example 12.2

Spatial Arrangements of Neem (Azadirachta indica) Trees in Windbreak Plantings, Majjia Valley, Niger, West Africa (Bognatteau-Verlinden 1980) The reforestation project in the Majjia Valley, Niger, included the planting of windbreaks to improve the microclimate, reduce wind and water erosion, and produce fuelwood (Example 6.3). Double rows of neem trees were planted in holes dug 4 m apart by local villagers. Trees were planted in a 4 × 4 m rectangular spacing pattern in the initial years of the project. However, a 4 × 4 × 4 m triangular spacing pattern was adopted subsequently to more efficiently reduce wind movements through the relatively narrow windbreaks. Windbreaks planted in the triangular spatial arrangements have proven more effective in reducing wind velocities and, at times, retaining soil moisture on the site.

Protection

To the extent possible, forest plantations must be protected from the detrimental effects of weather, fire, insects and fungi, grazing by livestock and browsing by wildlife species, and, in some situations, people. The strategies often followed in protecting plantations from these damaging agents are described in the following sections (Chapman and Allan 1978, FAO 1989, Goor and Barney 1976, Weber and Stoney 1986).

Weather The occurrences of damaging weather, such as a lack of rainfall or drying winds, are unpredictable. Therefore, foresters can do little to protect forest plantations against the damage caused by weather other than to grow tree and shrub species known to be resistant to the detrimental effects of local weather patterns or to establish plantations only in sheltered areas. For example, some tree and shrub species are more windfirm than others or less prone to crowns and branches breaking off in high winds. Other species are more tolerant of salt spray. Thick-barked species, in general, are less susceptible to salt damage than are other species.

Fire Damage by fire poses a serious threat to forest plantations. Even in relatively high rainfall areas, there can be warm and dry spells when the fire risk is high. Dangerous fires occur initially at ground level. Once they spread rapidly on the ground and increase their intensities, fires can move into crowns of trees and shrubs, causing even greater damage. The risk of fire, therefore, should be a major consideration from early stages of plantation development.

Fires originate from either natural causes such as lightning or the result of activities by people. The latter start from fires spreading from agricultural croplands on the perimeter, burning by herdsmen to improve livestock grazing conditions, and the activities of hunters. There also are instances of deliberate burning to create employment opportunities in fire suppression and subsequent replanting or to show disapproval of forest policies. It generally is not possible to prevent natural buildups of fuels and, as a consequence, conditions favorable for fire to occur. However, much can be done to minimize the risk of fire by involving local people in forestry activities and by pursuing policies that are sympathetic to the political, social, and economic needs of the community.

There is little or no fire risk where there are insufficient combustible materials to allow a fire to develop on the ground. A main principle in protecting forest plantations against fire, therefore, is to remove excessive buildups of fuels that have accumulated on the ground surface.

In many parts of the world, annual burning of vegetation is practiced to reduce buildups of fuels, improve grazing conditions, create seedbeds for natural regeneration, and improve soil fertility through accumulation of ash (Example 12.3). It is important, however, that these fires be prescribed carefully to satisfy the stated purposes of these controlled burns.

Example 12.3

Roles of Fire in the Management of West African Savannas (Mounkeila 1984) Fire is a tool in the management of game refugees and rangelands of West Africa. What is not so well known is that fire also can be used for seedbed preparation and to reduce the competition from noxious plants in silvicultural practices in the savannas. However, this practice favors growth of grasses on some sites and, as a consequence, can be detrimental to trees and shrubs. Many trees and shrubs on the savannas begin to sprout at this time, making them susceptible to fire. It has been concluded, therefore, that the state of knowledge on the use of fire as a silvicultural tool on the West African savannas is limited.

Insects and Fungi Most insects and fungi are selective of their host species. Trees and shrubs normally attain a state of equilibrium with indigenous pests in their natural environments. However, exotic pests can be introduced when exotic trees and shrubs are planted. These pests frequently adapt themselves to the conditions of their new habitats. In general, the risk of damage from pests is higher when plants are weakened physiologically from planting them on unsuitable sites, from improper site preparation, from inefficient planting, from adverse climatic conditions, or from neglect of weeding and other maintenance operations. However, even healthy trees and shrubs are attacked at times.

Care taken to attain vigorous trees or shrubs helps to make a forest plantation more resistant to attacks from insects and fungi. However, when evidence of attack appears, it should be investigated promptly and control initiated. Various control measures often are available.

Silvicultural control measures include well-timed, careful thinnings after the establishment of plantations. Poor, slow growing, and suppressed stems can be eliminated through thinning, maintaining the plantation in a vigorous growing condition. Prompt removal and destruction of infested trees and shrubs in newly established plantations is effective in preventing the spread of pest attacks to the rest of the plantation. Planting of a mixture of species also can be a silvicultural control measure when a threat of infection is known to exist. One disadvantage of planting a mixture of species is that subsequent forest management can become complicated. This complication can be avoided by planting different tree or shrub species in alternate blocks or wide belts, forming barriers to the spread of a pest or disease from the initial point of infection.

Insects and fungi often can be checked by applications of appropriate chemical insecticides or fungicides. These chemicals are available as liquids or wettable powders, dusts, or smokes. Spraying with hand-operated spray guns or portable mist blowers frequently is used in young plantations to control the attacks of insects and fungi. With canopy closure, aerial spraying and dusting or smoking can be more effective and cheaper. Only tested, environmentally sound, and locally accepted insecticides and fungicides should be prescribed for use.

Biological and mechanical control of insects has been used with success in some situations. In most cases, biological control involves introduction of a parasite to control the insects. Mechanical control, by either physically removing and destroying the pests or eliminating alternative hosts can be effective, although the costs can be high.

Livestock and Wildlife   Grazing and browsing by livestock and wildlife are a menace to forest plantations in the early stages of their development. Trees and shrubs can be eaten or trampled upon when these animals enter plantation areas. Hedges, fences, and ditches have been used with varying success to prevent intrusions by these animals. Where fencing costs are high, the trespass by livestock and wildlife can be controlled by guards or taking legal action against the owners of straying animals. Occasionally, the impoundment and confiscation of animals can prove to be an effective deterrent.

It was mentioned in Chapter 2 that the grazing of livestock is a traditional land use in many dryland regions. Enclosures of extensive forest plantations, therefore, can impose drastic changes in the habits and economies of livestock producers and the communities affected. In such situations, it can be unwise to initiate planting programs unless alternative means of livelihood are provided beforehand. This action generally requires the integration of community developmental schemes, for example, improved agriculture or animal husbandry; better communications, schools, or medical welfare; and increased opportunities for employment in rural industries, including afforestation programs and rural forest industries.

Damage to forest plantations by wildlife mainly takes the form of browsing or removing the bark of trees and shrubs. In general, there are three orders of wildlife responsible for this damage, *rodents* (rats, mice, moles, squirrels, chipmunks, and porcupines), *lagomophs* (hares and rabbits), and *artiodactyls* (deer, antelopes, pigs, and buffaloes). The methods of limiting damage by wildlife involve the use of fences, hedges or ditches, trapping and removal, poison baits, or controlled shooting.

People   Trespass by people onto forest plantations can take many forms, including encroachmental cultivation, attempts to divert water sources, taking of fuelwood and other wood products, unlawful hunting, and other recreational uses. In general, the risk of damage by the trespass of people is not too serious in recently established forest plantations, except that it can increase the fire hazard.

Cultural Treatments

Cultural operations promote conditions that are favorable to the survival and subsequent growth and yield of trees or shrubs in a forest plantation. Cultural operations in many forest plantations are concerned with preventing trees and shrubs from being suppressed by competing vegetation (Chapman and Allan 1978, FAO 1989, Goor and Barney 1976). Other cultural treatments include thinning to achieve the desired spacing among trees or shrubs, watering of the plants, and, in some cases, pruning and shaping of the plants.

Weeding   *Weeding* is a cultural operation that suppresses or eliminates the noxious plants that would impair growth of the plantation crop if no action were taken. This undesirable vegetation frequently competes with the trees and shrubs for light, water, and nutrients. Weeding increases the availability of these growth requirements to trees and shrubs. A primary objective of weeding treatments is to promote plantation development, while keeping the costs of the operation within acceptable limits.

One factor affecting the intensity and duration of weeding treatments is the relationship between the tree or shrub crop and undesirable vegetation. On some sites, the plantation crop eventually grows through the noxious plants, dominates the site, and eventually becomes established. The purpose of weeding is to increase the uniformity of the plantation crop and to increase growth on these sites. In other areas, the type and density of the noxious plants are such that they suppress and kill some or all of the planted trees or shrubs in the early stages of plantation development. The main purpose of weeding is to reduce mortality and maintain an adequate, proper stocking of trees or shrubs through establishment on these areas.

The methods of suppressing noxious plants include physically crushing or cutting them back at or immediately above ground level. Elimination is achieved through killing the plants by cultivation or use of chemicals. Weeding can be total or partial.

Thinning   *Thinning* of forest plantations, particularly those plantations established for wood production, is undertaken to obtain the desired spacing between trees or shrubs for maximum production of wood or biomass. This spacing is a compromise between a "wide" spacing to reduce the planting costs and intertree competition in times of drought and a "close" spacing to attain early canopy closure, suppression of noxious plants, a reduction of weeding costs, and natural pruning of branches through shading.

In "first-rotation" plantations established for wood production, an initial thinning objective frequently is to adjust the initial spacings among the trees or shrubs so that the size and quality of the trees or shrubs required at the time of harvesting is attained in a shorter rotational period, hopefully, without secondary thinning treatments. Where trees or shrubs of larger sizes and higher quality are specified, closer than final spacing often is prescribed in an initial thinning. Some form of secondary thinning usually is necessary as a subsequent treatment in these instances. The element of selection in thinning ensures that the growth of the final crop is concentrated on the best stems. Regardless of the purpose of a thinning operation, it should follow the timing and spacing requirements in a prescribed *thinning schedule* for the area.

Watering Forest plantations often need periodical watering in their first growing season to obtain satisfactory survival rates. Watering should begin after cessation of rains, before the moisture content of soil has fallen to the wilting coefficient (Chapman and Allan 1978, Weber and Stoney 1986). Watering can be repeated at intervals until onset of the next rainy season. The immediate area around the tree or shrub should be cleared of noxious plants before each watering. A shallow basin can be made around the stem of each plant to collect as much water as possible.

Watering is a capital-intensive operation, especially on terrain too steep or rough for the passage of tank vehicles. Pack animals can be required to carry water to the plantation site. Regular and frequent waterings can be uneconomical in large forest plantations, particularly when the source of water is a relatively long distance from the plantation. However, watering might be justified in the case of small production or amenity plantations.

Other Cultural Treatments Pruning is carried out to improve the quality of the wood and reduce the possibilities of fire spreading from ground level to the crown. For certain tree and shrub species, basal pruning is necessary to remove undesirable branches at ground level. However, with the exception of widely spaced plantation crops, pruning is not a common cultural treatment during the establishment phase of a plantation.

Tree- or shrub-shaping operations, including the excision of double leaders, are practiced in some kinds of forest plantations, particularly those grown from stumps or cuttings. Such work often can be combined with harvesting operations.

HARVESTING OPERATIONS

In plantations established for wood production, the trees and shrubs should not be cut until they have grown at least to the minimum size required for the specified product utilization. However, the question of when to harvest still must be answered after the minimum size has been attained.

Time of Harvesting

Foresters frequently are guided by the average annual growth rate of a forest plantation in determining when to harvest wood. In general, the average annual growth of trees and shrubs increases slowly during the initial years of plantation establishment, reaches a maximum, and then declines more gradually, as illustrated in Figure 12.4. From a biological standpoint, trees and shrubs should not be allowed to grow much beyond the point of maximum average annual growth, which is the age of maximum productivity. Foresters call this the *biological* rotation age of the forest plantation.

A forester must estimate the volume and know the age of the trees or shrubs in the plantation to determine the average annual growth rate of a forest plantation at a point in time. The average annual growth at the specified time is determined by

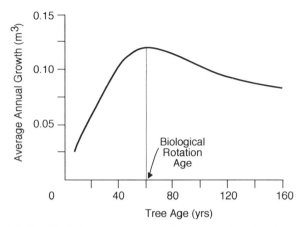

Figure 12.4. Relationship between tree age and tree growth, indicating the "biological" rotation age

dividing the estimated standing volume by the corresponding age. Careful measurements of volumes and known ages are necessary for this determination.

Unfortunately, the determination of tree or shrub age is difficult in many dryland regions, particularly those in the tropics. Unless a record of the date of plantation establishment is available, approximate ages must be estimated from the general size, shape, branching characteristics, and bark condition, and this can be done only for a few species (Avery and Burkhart 1983). Annual rings often are not formed in dryland environments, preventing the use of annual increment counts in estimating age.

Economic considerations also help to determine when to harvest trees and shrubs for wood products. When based solely on market conditions, the time to harvest is when the profit from the harvesting, processing, and selling the wood is maximized. The profit is maximized when the returns generated from selling the wood products minus the costs of harvesting and processing the wood into desired products are the greatest. The profit is maximized at some point in time before average annual growth is maximized in most situations.

Harvesting Techniques

The methods of felling trees and shrubs, cutting stems and branchwood into desired lengths for handling, and removing wood from the plantation to the place of processing, sale, or marketing should be chosen to minimize degradation of the site. Axes, saws, wedges, and sledges can be all that are necessary to fell trees and shrubs and to cut them into desired lengths. Power chain saws also are used in many instances. While their use makes harvesting easier, their high cost of operation can make the use of power chain saws uneconomical.

After the trees and shrubs are felled and cut into desired lengths, the merchantable segments are moved to loading points for their transport to processing sites or directly to a marketplace. A simple drag or sled can be used, pulled by a tractor or domesticated animal, when the stem lengths are too heavy for people to carry. The harvesting operation must be carried out carefully to prevent damage to any residual trees or shrubs remaining in the plantation after the harvesting.

The methods of harvesting should be selected to "match" the skills of the people who will harvest the trees or shrubs. Once again, planning is necessary to ensure that the labor and required equipment will be available for use at the needed time.

SUMMARY

Forest plantations are established and managed for production, protection, and amenity purposes in areas where natural forests and woodlands are inadequate to meet local demands on a sustainable basis. The emphasis of this chapter was placed on rainfed plantations, with irrigated plantations being the focus of the following chapter. Key points that you should be able to explain at this point are phrased in the following questions:

1. What are the general criteria for the selection of trees or shrubs for planting in a forest plantation? How is a site selected for the establishment of a forest plantation? What factors are considered in the selection process?
2. What can be accomplished by site preparation? What are some of the methods used in site preparation?
3. How are bare-rooted, ball-rooted, and containerized stock planted?
4. What are the strategies followed in protecting a forest plantation from the detrimental effects of weather, fire, insects and fungi, grazing by livestock, browsing by wildlife, and people?
5. In general, when should trees and shrubs be harvested in forest plantations that are established for production purposes?

REFERENCES

Avery, T. E., and H. E. Burkhart. 1983. *Forest measurements*. McGraw-Hill Book Co., New York.

Bognatteau-Verlinden, E. 1980. *Study on the impact of windbreaks in Majjia Valley, Niger*. CARE, Niamey, Niger.

Chapman, G. W., and T. F. Allan. 1978. Establishment techniques for forest plantations. *FAO Forestry Paper* 8, Rome.

Falker, P. 1987. *Tree plantings on semi-arid regions*. Elsevier Science Publishing Company, Amsterdam.

FAO. 1985. *Arid zone forestry programmes: State of knowledge and experience*. FAO, Rome.

FAO. 1989. Arid zone forestry: A guide for field technicians. *FAO Conservation Guide* 20, Rome, Italy.

Ffolliott, P. F., and J. L. Thames. 1983. *Environmentally sound small-scale forestry projects: Guidelines for planning*. VITA Publications, Arlington, Virginia.

Goor, A. Y., and C. W. Barney. 1976. *Forest tree planting in arid zones*. The Ronald Press, Co., New York.

Heidmann, L. J. 1967. Herbicides for preparing ponderosa pine planting sites in the Southwest. *USDA Forest Service, Research Note* RM-83.

Mounkeila, G. 1984. *Fire ecology and management in West African savannas and steppes*. Master's Thesis, University of Arizona, Tucson, Arizona.

NAS. 1990. *The improvement of tropical and subtropical rangelands*. National Academy Press, Washington, D.C.

Schubert, G. H. 1974. Silviculture of southwestern ponderosa pine: The status of our knowledge. *USDA Forest Service, Research Paper* RM-123.

Schubert, G. H., and R. S. Adams. 1971. *Reforestation practices for conifers in California*. Division of Forestry, Department of Conservation, State of California, Sacramento, California.

Schubert, G. H., R. W. Pearl, and L. J. Heidmann. 1969. Here's how: A guide to tree planting in the Southwest. *USDA Forest Service, Research Paper* RM-49.

Weber, F. R., and C. Stoney. 1986. *Reforestation in arid lands*. VITA Publications, Arlington, Virginia.

13 Irrigated Forest Plantations

Irrigation to increase production of food has been practiced in the dryland regions of the world since ancient times. The use of irrigation for production of wood is more recent, however, largely because the supplies of wood from natural forests and woodlands and rainfed forest plantations had been sufficient to meet the needs of people when populations were small in number and concentration. This situation has changed in many parts of the world, however, because increased population growth in many developing countries has expanded the demands for wood and other forest-based commodities. Unfortunately, wood resources in many regions have been and continue to be depleted at unsustainable levels. This situation is especially acute in dryland environments, where conditions for plant growth are severe.

A number of actions to intensify the practice of forestry in dryland regions have been initiated in response to the high demands and inadequate supplies of wood, including improved nursery operations, planting stock improvement programs, better site preparation techniques, and, where feasible, irrigation. It is to this latter action that this chapter addresses itself. The use of irrigation in the establishment and management of forest plantations has the potential to increase high yields of wood and, as a result, in some cases, counters the depletion of natural resources. Irrigation in forestry is a complex managerial activity, however, and its successful application requires inputs from a variety of specializations. This chapter discusses the feasibilities and potential benefits of forestry-related applications of irrigation in the establishment and management of irrigated forest plantations.

BACKGROUND KNOWLEDGE AND CONCEPTS

The growth of trees and shrubs in irrigated forest plantations is governed largely by biological, physical, and chemical processes that a forester must bear in mind while planning irrigation practices. For example, knowledge of plant-soil-atmospheric water relationships is basic to the design and operational features of irrigation systems (Armitage 1987, Doneen 1972). Movement of water in soil is affected by mechanical and molecular forces, and soil infiltration and retention capacities. Reduction of soil water below *field capacity* by evapotranspiration from plants leads to levels referred to as *incipient* and then *permanent wilting percentages*, both of which are affected by physical properties of the soil.

Water uptake by trees, shrubs, and other herbaceous plants depends largely upon the status of water within the soil, water potential at root surfaces, and efficiencies of root systems. Ascent of soil water into plants and then within the plants results from evapotranspiration at leaf surfaces, which is affected by atmospheric conditions and water availability. Climatological information can be used to estimate soil moisture conditions, potential evaporation, evapotranspiration, and, as a consequence, soil moisture surplus or deficiency.

Relationships of irrigation to soil properties, topographical characteristics, and hydrologic features also should be known. Soil structure, which can be modified by cultural practices, and texture influence infiltration and water-holding capacities of soils and, as a result, quantities and frequencies of irrigation applications (Yaron et al. 1973). Chemical and physical properties of soil affect one another and the movement of water-soluble salts (e.g., nitrate nitrogen, potassium, and phosphorus) in soil media. It is possible, as a consequence, to determine optimal combinations of amounts and salt contents of irrigation water and to manipulate both through the irrigation regimes used and, if necessary, through fertilization.

Topography is a major consideration in planning for irrigation and must be evaluated in designing and operating irrigation systems. Topography affects infiltration, surface runoff, and sedimentation. It also affects soil-forming processes, water-transported materials, and illuviations of clay materials (Armitage 1987). However, visible topographical characteristics alone may not be useful in deducing subsurface water-movement patterns on some sites, because barriers to subsurface drainage often are hidden beneath depositions of sediments.

Irrigation on a site can change the components of the hydrologic cycle. Most of the input of water to the system that is not precipitation is lost through evapotranspiration, with little left to become runoff or to recharge groundwater aquifers. Furthermore, irrigation water contains soil particles and chemical constituents from its source, whatever that might be.

When movements of excess irrigation water from a site are impeded, water tables can rise and *waterlogging* occur, bringing dissolved salts to the soil surface (Armitage 1987, Greenwood 1988). With this situation, plant growth can decline because of poor soil aeration and accumulations of salts. It is necessary, therefore, that irrigation water is not applied in excess of plant and periodical soil-leaching requirements. Inadvertently applied excess irrigation water must be drained quickly, assisted by pumps when necessary. Irrigation water also might have to be treated to reduce its salt content and maintain a desired quality standard. However, these treatments can be costly and, as a consequence, influence the feasibility of irrigation in the first place.

IRRIGATION WATER

Many systems are available to irrigate forest plantations, although there seldom is a ready-made system for application in a specific situation. Instead, irrigation systems are designed in relation to sources of water, site conditions, costs of equipment, and technical skills of available personnel. Regardless of the irrigation system ultimately selected, it is important that the system meets the requirements of minimal water losses in applications, prevention of site degradation, and sustained economic efficiency. Water for irrigation systems includes (FAO 1989):

- A dependable, permanent supply of water.
- An intermittent water supply.
- Wastewater.

Irrigation systems are selected on the basis of the source of water available. Permanent irrigation systems often are justified with a dependable, permanent water supply. Water harvesting, also referred to as *rainwater harvesting*, is used with an intermittent water supply. Waste water can be used to irrigate, although its use is more limited.

PERMANENT IRRIGATION SYSTEMS

Selection of permanent irrigation systems is possible with a dependable, permanent supply of water, for example, a well, reservoir, lake, or perennial river. Permanent irrigation systems chosen for implementation on the basis of local conditions include *gravity systems*, *sprinkler systems*, and *localized systems*, as described below.

Gravity Systems

The distribution of irrigation water in gravity systems is controlled largely by the land surface. Modifications in relief, when required to efficiently irrigate, are limited by the magnitude of topographical factors of the site in question and the costs. Examples of gravity systems are *surface flooding*, *border check*, *basin irrigation*, and *furrow irrigation* (Armitage 1987, FAO 1989).

Surface flooding, which resembles flooding that occurs on flat lands along rivers, is the simplest form of permanent irrigation, although it also is often the least efficient. In essence, irrigation water is released from ditches and allowed to spread over the land surfaces. Principally used on pasturelands and for agricultural crops, surface flooding generally is inadequate for applications on large forest plantations, because efficiencies in distributions of water are low and there is a risk of waterlogging.

In the border check method, parallel earthen ridges guide irrigation water as it flows downslope over strips of land that typically vary from 3 to 30 m in width and 100 m or more in length. Irrigated lands must have a uniform moderate slope that is parallel to the checks. Implementation of this method is suited to medium-textured, deep, and permeable soils. Infiltration on the upper end of the border of sandy soils can be excessive when the strips are long. Slow infiltration, causing water to stand on the surface for long periods of time, makes the method unsuitable on heavy soils. A ditch that is sited at the end of the strips carries away excess water. The border check method can be useful in agroforestry practices, with 1 or 2 rows of trees or shrubs grown along the ridges and agricultural crops in intervening strips.

Basin irrigation is a labor-intensive system in which land to be irrigated is divided into small basins, each of which has a level land surface. Basins are filled with irrigation water, which is allowed to infiltrate into soil, with the excess drained off. When leaching salts from the soil, the depth of water can be maintained for specified time periods through a continuous flow of water into the basins. The method, therefore, is suitable for saline forest plantations. The method also represents an efficient form of irrigation for agroforestry practices involving pasturelands, on which high rates of flow are available and with relatively large, flat basins.

Furrow irrigation is most suitable for forest plantations, especially on sites where topography is uniform, slopes are gentle, and soils not too porous. Furrows are built from main feeder channels in parallel lines at regular intervals to permit wetting of rooting zones for trees and shrubs, which are planted near the lips of furrows. Width and spacing of the furrows and ridges depend largely upon the infiltration capacity of the soil and plant species to be irrigated. The heavier the soil, the larger and wider apart the furrows must be built (FAO 1989). The opposite applies with more porous soils. Roots of trees and shrubs often develop linearly along furrows, and trees or shrubs tend to lean across the furrows and, consequently, windthrow can take place. Furrow irrigation is labor-intensive and requires both skill and experience in its application.

In deciding upon use of gravity systems, both advantages and disadvantages of the systems must be considered (Booher 1974). Principle advantages of gravity systems, regardless of the type, include:

- Their relatively low investment costs when the land is level initially.
- Water is not supplied under pressure.
- While the systems can be labor-intensive, maintenance costs are relatively low, provided that the systems are designed appropriately and installed properly.

Main disadvantage of gravity systems include:

- Soil fertility can be lowered when the topsoil must be removed in land-leveling operations.
- Small flaws in design can result in high labor costs, soil erosion, and wastage of irrigation water.

Sprinkler Systems

Sprinkler systems are employed in areas of irregular topography on which land leveling is not feasible or on which rapid applications of small quantities of irrigation water are desired. Applications of sprinkler systems in forest plantations generally are limited by the heights of trees or shrubs in the plantations, although sprinkler systems can be applicable in the early stages of plantation establishment. All sprinkler systems need a source of water to be supplied under pressure, a distribution of pipelines to deliver the water, and nozzles to discharge the water (Armitage 1987, FAO 1989, Pillsbury 1968).

Distribution systems with pipelines permanently buried in the ground, and with the heads and risers also permanently in place, have high installation, but low operating, costs. These distribution systems are best adapted to perennial crops of trees or shrubs. Semipermanent distribution systems are similar to permanent systems, except that the laterals are portable. In fully portable distribution systems, all of the components (including the pumps) are portable. These latter systems have low installation and high operating costs.

There are three types of discharge devices, namely, rotating sprinklers, static sprinklers, and nozzle lines. Use of rotating sprinklers is the most common, however. The design of a sprinkler system should involve consultations with specialists (Pillsbury 1968).

Advantages of sprinkler systems include:

- Applicability in areas of irregular topography and slope without a need for land leveling.
- Applicability in areas of high water tables or where there is a hard pan near the land surface.
- Amounts and rates of irrigation water application are controlled easily, so surface runoff and deep percolation are avoided.
- Small, continuous supplies of irrigation water can be more efficiently utilized than is the case with gravity systems.
- Land is not required for channels, ditches, and borders, saving land and maintenance costs of open distribution systems.
- Operators are trained easily.

Disadvantages of sprinkler systems include:

- Initial costs often are greater than those of gravity systems.
- Irrigation water must be supplied under pressure, requiring operating and maintenance costs not incurred with gravity systems.
- Applications of irrigation water can be affected by wind, resulting in drift and an aerosol effect, deep percolation, and losses from evaporation.
- There can be adverse effects on the foliage of some plant species, for example, when irrigation water with a high bicarbonate content is applied when atmospheric humidity is low and evaporation is high (Ayers and Westcot 1976, Doneen 1972, Yaron et al. 1973).

Localized Systems

Localized systems are those in which only a small part of the soil is wetted, for example, at the base of plants and surrounding root systems. Localized systems, which include *trickle* and *drip* irrigation methods, are characterized by slow, low rates of applying water through distribution pipelines and orifices or nozzles placed either under or above the land surface (FAO 1989, NAS 1974, Vermeiren and Jobling 1980). Localized systems have been used successfully in the establishment and management of forest plantations in the Sahelian region of West Africa (Armitage 1987), windbreak plantings in the Great Plains of the United States (Thomas et al. 1981), and forest plantations irrigated with saline water in the desert conditions of Abu Dhabi (Wood et al. 1975).

Components of localized systems include a supply of water under pressure, a control head, a main line, sublines, laterals, and the necessary emitters or distributors. A pump and storage tank or a reservoir is needed to deliver water to the system. The control head, located at the highest point of land in the forest plantation, is connected to the pump to regulate the pressure and amounts of irrigation water applied, filter water before it enters the system, and permit additions of nutrients. The main line leads water to sublines, which supply laterals with distributors opposite trees or shrubs. Irrigation water trickles or drips at constant low discharges under pressure from the emitters. The ends of the sublines and laterals often are open to allow the system to be flushed.

Advantages of localized systems include:

- A capacity to irrigate undulating land surfaces.
- Successful applications on sites that have excessively heavy or light soils.
- An economy of water use, easy control of competing plants, and an ability to keep the soil moisture content near field capacity, reducing a buildup of salinity.
- Easy management, relatively low labor costs, and simple operations.

Disadvantages of localized systems include:

- Susceptibility of small pipes and distributors to clogging.
- A possible restriction of root development through inadequate amounts of watering.

WATER HARVESTING

In the absence of permanent water, a water supply obtained largely from intermittent and often unreliable rainfall is a means of providing irrigation water on a seasonal basis or for longer periods of time if there is a storage facility. *Water harvesting*, as this method of irrigation generally is called, has been used historically in many dryland regions of the world (Brooks et al. 1991, NAS 1974, Thames 1989). In one form or another, water harvesting continues to be used for subsistence farming, watering livestock and wildlife, and domestic use in Australia, India and Pakistan, the United States, and countries in the Near East and the Sahelian region (Armitage 1987), often in areas where annual precipitation is less than 100 mm. Water harvesting also is used in establishing trees and shrubs in plantations (Example 13.1), as discussed below.

Systems and Techniques

Water-harvesting systems include a *catchment area*, usually prepared by removal of rocks and vegetation, compacting the soil, and applying waterproof covers of latex, asphalt, or wax to improve runoff efficiency, and a smaller *storage facility* for the harvested water, unless the water is concentrated immediately in the soil profile or a smaller area for growing drought-hardy trees or shrubs (Brooks et al. 1991, Frasier and Myers 1983, NAS 1974, Thames 1989). A distribution scheme also is required for systems that are designed to irrigate during long dry periods.

The collected water often is used directly without a storage requirement in establishing and maintaining forest plantations (FAO 1989, NAS 1974)). Four techniques use for this purpose are *runoff farming*, *desert-strip farming*, *contour terrace farming*, and *water spreading*.

In runoff farming, a site is divided into small catchments, the size of which is based upon the area required to grow the planted tree or shrub. Collection areas for each catchment range from 20 to 1,000 m^2, depending upon rainfall regimes and water requirements for the tree or shrub planted in the catchment. A basin about 40 cm deep is dug and the tree or shrub planted at the lowest point in each catchment. The depression collects and stores runoff from the rest of the catchment. At the root zone, soil depth should be 1.5 m or more. Diagonal distance from the lowest corner to farthest contributing area generally is between 5 and 30 m. A series of catchment areas with appropriate dimensions is prepared in a typical situation.

Desert-strip farming makes use of runoff from gently sloping watersheds by using a series of terraces to deflect runoff water onto neighboring strips of planted trees or shrubs. Depending upon the topography, soil characteristics, and climate, either a *one-sided microwatershed* for sites with moderately permeable soil and slope greater than 5 percent or a *two-sided microwatershed* for sites with highly permeable soil and slope 5 percent or less, is used. Desert-strip farming is practiced commonly in areas in which only small amounts of rainfall runoff reach major drainage channels.

Contour terrace farming is designed to retard and collect runoff and sediment between parallel terraces along contour lines. If the runoff is properly managed, enough water is added to the soil to improve growth of trees and shrubs significantly. The terraces, built of stones, logs, or earth, must be large enough to hold specified runoff amounts, for example, that expected to occur 1 year in 10. Contour terrace farming can be essential on steep slopes without protective trees,

Example 13.1

Water Harvesting and Tree Establishment: Some Examples

Iran

Asphalt covering has been applied at a rate of 1 l/m^2 to slopes above experimental runoff plots and terraces (2 m wide) on a hillside near Tehran, Iran, to harvest rainwater for growing *Robinia pseudoacacia, Cupresses arizonica,* and *Fraxinus rotundifolia* trees (Mehdizadeh et al. 1978). Rainfall runoff onto the plots over a 5-year test period was substantial. There was a significant increase in stem diameter, height, and crown development of trees in the asphalt-treated plots, as compared to controls.

Israel

A long-term project to select appropriate tree species, develop management practices, and evaluate the potentials for growing fuelwood trees in agroforestry systems using rainfall harvesting techniques in southern Israel has been reported upon by Zohar et al. (1988). It was found that the annual biomass production of individual *Eucalyptus occidentalis* and *Acacia salicina* trees grown in 2-year rotations without supplementary irrigation was 30 and 25 kg, respectively, and 60 and 30 kg in 4-year rotations. It was concluded, therefore, that fuelwood plantations could be established and sustained by relying entirely on rainfall runoff water.

Pakistan

The Pakistan Forest Institute installed a system of microcatchments on more than 40 ha in an area that received 250–300 mm of annual rainfall in 1982. The purpose of the project was to establish forest plantations of *Acacia, Prosopis, Tecoma,* and *Parkinsonia* species. Survival of these species when planted in the microcatchments was 80–90 percent, while their survival on sites without microcatchments was only 10 percent. *Acacia tortilis* had the highest survival rate and grew more than 1 m in height annually.

Southwestern United States

A water-harvesting system consisting of a gravity-fed sump, a storage reservoir, a series of catchments, and an irrigation system occupies nearly 2 ha of retired farmland near Tucson, Arizona (Karpiscak et al. 1984). The combined designed capacity of the sump and reservoir, treated with sodium chloride (NaCl) to decrease infiltration, is approximately 2,400 m^3 of water. The reservoir was covered with 250,000 empty plastic film cans to decrease evaporation. The catchments, also treated with NaCl to decrease infiltration, have been used to concentrate rainfall runoff around planted agricultural crops and tree species in untreated planting areas at the base of the catchments.

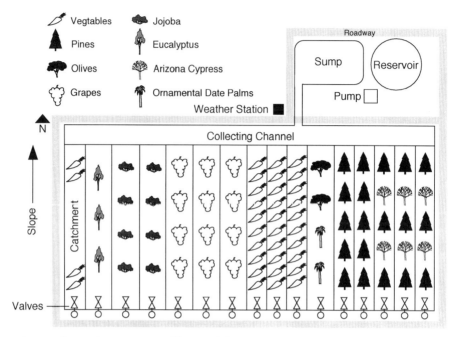

A water-harvesting system near Tucson, Arizona

Survival of Aleppo (*Pinus halepensis*) and Brutia pine (*P. brutia*), commonly found throughout southern Europe into Asia Minor, after a 3-year evaluation period suggested that both species can be planted with relative success in a water-harvesting system such as the one used in this study (Ffolliott 1988). Survival ranged from 50–80 percent, although growth was relatively low. Long-term survival and growth of these tree species has been monitored to ascertain the feasibility of planting Aleppo and Brutia pine in dryland environments of the southwestern United States.

---

shrubs, or other herbaceous plants and where it is unlikely that trees or shrubs can be established before severe erosion takes place.

Rain usually falls in short, intense storms in dryland regions. Runoff from these events swiftly flows away into drainage channels and is lost to the site. Sometimes, flooding occurs in areas not affected directly by extreme rainfall events. Water spreading diverts floodwaters from natural drainage channels and spreads the water onto adjacent floodplains or retains the water on valley floors for later use. Wet floodplains or valley floors then are used to grow trees or shrubs. The sites preferred for water spreading are slopes below escarpments, alluvial deltas, and floodplains, all of which must be able to withstand the onslaught of floodwaters.

Microcatchments

Water harvesting also can be practiced in microscale. For example, small catchments, often called *microcatchments*, can be built around an individual tree or shrub, forcing rainfall runoff from a larger than normal area to the plant, where water infiltrates into the soil and percolates to sufficient depths to keep the tree or shrub alive (NAS 1974). A small depression usually is made around the plant to act as a reservoir, and mulch is used to reduce evaporation. Microcatchments have been used successfully in the Near East, Africa, and the Americas for this purpose. One example of a microcatchment design is that used in the Negev Desert of Israel, illustrated in Figure 13.1.

Advantages of water harvesting, regardless of the technique employed, include the following (Armitage 1987, Brooks et al. 1991, NAS 1974, Thames 1989):

- Existing water supplies can be augmented or water sources can be provided when other sources of water are not available or when the obtaining of sources entail prohibitive development costs.
- Small-scale methods of irrigation can be adapted to the resources and needs of people for which large-scale irrigation projects are not possible.

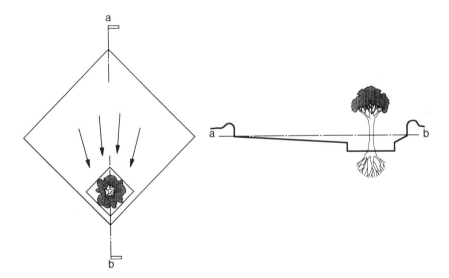

Figure 13.1. A successful microcatchment design in Israel (adapted from Evenari et al. 1968, with permission of the American Society of Agronomy, Inc.) (Arrows indicate the direction of runoff flow. The cultivated plot is placed at the lowest point of the natural terrain in the catchment. Walls are 15–20 cm high. The bottom is about 40 cm below the catchment, holding seeping water close to the plant. Root-zone soil must be at least 1.5 deep. The distance (a–b) can be less than 5 m to more than 30 m, depending upon the tree or shrub species and climate.)

Disadvantages of water harvesting include (NAS 1974):

- Uncertainties of rainfall.
- Possibilities of soil erosion.
- Maintenance or replacement of materials is a constant necessity.
- New skills, though relatively simple, can be required.

WASTEWATER

A number of trials have shown that irrigation with wastewater improves the growth of trees and shrubs (FAO 1989, NAS 1974). However, the optimal types of equipment, most appropriate techniques, and resolution of health problems that are associated with irrigation with wastewater often remain to be resolved. Three types of wastewater have potentials for irrigated forest plantations—untreated, partially treated, and completely treated wastewater—each of which must be evaluated thoroughly before deciding upon its use.

The use of wastewater, regardless of its type, to irrigate forest plantations requires periodical chemical analysis, because the quality of wastewater varies considerably. Soils to be irrigated should have high porosity and moderate infiltration rates. Absorption capacities of the soils should be monitored carefully.

There are potential health problems in irrigating with wastewater, including possible contamination of soils and plants, effluents polluting surface water systems, and wastewater infiltrating to groundwater aquifers. When these problems occur, the use of untreated or partially treated wastewater is limited to sites with low slopes, moderately permeable soils, and away from settlements of people. Irrigation by gravity systems limits contact of wastewater with trees and shrubs, although these systems have a disadvantage of contaminating groundwater aquifers if the wastewater is applied in large quantities. Sprinkler systems limit risks of groundwater pollution but lead to contact of wastewater with the trees and shrubs. Water harvesting, therefore, can be the most apt method of irrigation with wastewater, provided that the problem of clogging hoses is solved.

Security from health problems can be achieved through implementation of the following preventative measures (FAO 1989, NAS 1974):

- Selection of suitable tree and shrub species that are least affected by contact with wastewater.
- Selection of appropriate sites for establishment of forest plantations and the irrigation techniques to be applied.
- Addition of decontaminates to wastewater whenever possible and feasible.

ESTABLISHMENT AND MANAGEMENT OF IRRIGATED FOREST PLANTATIONS

Many of the points that were made in relation to the establishment and management of rainfed forest plantations also apply to irrigated forest plantations. After a site has been selected, the establishment of irrigated forest plantations depends upon the proper installation of the irrigation systems, species selection, the obtaining of planting stock suitable to irrigation, site preparation, and establishment techniques.

Installation of Irrigation Systems

High standards of work are required in installation of irrigation systems to reduce losses of water and maintenance costs and to ensure desirable distributions of irrigation water. It is necessary to ensure a uniform flow and applications of specified amounts of irrigation water with a minimum of unscheduled interruptions. The successful irrigation of forest plantations also calls for efficient drainage systems to remove excess water. Excess irrigation water occurs inadvertently or through deliberate leaching.

It is beyond the scope of this chapter to elaborate in detail upon design criteria and engineering and construction specifications for irrigation systems applicable to forest plantations. Alternative irrigation systems usually are considered for installation at a site, each with a range of criteria and specifications. It is recommended that appropriate references about irrigation systems for forest plantations be consulted for installation guidelines (Booher 1974, Doneen 1972, Pillsbury 1968, NAS 1974, Thomas et al. 1981, Vermeiren and Jobling 1980; Yaron et al. 1973).

Establishment of Irrigated Forest Plantations

Information about the establishment of forest plantations in dryland regions is found in the previous chapter of this book and elsewhere in the literature (Armitage 1987, Goor and Barney 1968, Kaul 1970, FAO 1989, Laurie 1974, Weber and Stoney 1986) and, therefore, need not be repeated here. There are techniques, methods, and other considerations that are important specifically to the successful establishment of irrigated forest plantations worth mentioning, however, including those relating to species selection, production of planting stock, site preparation, and establishment techniques.

Species Selection   Environments in which trees and shrubs are grown in irrigated forest plantations and the purposes for which they are grown are diverse. It is not surprising, therefore, that listings of suitable tree and shrub species are extensive but not comprehensive (Armitage 1987, FAO 1989, Goor and Barney 1968, Kaul 1970, Weber and Stoney 1986). The criteria for species selection varies greatly in terms of objectives that apply in specific situations.

Tree and shrub species that are adapted to the environment in question and to the silvicultural treatments to be used and which have water requirements that can be met with the available supplies of irrigation water usually are chosen for planting. In some instances, however, special-purpose species dictate the selection process (Example 13.2). Criteria of importance in testing the suitabilities of tree and shrub species for irrigation in dryland regions include (NAS 1974):

- Satisfy stated purpose.
- Adapted to environment and silvicultural system to be applied.
- Economy of water use through stomatal mechanisms that reduce evapotranspiration losses.
- Water requirements that can be met with available amounts of irrigation water.
- Tolerance to saline or alkaline conditions of the soil, irrigation water, or both.

Example 13.2

Special Purpose Species for Irrigated Forest Plantations (Armitage 1987, Goor and Barney 1976) In addition to general guidelines for the selection of trees and shrubs for irrigated forest plantations, special-purpose species often must be considered, as indicated by the following examples:

- Species such as *Acer negundo* that have dense root systems are recommended for "binding" the banks of unlined canals or helping to stabilize stream banks in riparian ecosystems.
- In some situations, "negative" selection factors are important. For example, some species have spreading crowns that make them unsuitable in high-yielding forest plantations, although they can be valuable for other applications. Many *Albizia* and *Terminalia* species fall into this category.
- Trees or shrubs that seed themselves or sucker "strongly" sometimes are undesirable, especially where they invade agricultural croplands or other forest plantations. *Robinia pseudoacacia* is a vigorous suckering species, along with certain poplars such as *Populus alba*. Other species that have become "weeds" in irrigated forest plantations are *Morus alba*, *Prosopis cineraria*, and *P. juliflora*.
- Species that encourage seed-eating birds by providing nesting sites and cover, for example, the multipurpose *Acacia nilotica*, are shunned by local farmers. At times, counterclaims are made that birds feeding on insect pests in plantations are beneficial. It is obvious, therefore, that a compromise often is necessary in species selection.

Production of Planting Stock   Planting stock for irrigated forest plantations must be high quality, with well-developed root systems free of malformation, disease, and mechanical damage. The planting stock also must be able to grow rapidly and vigorously once planted. Cultural treatments must be prescribed in the nursery to produce planting stock that meets established *acceptance criteria*, with a culling of the stock not meeting these standards. In general, planting stock of insufficient standards at the time of planting should not be "held over" in nurseries for subsequent planting periods but treated as culls and discarded.

It often is recommended that planting stock for irrigation be 30 cm or more in height when planted (Armitage 1987). Smaller stock frequently suffers from wind damage, blowing sand, salt (when it is a factor), and a variety of pests. Even if smaller planting stock survives planting, low initial growth rates can place the stock at a disadvantage in achieving the objectives of a plantation.

When containers are to be used in producing tree or shrub seedlings, the containers should be open at the bottom to prevent waterlogging, a lack of aeration, and coiling of root systems (Laurie 1974). These containers also should allow protruding roots to be pruned at regular intervals. Growing of seedlings in this manner leads to development of fibrous root systems that can be maintained in a vigorous physiological condition, and it ensures that roots will be free of mechanical damage and not prone to diseases that often are found in irrigated soils.

Other considerations include watering in a manner to eliminate salt layering at the surface of soils. Drainage of potting media is necessary to prevent waterlogging. Care in fertilization treatments, when part of the nursery operations, is important. Some mineral elements can be lethal to seedlings when applied improperly.

Site Preparation   The establishment of irrigated forest plantations generally requires high investments (Armitage 1987, FAO 1989, Weber and Stoney 1986). Careful site preparation is necessary to protect this investment. Sites should be graded to remove unlevel terrain before other preparations, such as the plowing of soil or the construction of ridges to control flows of irrigation water. Plowing and ridging are prescribed in attempting to meet specified planting survival rates. The depth of plowing is dictated largely by local soil conditions and the character of rooting systems of the planting stock. The heights of ridges and intervals between furrows, when constructed as part of the irrigation system, also vary (Example 13.3).

Ripping of heavy soils or soils with impeding horizons to allow irrigation water to penetrate and improve drainage has value at times (Edgar and Stewart 1979). When prescribed, this operation should be done at specified spacings in two directions at right angles to one another, with seedlings planted at the intersections. The ripping of soils often is undertaken in combination with grading activities, while the necessary heavy equipment is still on-site. Ripping might be repeated as a cultural treatment during the life of a forest plantation.

Example 13.3

Site Preparation for the Establishment of Irrigated Forest Plantations (Armitage 1987, Laurie 1974)   A traditional method of site preparation in the Gezira and Khartoum greenbelt plantings in the Sudan includes construction of a series of ridges that are 2.5–3.0 m apart, with the height between tops of ridges and bottoms of intervening furrows being about 60 cm. Furrows 20–30 cm in depth and 3 m apart are used successfully in the Indus Basin of Pakistan, with planting spots located on notches cut one-half the way down the sides of the furrows to provide a planting shelf. In Kuwait, where sewage effluent and untreated sewage have been applied as irrigation water, trenches are made 0.8 m wide, 1 m deep, and 6 m apart, with seedlings planted at relatively wide spacings in 1 m^3 planting holes. Regardless of the specifications, however, planting too close to the furrows can result in malformed root systems, often leading to leaning or windthrow of the trees or shrubs.

Establishment Techniques   The establishment of irrigated forest plantations involves planting of seedlings, insertion of vegetative plant sections, or, with favorable conditions, direct sowing of seeds. Regardless of the establishment technique used, details of implementation depend largely upon the silvical characteristics of tree or shrub species to be planted, subsequent thinning regimes and rotational intervals prescribed, and whether the forest plantation in question is a block or linear in form.

Planting of bare-root seedlings is successful sometimes, although the seedlings can become desiccated or suffer damage to their root systems when handling and transporting them from nurseries to planting sites. Container seedlings, therefore, usually are preferred. In the planting of containerized seedlings, the containers should be removed immediately before planting to allow root systems to grow outward into the soil after planting. It is important that the balls of potting media around the root systems are not broken up in planting. Coiled roots should be extended and pruned where they emerge from the ball, however. The protection of seedlings from browsing and blowing sand can be achieved by inserting thorny twigs, palm fronds, or similar materials around the base of the plants.

Inserting unrooted cutting or other vegetative plant sections is an established alternative with tree and shrub species that root relatively easily, such as most *Tamarix* species, and many poplars, willows, and mulberries. However, mixed results have been reported with this establishment technique (Armitage 1987). One successful method in Kuwait involves insertion of *Tamarix aphylla* cuttings into trenches or pits and irrigated with sewage effluent and untreated sewage water. However, only "average" results were obtained with the same species in the Khartoum greenbelt plantations in the Sudan. Poor results have been reported with other species in the Sudan, including *A. indica, A. nilotica, Ceiba pentandra, E.*

tirucalli, Poinciana regia, Melia azaderach, and *Peltophorum pterocarpum.* Poor results frequently occur with unrooted cuttings or other vegetative plant sections when the stock tends to rot because the irrigation water is applied in improper amounts and at incorrect intervals.

Broadcast or spot sowing of seeds, while generally unsuccessful in rainfed conditions, can be successful at times with irrigation. For success, however, species that produce large quantities of easily germinating seeds should be used. The depth of sowing can be critical, especially in soil with a high proportion of silt. It is often that the germinants, once established, require a longer time period to reach the size for the purpose for which the trees or shrubs are grown.

It is important that irrigated forest plantations attain specified levels of stocking as quickly as possible after planting. A stocking *standard* of 90 percent with evenly distributed trees or shrubs commonly is suggested (Armitage 1987). To ensure that standards are approached in a timely manner, inspections of survival should be scheduled within a month or 6 weeks of establishment, with low vigor or dead plants replaced as necessary.

Management of the Forest Plantations

Irrigated forest plantations, similar to rainfed plantations, are managed to provide a variety of products, including fuelwood, poles and posts, building materials, or fodder for livestock and food for people. However, irrigation often allows for the establishment of faster growing tree and shrub species than normally is possible in rainfed forest plantations, the latter being limited often by low levels of available water. Furthermore, in many instances, the availability of wood from irrigated forest plantations lessens the destruction of fragile natural forests and woodlands.

Once they are established in irrigated forest plantations, the trees and shrubs are managed generally in a manner that is similar to that of rainfed forest plantations. It is necessary to protect irrigated plantations against fire, insects, and diseases and to apply appropriate weeding, thinning, and other cultural treatments when required. In addition, one must specify the time of harvesting and the harvesting techniques to be used for plantations that produce wood for products. These considerations are important, particularly in protecting the relatively large investments already made in installing irrigation systems and establishing forest plantations. The anticipated benefits of irrigated forest plantations are realized largely through intensive, carefully prescribed, and properly implemented management practices.

Management and Operation of Irrigation Systems

Irrigated forest plantations often fail to achieve anticipated benefits because of inappropriate management and operation of the irrigation systems. Information about irrigation practices for agricultural crops is available, but little of this information applies directly to irrigation practices for perennial trees and shrubs in forest plantations (Armitage 1987, FAO 1989, NAS 1974). More might be learned from irrigation practices for plantations of fruit trees than for agricultural crops.

Whatever the circumstances, the irrigation practices are determined largely by the local conditions and economic situations. Of particular importance in irrigating forest plantations are the rates and methods of application, the efficiency of water use, and the maintenance of the irrigation systems.

Rates and Methods of Applying Water Empirical studies can help to determine water requirements for trees and shrubs, rather than theoretical approaches, which may be based upon annual agricultural crops that generally do not address questions relating to actual water availability at a site (Armitage 1987, NAS 1974). Among the questions that frequently can be answered empirically are, *How much water do trees and shrubs actually need? When and for how long is this water needed?* and *For how long can a tree or shrub tolerate a lack of water and at what time of year?* It also is important to distinguish between *water requirements* of trees and shrubs for sustained growth and *potential water consumption*, which is the amount of water that would be used if it were available in unlimited quantities but would not necessarily result in significant increases in growth rates. Studies on rates and methods of applying irrigation should include:

- Evaluation of irrigation methods and alternative schedules in reference to the specific tree and shrub species and their stages of development.
- Determination of the frequencies of irrigation and the amounts of water applied.
- Development of cultural practices to control problems of salinity.
- Determination of the irrigation scheduling and periodical seasonal water deficits on growth rates and subsequent yields of tree and shrub species.
- Evaluation of irrigation methods, including alternative layouts, lengths of run, and permissible stream sizes.
- Possible irrigation-fertilization interactions.

The results from these empirical studies generally are translated into recommendations for amounts and depths of irrigation at different times of the year and for different sites and stages of plant growth. The irrigation schedules and operations of distribution systems are modified subsequently and accordingly. General guidelines are often to irrigate immediately before occurrence of wilting and to apply the amount of irrigation water necessary to bring soil in the rooting zone to field capacity (Armitage 1987, Doneen 1972, Doorenbos and Pruitt 1977, NAS 1974, Yaron et al. 1973). Inadequate irrigation reduces growth rates of trees and shrubs and, with leaching, can result in a loss of nutrients. In general, irrigation schedules should reflect the following facts:

- Sandy soils are irrigated more frequently and with lesser amounts of water in an irrigation period than heavier soils.
- Water use by trees and shrubs varies with stages of development.

- Water use is lower in cool, cloudy, still, and humid days than when it is hot, clear, windy, and dry.

In time and with continual study, irrigation schedules for specific sites can become refined in terms of satisfying objectives for management of forest plantations. The ultimate aim in irrigation is to use water efficiently, to optimize growth rates and subsequent yields of trees and shrubs, and to maintain soil fertility properties. Therefore, irrigation schedules should be refined by continuous monitoring, adaptive research efforts, and making adjustments throughout the life of the forest plantation.

Efficiency of Water Use   *Efficiency* of water use in irrigation, that is, the ratio between the calculated amount of water added to the soil to bring the moisture content in the rooting zone to field capacity and the amount of water actually applied, depends largely upon the irrigation method and skill of the irrigationist. When the amount of irrigation water applied exceeds that needed to replenish water depleted by evapotranspiration, efficiency is low, while applications of less than the required amount of water often have detrimental effects on available nutrients and result in sub-optimal growth rates. Even with controls, some irrigation water will be lost through percolation below the rooting zone, surface runoff, evaporation, or seepage from distribution channels (Armitage 1987, NAS 1974). These losses should be minimized, however, to prevent a raising of water tables, control costs of operation, and limit the loss of nutrients in irrigation water.

It is necessary to maintain a uniform distribution of water on the irrigated area. Therefore, continual monitoring is required to optimize the efficiency of irrigation. Guidelines for this purpose include (Armitage 1987, Doorenbos and Pruitt 1977, NAS 1974, Yaron et al. 1973):

- Check soil moisture in the rooting zone at several locations before irrigation, estimating the amount of water needed to bring soil moisture content to field capacity within 2 or 3 days of irrigation.
- Check soil moisture again after irrigation to determine whether it is close to field capacity throughout the rooting zone, with no dry spots or layering in the profile.
- Calculate the efficiency ratio, making changes in the irrigation schedules when necessary.
- During irrigation, determine whether water is percolating uniformly into the soil, whether basins and level borders are filled quickly, and, if furrows are used, whether water reaches the lower end in about one-quarter of the time it occurs above the bottom of the furrows at the upper end.
- If excessive surface runoff occurs at the lower end of a border or furrow, the stream of water at the upper end is not being reduced properly or cut off soon enough. When this happens, it is necessary to adjust the magnitude of

the stream or to reduce or cut off the water earlier in subsequent irrigations in order to approach a uniform distribution of water.

Economic use of irrigation water and the general efficiency of irrigation are improved when a flexible approach is adopted to operation of the system. Once again, continuous monitoring of the applications of irrigation water and the subsequent effects is necessary. Irrigation water should not be applied arbitrarily. Those responsible for supplying the water should be sensitive to the local situation and not adhere to irrigation schedules that are not efficient.

Maintenance   Maintenance of main and lateral canals, channels and pipes delivering irrigation water, and control and outlet devices is imperative to a reliable supply of water. Maintenance is important, particularly at points of consumption at the lower end of irrigation systems and in preventing seepage. The tasks in a maintenance program include (Armitage 1987):

- Removal of accumulated sediments.
- Repair of leaks, cracks, and other "breakdowns" in the system.
- Attention to pumping and distribution equipment, making repairs or replacements when necessary.

Maintenance work should be undertaken so that it will not disrupt irrigation schedules. However, maintenance shutdowns of entire irrigation systems for specified time periods at regular intervals are part of the operations of larger irrigation systems. Maintenance shutdowns frequently are planned for a dry season and, as a consequence, cause setbacks to growth rates or damage to trees and shrubs that depend upon irrigation water at the time. Therefore, large-scale maintenance functions must be considered in determining the feasibility of proposed irrigation programs (Armitage 1987, NAS 1974) and, in some instances, can "tip the balance" against establishing irrigated forest plantations.

PROBLEMS RELATED TO IRRIGATED FOREST PLANTATIONS

Problems frequently related to irrigated forest plantations include waterlogging and salinity; malformations of root systems; occurrences of birds, insects, and other animals; and potential environmental and health-related problems. The most important problems are those of waterlogging from applications of excessive amounts of irrigation water and, as a result, water tables rising to cause increases in soil salinity in the absence of proper underground drainage (Armitage 1987, Eckholm 1973, Greenwood 1988, Yaron et al. 1973). Salinity also is caused by direct applications of saline irrigation water. These problems are prevented largely by appropriate design, implementation, and operation of irrigation systems. Once problems occur, however, reclamation generally is costly and can limit plant productivity.

Healthy root systems for the planting stock depend upon "good" aeration of the soil. A lack of soil aeration can create conditions favorable to diseases and, in extreme instances, the death of plants. Uniformity of irrigation in terms of amount and frequency is important in ensuring the necessary soil aeration (Armitage 1987, Doneen 1972, Yaron et al. 1973).

Birds, insects, and browsing animals can be found in disproportionate numbers in irrigated forest plantations. Seed-eating birds inhabiting these plantations can "spillover" and damage adjacent agricultural crops. Selecting alternative tree or shrub species for planting or use of agricultural crops that frustrate removal of grains by birds are among the corrective actions prescribed in these situations (Armitage 1987). Damage to trees and shrubs in plantations can occur from browsing by livestock and other animals. Direct control of these animals is likely the best control of this kind of damage. In general, the impacts of animals usually is local in extent.

Irrigating with sewage and untreated industrial effluent has environmental implications. These kinds of irrigation waters contain minerals and ions that can accumulate in soils and, in doing so, affect the productivity potential of soils and properties of groundwater. Irrigation areas are notorious sites for human parasites and a number of disease vectors. The control of these parasites and vectors through chemical methods and environmental management, including the use and management of irrigation water, of the nature and manipulation of vegetation, and of measures related to human habitation and behavioral patterns, is recommended (Armitage 1987, NAS 1974).

A final point on possible environmental implications of irrigated forest plantations relates to the effects of large-scale irrigation programs on climate. It is believed that widespread climatological effects are minimal (Fowler and Helvey 1974). However, localized microclimatological effects likely will occur, particularly increases in atmospheric humidity.

SUMMARY

Irrigated forest plantations offer the potential of increased wood production in situations where it is feasible, both technically and economically. However, irrigation in forestry requires that a variety of specialists be involved in the planning and managing of irrigated plantations. The purpose of this chapter, therefore, was to introduce the subject of irrigated forest plantations and to provide sufficient information so that you should be able to:

1. Describe the sources of water for irrigation systems and the types of irrigations systems best adapted for these sources.

2. Describe the advantages and disadvantages of the different irrigation systems considered in the chapter.

3. Explain how the establishment and management of irrigated forest plantations differ from that of rainfed plantations.

4. Discuss the biological, physical, environmental, and socioeconomic problems that are related to irrigated forest plantations.

REFERENCES

Armitage, F. B. 1987. *Irrigated forestry in arid and semi-arid lands: A syntheses.* International Development Research Center, Ottawa, Canada.

Ayers, R. S., and D. W. Westcot. 1976. Water quality for irrigation. *FAO Irrigation and Drainage Paper* 29, Rome.

Booher, L. T. 1974. Surface irrigation. *FAO Agricultural Development Paper* 95, Rome.

Brooks, K. N., P. F. Ffolliott, H. M. Gregersen, and J. L. Thames. 1991. *Hydrology and the management of watersheds.* Iowa State University Press, Ames, Iowa.

Doneen, I. D. 1972. Irrigation practice and water management. *FAO Irrigation and Drainage Paper* 1, Rome.

Doorenbos, J., and W. O. Pruitt. 1977. Guidelines for predicting crop water requirements. *FAO Drainage and Irrigation Paper* 24, Rome.

Eckholm, E. P. C. 1975. *Losing ground: Environmental stress and world food prospects.* W. W. Norton, New York.

Edgar, J. G., and H. T. L. Stewart. 1979. Wastewater disposal and reclamation using *Eucalyptus* and other trees. *Progress in Water Technology* 11:163–73.

Evenari, M., L. Shanan, and N. H. Tadmor. 1968. Runoff farming in the desert. I. Experimental layout. *Agronomy Journal* 60:29–32.

FAO. 1989. Arid zone forestry: A guide for field technicians. *FAO Conservation Guide* 20, Rome.

Ffolliott, P. F. 1988. Initial survival and growth of tree seedlings in a water harvesting agrisystem. *Hydrology and Water Resources in Arizona and the Southwest* 18:43–7.

Fowler, W. B., and J. D. Helvey. 1974. Effect of large scale irrigation on climate in the Columbia Basin. *Science* 184(4133):121–27.

Frasier, G. W., and L. E. Myers. 1983. Handbook of water harvesting. USDA Agricultural Research Service, *Agricultural Handbook* 600.

Greenwood, E. A. C. 1988. The hydrologic role of vegetation in the development and reclamation of dryland salinity. In Allen, E. B. (ed.). 1988. *The reconstruction of disturbed lands: An ecological approach.* American Association for the Advancement of Science, Washington, D.C., pp. 205–33.

Goor, A. Y., and C. W. Barney. 1968. *Forest tree planting in arid zones.* The Ronald Press, New York.

Karpiscak, M. M., K. E. Foster, R. L. Rawles, N. G. Wright, and P. Hataway. 1984. *Water harvesting agrisystem: An alternative to ground water use in the Avra Valley Area, Arizona.* Office of Arid Lands Studies, University of Arizona, Tucson, Arizona.

Kaul, R. N. 1970. *Afforestation in arid zones.* Junk N.V., The Hague.

Laurie, M. V. 1974. Tree planting practices in African savannas. *FAO Forestry Development Paper* 19, Rome.

Mehdizadeh, P., A. Varizi, and L. Boersma. 1978. Water harvesting for afforestation, efficiency and life span of asphalt cover 11, survival and growth of forest trees. *Soil Science Society of America Journal* 42:644–57.

NAS. 1974. *More water for arid lands: Promising technologies and research opportunities.* National Academy of Sciences, Washington, D.C.

Pillsbury, A. F. 1968. Sprinkler irrigation. *FAO Agricultural Development Paper* 88, Rome.

Thames, J. L. 1989. Water harvesting. In FAO. 1989. Role of forestry in combating desertification, *FAO Conservation Guide* 21, Rome, pp. 234–52.

Thomas, J. G., D. A. Starkey, and R. G. Aslin. 1981. *Drip irrigation for windbreaks.* Cooperative Extension Service, Kansas State University, Manhattan, Kansas.

Vermeiren, J., and G. A. Jobling. 1980. Localized irrigation—design, installation, operation, evaluation. *FAO Irrigation and Drainage Paper* 36, Rome.

Weber, F. R., and C. Stoney. 1986. *Reforestation in arid lands.* VITA Publications, Arlington, Virginia.

Wood, P. J., A. F. Willens, and G. A. Willens. 1975. An irrigation plantation project in Abu Dhabi. *Commonwealth Forestry Review* 54:139–46.

Yaron, B., E. Daufors, and Y. Vaadia (eds.). 1973. *Arid zone irrigation.* Springer-Verlag, New York.

Zohar, Y., J. A. Aronson, and H. Lovenstein. 1988. Cultivation of multipurpose trees in rain water harvesting systems in the arid zone of Israel. *Commonwealth Forestry Review* 67:339–49.

14 Management of Natural Forests and Woodlands

Natural forests and woodlands in the dryland regions of the world have been and continue to be harvested for fuel, building materials, poles, and other wood products. However, the rates of removals of trees and shrubs for purposes of meeting the demands for these wood products, converting to agricultural lands, and grazing by livestock only can be estimated. It is true, moreover, that the continuing depletions of growing stock from these fragile ecosystems is alarming. Therefore, the remaining natural forests and woodlands must be managed carefully, to the extent that is possible, to ensure sustainable flows of wood and needed site protection and amenities.

Management of natural forests and woodlands to meet the needs of people living in dryland environments is the topic of this chapter. These forests and woodlands often were more "mined" than "managed" in the past, and, as a consequence, management prescriptions for sustainable production and conservation are incomplete at best. Nevertheless, improved management practices are requisite to move away from mining and toward management. Many of the considerations presented in reference to the management of forest plantations also are important for natural forests and woodlands. However, there are differences in the characteristics of natural forests and woodlands and those of forest plantations, which can dictate the nature of management practices to be implemented.

STATE OF KNOWLEDGE AND EXPERIENCE

With few exceptions, little investment in the management of natural forests and woodlands in dryland regions has been made in the past. As a consequence, the states of knowledge and experience in management of natural forests and woodlands are limited. Pakistan is one country that has a formal system of management (FAO 1989b). Tropical thorn and subtropical broad-leaved forests in Pakistan are harvested on regular 30-year coppicing cycles. A selection system of silviculture also is applied in broad-leaved forests, supplemented by planting of trees when protection from grazing by livestock is achieved.

Investments in management of natural forests and woodlands in dryland regions have been minimal, largely because of inherently low levels of annual wood production, usually less than 0.5 m³/ha. Nevertheless, there is increasing interest in the management of natural forests and woodlands in dryland regions. Many of these natural ecosystems could offer greater possibilities than forest plantations for meeting increasing needs of local people for fuelwood, service timbers, fodder, and minor forest products (FAO 1985, Salem 1988), if they are managed for sustainable production.

Unfortunately, there is a limited basis to prescribe management practices, as there is little "history" of the proper management of natural forests and woodlands in these regions. Normally, the level of management that occurs is not intensive, even in forest reserves. Management involves little more than early burning to encourage natural regeneration and subsequent regulation of fuelwood harvesting, grazing by livestock, and, on many lands, agricultural encroachment in many instances (FAO 1989b). Ecological degradation frequently continues through often conflicting demands for fuelwood, grazing lands, and agricultural crop production. Improved management for sustainable production and conservation is essential to reduce this degradation. An objective of management, therefore, should be to ensure multiple uses of natural resources rather than to maximize returns on any one product and, in doing so, risk further degradation and destruction of these fragile ecosystems.

Applications of silvicultural treatments and management generally presuppose a knowledge of the inherent characteristics of the natural ecosystems in question, which is not always the case in dryland regions. However, inventories and ecological studies have been conducted to determine these characteristics in the southwestern United States and northern Mexico (Conner et al. 1990, Ffolliott 1989). Limited efforts to obtain this knowledge have been initiated in Australia, many countries in the Sahelian region of West Africa, and the dryland regions of South America and Asia (FAO 1985, FAO 1989b). Without this information from inventories and ecological studies, it is difficult to develop a foundation for planning and implementing silvicultural practices to meet desired management goals.

The more "traditional" silvicultural methods developed in more temperate regions, for example, seed tree, shelterwood, and selection methods (Daniel et al. 1979, Lorimer 1990, Smith 1986), often must be modified for use in dryland regions because of unique characteristics of tree and shrub species in these ecosystems. To illustrate this point, some species have large seeds that are dispersed largely by animals and, as a consequence, not suitable to "traditional" European-North American silviculture.

CHARACTERISTICS OF NATURAL FORESTS AND WOODLANDS

Natural forests and woodlands evolve into either *even-aged* or *uneven-aged* structures, depending upon frequency distributions of tree and shrub age classes. All of the trees or shrubs are essentially the same age class in even-aged structures, as observed in most forest plantations. Uneven-aged stand structures are those in which trees or shrubs differ markedly in age classes. A minimum difference of 10–20 years in age classes is accepted generally as the definition of uneven-aged structures in the United States (Ford-Robertson 1983). Even-aged or uneven-aged management practices are prescribed in natural forests and woodlands, depending upon the situation. Regenerative opportunities, compositions and structures of stands, and growth rates and yields are inputs to formulation of the respective management practices.

Regenerative Opportunities

Natural forests and woodlands regenerate naturally by seeding or vegetative reproduction of the trees and shrubs on-site. Tree and shrub species already present in an area largely dictate compositions of these forests and woodlands. As a consequence, foresters can have little choice but to implement forestry practices with indigenous species. In contrast, tree and shrub species are selected purposely to meet specified management goals in forest plantations.

Even-aged stand structures evolve when natural regeneration occurs in one short time period within a rotational cycle, either prior to or shortly after final harvesting of trees or shrubs. Regeneration is a continuing or recurring processes that occurs intermittently, to some degree, through time in uneven-aged stand structures (Gibbs 1977, Lorimer 1990, Smith 1986). Adequate natural regeneration frequently is unreliable in many dryland regions, in either case.

The spacings and arrangements of trees and shrubs in natural forests and woodlands typically are irregular and largely random. As a consequence, the costs of management and harvesting of wood can be greater in natural forests and woodlands than in forest plantations, particularly in those represented by uneven-aged structures.

Compositions and Structures of Stands

Stands are aggregations of trees or shrubs occupying the same area and distinguishable, in some way, from the trees or shrubs found on adjacent areas. Stands are often the primary units of planning and implementation of the management practices in general applications of forest management (Clutter et al. 1983). Species composition and size class structures of natural forests and woodlands determine the potential of stands to meet management goals. A mosaic of stands frequently develops in an area, offering a variety of stand characteristics and, therefore, management opportunities.

Stand Compositions Trees and shrubs can be tolerant, intolerant, or combinations of both in even-aged stand compositions (Gibbs 1977, Lorimer 1990, Smith 1986). *Tolerance* is a measure of capacities of plants to grow in the shade of other plants. Trees and shrubs often are more tolerant species in uneven-aged stands, although an overstory of seral intolerant species related to past disturbances can be found in some situations. Regardless of stand composition, natural forests and woodlands in dryland regions are characterized frequently by wide spacing patterns between trees or shrubs, indicating competition for soil moisture on dry sites.

Stand Structures All of the trees or shrubs in even-aged stand structures are essentially the same age class, although several size classes might be found because of differences in growth rates. On the other hand, uneven-aged stand structures include two, three, or four age classes and, in most situations, size classes of trees or shrubs. Each age or size class generally represents establishment success in a year of natural regeneration.

Stand structures can be the most important factor in applications of silviculture and management to natural forests and woodlands. In harvesting stands of even-aged structures, for example, all, or nearly all, of the trees or shrubs are harvested at one time. However, trees or shrubs should be removed in each of the size classes represented at each cutting cycle to maintain a specified uneven-aged structure. In doing so, it is anticipated that an environment favorable to subsequent natural regeneration will be created and growth of the residual stand promoted.

It frequently is thought that only the largest trees or shrubs should be harvested in uneven-aged stands (Gibbs 1977, Leuschner et al. 1990), although this action is not necessarily appropriate. The sustainable production of wood can be compromised when only large trees or shrubs are removed. Furthermore, stands of irregular or even-aged structures also can be created, which likely will be counter to uneven-aged management goals.

Growth Rates and Yields

Competition for light, space, and soil moisture is largely horizontal between codominant trees or shrubs in even-aged stands. However, the growth rates and yields of wood in uneven-aged stands are affected by competition both vertically and horizontally. Depending upon stand structures, the trees or shrubs in uneven-aged stands that are affected by competition can be *dominant, codominant, intermediate,* or *suppressed* in their respective vertical positions within the stands. Often, "overstory-understory" stratifications evolve in uneven-aged structures, with overstories consisting of dominant or codominant trees and understories being comprised of intermediate or suppressed smaller trees or shrubs (Gibbs 1977, Lorimer et al. 1990, Smith 1986).

Growth Rates Effects of competition from other trees or shrubs on growth rates can be predicted more easily in even-aged stands and, consequently, are better known than for uneven-aged stand structures. The presence of vertical competition is reflected in the management of uneven-aged stands being limited to more tolerant tree and shrub species in many cases. However, the capacities of tolerant tree and shrub species to regenerate and survive in situations of vertical competition is not necessarily equated with capacities to grow rapidly in these conditions (Gibbs 1977, Lorimer 1990, Smith 1986). Obtaining acceptable growth of understory trees and shrubs in uneven-aged stands frequently requires relatively low densities of stand structures.

Estimates of growth rates in natural forests and woodlands in the dryland regions of the world are few. Nevertheless, some information is available to illustrate the relatively slow growth rates that characterize these ecosystems. Annual growth rates in the woodlands of the southwestern United States and northern Mexico range from 0.25 to 0.50 m³/ha, depending upon species composition, site productivities, age of the woodlands, and densities of trees and shrubs (Conner et al. 1990, Everett 1987, Ffolliott 1989).

Annual growth in the generally uneven-aged stands of pinyon-juniper woodlands averages from 0.35 to 0.50 m³/ha, which translates into annual growth rates of less than 1 percent. Annual growth in oak woodlands, also called *encinal* woodlands, from the Spanish designation to describe evergreen woodlands that are wholly or partially *Quercus* spp., rarely is greater than 0.25 m³/ha. Stands of oak woodlands are either even-aged or uneven-aged in structure, depending largely upon the past fuelwood-harvesting practices. Annual growth rates in stands of *Prosopis juliflora* also are slow, averaging less than 0.50 m³/ha on better sites. These estimates of growth largely represent sites in the southwestern United States and northern Mexico that are managed for livestock production, diversities in wildlife habitats, and watershed protection and, as a consequence, are not solely managed for the sustainable production of wood.

Estimates of growth rates obtained elsewhere suggest that the inherent productivities can be higher than those reported above. In the Sahelian region of West Africa, for example, protected and largely even-aged stands of *Acacia senegal* in Chad grow at annual rates of from 4 to 5 m³/ha (FAO 1985, FAO 1989b). Annual growth rates of *Acacia senegal* in the classified forests of Senegal range from less than 1 to about 2.5 m³/ha. In the East African drylands, annual growth rates of native tree and shrub species vary from 2.8 m³/ha in the Rift Valley of Kenya to between 1.1 and 2.1 m³/ha in savannas. Annual growth rates of indigenous woodlands in Tanzania average 1 m³/ha and less than 0.5 m³/ha in bushlands. These estimates of growth generally represent sites supporting overmature forests or woodlands on which forest management is not practiced intensively. However, the mere protection of these sites against browsing by livestock and fire has been found to increase growth rates in many of these forests and woodlands by as much as 25 percent (FAO 1985).

Yields The yields of wood, measured in terms of standing volumes of trees and shrubs, largely are unknown. Inventories of natural forests and woodlands in dryland regions, from which baseline information about growth rates and yields can be obtained, are lacking or incomplete. Mensurational techniques and sampling methods for these inventories often are not developed fully, and areal delineations of these natural formations remain a task to be completed, in many instances. Better information about yields is needed.

Some measures of yields are available, however. In reference to the southwestern United States and northern Mexico, the yields in pinyon-juniper woodlands vary considerably, ranging from less than 2 to nearly 100 m³/ha (Conner et al. 1990, Everett 1987, Ffolliott 1989). Extrapolating average values to a total area basis, these pinyon-juniper woodlands are estimated to contain 1.45×10^9 m³ of standing volume. Yields are from less than 2 to about 65 m³/ha in oak woodlands.

Example 14.1

Mesquite: A Woodland Type in the Southwestern United States (Conner et al. 1990) Mesquite (*Prosopis juliflora*) is classified primarily as a component of the desert-shrub ecosystem in the region. However, it is a recognized woodland type on flood plains, where the species can form dense communities of sizable trees. On these sites, mesquite attains "product" size of 10 m in height and 30–45 cm in diameter and, as such, can be a valuable commodity. Trends toward increasing wood utilization in the southwestern United States dictate a need for more information about this potential emerging resource.

The USDA Forest Service estimated that mesquite, as a woodland type in Arizona, occupied nearly 514,000 ha in 1985. In excess of 4,225,000 m^3 of net volume was located on these lands, with over 95 percent of this volume on "high site" lands capable of producing fuelwood on a sustainable basis. Net annual growth was estimated to be 178,350 m^3.

However, extrapolation is difficult, largely because of insufficient knowledge of the extent of oak woodlands in northern Mexico. Estimates of yields in *Prosopis juliflora* stands are difficult to obtain because of a lack of adequate inventory data (Example 14.1).

BASIC MANAGEMENT CONCEPTS

As mentioned above, either even-aged or uneven-aged management is selected as a managerial basis in natural forests and woodlands in dryland regions. The principles and applications of even-aged management are related, in many respects, to those followed generally in management of forest plantations. A different situation exists in reference to uneven-aged management, however, where knowledge and experiences are limited even more. Most of the experience in uneven-aged management of natural forests and woodlands has been obtained in stands of irregular structures that have evolved from earlier removals of desirable tree and shrub species. It is likely, therefore, that these stands subsequently do not express the "full capacities" of the site in question for a period of time.

In actuality, it frequently is immaterial as to whether even-aged or uneven-aged management systems yield the most wood for harvesting. The management practices used in specific cases are dictated by the local demands for wood, managerial objectives to meet these demands, and biological constraints to sustainable production and conservation. Of particular importance in formulating uneven-aged management practices for natural forests and woodlands in dryland regions are the protection strategies, the silvicultural practices and treatments, and the time of harvesting.

Protection Strategies

Protection strategies for natural forests and woodlands in dryland regions are similar to those for forest plantations. However, the risks that are associated with protecting *monocultures*, the composition and structure of many forest plantations, are lessened considerably in these natural ecosystems, largely because of the frequently encountered mixtures of tree and shrubs species of different age classes. Nevertheless, repeated occurrences of fire, diseases, and insect infestations in natural forests or woodlands, which often are proportional to the degree of misuse, can result in serious losses.

The use of fungicides or insecticides to control diseases and insects requires considerable care. These chemicals can be more damaging to the environment than the pests being controlled. When large-scale fires or epidemics occur, there is little practical control other than to remove and, if possible, utilize the killed, diseased, or infested trees and shrubs.

Extensive areas of natural forests and woodlands continue to be subjected to removals of trees and shrubs for wood products, fire to improve forage production, and clearings for agricultural crop production. It is important, therefore, that preventive and protective measures against these actions also become part of management plans for those forests and woodlands so affected if these ecosystems are to be retained in the landscape. In some instances, it becomes necessary to issue governmental decrees to protect tree or shrub species from possible extinction. One example of this complete protection is the case of *Prosopis tamarugo* and *P. atamensis* in northern Peru (FAO 1989b).

Silvicultural Treatments

Few silvicultural treatments are incorporated into management of natural forests and woodlands in dryland regions. The information necessary for these silvicultural prescriptions usually is insufficient. Specified coppicing cycles in Pakistan and the *depressage de chene vert* in Morocco represent two examples of silvicultural treatments that are found, but such examples are rare (FAO 1989b). Nevertheless, silvicultural treatments must be considered in improving the production of these forests and woodlands on a sustainable basis.

As a starting point in considering the roles of silviculture, some definitions are in order. A distinction is made in European-North American silviculture between *reproductive methods* and *silvicultural systems*. Reproductive methods are orderly ways by which forests or woodlands are established or renewed (Daniel et al. 1979, Lorimer 1990, Smith 1986). Silvicultural systems are more comprehensive in scope, including applications of intermediate cuttings throughout the rotational cycle of a forest or woodland.

Reproductive Methods   Two broad categories of reproductive methods are recognized, *natural reproductive methods* and *artificial reproductive methods*. The purpose of this chapter is to consider natural reproductive methods. Artificial reproductive methods were discussed in the chapters on the establishment and management of forest plantations. A number of natural reproductive methods are recognized in forestry (Daniel et al. 1979, Lorimer 1990, Smith 1986), some of which are applicable to some of the natural forests and woodlands in dryland regions. These natural reproductive methods include:

- High forest methods—producing forests or woodlands from seed.
- Even-aged stands—age class differential is less than 10–20 years.
- Clearcutting methods—removal of entire stand in one cutting, with reproduction obtained naturally or, when natural regeneration is not possible, artificially.
- Seed tree methods—removal of mature trees in one cutting, except for a specified number of seed trees left singly or in small groups to provide required seed.
- Shelterwood methods—removal of mature trees in a series of cuttings extending over a relatively short time period, by means of which establishment of essentially even-aged reproduction, under partial shade of seed trees, is obtained. (An area can receive two or more harvests before the overstory is removed completely.)
- Uneven-aged stands—age class differential in stands is 20 years or more.
- Selection methods—removal of trees, usually the largest or oldest trees, either as single scattered individuals or in small groups, repeated indefinitely, by means of which continuous establishment of reproduction is encouraged and uneven-aged stand structures are maintained.
- Low or coppice forest methods—producing forests or woodlands by vegetative regeneration.
- Coppice methods—a type of cutting in which dependence is placed mainly on vegetative reproduction, for example, by stump-sprouts or root-sprouts.
- Coppice-with-standards methods—production of coppice and high forests on the same site, with trees or shrubs originating from seed origin being "carried through" a much longer time than those of vegetative origin.
- Pollarding—a modification of coppice methods, used commonly in dryland regions, where branches of trees or shrubs are cut to produce sprouts at the top of "very high" stumps.

There are many variations and combinations of natural reproductive methods, especially when these methods are applied in dryland regions. In selecting a method for implementation, therefore, foresters must consider the origin of reproduction that is possible to obtain from seed or vegetatively and the arrangements of the cuttings to be imposed in time and space.

Intermediate Cuttings Cultural treatments can include *intermediate cuttings* that either eliminate or suppress vegetation that impairs growth of residual trees or

shrubs or are designed to achieve prescribed spacing patterns. Six types of intermediate cuttings generally are recognized (FAO 1989a, Lorimer 1990, Smith
1986):

- *Weedings or cleanings*—cuttings that are made to free "crop" trees or
  shrubs not past the sapling stage in growth from undesirable competing
  vegetation of the same stage that overtop them or are likely to do so in the
  future.
- *Liberation cuttings*—cuttings made to free immature stands of trees or
  shrubs not past the sapling stage from competition of older, overtopping
  trees and shrubs.
- *Thinnings*—cuttings made in immature stands of trees or shrubs to stimulate
  growth rates of trees or shrubs that remain and increase total production of
  the stand.
- *Improvement cuttings*—cuttings made in stands of trees or shrubs that are
  past sapling stage for the purpose of improving composition and quality by
  removing trees and shrubs of undesirable species, form, or vigor.
- *Salvage cuttings*—cuttings made to remove trees or shrubs damaged or
  killed by fire, insects, or diseases. When cuttings are made to prevent
  spread of insects or diseases from damaged trees or shrubs, these cuttings
  are called *sanitation cuttings*.
- *Prunings*—cuttings of branchwood on standing trees or shrubs to increase
  the quality of wood that ultimately will be produced.

Although commonly prescribed in commercial forests of the more temperate
and moist tropical environments, intermediate cuttings frequently cannot be justified economically in dryland regions, even though these cuttings ultimately might
increase the volume of wood produced. Nevertheless, it is conceivable that intermediate cuttings and other cultural treatments will be considered in future management plans, with increasing interest in more intensive management of natural
forests and woodlands in dryland regions.

Other Cultural Treatments   Site preparation, including the use of fire to create a
"favorable" seedbed for natural regeneration, applications of fertilizers, and periodical waterings of trees and shrubs often are employed in the intensive management of forest plantations (FAO 1989a). However, the cultural treatments are not
common in natural forests and woodlands in dryland regions. The investments
involved in the use of these treatments usually preclude their large-scale use,
although adaptations in applications, with a view to increasing productivities, can
be warranted in some instances.

Time of Harvesting

The time of harvesting the trees or shrubs in even-aged stands that are managed
primarily for wood production is based upon *rotational periods*. As mentioned in

Chapter 12, foresters often use average annual growth rates to guide themselves in determining the rotational periods of forest plantations. A similar approach is followed in estimating time of harvesting even-aged stands in natural forests and woodlands. In general, the trees or shrubs should not be allowed to grow beyond the point where average annual growth rates are maximized. Other factors also must be considered in estimating time of harvesting, for example, maximizing profits from harvesting of wood or minimizing potential risks of disease or insect infestations that are incurred when trees and shrubs increase in age.

Estimating the time of harvesting is more complicated in uneven-aged stands, however, because of the common occurrences of more than one species of different ages and, therefore, sizes. When trees or shrubs of one species, age, and size should be harvested, other trees or shrubs often should not. There are three interrelated factors that must be taken into account in estimating the time of harvesting under uneven-aged management (Gibbs 1977, Leuschner et al. 1990). These factors are:

- Size of trees or shrubs to be grown, recognizing the fact that trees and shrubs of different species and age classes frequently occur together.
- Residual volume of trees or shrubs, referred to as the *growing stock*, that must be maintained to provide adequate growth rates and yields in the future.
- Structure of stands necessary to provide opportunities for recurring natural regeneration and, subsequently, orderly growth and development of smaller trees or shrubs to replace those to be harvested.

Continuous inventories of trees and shrubs are necessary in evaluating these factors. Inventories of trees or shrubs in uneven-aged stands should be more frequent and more detailed than those in even-aged stands because of the greater complexities of uneven-aged structures.

IMPROVED MANAGEMENT OF NATURAL FORESTS AND WOODLANDS

The difficult conditions that confront people in dryland environments necessitate a renewable resource base to meet the requirements of life. It is important, therefore, to improve management of natural forests and woodlands to achieve sustainable production and conservation of these fragile natural ecosystems. The issues that should be addressed for this purpose can be grouped into three general categories: *production, utilization, and processing*; *conservation and restoration*; and *policy-making, institutional, and socioeconomic considerations* (FAO 1985, FAO 1989b, Salem 1988). Some of these issues are presented below.

Production, Utilization, and Processing

One of the more critical issues for improved management of natural forests and woodlands is obtaining baseline information about growth rates and yields of indigenous trees and shrubs from comprehensive, countrywide inventories. A significant challenge is specification of rotational cycles, which requires the knowledge of growth rates. Unfortunately, annual growth rates of natural forests and woodlands in dryland regions can be difficult to measure, resulting in problems in the determination of rotational cycles. It is difficult, if not impossible, to manage natural forests and woodlands for sustainable production and conservation in the absence of specified rotational periods.

Improved silvicultural treatments also are necessary to attain "optimal" production of natural forests and woodlands, regardless of the management goals (Example 14.2). As mentioned earlier, it is difficult and often inappropriate to extrapolate silvicultural treatments from temperate and humid forest ecosystems to dryland regions in the absence of rigorous testings and without extensive modifications. A priority is the improvement of natural regenerative methods, including the identifications of "superior" trees and shrubs for retention as seed sources, determinations of natural seeding cycles, and intervals of environmental conditions favorable to germination and initial survival of native tree and shrub seedlings. Soil-site quality analyses are needed to identify areas in which probabilities of obtaining successful regeneration are highest.

Efforts to genetically improve native tree and shrub species are needed to obtain drought-resistant, high-quality plants. Attention to indigenous nitrogen-fixing trees and shrubs is suggested. Among the factors that indicate potentials for improvement are relatively short seed-to-seed cycles, often less than 2 years. Many

---

Example 14.2

Improvement of Silvicultural Treatments in the Pinyon-Juniper Woodlands of the Southwestern United States (Gottfried 1992) Pinyon-juniper woodlands occur over large areas of North America, from Mexico to Canada and from California to Texas. Historically, these woodlands have been misused, largely because of inadequate managerial guidelines. Significant management problems are identifying and classifying productive woodland sites, understanding woodland ecology, and prescribing proper management for sustained productivity (Everett 1987). Land managers and scientists alike have recognized the need to improve their knowledge of pinyon-juniper woodlands and their management.

In response to the above, the Rocky Mountain Forest and Range Experiment Station, USDA Forest Service, is attempting to fill information gaps by conducting simultaneous studies concerned with silvics and silviculture. Investigations also are made of woodland mensuration, livestock and wildlife management, and watershed protection. Managers are developing silvicultural prescriptions to sustain wood production in pinyon-juniper woodlands, while benefiting livestock, wildlife, and watershed values from the results of this integrated research approach.

---

nitrogen-fixing plants are self-sterile and highly variable genetically, and hybridization can occur readily, allowing wide crossing and exploitation of tracts such as vigor and resistance to diseases. Indigenous nitrogen-fixing trees and shrubs commonly have multiple uses, such as providing wood, fodder, food, shade, and green manure. Nitrogen-fixing plants also are easily propagated vegetatively and grow rapidly in relatively short rotational periods.

Analyses of available technologies for agroforestry production systems involving trees and shrubs indigenous to dryland regions and agricultural crop and livestock production is necessary. The potential products from these trees and shrubs in agroforestry include wood, fodder, food, and mulching materials for agricultural crop production (Vanderbeldt 1990, Nair 1989, Rocheleau et al. 1988). However, further research is needed to more fully realize potentials for these products. Studies of compatibility among native tree and shrub species, agricultural crops, and forage plants are required to attain full potentials of agroforestry in dryland regions. The performances of native, multipurpose trees and shrubs need to be catalogued by species and use to provide, for example, fuelwood, fodder, or fruit production.

Studies are needed to determine physical properties of wood to efficiently process and utilize trees and shrubs from natural forests and woodlands. The opportunities for utilizing tree and shrub species from dryland regions, and generally elsewhere, depend largely upon wood densities, mechanical strengths, shrinkage characteristics, and visual features, including texture and color. This information is available for major woodland tree species in the southwestern United States and northern Mexico (Barger and Ffolliott 1972, Maingi and Ffolliott 1992). Increased use of harvesting and processing residues is proposed to enhance availability of wood resources. The potential uses of leaves, flowers, and other plant parts should be determined. Promotion of small-scale cottage industries is needed to enhance the economic status of local people in dryland regions.

Conservation and Restoration

Natural forests and woodlands play an important role in controlling soil erosion, in providing soil and water conservation, and in land restoration and revegetation. Investigative efforts designed to determine values of indigenous trees and shrubs in sand dune stabilization should be undertaken. Developments of appropriate silvicultural systems and management practices for long-term protection and, where possible, profitable use of rehabilitated sand dune formations also are required. Use of native trees and shrubs in stabilization of streambanks and other sites potentially eroded by flowing water must be explored in more detail.

Further studies are needed into the protective roles of native trees and shrubs in soil and water conservation. The ecological and managerial needs in riparian areas are other topics for intensive studies. Integrated management of natural forests and woodlands on critical watersheds also is necessary to ensure environmental stability. Watershed management practices in dryland regions largely include protecting fragile sites, increasing available water supplies, and rehabilitating landscapes (Brooks et al. 1991). In most instances, these practices are linked intrinsically to forestry-related activities.

Sites to demonstrate managerial techniques for rehabilitation and restoration of natural forests and woodlands, when needed, should be established at village levels. It is suggested that these demonstrations include appropriate combinations of forestry, livestock, agricultural production, and industrial activities, with the details to be specified locally. Because of the frequently encountered problems of waterlogging and salt-affected lands, it is imperative that representative demonstrations be established on these latter sites.

Policy-making, Institutional, and Socioeconomic Considerations

The third category of issues calls for actions in guiding policy formulations, strengthening forestry administration, education and training, information and extension services, and strategies for increasing the levels of investment. The implemental details of these proposals relate largely to in-country policies and the institutions affected. In terms of education and training, and information and extension services, however, the following points warrant attention.

The desirable levels of education and training in a country need to be recognized. Following this, curricula must be structured at different levels, with the emphasis on problems in sustainable production and conservation of natural forests and woodlands. Strengthening or, where necessary, establishment of schools and training centers in forestry at the identified levels is recommended. The integration of education and training in forestry at professional levels on a regional basis is proposed to efficiently accomplish these tasks.

Seminars and workshops about forestry topics of common interest and concern should be organized at national and regional levels. Publications of the resultant proceedings, pamphlets, and other informational documents are encouraged. Responsible personnel must be kept abreast of technological progress in forestry-related development of natural forests and woodlands in dryland regions. Specified informational and extension services, including the training of staff and provisions for needed materials and equipment, should be strengthened to attain the hoped for success.

THE FUTURE

After they have been formulated for an area, the appropriate management practices for natural forests and woodlands in dryland regions should be implemented initially on a small-scale and then increasing the areas of management with increasing managerial experience. Implementation of management practices also should be initiated near metropolitan centers, where pressures placed on these fragile ecosystems for production, protection, and amenities often is greatest. Inventories and applied studies on effects of alternative management practices on wood, forage, and water production, and rehabilitative technologies are important.

In general, the problems of implementing management practices are essentially of a social nature, which likely can be solved only through appropriately structured demonstrations, educational and training activities, and extension efforts.

SUMMARY

In the past, the natural forests and woodlands in the dryland regions of the world have been "mined" more than "managed" and, as a result, management prescriptions for sustainable development are incomplete. It is important, therefore, that the remaining natural forests and woodlands be managed carefully to reduce the continuing depletions of growing stock. After you have read this chapter, you should be able to:

1. Discuss the regenerative opportunities, compositions and structures of stands, and growth rates and yields of natural forests and woodlands in relation to even-aged and uneven-aged structures.
2. Discuss the importance of protective strategies, silvicultural treatments, and time of harvesting for natural forests and woodlands.
3. Appreciate the issues to address for the improved management of natural forests and woodlands, specifically in reference to production, utilization, and processing; conservation and restoration; and policy-making, institutional, and socioeconomic considerations.

REFERENCES

Barger, R. L., and P. F. Ffolliott, 1972. Physical characteristics and utilization of major woodland tree species in Arizona. *USDA Forest Service, Research Paper* RM-83.

Brooks, K. N., P. F. Ffolliott, H. M. Gregersen, and J. L. Thames. 1991. *Hydrology and the management of watersheds.* Iowa State University Press, Ames, Iowa.

Clutter, J. L., J. C. Fortson, L. V. Pienaar, G. H. Brister, and R. L. Bailey. 1983. *Timber management: A quantitative approach.* John Wiley & Sons, Inc., New York.

Conner, R. C., J. D. Born, A. W. Green, and R. A. O'Brien. 1990. Forest resources of Arizona. *USDA Forest Service, Resource Bulletin* INT-69.

Daniel, T. W., J. A. Helms, and F. S. Baker. 1979. *Principles of silviculture.* McGraw-Hill Book Company, New York.

Everett, R. L. (compiler). 1987. Proceedings—pinyon-juniper conference. *USDA Forest Service, General Technical Report*, INT-215.

FAO. 1985. *Arid zone forestry programs: State of knowledge and experience: An overview.* FAO, Rome.

FAO. 1989a. Arid zone forestry: A guide for field technicians. *FAO Conservation Guide* 20, Rome.

FAO. 1989b. Role of forestry in combating desertification. *FAO Conservation Guide* 21, Rome.

Ffolliott, P. F. 1989. Arid zone forestry program: State of knowledge and experience in North America. *Arizona Agricultural Experiment Station, Technical Bulletin* 264, Tucson, Arizona.

Ford-Robertson, F. C. (ed.). 1983. *Terminology of forest science, technology, practices and products.* Society of American Foresters, Washington, D. C.

Gibbs, C. B. 1977. Uneven-aged silviculture and management? Even-aged silviculture and management? Definitions and differences. In USDA Forest Service. 1977. *Uneven-aged silviculture and management in the western United States.* USDA Forest Service, Washington, D.C., pp. 12–19.

Gottfried, G. J. 1992. Ecology and management of the southwestern pinyon-juniper woodlands. In Ffolliott, P. F., G. J. Gottfried, D. A. Bennett, V. M. Hernandez, A. Ortega, and R. H. Hamre (technical coordinators). 1992. Ecology and management of oak and associated woodlands: Perspectives in the southwestern United States and northern Mexico. *USDA Forest Service, General Technical Report* RM 218, pp. 78–86.

Leuschner, W. A., H. W. Wisdom, and W. D. Klemperer. 1990. Timber management. In Young, R. A., and R. L. Giese (eds.). 1990. *Introduction to forest science.* John Wiley & Sons, Inc., New York, pp. 326–39.

Lorimer, C. G. 1990. Silviculture. 1990. In Young, R. A., and R. L. Giese (eds.). 1990. *Introduction to forest sciences.* John Wiley & Sons, Inc., New York, pp. 300–25.

Maingi, J. K., and P. F. Ffolliott. 1992. Specific gravity and estimates of physical properties of Emory oak in southeastern Arizona. In Ffolliott, P. F., G. J. Gottfried, D. A. Bennett, V. M. Hernandez, A. Ortega, and R. H. Hamre (technical coordinators). 1992. Ecology and management of oak and associated woodlands: Perspectives in the southwestern United States and northern Mexico. *USDA Forest Service, General Technical Report* RM-218, pp. 147–49.

Nair, P. K. R. 1989. *Agroforestry in the tropics.* Kluwer Academic Publishers, Boston.

Rocheleau, D., F. Weber, and A. Field-Juma. 1988. *Agroforestry in dryland Africa.* International Council for Research in Agroforestry, Nairobi, Kenya.

Salem, B. B. 1988. A strategy on the role of forestry in combating desertification. In Whitehead, E. F., C. F. Hutchinson, B. N. Timmermann, and R. G. Varady (eds.). 1988. *Arid lands: Today and tomorrow.* Westview Press, Boulder, Colorado, pp. 841–49.

Smith, D. M. 1986. *The practice of silviculture.* John Wiley & Sons, Inc., New York.

Vanderbeldt, R. J. 1990. Agroforestry in the semiarid tropics. In MacDicken, K. G., and N. T. Vergara (eds.). 1990. *Agroforestry classification and management.* John Wiley & Sons, Inc., New York, pp. 150–94.

PART IV
Special Topics

15 Fuelwood Production

Demands for fuelwood are increasing throughout the world. Many households and, in some cases, entire communities, are entirely dependent upon wood for cooking, heating, or both. With these increasing demands for fuelwood, natural forests and woodlands and forest plantations often are managed improperly for fuelwood production. Frequent and continuous harvesting of fuelwood can result in soil compaction, soil erosion by both water and wind, and depletions in nutrients and organic materials. The environmental consequences of these effects include the dislodging of plant, animal, and human populations; the degrading of soils and site productivities; and the reducing of biological diversities of indigenous species.

The establishment and management of forest plantations and the management of natural forests and woodlands for sustainable production and conservation were the topics, in general, of earlier chapters in this book. Here, we will enlarge upon these general discussions of forest management practices, specifically in reference to use of these ecosystems for production and utilization of fuelwood. To achieve sustainability, it is important to understand the role of fuelwood in meeting people's energy requirements, the advantages and disadvantages of fuelwood management in different ecosystems, and the biological and socioeconomic considerations in implementing environmentally sound fuelwood management practices.

ROLE OF FUELWOOD IN ENERGY REQUIREMENTS

Fossil fuels, natural gas, geothermal sources, and uranium account for approximately 95 percent of the energy production on a worldwide basis. This fact is misleading, though, in that more than one-third of the world's population depends upon fuelwood for cooking, heating, or both (FAO 1986, Jacobson and Price 1991, Smith 1982). Consequently, the levels of fuelwood consumption are high in many countries (Example 15.1). However, the consumption of fuelwood per inhabitant and the percentage of the total energy demanded that is represented by fuelwood differ greatly among countries of the world.

The use of wood for energy purposes has many environmental and socioeconomic implications, and raises technical questions concerning growth, management, harvesting, and subsequent regeneration of the trees and shrubs utilized for energy purposes. Nevertheless, wood can be utilized effectively and efficiently as a source of energy through carefully formulated fuelwood management practices.

Example 15.1

Fuelwood Consumption in the Sahelian Region of West Africa (Anderson and Fishwick 1984, Eckholm et al. 1984)   In the Sahelian region, between 75 and 85 percent of the energy needs are satisfied by fuelwood, placing intense pressures on the limited fuelwood resources. In many instances, people spend several days collecting fuelwood that frequently lasts less than 1 week. Fuelwood gathering around the larger cities has created extensive deforestation. Fuelwood must be transported from more than 100 km around some of these cities. Up to one-fourth of an average family's income can be spent on obtaining the required fuelwood for cooking and heating. It is likely, therefore, that, in many instances, more energy is used in gathering fuelwood than is obtained in the combustion of the fuelwood.

ADVANTAGES OF WOOD AS A SOURCE OF ENERGY

It is likely in the future that more people throughout the world will become dependent upon fuelwood for energy. When properly managed, the use of wood as a source of energy has advantages over other sources of energy, including the following (Boyce 1979, FAO 1984, NAS 1976, Smith 1982):

- It is dependable and renewable.
- With appropriate planning, an "even spread" of development activities can be achieved through the planting of fuelwood crops on marginal lands.
- Through management of fuelwood resources, employment opportunities are increased in rural areas, which generally are closer to forests and woodlands.

People throughout the world, therefore, can gain from proper utilization of fuelwood resources and other forest biomass for energy purposes. However, environmentally sound planning is necessary to achieve these gains. An understanding of the dynamics of forests, woodlands, and plantations in converting solar inputs into energy storehouses is important to this planning effort. Converting wood into energy for human use also requires an energy input, the latter being human efforts or the use of other types of fuels to obtain wood for conversion. In an energy balance calculation, this energy input should be subtracted from the total energy that is stored in a forest, woodland, or plantation to determine the net energy gain through fuelwood utilization. The situations in which a net energy gain is anticipated should be stressed in fuelwood management.

Some ecosystems in which fuelwood is produced require energy inputs only at the time of fuelwood harvesting and during its transportation to places of combustion. Other more intensively managed ecosystems require continuous energy inputs from the beginning to the end of a rotational cycle. In all likelihood, energy also is needed in the harvesting, transporting, and, if necessary, processing of fuelwood crops. To plan environmentally sound fuelwood management practices that produce a net energy gain, therefore, a forester and the local people should recognize the relative advantages and disadvantages associated with fuelwood production in natural forests and woodlands, forest plantations, and agroforestry systems (Boyce 1979, Ffolliott and Thames 1983).

Natural Forests and Woodlands

Natural forests and woodlands usually have a mixture of indigenous tree and shrub species of varying ages and sizes growing on a relatively large area. In reference to yielding fuelwood and other biomass for energy, these ecosystems have several advantages, including:

- People need to invest only little energy in establishment of the forest or woodland, since the ecosystem regenerates itself naturally.
- Less energy usually is needed to maintain a sustainable forest or woodland in an "acceptable" growing condition.
- Net energy production can be relatively high, particularly in young stands.

However, there are disadvantages in managing natural forests and woodlands of multiple tree and shrub species and age classes for fuelwood. Included among the disadvantages:

- Little information may be available to describe growth rates of all of the tree and shrub species and age classes throughout a rotational cycle.
- Management is relatively complex and silvicultural treatments and managerial techniques are developed only partially in many areas.
- Harvesting of trees and shrubs for fuelwood and other wood products in an environmentally sound manner often is difficult.
- Reproduction of shade-tolerant species, which frequently are found in natural forests and woodlands, can present a problem.
- A relatively large energy investment of human resources generally occurs at the end of a rotational cycle, primarily for harvesting, transporting, and processing the fuelwood crop.

Forest Plantations

Forest plantations, either rainfed or irrigated, usually consist of one-aged blocks of a single tree or shrub species planted in specified spacing patterns. These ecosystems can be attractive as a source of biomass for energy because:

- Management often can be prescribed relatively precisely and, as a consequence, can be carried out by skilled workers.
- Tree or shrub growth over a rotational cycle generally can be forecast more accurately than in natural forests and woodlands. Rotational lengths often can be adjusted to provide optimum fuelwood production to meet specified energy needs.
- In many situations, net energy production is greater than is the case for natural forests and woodlands.
- Management and utilization can be mechanized more easily than in natural forests or woodlands.
- Management of forest plantations often is founded on a history of research. Fortunately, there is an increasing body of information about the management of these ecosystems in the dryland regions of the world.

Nevertheless, questions about the use of forest plantations as a source of fuelwood on a sustainable basis also arise, mainly from the following concerns:

- Forest plantations can present a greater risk of loss to fire, insects, and disease and loss of soil fertility because of their tendency to be monocultures.
- Wildlife habitats and recreational values can be diminished.
- There often is a relatively large investment of money and energy in the establishment and maintenance of forest plantations.
- Once planted, options for alternative land and resource uses can be restricted.
- Relatively large investments of human energy are required to manage throughout rotational cycles and to harvest, transport, and process the fuelwood crop.

Agroforestry Systems

Growing trees and shrubs with agricultural crops and, at times, livestock is *agroforestry*, a topic to be discussed in the following chapter. Trees and shrubs that are grown in many agroforestry systems also are harvested as fuelwood (MacDicken and Vergara 1990, Nair 1989). Examples of advantages of fuelwood production in agroforestry systems include:

- Tree and shrub species used in agroforestry frequently are either self-regenerating or readily available for planting.
- Maintenance and protection costs usually are minimal.
- Energy outputs can be "profitable" at the village level, even for a single family.

- No major investments of money normally are needed. Harvesting and transportation costs are small.
- Multiple benefits are achieved.

However, there can be disadvantages to obtaining fuelwood from trees and shrubs in agroforestry systems, including:

- Planting of trees or shrubs in proximity to agricultural crops or forage plants can reduce the yields and qualities of all crops in some cases.
- Harvesting of trees or shrubs for fuelwood can be difficult, depending upon the stage of development of the agricultural crops or forage plants.
- Soil fertility can be reduced, particularly in "slash-and-burn" situations.

It can be seen that a series of energy inputs and outputs need to be identified in evaluating fuelwood potentials, regardless of whether a forest, woodland, or plantation is the fuelwood production system. The major energy input and output components of a fuelwood production system are listed in Table 15.1. These components, in theory, can be estimated quantitatively and used as a summary balance sheet for decision-making purposes, as suggested by the format in Table 15.2.

BIOLOGICAL CONSIDERATIONS IN FUELWOOD MANAGEMENT

It is important to consider the selection of trees and shrubs for fuelwood, the appropriate silvicultural practices to apply, the growth and yield of the fuelwood

TABLE 15.1. Major Energy Components of a Fuelwood Resource System

Capital	*Removal*
Trees and shrubs	Trees and shrubs
above ground	Herbaceous plants
below ground	Secondary producers
Other living organisms	*Changes in capital*
herbaceous plants	Trees and shrubs
animals	Other living organisms
Dead organic materials	Dead organic materials
Solar input	*Management costs*
Trees and shrubs	Establishment
above ground	Maintenance
below ground	Harvesting
Herbaceous plants	Transportation
Biological drain	Infrastructure
Decomposition	Administration
Conversion to secondary producers	

Source: Adapted from Boyce (1979).

TABLE 15.2. Format of a Summary Balance Sheet of Energy Components for Fuelwood Resource Systems

	Natural Forest or Woodland	Forest Plantation	Agroforests
Solar input[a]			
Management costs			
Establishment			
Maintenance			
Harvesting			
Transportation			
Processing			
Changes in capital			
Removal			

[a]A common energy unit for all of the energy components must be used in preparing this balance sheet. Calories per square meter per year is one constant applicable to all aspects of energy production and use. Conversion factors and appropriate formulas can be developed to convert available data, for example, hours of labor or costs per day, to this constant unit.
Source: Adapted from Boyce (1979).

resources, and the methods to be employed in the harvesting of fuelwood crops when planning fuelwood management practices. While some of these topics have been considered in a general context in earlier chapters, specifics in relation to fuelwood management are considered below.

Selection of Trees and Shrubs

Regeneration of indigenous woody plants dictates the tree and shrub species to be grown for fuelwood in natural forests or woodlands. In these situations, a forester may have little choice but to develop a management strategy with indigenous tree and shrub species in mind. Elsewhere, artificial regeneration through the planting of seedlings or vegetative plant sections can be required, in which case a selection of tree or shrub species must be made.

Attention must be given to the value of the wood as energy in selecting trees and shrubs for fuelwood. A practical indication of the energy value of wood is the density of the wood itself (Harris et al. 1986, Reineke 1960). The heavier the wood when it is dry, the greater is its heat content (Example 15.2). Woods of slower-growing tree and shrub species generally are denser than the wood of faster-growing species, which means that slower-growing species can produce wood of relatively high energy value.

The value of wood as fuel also is dependent upon its moisture content, because energy is used in evaporating moisture in the wood (Harris et al. 1986). Fast, natu-

Example 15.2

Heat Content of Woodland Tree Species in the Southwestern United States (Barger and Ffolliott 1972, Reineke 1960) Heat content of wood is proportional to the density of wood. Laboratory tests have shown that *gross* heat contents of a kilogram of oven-dry wood are approximately 4.08×10^6 joules (J) for nonresinous species and 4.34×10^6 J for resinous species. *Net* heat per kilogram amounts to approximately 3.44×10^6 and 3.70×10^6 J, respectively. The following are estimates of the gross heat contents of major woodland tree species in the southwestern United States:

Species	J/m^3
Pinyon (*Pinus edulis*)	3.967×10^{12}
Utah juniper (*Juniperus osteosperma*)	3.762×10^{12}
Alligator juniper (*J. deppeana*)	3.336×10^{12}
Gambel oak (*Quercus gambelii*)	4.668×10^{12}

Comparative values such as those presented above are helpful in determining the potentials of tree and shrub species for fuelwood in a region.

ral drying ability of wood can be important when it is possible to dry the wood before it is used. However, too often, fuelwood in short supply will be burned soon after harvesting. Wood that burns well, even with a high moisture content, has a clear advantage. The resins found in coniferous wood, and oils and gums found in hardwoods enhance the heat given off. A slow rate of burning is preferred for cooking and heating purposes, a characteristic possessed by many high-density woods.

Fuelwood should be easy to handle, free from thorns, and easy to cut. When burned, heavy smoke or odor that affects the taste of food may not be desired. An exception is where the intention is to smoke meat or to control the occurrence of insects. The sparks from burning wood are regarded as a nuisance by many people.

There are desirable characteristics that should be stressed in choosing tree or shrub species for fuelwood. Although the question of what species should be grown is best answered on a local basis, desirable characteristics include:

- A relatively high wood density value and, as a consequence, a potentially high energy yield should be favored whenever possible.
- A relatively short rotational cycle is often an objective of fuelwood management, requiring the selection of an easily established and rapidly growing tree or shrub species. Species that resprout from stumps are favored in some situations, sparing the grower the need for replanting.

- Production of wood for energy is sometimes a secondary objective of a development activity. With some species of *Prosopis* and *Acacia*, for example, branches are harvested for fuelwood, although the trees or shrubs themselves are used as live fencing, to provide fodder, or to fix nitrogen in the soil.

It is beyond the scope of this chapter to identify all of the tree and shrub species that might be fuelwood resources in particular dryland regions of the world. However, some of the more important tree and shrub species commonly used for fuelwood are listed in Appendix II. Other tree and shrub species suitable for fuelwood are found in the literature (NAS 1980, 1983, Weber 1986).

Silvicultural Treatments

In considering silvicultural treatments for the management of fuelwood resources, foresters frequently extrapolate "traditional" silvicultural treatments commonly employed in "commercial" forestry to fuelwood management. In other instances, innovative forms of silviculture are needed to manage fuelwood resources on a particular site.

Cultural treatments are required to promote the conditions that are favorable to the growth of trees and shrubs in a natural forest or woodland, or a forest plantation, as discussed elsewhere. In most instances, cultural treatments in fuelwood management, when warranted, are concerned with preventing the trees and shrubs from being suppressed by competing vegetation, attacked by pests, or lost to fire. Other cultural treatments are designed to achieve the desired spacings among the trees or shrubs through weedings and thinnings and to provide for periodical watering of the plants, when needed.

Growth and Yield

The growth and yield of a fuelwood species should be known at different intensities of management. In fuelwood management, this estimate often is based on interpretations of *yield tables*, which are tabular expressions of the expected volumes of wood in relation to age, site quality, and density of forests, woodlands, or plantations (Clutter et al. 1983, Curtis 1972). Yield tables for even-aged stands of trees or shrubs, which are common stand structures in fuelwood management, relate an estimate of per-unit-area volume of standing trees or shrubs to measures of age, site quality, and stand density, that is:

$$\text{Volume} = f(\text{Age, Site Quality, Density}) \qquad (15.1)$$

A forester uses yield tables to make estimates of the level of *current* volume of a fuelwood resource. Numerous examples of this application are found in the literature (Example 15.3). It becomes necessary to adjust "technical coefficients" to reflect local situations in many instances. To predict *future* yield of a fuelwood resource usually involves one of three different methods (Clutter et al. 1983, Curtis 1972):

- *Method (1)*—predict volume growth and then add this prediction to the estimate of current fuelwood volume.
- *Method (2)*—specify or predict values of input variables that represent the future and then solve the same yield table relationships that are used to estimate current yields.

Example 15.3

A Yield Table for Fuelwood Resources in Southeastern Arizona (Fowler 1990, Fowler and Ffolliott 1992)   One example of a yield table developed for a fuel-wood species is that derived to estimate volumes in the oak woodlands of southeastern Arizona. Emory oak (*Quercus emoryii*) is a preferred fuelwood species by local people in this region, largely because of its dense wood. An estimate of the volume of Emory oak can be obtained through solution of the following yield table equation:

$$\ln V = 1.25 - 8.83(A^{-1}) + 0.565(\ln SI) + 1.0(\ln BA)$$

where V = Volume of standing trees in cubic feet per acre
        A = Age of stand in years
        SI = Site index (Callison 1988)
        BA = Density in square feet of basal area per acre

Application of this yield table in estimating current yield, future yield, and growth is illustrated by the following example. From independent inventory data, it was determined that a stand of Emory oak is 25 years old, the site index is 15, and its current basal area is 15.9 ft^2 per acre. The current yield of this stand, estimated by solving the yield table equation in terms of these input variables, is 185 ft^3 per acre.

Future yield at age 40, for example, is estimated by changing the age variable accordingly, using the site index value of 15, as site index is considered to be a characteristic of the site, and adjusting the basal area value by solving a supplementary equation that relates future basal area values to the time of the projection period and the site index. These variables are used to solve the yield table equation once again, this time to estimate future yield. Future yield is 340 ft^3 per acre in this example.

Growth is expressed on an annual basis by dividing total growth by number of years in the projection period, in this case 15 years. Annual growth in this example is estimated to be about 10.5 ft^3 per acre.

- *Method (3)*—predict future volume directly, using current measures of age, site quality, and density, and the length of the selected projection period as predictor variables.

Methods (2) and (3) are employed more generally than Method (1) to predict future yields. Methods (2) and (3) are related in that a large number of equations used in Method (3) are obtained by incorporating *stand density projections* into an estimating equation for current yield. Whenever possible, emphasis generally is placed on the application of Method (2) in estimating growth and yield of fuelwood resources.

The values of input variables that will be present at the end of the projection period are either specified or predicted in applying Method (2). A forester then solves the same equation or set of equations that are used to estimate current volume. Two estimates of per-unit-area volume are derived as a result, one for current conditions and one for the future (Example 15.3). From these estimates, periodical annual growth is determined as follows:

$$pag = \frac{V_2 - V_1}{t} \qquad (15.2)$$

where pag = Periodical annual growth
V_2 = Volume in future
V_1 = Volume for current conditions
t = Time of projection period

In situations in which a yield table is not available for a particular fuelwood resource, one course of action is to use inventory procedures that estimate the future growth of a forest, woodland, or plantation from incremental measurements of past growth rates. In general, these estimation methods are referred to as *stand table projection* methods, of which there are many. The details about applications of these methods are found in references on forest mensurational techniques (Avery and Burkhart 1983, Husch et al. 1982).

Harvesting of Fuelwood Crops

Two important questions must be answered in planning the harvesting of fuelwood crops. When should harvesting take place, and what harvesting techniques should be specified? Only generalizations are presented here, as local rates of growth, demands for fuelwood, and available labor and types of equipment will provide the specific answers to these questions.

Time of Harvesting The time of harvesting fuelwood, when sustainable forest management is the sole basis for this decision, should be somewhere between the time required for the trees or shrubs to attain the minimum size locally acceptable for utilization and the point of maximum average annual growth. Foresters refer to the latter point as the "biological" rotational age, a concept presented in Chapter 12. The time of harvesting Emory oak (*Quercus emoryii*) sprouts for fuelwood in southeastern Arizona, for example, is illustrated in Figure 15.1.

Economic considerations also determine when to harvest trees or shrubs for fuelwood. When the decision to harvest is based only on market factors, the time to harvest is when the profit is maximized. Profit is maximized when the returns generated from harvesting fuelwood minus the costs of harvesting the fuelwood are the greatest. Other economic factors to consider in deciding when to harvest trees and shrubs for fuelwood include:

- *Local harvesting techniques*—labor-intensive techniques could limit handling of large trees and shrubs.
- *Available labor*—when labor must be allocated to other tasks, for example, the tending of agricultural crops, the extent of harvesting can be restricted.
- *Market outlets*—in large part, market outlets can dictate the kind of wood desired for fuel and, therefore, affect demands for particular tree and shrub species.

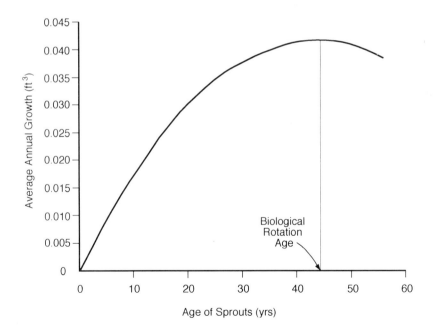

Figure 15.1. Time of harvesting Emory oak (*Quercus emoryii*) sprouts for fuelwood in southeastern Arizona (adapted from Touchan 1991)

Harvesting Techniques Harvesting of fuelwood on a large scale involves skill and the appropriate type of equipment. In general, fuelwood harvesting differs from commercial harvesting methods for lumber or pulpwood only if it alters the frequency, technique, or intensity of the harvest (Saucier 1980). Sequential tasks of harvesting fuelwood resources typically involve:

- Using axes, saws, wedges, and sledges, trees and shrubs are felled and cut into desired lengths for utilization. Occasionally, power chain saws are used for this purpose.
- Desired lengths of fuelwood are carried or pulled to a loading point.
- Fuelwood is loaded onto animals, wagons, or trucks and transported from the forest, woodland, or plantation to the marketplace, where it is unloaded and made available to consumers. Fuelwood also can be transported directly to a home or other points of use.

Dead wood is gathered from the ground for fuel in many dryland countries, with women and children frequently responsible for this task. It is common, therefore, that women and children are away from the house for extended periods of time while collecting fuelwood, often disrupting schedules of household activities (Anderson and Fishwick 1984, Boyce 1979, Wood et al. 1980). Considerable expenditure of human energy also is necessary in collecting the fuelwood. The large expenditures of energy required in gathering fuelwood and carrying it to its point of use can represent greater levels than obtained through combustion of the fuelwood.

SOCIOECONOMIC CONSIDERATIONS

Along with biological considerations, socioeconomic factors must be incorporated into fuelwood management plans. Included among these factors are the policy issues that place the management of fuelwood resources in developing countries and industrialized societies into perspective, the role of incentives in fuelwood management practices, and supply and demand comparisons of fuelwood resources.

Policy Issues

Emphasis and priorities for use of fuelwood for energy purposes vary greatly from country to country. A global view of energy sources conceals the significant differences between people in developing countries and in industrialized societies. The energy use per capita in India, for example, amounts to only one-thousandth of the energy consumption in the United States (Boyce 1979, Wood et al. 1980). More importantly, fuelwood provides about 60 percent of the total energy consumption in India and less than 5 percent in the United States. Wood will continue to be the primary energy source that satisfies the basic needs of cooking and heating in many of the developing countries in dryland regions.

Individual countries have developed unique, though possibly complementary, approaches to energy use that become necessary in view of the peculiarities of socioeconomic circumstances in each country. The approaches adopted by people in developing countries and industrialized societies generally are different, in degree, if not in kind, because of varying levels of technological development and industrial needs. Developing countries usually focus on the necessary use of fuelwood for cooking and heating purposes. However, approaches are determined largely by the fact that, in industrialized societies, the common source of energy is fossil fuels.

There is a difference between the degree of socioeconomic significance that fuelwood resources play in developing countries and in industrialized societies. In the former, fuelwood remains the primary, if not total, source of energy for cooking and heating. Fuelwood constitutes more than 90 percent of the total energy requirement in some cases (FAO 1986, Smith 1982, Wood et al. 1980). On the other hand, energy from wood to sustain economic development in industrialized societies is unlikely in the immediate future and, at best, likely to be only a supplementary source of energy. However, industrialized societies will continue to use large quantities of wood for purposes other than fuel. The changes affecting fuelwood resources, therefore, have more far-reaching effects in the socioeconomic milieu of developing countries than in industrialized societies.

Differences portrayed by developing countries and industrialized societies in relation to the importance of fuelwood resources are similar to differences between the rural and urban areas in many countries. Fuelwood is more important in meeting the energy requirements of people in rural areas of developing countries than it generally is in urban areas. Socioeconomic consequences and constraints on the use of forests, woodlands, and plantations for energy also are more important in rural areas than in urban areas, as witnessed by the fuelwood situations in the Sahelian region of West Africa (Anderson and Fishwick 1984, Falloux and Mukendi 1988). Rural people are less likely able to cope with limited fuelwood resources than people in urban areas, largely because the latter more commonly are in a position to locate substitutes for fuelwood.

Socioeconomic circumstances of development activities in general, and those of the use of forests and woodlands as a source of energy in particular, are being affected constantly by demographical changes in different parts of the world. As populations increase, the pressures on fuelwood resources also increase. A consequence of these changes is that natural forests and woodlands that are available for fuelwood extraction at one time might become inadequate at a later date simply because of increasing populations. The populations in developing countries have been increasing out of proportion to food, energy, and a large number of other resources in recent decades (World Resources Institute 1990). Furthermore, the technical skills of populations have been upgraded significantly through increasing educational opportunities in the last few decades, resulting in increased incomes for people who likely will substitute electricity or gas for fuelwood, whenever possible. There seems to be a correlation, in many countries, between income and upliftment status vis-à-vis the type of energy sources being utilized by people (Boyce 1979).

One other socioeconomic issue warrants consideration. Numerous technologies have been transferred, either consciously or inadvertently, from industrialized societies to developing countries. In many instances, applications of these technologies have led to environmental damage. To illustrate this point, in many developing countries, power saws have become available for people. These power saws and other mechanized harvesting methods provide users with an advantage in harvesting fuelwood resources efficiently but in a manner that can devastate environments in the absence of sound planning and careful administration. However, the consumption of goods, to which standards of living generally are equated, depends largely upon abundant supplies of energy. The dilemma, therefore, is to strike an acceptable balance among the availability of technologies, the increasing standards of living, and the maintenance of the qualities of fragile dryland environments.

Role of Incentives

One important socioeconomic issue that is frequently an integral part of the proper management and utilization of fuelwood resources on a sustainable basis is incentives. Of all of the technical, institutional, and political constraints to sustained fuelwood management, the lack of the necessary resources to undertake this management is the most commonly encountered limitation, especially in the case of rural settings in developing countries. These people often need some form of incentive to become partners in sustainable fuelwood management (Example 15.4).

Incentives to involve rural people in forestry practices in general will be considered in Chapter 20. In the case of making people partners in fuelwood management practices, incentives frequently are made available through governmental institutions, donor agencies, or combinations thereof. Examples of these incentives include:

- Cash payments for work accomplished.
- In-kind payments in the form of commodities that otherwise would have to be purchased in marketplaces, for example, "food for work" programs.
- Loans or "in-kind" payments that are repaid in the future.
- Credit in lieu of cash payments in the form of subsidies to be collected in the future, credit against payment of a tax, and so forth.
- Promise of future benefits, for example, accessibility to future market goods, assurances of future land tenure, and so forth.

Incentives are employed frequently as "trickle-down" benefits to people who are not capable of developing fuelwood resources themselves. One difficulty with

Example 15.4

Incentives for Establishment of "Energy Plantations" in India (Eckholm 1979, Wood et al. 1980)   People have become involved in raising, exploiting, and marketing fuelwood resources as part of the social forestry programs in Gujarat. In 1973, governmental forestry officers proposed to the panchayats, elected councils that govern villages in the state, that a village set aside a minimum of 4 ha for establishment of "energy plantations" on communal lands. If this proposal was agreed to, the local forestry officers would supply tree and shrub seedlings, technical assistance, and, through governmental allocations, pay poorer villagers to prepare sites for plantings and plant and maintain the trees and shrubs. Villagers would protect the plantations from grazing by livestock and unauthorized gathering of fuelwood.

The villagers were granted permission to harvest forage plants and fruit from the plantations free of charge. When it became time to harvest fuelwood, panchayats and the governmental forestry department would split the proceeds generated. Furthermore, the harvested fuelwood would be sold through governmental controlled depots at prices below those of common marketplaces, providing a competitive edge to the operations.

Use of cash for wages, in-kind payments in this case, seedlings that otherwise would have to be purchased, technical assistance, and a marketing advantage as incentives have proven to be successful in this program. One reason for the program's popularity with rural people was the "quick" returns it generates. It commonly is thought that forestry enterprises take too long to be attractive to poor villagers. This notion was disproved in Gujarat. Most of the communal lands planted with fuelwood species had been called "grazing lands" before establishment of the plantations, but in reality they were nothing more than "exercise grounds" that scarcely produced a blade of edible grass. Nevertheless, after one year of protection from livestock, forage plants that could be harvested manually became available on these same lands. Villagers suddenly were receiving economic benefits from areas that formerly were considered worthless. The planted fruit trees in the plantations began to produce in the second year. And, even in the absence of irrigation, most of the tree and shrub species planted grew quickly enough to convey an obvious message to rural people.

Discussions about improving environments and qualities of life do not always make sense to the rural poor. However, one exception was the establishment of an energy plantation in Gujarat. It did not require much time for "hardened realists" to recognize real benefits from this intervention materializing before their eyes, justifying the use of incentives.

incentives, however, is understanding clearly the requirements to be met to obtain the incentives. Additionally, the duration of time that the incentives are available to people often is unclear. The incentives sometimes make people dependent upon this form of external support. Prolonged issuance of incentives also can be a detriment to the implementation of other projects requiring the involvement of people. Therefore, these considerations must be kept in mind to be effective as a source of external support.

Supply and Demand Comparisons

Supply and demand comparisons are helpful in placing the perspectives that people may have of an available fuelwood resource into a context of sustainable production. However, it is impossible to describe in detail the supplies and demands for fuelwood in the world. Each region, country, and locale exhibits its own supply and demand functions, most of which are not well defined. To illustrate supplies and demands for fuelwood resources in qualitative perspectives, general comparisons for the southwestern United States and, in aggregate, the dryland regions of the world are presented below.

Southwestern United States Source data to describe the supply and demand functions for fuelwood resources in the southwestern United States are available only partially. However, with increasing interest in fuelwood as a source of energy since the early 1970s, efforts in obtaining necessary information about the supplies and demands have been made (Ffolliott et al. 1979, Olsen and Betters 1989, Sampson 1979). It is believed that the supplies of fuelwood will remain constant, or essentially so, in the near future. There is little reason to expect that these supplies, obtained mostly from natural forests and woodlands located on public lands, will increase in response to the higher prices for fuelwood being experienced. Furthermore, it is anticipated that demands for other products and amenities derived from these publicly owned lands will prevent significant increases in supplies.

It is likely that the "relatively strong" demands for fuelwood that have been experienced since the early 1970s will continue. Woody biomass contributes only 5 percent or less of the energy needs in the southwestern United States (Ffolliott et al. 1980). But, residential use of fuelwood for supplementary heating and cooking is increasing at the approximate rate of 10 percent annually.

With the above supply and demand situations, fuelwood markets in the southwestern United States are best characterized in terms of individuals attempting to enter into fuelwood business for short-term profit motives. (Large-scale fuelwood operators are not common in the region.) In all likelihood, therefore, individuals will operate in a manner to attain a short-term equilibrium between supply and demand points that largely control an individual's activities. This situation is a representation of short-term equilibrium with the supply fixed and, as a consequence, the prices for fuelwood increasing as demands continue to increase, as illustrated by Figure 15.2. It is not surprising, as a consequence, that fuelwood prices have

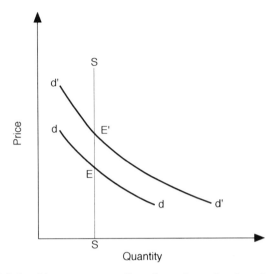

Figure 15.2. Relationships among supplies, demands, and prices for fuelwood in the southwestern United States (Interval between E and E^1 represents a price increase when supply (S) is fixed and demands increase from d to d^1.)

been increasing dramatically in the southwestern United States. These increasing prices frequently cause consumers to seek alternative energy sources.

Dryland Regions of the World   Information about the consumption of fuelwood for individual countries in the dryland regions of the world is fragmented and limited. As a consequence, the aggregations of consumption for regions are unreliable and, therefore, only general statements on supplies and demands can be presented (Example 15.5). Nevertheless, these statements provide insights into critical fuelwood scarcities that confront many developing countries in the dryland regions.

The extent of natural forests and woodlands in the dryland regions has been estimated by country in terms of *closed* and *open* forest structures (World Resources Institute 1990). Closed forests are those in which the trees and shrubs cover more than 20 percent of the ground, while open forests consist of mixtures of trees, shrubs, and grasslands, with from 5 to 20 percent in tree and shrub cover. Many of the natural forests and woodlands in dryland regions fall into the second category. However, it is difficult to translate these estimates of extent into estimates of fuelwood volumes, largely because baseline inventories of the fuelwood resources are incomplete.

Classifications of trees and shrubs as fuelwood species also are incomplete. Nevertheless, it is recognized that supplies of fuelwood from natural forests and woodlands in dryland regions are diminishing at alarming rates, with ineffective efforts to replenish these stocks on a sustainable basis (Anderson and Fishwick

---

Example 15.5

*Estimates of Fuelwood Consumption in the Sahelian Region of West Africa
(Aw 1986)* Data on fuelwood consumption in the Sahelian region are limited
and largely unreliable. Estimates of noncommercial consumption of fuelwood
are unavailable in many countries, but even for those countries where information is available, there are major problems stemming from the inaccuracy of the
data, definitional constraints, and choice of conversion factors to aggregate
fuelwood use into a comparable basis. Nevertheless, simulations have been
developed to approximate fuelwood consumption in the region.

On a countrywide basis, for example, per capita consumption of fuelwood on
an annual basis has been related to measures of GNP, population characteristics,
and measures of income and wood accessibility. Correlations between fuelwood
consumption and these measures were found in Chad, The Gambia, Mauritania,
Niger, Senegal, Burkina Faso, and Mali, although the "quality" of the data limited large-scale extrapolations. A pooling of the available data for all of the
countries analyzed indicated that the human population was the single most
important factor in determining fuelwood consumption in the region.

1984, Eckholm et al. 1984). It largely is because of this situation that "energy
plantations" are being established at increasing rates in many regions of the world.

The cutting of wood for fuel is a significant form of exploitation and, in many
situations, deforestation throughout dryland regions. Four-fifths of the wood harvested annually in the dry tropics is utilized as fuel, leaving large areas devoid of
trees and shrubs (Boyce 1979). Demands for fuelwood often are considered to be
expressed locally, because wood is more expensive to transport to outside regions
than other forms of fuel.

With demands greatly exceeding supplies in many areas, many countries in the
dryland regions of the world are experiencing fuelwood scarcities or deficits, as
indicated in Table 15.3. On a worldwide basis, to meet anticipated deficits in fuelwood resources requires establishment of an additional 50 million hectares of
fuelwood plantations (Boyce 1979). A fivefold increase in planting programs
would be necessary to achieve this goal by the year 2000, an unlikely possibility
because of the large labor and money requirements anticipated. Nevertheless,
experimental work is underway to help in alleviating these deficits. Included in
these efforts are the identification of potential roles for multipurpose, fast-growing
tree and shrub species suitable for fuelwood plantations, more efficient recoveries
of harvesting residues as sources of energy, and more efficient combustion and
carbonization technologies.

TABLE 15.3. Countries with Fuelwood Scarcities or Deficits

	Acute Scarcity	Deficit	Potential Deficit
Africa	[a]Botswana	Gambia	Ghana
	[a]Burkina Faso	[a]Malawi	[a]Sierra Leone
	[a]Cape Verde	[a]Mozambique	Zimbabwe
	[a]Chad	Nigeria	
	Djibouti	Cameroon	
	[a]Ethiopia	Senegal	
	[a]Kenya	Togo	
	Lesotho	Zambia	
	[a]Mali		
	Mauritania		
	[a]Niger		
	[a]Somalia		
	[a]Sudan		
	Swaziland		
Near East		Yemen	
Asia	[a]Afghanistan	India	
		Pakistan	
Latin America	Bolivia	Brazil	Argentina
	Peru	Chile	
		[a]Paraguay	

[a]Depending upon fuelwood for over two-thirds of its total primary energy requirement in the early 1980s

Source: Adapted from the Food and Agriculture Organization of the United Nations (1986).

FUTURE MANAGEMENT OF FUELWOOD RESOURCES

Many of the sites potentially suited to fuelwood production also are managed to provide forage for livestock and habitats for wildlife species. Water resources also may be given consideration in the management scheme of these areas. As a result, the forest management practices implemented to improve the potentials for obtaining fuelwood must be designed to maintain a balance among all of the natural resource objectives on these lands, a multiple use concept presented earlier in Chapter 10.

Specific forest management practices that can improve the recoveries of fuelwood resources involve two broad forms of considerations. Initially, biological considerations, for example, increasing the growth rates of tree and shrub species to be used as fuelwood, must be incorporated into the management plans. Secondly, administrative considerations, such as specifications for the harvesting techniques and restrictions on lands open to fuelwood harvesting in a particular season, should be analyzed. As governmental agencies generally are responsible for establishing the administrative framework, biological considerations are emphasized below.

Biomass resources used for fuel have been "more mined than managed" in the past, meaning that the tendencies have been to harvest or gather fuelwood on sites without concern for renewing the fuelwood resources for future use. However, if demands increase and markets expand, as they are expected to do, attempts will have to be made to place fuelwood resources into integrated multiple-purpose forest management plans. In other words, it will become necessary that fuelwood resources are "more managed than mined" in the future. To this end, the following considerations are important:

- Increase the growth rates of tree and shrub species utilized, currently or potentially, as fuelwood.
- Place forests, woodlands, and plantations to be utilized for fuelwood under a "sustained yield" form of management.
- Insure that sufficient tree and shrub regeneration is attained to maintain a renewable flow of wood on the lands harvested for fuelwood.

SUMMARY

Increasing numbers of households and communities in dryland regions are dependent entirely upon wood for fuel. However, the frequent and continuous harvesting of fuelwood can have serious environmental consequences, including the dislodging of plant, animal, and human populations; degrading of soil and site productivities; and reducing the biological diversities of indigenous species. The purpose of this chapter was to present information so that one can understand the:

1. Role of fuelwood in meeting people's energy requirements.
2. Advantages and disadvantages of fuelwood management in different types of ecosystems.
3. Biological and socioeconomic considerations in implementing environmentally sound fuelwood management practices.

At this point, you should be able to answer the following questions:

1. What are the advantages of using fuelwood (rather than fossil fuels) for cooking and heating?
2. What are the input and output components of fuelwood resource systems in natural forests and woodlands, forest plantations, and agroforestry systems?
3. What criteria are used to select tree and shrub species for fuelwood? What is the role of silvicultural treatments in fuelwood management? How can the growth and yield of a fuelwood resource be estimated? When and how should fuelwood be harvested?
4. What policy issues are important in implementing fuelwood management practices? What is the role of incentives? How do the supplies of and

demands for fuelwood in the southwestern United States and other dryland regions of the world compare?

5. What is the future for fuelwood management in dryland regions?

REFERENCES

Anderson, D., and R. Fishwick. 1984. Fuelwood consumption and deforestation in African countries. *The World Bank, Staff Working Papers* 704, Washington, D.C.

Avery, T. E., and H. E. Burkhart. 1983. *Forest measurements*. McGraw-Hill Book Company, New York.

Aw, O. 1986. *Status and perspectives of the wood energy crisis in the Sahel*. PhD Dissertation, University of Arizona, Tucson, Arizona.

Barger, R. L., and P. F. Ffolliott. 1972. Physical characteristics and utilization of major woodland tree species in Arizona. *USDA Forest Service, Research Paper* RM-83.

Boyce, S. G. (ed.). 1979. *Biological and sociological basis for a rational use of forest resources for energy and organics*. USDA Forest Service, Southeastern Forest Experiment Station, Asheville, North Carolina.

Callison, J. C. 1988. Site quality indices for Emory oak. In Ffolliott, P. F., and J. D. Hasbrouck (eds.). 1988. *Oak woodland management: Proceedings of the workshop*. School of Renewable Natural Resources, University of Arizona, Tucson, Arizona, pp. 39–43.

Clutter, J. L., J. C. Fortson, L. V. Pienaar, G. H. Brister, and R. L. Bailey. 1983. *Timber management: A quantitative approach*. John Wiley & Sons, Inc., New York.

Curtis, R. O. 1972. Yield tables past and present. *Journal of Forestry* 70:28–32.

Eckholm, E. 1979. Planting for the future: Forestry for human needs. *Worldwatch Paper* 26, Washington, D.C.

Eckholm, E., G. Foley, G. Barnard, and L. Timberlake. 1984. *Fuelwood: The energy crisis that won't go away*. Earthscan, Washington, D.C.

Falloux, F., and A. Mukendi. 1988. Desertification control and resource management in the Sahelian and Sudanian zones of West Africa. *The World Bank, Technical Paper* 70, Washington, D.C.

FAO. 1984. *Wood energy development*. FAO, Bangkok, Thailand.

FAO. 1986. FAO's tropical forestry action plan. *Unasylva* 38:64.

Ffolliott, P. F., and J. L. Thames. 1983. *Environmentally sound small-scale forestry projects: Guidelines for planning*. VITA Publications, Arlington, Virginia.

Ffolliott, P. F., W. O. Rasmussen, and J. G. Patterson. 1980. Biomass for energy: Potentials in Arizona. *Biosources Digest* 2:240–47.

Ffolliott, P. F., W. O. Rasmussen, T. K. Warfield, and D. S. Borland. 1979. Supply, demand, and economics of fuelwood markets in selected population centers of Arizona. *Arizona Land Marks*, Volume 9, Number 2, Phoenix, Arizona.

Fowler, W. P. 1990. *Variable-density yield tables for Emory oak of southeastern Arizona*. PhD Dissertation, University of Arizona, Tucson, Arizona.

Fowler, W. P., and P. F. Ffolliott. 1992. Structure of a variable-density yield table for Emory oak. In Ffolliott, P. F., G. J. Gottfried, D. A. Bennett, V. M. Hernandez, A. Ortega, and R. H. Hamre (technical coordinators). 1992. Ecology and management of oak and associated woodlands: Perspectives in the southwestern United States and northern Mexico. *USDA Forest Service, General Technical Report* RM 218, pp. 141–43.

Harris, R. A., J. W. McMinn, and F. A. Payne. 1986. Calculating and reporting changes in net heat of combustion of wood fuel. *Forest Products Journal* 36:57–60.

Husch, B., C. I. Miller, and T. W. Beers. 1982. *Forest mensuration.* John Wiley & Sons, Inc., New York.

Jacobson, H. K., and M. F. Price. 1991. *A framework for research on the human dimensions of global environmental change.* International Social Science Council, UNESCO, Paris.

MacDicken, K. G., and N. T. Vergara (eds.). 1990. *Agroforestry: Classification and management.* John Wiley & Sons, Inc., New York.

Nair, P. K. R. (ed.). 1989. *Agroforestry in the tropics.* Kluwer Academic Publishers, Boston.

NAS. 1976. *Energy for rural development: Renewable resources and alternative technologies for developing countries.* National Academy of Sciences, Washington, D.C.

NAS. 1980. *Firewood crops: Shrub and tree species for energy production.* National Academy of Sciences, Washington, D.C.

Olsen, W. K., and D. R. Betters. 1989. Domestic fuelwood consumption and supply in Colorado: Characteristics, trends and projections. *Colorado Agricultural Experiment Station, Technical Bulletin* 89-1, Fort Collins, Colorado.

Reineke, L. H. 1960. Wood fuel combustion practice. *USDA Forest Service, Forest Products Laboratory Report* 1666-18, Madison, Wisconsin.

Sampson, G. R. 1979. Energy potential from central and southern Rocky Mountain timber. *USDA Forest Service, Research Note* RM-368.

Saucier, J. R. 1980. Environmental effects of harvesting fuelwood. In *Safe and clean wood energy.* Engineering Experimental Station, Georgia Institute of Technology, Atlanta, Georgia, pp. 2–6.

Smith, W. R. 1982. *Energy from forest biomass.* Academic Press, New York.

Touchan, R. 1991. *Effects of coppice thinning on growth and yield of Emory oak in southeastern Arizona.* PhD Dissertation, University of Arizona, Tucson, Arizona.

Weber, F. R. 1986. *Reforestation in arid lands.* VITA Publications, Arlington, Virginia.

Wood, D. H., D. Brokensha, A. P. Castro, M. S. Gamser, B. A. Jackson, B. W. Riley, and D. M. Schraft. 1980. *The socio-economic context of fuelwood use in small rural communities.* U.S. Agency for International Development, Evaluation Special Study 1, Washington, D.C.

World Resources Institute. 1990. *World resources 1990–91.* Oxford University Press, New York.

16 Agroforestry

A variety of agricultural and natural resource production systems are recognized and practiced in the dryland regions of the world. Depending upon the environmental and socioeconomic situation, these production systems vary from traditional agricultural crop and livestock production systems to different combinations of agricultural, livestock, forestry, and other productions systems that are practiced either rotationally, simultaneously, or spatially on the same piece of land. Regardless of the nature of these combined production systems, their goal is to provide ecological stability and sustainable benefits to users of the land.

Combined production systems that involve trees or shrubs are known more commonly as *agroforestry systems*. Although new to many people, agroforestry is not a new concept of land use. Historically, it has been a common practice to cultivate tree or shrub species and agricultural crops in intimate combinations. Worldwide examples of agroforestry are numerous, ranging from practices in the Middle Ages in Europe to before colonial times in America, Asia, and Africa (King 1989). Agroforestry was largely a "handmaiden" of forestry in its early history, while today it is a recognized set of systems that are capable of yielding food and wood and at the same time conserving and, when necessary, rehabilitating ecosystems.

DEFINITIONS

Agroforestry has been defined as "trees plus any other food crop" or, alternatively, as land management "combining trees with a form of food crops" (MacDicken and Vergara 1990, Vergara 1985). *Agroforestry* also is considered a collective term for those land use practices in which trees and shrubs are combined deliberately on a land unit with agricultural crops and/or livestock in spatial arrangements or temporal sequences (Raintree 1987). A more comprehensive definition follows:

> Agroforestry is considered to be any land use that maintains or increases total yields by combining food crops, livestock production, and forest crops on the same unit of land, alternately or simultaneously, using management practices that suit the social and cultural characteristics of the local people, and the ecological and economic conditions of the area (Young 1983).

Agroforestry, therefore, consists of all land use practices that involve ecological and economic associations of trees or shrubs with agricultural crops and/or livestock production on the same piece of land. It makes little difference if the piece of land in question is as small as one home garden or as extensive as a large tract of communal grazing land. If agroforestry is to serve people's needs, it is important to see it as an approach to land use rather than as a predetermined arrangement of plants and animals or particular combinations of species (Rocheleau 1988). A review of how agroforestry systems are classified provides a basis for thinking about the agroforestry systems that are found in the dryland regions of the world.

CLASSIFICATIONS OF AGROFORESTRY SYSTEMS

To evaluate the effectiveness of agroforestry systems and prepare plans for their implementation or improvement, it is helpful to classify them in a practical frame-work. Most of the available information about agroforestry is descriptive in nature, and, as a consequence, agroforestry systems are classified commonly in terms of descriptive criteria. As pointed out by Nair (1989b, 1990), most agroforestry systems have been classified on the bases of the following:

- *Structural basis*—refers to the composition of components in agroforestry systems, including spatial mixtures, vertical stratifications, and temporal arrangements of the components.
- *Functional basis*—refers to the functions or roles of the systems. For example, there are productive functions (food, fodder, and fuelwood) or protective functions (windbreaks, soil and water conservation, and shade for livestock).
- *Ecological basis*—refers to the environmental conditions and ecological stabilities of the systems in geographical regions, that is, agroforestry systems for arid lands, semiarid lands, and subhumid margins.
- *Socioeconomic basis*—refers to the level of managerial inputs into the systems (low inputs, high inputs) or benefit-cost relationships (subsistence, commercial, or intermediate).

These broad bases of classification are neither independent nor mutually exclusive. In fact, they often are interrelated closely. Structural and functional bases relate to components in the systems, while ecological and socioeconomic bases relate to the organization of the systems in relation to ecological or socioeconomic conditions.

Structural Basis for Classification

The structure of agroforestry systems can be described in terms of the nature of the components of the systems and, subsequently, their arrangements in space and time.

Nature of Components In general, three sets of components are managed by people in agroforestry, namely, herbage (agricultural or forage crops), trees or shrubs (forestry), and animals (livestock). Unfortunately, a profusion of names and terms has evolved throughout the world in classifying agroforestry systems consisting of combinations of these components, leading to frequent confusion (Combre and Budowski 1979, Vergara 1985). The term *agrisilviculture*, for example, has come to be regarded by many people as a similar term as *agroforestry*. However, it has a different and more precise meaning than other compound words, such as *silvoagricultural*, *silvopastoral*, and *agrosilvipastoral*. A closer examination of these terms indicates that the order of the component crops in the compound names reflects an order of dominance among these crops. *Agrisilviculture* implies that agricultural crops dominate over forest crops, while *silvoagricultural* means that forest crops dominate. This order of dominance is illustrated in Figure 16.1, in which agroforestry cropping systems are shown as a continuum over which a range of varying crop combinations appears.

Because of the competition for space between two component crops, such as agriculture and forestry, an increase in the area allocated to one automatically results in a reduction in the area allocated to the other, assuming that the entire area is always the sum of the two allocations. This idea is best presented through an example.

In Figure 16.1, point *A* shows that 100 percent of the area is allocated to agricultural crop production. Similarly, on the extreme right, point *E*, the area is totally assigned to forestry. At any point between these two extremes are agroforestry systems with varying proportions of land allocation. At point *B*, for example, agricultural crop production dominates, so the system is *agrisilvicultural*. On the other hand, at point *D*, forestry is the dominant crop, so the system can be properly termed *silvoagricultural*. A situation might arise in which the component crops receive an equal share of the land, as shown at point *C*. In this case, either of the two terms could be employed.

One problem with the use of Figure 16.1 is that it is only two-dimensional. It is difficult, therefore, to use it in illustrating more than two components in agro-

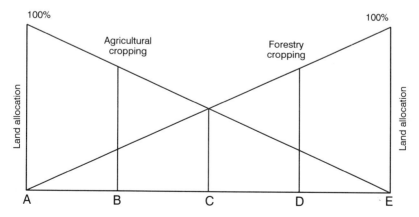

Figure 16.1. Allocation of crop components in agroforestry (adapted from Vergara 1985, by permission of the Food and Agriculture Organization of the United Nations)

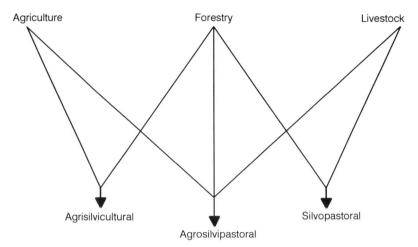

Figure 16.2. Three types of agroforestry (adapted from Vergara 1985, by permission of the Food and Agriculture Organization of the United Nations)

forestry, such as when livestock production is added to the system. The graphical presentation in Figure 16.2 can be used to describe multicomponent agroforestry systems. However, while this second graph shows more than two components, it does not show the degree of dominance of the components involved.

The hierarchical order of components presented above is based only on the allocations of land to the respective agroforestry crops. Theoretically, the hierarchical order also could be based upon the respective economic values of the crops, if these values are known. Unfortunately, economic values of the crops often are difficult to estimate, especially when agroforestry is practiced at a subsistence level. The use of this approach to determine hierarchical order of crops, therefore, is limited.

Divisions among the categories of agroforestry systems are not discrete. Rather, they represent a continuum of combined production systems. It should be seen from this discussion that agroforestry can be classified in a number of different ways, including physical structure, temporal arrangements, relative importance and roles of components, production outputs, and social and economic features.

Arrangements   Arrangements of the components of agroforestry systems might be made in space and time, as mentioned above. The spatial arrangements can include all of the components in place at one time, but they are spaced in a manner that, hopefully, become supportive rather than competitive (Vergara 1985). Considering agricultural crops and forestry for illustration, there are four arrangements of the components.

A *random mixture* of components displays little orderly placement, although the components can occupy their own ecological niches and, therefore, are able to coexist. *Alternative rows* or *alternative strips* of two or more rows are effective in erosion control and maintaining slope stability when positioned along contours.

(These spatial arrangements also are referred to as *alley* or *hedgerow* croppings in the literature.) *Border tree plantings* are found where people use lines of trees or shrubs as windbreaks, live fences, or boundary markers. These trees and shrubs often produce fuelwood and other wood products, fodder for livestock, and green manure as organic fertilizer. Collectively, all of these spatial arrangements are forms of *intercropping systems*, and are illustrated in Figure 16.3.

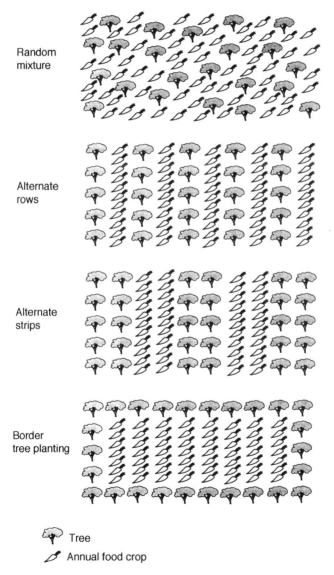

Random mixture

Alternate rows

Alternate strips

Border tree planting

Tree
Annual food crop

Figure 16.3. Intercropping systems, including (a) random mixture, (b) alternate rows, (c) alternate strips, and (d) border tree planting (adapted from Vergara 1982)

Temporal arrangements, as the name implies, are rotational systems in which the components of agroforestry are alternated through time. One example is the shifting of cultivation, when agricultural crops are grown for a few years, with longer periods of fallow, when trees or shrubs are planted and grown. Alternating grazing by livestock in the fallow, with the growing of agricultural crops at other times is another example. Temporal arrangements have been described in the literature with such terms as *coincident, concomitant, overlapping,* and *sequential* by different authors (Kronick 1984, Nair 1989b, 1990). Temporal arrangements, collectively, are *crop rotational systems.*

Functional Classification

Agroforestry systems can be grouped according to functional categories, namely, *productive* and *protective.* Agroforestry systems with productive functions are those producing one or more of the needs for people, such as food, energy, shelter, raw materials, and, in some instances, cash. Protective functions of agroforestry systems often contribute to these productive functions by sustaining and, at times, augmenting the production through amelioration of microclimates and the retaining of soil and water resources. All agroforestry systems are multipurpose and, in general, have both productive and protective functions (Nair 1989b, 1990). A particular agroforestry system can be termed either *productive* or *protective* functionally, however, depending upon the relative dominance of the respective roles.

Ecological and Socioeconomic Classifications

Many descriptions of agroforestry systems in specific ecological settings within geographical regions are found in the literature. *Acacia albida* interspersed on sorghum and maize croplands in the Sahelian region of West Africa (Rocheleau et al. 1988); the *Dehesa* agrosilvipastoral systems in the Mediterranean region, including the growing of *Quercus* spp. and recurrent cropping of cereals on grazing lands (Joffre et al. 1989); and intercropping of *Prosopis juliflora* and barley by indigenous people of the southwestern United States (Fowler and Ffolliott 1986) are a few examples. The usefulness of these descriptions in classification of agroforestry systems is limited, however.

Several agroforestry systems can be relevant to a particular agro-ecological region, regardless of how they are defined. Also, the functional emphasis of a system can vary, depending upon the environmental conditions and ecological stabilities in the region. In some situations, in which the basic needs of people are not being met, emphasis likely will be placed on production. Where sustainability is paramount, emphasis might be placed on protection.

Socioeconomic criteria, such as the scale of production or level of technological inputs and management, also have been used as a basis to classify agroforestry systems. Systems have been grouped, somewhat arbitrarily, into *subsistence, commercial*, or *intermediate* categories, depending upon whether the outputs are used

TABLE 16.1. A Framework for Classification of Agroforestry Systems

Classification Based upon the Nature of the Components	Other Characteristics

Agrisilvicultural	Arrangements of components
	    In space
	    In time

Silvopastoral	Function
	    Production
	    Protective

Agrosilvipastoral	Agro-ecological region

Other (specify)	Socioeconomic criteria
	    Subsistence
	    Commercial
	    Intermediate

Source: Adapted from Nair (1989b, 1990)

to satisfy the basic needs of people, are made available for sale in a marketplace, or a combination thereof (Nair 1989b, 1990). A drawback to this classification scheme is that the groupings are not quantifiable; standards for differentiation in one locality often do not apply in another. The "boundaries" of groupings also can change in time, reflecting changing economic conditions in an area. Therefore, socioeconomic criteria in themselves usually are not adopted as a classification basis.

A Framework for Classification of Agroforestry Systems

The complexity of classification can be reduced if the nature of the components in agroforestry systems receives primary consideration in classification, and then information on other characteristics of the systems is used as criteria for subsequently grouping them for specified purposes (Nair 1989b, 1990). A framework for the classification of agroforestry systems based upon these considerations is presented in Table 16.1. This framework presents a logical, simple, and purpose-oriented approach to classification.

SYSTEMS, PRACTICES, TECHNOLOGIES

As pointed out by Nair (1989a, 1990), the terms *systems* and *practices* are used commonly in agroforestry literature, which has caused confusion in classification. A system is a type of land use that is specific to a locality and described in terms of its biological composition and management, level of technical management, or socioeconomic features. Examples of agroforestry systems, as described above, are agrisilvicultural, silvopastoral, and agrosilvipastoral. A practice is a specific land management activity of an agroforestry nature on a farm or other land management unit that consists of agroforestry components. Agricultural crops in combinations with forest plantations, trees and shrubs in pastures, and woody hedges for fodder and browse, mulch, green manure, and soil conservation are agroforestry practices. Practices become systems when they are developed to form definite land-utilization types in a specific area.

Another term used in agroforestry literature is *technology*, which usually is used in combination with a production system, for example, agricultural technology, wood production technology, and agroforestry technology. The word *technology* often indicates a form of improvement through scientifically based intervention. In this chapter, the emphasis is placed on systems, with practices used to illustrate the systems. However, as suggested above, systems and practices commonly are used interchangeably in agroforestry.

AGROFORESTRY SYSTEMS IN DRYLAND REGIONS

Agrisilvicultural, silvopastoral, and agrosilvipastoral systems are found commonly in many forms throughout the dryland regions of the world. The general nature of these specific agroforestry systems is discussed below, with some examples presented in Table 16.2.

Agrisilvicultural Systems

Agrisilvicultural systems are a form of land use system in which both agricultural crops and products from trees or shrubs are produced either simultaneously or sequentially. This form of land use generally represents an improvement over the traditional systems of "shifting cultivation," a method in which farmers cut some or all of the trees and shrubs, burn them, and raise agricultural crops for one or more years before moving on to another site and repeating the process. Agrisilviculture is sound ecologically, provided that the fallow is long enough to allow the trees or shrubs to restore soil fertility. To shorten the fallow period, trees or shrubs often are planted instead of allowing a forest or woodland to reestablish itself by natural regeneration when shifting cultivators abandon the land.

One example of agrisilviculture is the *Acacia senegal*-millet-sesame-ground-nut cropping combination that is practiced in the Kordofan region of the Sudan. A primary feature of this practice is a 16-year rotation, in which the land is under tree cover for 12 years (FAO 1989). Gum arabic is obtained from mature *Acacia senegal* trees as a marketable product in the last of these 12 years. The trees are cut for fuelwood at the end of a rotation. The subsequent rotation begins with the land being cultivated for 4 years in a combination of millet, sesame, or ground nut crops. This agroforestry practice requires 24 ha of land to support a family. The land is arranged in 16 plots of 1.5 ha each, one plot for each year in the rotation, representing a series of normal age classes.

TABLE 16.2. Examples of Agroforestry Practices in Dryland Regions

Southern Asia	Mediterranean and Middle East	West Africa	United States
Agrisilvicultural			
Timber/fruit trees and crops	Olive and cereals	Windbreaks	Windbreaks
Windbreaks	Poplars along irrigation canals	Trees and shrubs in sand dune stabilization	Fruit trees and irrigated crops
Live fences	Trees and shrubs in sand dune stabilization	Fuelwood trees and crops	Multipurpose trees and crops
Shifting cultivation	Multipurpose trees and crops	Multipurpose trees and crops	
Medicinal trees and crops	Fruit trees and irrigated crops		
Silvopastoral			
Timber/fruit trees and pasture forage	Oak forests and grazing	Nomadic/seminomadic/transhuman grazing systems	Tree crops and grazing
Forest plantation crops and pasture forage	Fodder trees and shrubs	Fuelwood and fodder trees and shrubs	
Fodder trees and shrubs			
Agrosilvipastoral			
Forest plantation crops, arable agricultural crops, livestock	Multiple use management systems on grazing lands	Multiple use with tree crops, agriculture, or livestock dominating	Multiple use on management
Agricultural tree and shrub crops and pasture forage			
Others			
Mixed perennial intercropping	Spice plantation and erosion control	Oasis	Mixed perennial intercropping
Irrigation systems	Fruit trees in deserts	Irrigation systems	Irrigation systems
Fuelwood systems	Mushroom cultivation in forest plantations	Various site-specific systems	

Source: Adapted from Anonymous (1983).

Silvopastoral Systems

Silvopastoral systems, practiced when the land use is primarily the growing of forest products and the raising of livestock through grazing, involves controlled grazing in natural forests, woodlands, or forest plantations. As mentioned earlier, dryland regions generally are livestock-raising areas, with silvopastoral systems as a dominant land use. The vegetative resources of these vast, low-yielding areas frequently are best utilized through grazing. Under this type of agroforestry, the main sources of forage and fodder for livestock consist of grasses, forbs, trees, and shrubs.

Multipurpose tree or shrub species that produce fodder in silvopastoral systems have gained considerable attention in many dryland regions of the world, as illustrated by the examples in Table 16.3. In addition to furnishing fuelwood and other wood products, these trees and shrubs offer a level of "insurance" to pastoralists during droughts and other periods of forage shortages by providing a source of fodder, as shown in Figure 16.4. The advantages of using trees and shrubs for fodder production in dry seasons include:

- Forage production remains higher for longer periods of time into dry seasons than is the case with herbaceous plants because of the deeper rooting systems and longer growing seasons.
- Nutrient and crude protein contents of many tree and shrub species are higher than that of herbaceous forage in dry seasons, resulting in higher weight gains in livestock and improved conception rates (Von Carlowitz 1989).
- Trees and shrubs often are the only source of forage for livestock in the severest of drought. Herbaceous vegetation can be reduced to less than 20 percent of the total cover at these times. This situation was observed in the short-grass prairies of the Great Plains in the midwestern United States during the droughts of the 1930s (Branson 1985).

At times, silvopastoral systems involve the controlled utilization of forest or woodland vegetation as fodder. However, it must be realized that there is a limit to the number of livestock the land can support. Proper management to prevent overgrazing is vitally important, as mentioned in Chapter 2. Sometimes, introducing trees and shrubs onto natural grasslands can be feasible, since a combination of trees, shrubs, and grasses often offers optimal benefits. The individual trees and large shrubs on grazing lands offer additional benefits of providing shade and shelter for animals.

Agrosilvipastoral Systems

This type of agroforestry is a combination of agricultural crop production and silvopastoral practices. The land use is often a mixture of agriculture and livestock raising, relying heavily on fodder from tree and shrub species. Agrosilvipastoral

TABLE 16.3. Silvopastoral Practices, Including Tree and Shrub Species for Fodder Production

Practice	Description
Hedgerow intercropping for fodder	Medium- to densely spaced lines of trees or shrubs intercropped with grains to provide fodder, fuelwood, and erosion control
Tree-line fodder bank	Medium-spaced lines of trees or shrubs for fodder, fuelwood, and improvement of soil fertility
Scattered fodder trees in pasture	Widely spaced, scattered trees or shrubs for fodder, fuelwood, and shade for livestock
Boundary planting	Widely spaced lines of trees and shrubs to furnish fodder, fuelwood, and timber and poles on property lines
Live fences	Densely spaced lines of trees or shrubs for fodder, fuelwood, protection, and demarcation of agricultural fields and homes

Source: Adapted from Von Carlowitz (1989)

systems should be practiced in areas that can support limited agriculture. They are not necessarily applicable to dryland regions that are best suited for livestock raising. Quite often, agrosilvipastoral systems of land use take place in a valley, where agriculture is practiced on the valley floor and silvopastoral agroforestry is employed on forest-covered slopes around the valley. The agrosilvipastoral method also can be practiced on the same piece of land but not always at the same time. In some cases, fields in which trees or shrubs are growing can be farmed only during certain periods of the year and grazed during other periods. Any integration

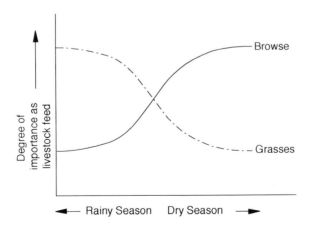

Figure 16.4. Relative importance of different forage types in periods with adequate moisture in comparison to dry periods (adapted from Von Carlowitz 1989)

of livestock raising and agricultural crop production must be considered with care. In general, traditional grazing lands are not well suited for intensive agricultural crop production.

The *Dehesa* system in southwestern Spain, also known by the name of *Montado* in southern Portugal, essentially consists of two agroforestry systems (Joffre et al. 1989, Maranon 1988). Livestock are grazed in oak woodlands, dominantly comprised of *Quercus ilex*, with *Q. suber* and *Q. faginea* occasionally intermingled, at which time the system is silvopastoral in nature. Cereals are cropped on one-fifth or one-sixth of the areas every 5 or 6 years, when the system of land use is agrosilvipastoral. Mature *Q. ilex* trees are harvested for fuelwood, other wood products, and acorns; and *Q. suber.* when present, is harvested for cork every 10 years. *Q. ilex* is lopped every 8–12 years to enhance production of acorns.

Multipurpose Trees and Shrubs

Multipurpose trees and shrubs in themselves are also agroforestry systems. In essence, these plants represent combined production systems in which wood might be used for fuel or fence posts, leaves and small branches for fodder or browse, and fruit and nuts as food for people. That this is feasible can be illustrated by Example 16.1 and below.

Example 16.1

Fodder and Fuelwood from Multipurpose Shrubs (Orev 1988)   The area near Eilat, Israel, on the Gulf of the Red Sea, has an annual precipitation amount of less than 35 mm. The area historically suffered from overgrazing by camels, although it has been protected from grazing for over 30 years. As a result of the original overgrazing, a browse shrub, *Haloxylon persicum* var. *idumaneum*, has spread onto sand dunes and gravel flats, attaining heights of 25 m. Short-lived flash floods periodically replenish soil moisture on the gravel flats, so that "reasonable" browse production from the shrubs occurs. Browse production varies from 300 to 800 kg/ha, with the first year's growth possessing a digestibility of about 75 and 50 percent for early green and dormant stages of growth, respectively. Unbrowsed stems from 2-year growth provide valuable fuelwood supplies. With an annual production of 400 kg/ha of fuelwood, 3 ha of a good stand of *Haloxylon* can furnish fuelwood sufficient to support a family of five. Furthermore, the shrub has value in stabilizing sand dunes, an added benefit of a truly multipurpose shrub.

By promoting *Atriplex halimus*, a slow-growing but more nutritious shrub, in mixed stands of *Haloxylon*, the grazing season in the region can be prolonged, because *Atriplex* is at its peak of palatability when *Haloxylon* is dormant. In areas that receive in excess of 70 mm of precipitation annually, other shrubs and perennial grasses become viable options for developing more diversified agroforestry practices.

A well-known multipurpose tree in the Sahelian region and other drylands throughout Africa is *Acacia albida*. Farmers value this leguminous tree for its green manure and fodder, and it is harvested for tannins and gums, charcoal, and wood for general carpentry (Hocking 1987). A unique feature of *A. albida* is its leaflessness in rainy seasons, which minimizes competition with agricultural crops for light. The tree also provides shelter and shade, and it is a frequent choice in amenity plantings.

Some trees have value simply because "they are there," filling vacuums in nature. Such is the case with *Prosopis pallida*, which inhabits the hot, dry, and saline environments along the coastlines of Peru and Ecuador (Brewbacker 1987). This tree also has multipurpose values, however, in that it yields nutrient-rich pods for livestock consumption, high-valued fuelwood and charcoal, and a nectar which makes honey that sometimes is produced as a commercial product. Similar to many other multipurpose trees and shrubs, *P. pallida* trees fix nitrogen to enrich the soil for agricultural purposes.

A final example of a multipurpose tree serving a role in agroforestry is *Albizia lebbeck*, which provides fodder during dry seasons in the semiarid regions of the tropics and subtropics (Prinsen 1988). The tree also has value as fuelwood, pulp, and a source of construction materials. Soil-binding characteristics make it useful in soil conservation, and the tree is planted along roadways and, occasionally, to shade coffee or tea plantations.

A listing of other tree and shrub species with multipurpose potentials is presented in Appendix II. Other listings are found in the literature (Huke and Plecan 1988, Nair 1989a, Rocheleau et al. 1988, Weber 1986).

Efforts to genetically improve multipurpose tree and shrub species have been initiated recently, with a primary emphasis placed on fast-growing, nitrogen-fixing species (Brewbacker 1990).

BENEFITS AND LIMITATIONS OF AGROFORESTRY

Agroforestry systems attempt to optimize ecological and economic concerns to obtain a higher, more diversified, and more sustainable total production than is possible with a single land use. It is necessary, however, to consider both the benefits and limitations of agroforestry interventions to assess the advantages of agroforestry, if there are any, relative to monocultural cropping methods of land use.

Benefits of Agroforestry

Agroforestry systems can provide many goods and services to people (Budowski 1981, Vergara 1982, Wiersum 1988). Depending upon the situation, agroforestry can:

- Make more efficient use of natural resources, for example, several vegetative layers utilize solar radiation inputs more efficiently, different depths of rooting systems increase cycling of nutrients, and, when livestock are included, unused primary production (forage plants) is utilized for secondary production (livestock).

- Increase yields and improve the qualities of food production.
- Produce fuelwood plus a variety of other raw materials from trees and shrubs for a farmer's subsistence, local sale in rural communities, and, sometimes, export.
- Protect and improve a soil's productive potential.
- Improve the socioeconomic conditions in rural areas by creating employment and income, and by reducing risks of food production and monetary losses.
- Develop land use systems that combine both modern technology and traditional local experience, and that are compatible with the cultural and social life of the people involved.
- Be a tool for the settlement of shifting cultivators, providing people with better social services and improved living conditions.

Limitations of Agroforestry

Although there are environmental, economic, and social benefits of agroforestry, there also can be limitations that must be considered and, when possible, overcome. Limitations of agroforestry include:

- Possible competition of trees and shrubs with food crops and forage species for space, sunlight, soil moisture, and nutrients, which can reduce food crop yields. (Competition for soil moisture is a particular concern in dryland regions.)
- Adverse effects through introductions of chemical substances from one component to another, a process known as *allelopathy*. (Some eucalyptus species, for example, have this trait.)
- Rapid regeneration by prolific tree and shrub species, which can displace food crops and forage species and take over entire agricultural fields and pastures.
- A potential of trees and shrubs to serve as hosts to insects and diseases that are harmful to food crops and forage species.
- Requirements of more labor input, which can result in labor scarcities at times for other agricultural activities.
- Resistance by farmers to the displacement of food crops and forage resources with trees and shrubs, especially where land is scarce.
- A general lack of knowledge and experience about the establishment and management of sustainable agroforestry systems and practices in specified conditions.

It should be noted that most of the limitations are related to the fact that agro-forestry is a land use that is geared to meeting the needs of rural people and, in general, is managed by rural people. In analyzing the advantages of agroforestry in a specific area, therefore, usually more attention must be paid to the various kinds of socioeconomic constraints to land use than usually is directed to "classical" forestry development, which leads to relatively large tracts of land being managed by centralized organizations to meet the needs of a region or country at large.

Assessment of Advantages of Agroforestry

It is not easy to assess the benefits and limitations and, therefore, the advantages of agroforestry. The most straightforward method is to compare benefits and costs of the agroforestry system or practice in question with traditional agricultural, live-stock or forestry monocultural production systems. The problem encountered is to express multiple resource benefits, including the ecological benefits and costs in monetary terms.

One approach to assessing the advantages of agroforestry is to use the land equivalent ratio (*LER*), which is a measure of the relative land area under tradi-tional monocultural production that is required to produce the same yield as obtained in agroforestry under the same level of management (Agricultural Uni-versity Wageningen 1988, Newman 1990). The *LER* is a summation of the frac-tions of yields of agroforestry in relation to the monocultural yields; that is:

$$LER = \sum_{i=1}^{n} \frac{Ym_i}{Yp_i} \tag{16.1}$$

where Ym_i = Yield of crop component in agroforestry
 Yp_i = Yield of same crop in monoculture
 n = Number of crop components in agroforestry

There is a yield advantage in agroforestry in those cases where *LER* >1. For example, Newman (1986) reported a *LER* value of >2 was obtained for a pear tree and vegetable combination, indicating a yield advantage to this agroforestry com-bination.

Although the *LER* is useful to indicate whether a yield advantage can be obtained, it is not a measure of economic value. The income equivalent ratio (*IER*) is more appropriate for this measure. The *IER* is the ratio of the area needed under monocultural cropping to that of agroforestry, at the same level of management, to produce the same amount of income (Agricultural University Wageningen 1988). It should be realized, however, that the outcome of a benefit-cost comparison of agroforestry and monocultural cropping is dependent largely upon the relative prices of the component crops.

The output of the monoculture should be the optimal one for a valid comparison of agroforestry with monocultural cropping. Optimal plant species, spacing patterns, and irrigation schedules should be considered. Unfortunately, it often is difficult to know optimal conditions, which vary spatially and temporally.

PLANNING AGROFORESTRY INTERVENTIONS

A general planning process framework was presented in Chapter 8 to guide people interested in the planning of dryland forestry projects for sustainable development. Here, we will look specifically at planning for agroforestry interventions, which is unique in that agroforestry often is a means of ameliorating detrimental land use impacts while addressing the needs of people (Duchhart 1988). However, planning for agroforestry cannot be limited to individual landowners or land occupants and, importantly, must consider all units of a landscape in terms of both the constraints and opportunities for future development.

Diagnosis and Design Methodology

The International Council for Research in Agroforestry (ICRAF), Nairobi, Kenya, has developed a detailed planning procedure referred to as the Diagnosis and Design (D&D) methodology (Raintree 1987), which has been implemented by countries in ICRAF's Agroforestry Research Network for Africa (AFRENA) and elsewhere in Asia and Latin America. This basic planning methodology is comprised of 6 stages with 15 steps, as shown in Figure 16.5. The steps are used selectively for varying purposes, although the hierarchical process is relatively robust and generally applicable to most problems in agroforestry technology design.

The D&D methodology is repeated throughout the implementational stage of an agroforestry intervention to refine the original diagnosis and improve the technology design when new information becomes available. It, therefore, is an iterative process that provides feedback and complimentarity among project components and activities (Figure 16.6). The D&D process is "self-corrective" in that it adjusts a plan of action to newly obtained information, with pivotal decisions made at regularly scheduled meetings, where new results are evaluated and the plan revised accordingly. The planning cycle illustrated in Figure 16.6 can be entered at any point, although dissemination of technology is accomplished most likely by landowners or land occupants themselves.

Prior to development of the current D&D methodology, a land evaluation system similar to that proposed by FAO (1976, 1984) was tested by ICRAF. The land evaluation approach of FAO was sensitive to broader environmental issues, while a strength of the D&D process is its consideration of social factors at the level of a landowner or land occupant (Young 1985). These two planning philosophies have been combined into the present version of the D&D methodology to permit applications on a regional scale to areas possessing a variety of local environmental conditions.

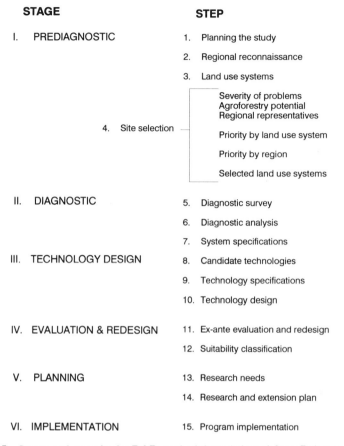

Figure 16.5. Stages and steps in the D&D methodology (adapted from Raintree 1987, by permission of the International Centre for Research in Agroforestry)

Other Planning Methods

Planning for the implementation of agroforestry technologies throughout the world has indicated that:

- Problem solving cannot be limited to individual landowners or land occupants from an ecological or socioeconomic viewpoint.
- Landscapes present both constraints and opportunities for future development, regardless of the region.
- More appropriate agroforestry technology is applied by initially classifying land units and land use systems in terms of capabilities and suitabilities.
- Planning, therefore, is essential, considering the inherent complexity and long-term implications of agroforestry interventions.

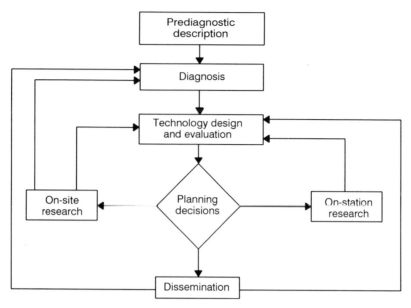

Figure 16.6. Flowchart of iterative activities and feedback in a D&D planned agroforestry project (adapted from Raintree 1987, by permission of the International Centre for Research in Agroforestry)

For these reasons, a number of agroforestry planning methods in addition to the D&D methodology has evolved. These planning methods will not be elaborated upon, other than to indicate that they all address two essential concerns: sustainability of land use and fulfillment of the needs of rural people. Many of these methods concentrate largely upon agricultural production. However, they also form effective planning frameworks for agroforestry because of their integrated basis.

Three examples of other planning methods for agroforestry interventions are *land evaluation, farming systems research and development*, and *agro-ecosystem analysis*, the details of which are found in references about these methods (Duchhart 1988, Duchhart et al. 1990).

Species Selection

One final comment on planning for agroforestry interventions is warranted. It is necessary that something be said about the selection of trees and shrubs for inclusion in agroforestry schemes. As previously mentioned, trees and shrubs have a variety of roles in agroforestry, including production, protection, and amenity purposes. Therefore, the selection of species that accomplish these roles is a primary concern.

Trees and shrubs with potential roles in agroforestry are listed in Appendix II and elsewhere in the literature. However, the usefulness of a specific species in a particular environment must be left largely to rural people to observe, test, evaluate, and judge the usefulness of the species for themselves (Rocheleau et al. 1988, Wood 1990). General listings of trees and shrubs, consequently, can be misleading. In this regard, the following "warnings" merit close attention:

- Information on a *specific* tree or shrub species often is incomplete, conflicting, unreliable, or useful only to a particular site. Important environmental and social variables may not be indicated, and techniques of measurement may not be explained fully.
- Trees and shrubs react differently to different environments. The quality of a tree or shrub in relation to its role in agroforestry is best when the tree or shrub is grown in its most suitable habitat. When a species is planted at the edge of its natural range, it can survive but not perform as expected.
- A tree or shrub normally is used by rural people to meet their specific needs and preferences. General listings typically only show how *some* people might use the trees and shrubs, not necessarily how one might use them in a particular situation.
- Only a small sample of indigenous and exotic trees and shrubs with some of their possible uses and environmental requirements are presented in general listings. These listings, therefore, are meant to suggest a few species, uses, and environmental conditions for consideration. There likely are other tree and shrub species growing locally that also should be taken into account.

PROSPECTS FOR SUSTAINABLE AGROFORESTRY IN DRYLAND REGIONS

Empirical and scientific information has indicated a number of reasons for a greater stability and higher level of productivity of agroforestry in comparison with monocropping. Using these same bases, it is likely that modified and improved agroforestry practices can be designed and disseminated among rural people for possible adoption. For example, a random mixture of component crops can be modified into contour hedges, or alternate rows or alley cropping, for better site protection and, hopefully, for greater and more steady productivity. It is important, however, that people are able to participate actively in the conceptualization, planning, and development of agroforestry practices. By doing so, the people can become more inclined to adopt the project or program and, therefore, move closer to achieving ecological stabilization and sustained yields in agroforestry. The prospects for attaining this goal in the dryland regions of the world appear promising, assuming that participatory planning, implementation, and monitoring is attained.

SUMMARY

Agroforestry is a collective term for land use practices that maintain or increase total yields by combining food crops, livestock production, and crops from trees and shrubs on the same piece of land, either alternatively or simultaneously, using management practices that suit the characteristics of the rural people and the ecological and economic conditions of the area. Agroforestry systems are implemented to provide stability and sustainable benefits to the users of the land. After you have read this chapter, you should have a better appreciation of agroforestry as a land use strategy in dryland regions. Specifically, you should be able to:

1. Explain how agroforestry systems are classified in terms of structural, functional, ecological, and socioeconomic bases.
2. Answer the following questions:
   - What are the characteristics of the agrisilvicultural, silvopastoral, and agrosilvipastoral systems that are found throughout the dryland regions of the world?
   - Why are multipurpose trees and shrubs in themselves agroforestry systems?
   - How are the advantages of agroforestry assessed?
3. Discuss the D&D methodology as a planning process for agroforestry.

REFERENCES

Agricultural University Wageningen. 1988. Agricultural aspects of agroforestry with special reference to the humid tropics. In Wiersum, K. F. (ed.). 1988. *Viewpoints on agroforestry*. Agricultural University Wageningen, Netherlands, pp. 69–89.

Anonymous. 1983. A global inventory of agroforestry systems. *Biomass* 3:241–45.

Branson, F. A. 1985. Vegetation changes on western rangelands. *Range Monographs* No. 2, Society for Range Management, Denver, Colorado.

Brewbacker, J. L. 1987. *Prosopis pallida*—pioneer species for dry, saline shores. Nitrogen Fixing Tree Association, *NFT Highlights* 87-05, Waimanalo, Hawaii.

Brewbacker, J. L. 1990. Genetic improvement of multipurpose trees for agroforestry systems. *XIX World Congress Report B*, IUFRO, pp. 304–15.

Budowski, G. 1981. Applicability of agroforestry systems. In MacDonald, L. H. (ed.). 1981. *Agroforestry in the African humid tropics*. United Nations University, Tokyo, Japan, pp. 13–16.

Combre, J., and G. Budowski. 1979. *Classification of agroforestry techniques*. Workshop on Agroforestry Systems in Latin America, CATIE, Turrialba, Costa Rica.

Duchhart, I. 1988. Towards an integrated planning method for agroforestry development. In Wiersum, K. F. (ed.). 1988. *Viewpoints on agroforestry*. Agricultural University Wageningen, Netherlands, pp. 215–42.

Duchhart, I., R. Van Haeringen, and F. Steiner. 1990. Introduction: Integrated planning for agroforestry. In Budd, W. W., I. Duchhart, L. H. Hardesty, and F. Steiner (eds.). 1990. *Planning for agroforestry*. Elsevier, New York, pp. 1–17.

FAO. 1976. A framework for land evaluation. *FAO Soil Bulletin* 32, Rome.

FAO. 1984. Land evaluation for forestry. *FAO Forestry Paper* 48, Rome.

FAO. 1989. The role of forestry in combating desertification. *FAO Conservation Guide* 21, Rome.

Fowler, W. P., and P. F. Ffolliott. 1986. An agroforestry demonstration in Avra Valley of southeastern Arizona. *Hydrology and Water Resources in Arizona and the Southwest* 16:1–9.

Hocking, D. 1987. *Acacia albida*—the farmers choice for semi-arid and arid zones. Nitrogen Fixing Tree Association, *NFT Highlights* 98-02, Waimanalo, Hawaii.

Huke, S., and J. Plecan. 1988. *Planning for agroforestry*. Save the Children, Westport, Connecticut.

Joffre, R., J. Vacher, C. de los Llanos, and G. Long. 1989. The Dehesa: An agrosilvipastoral system of the Mediterranean region with special reference to the Sierra Morena area of Spain. In Nair, P. K. R. (ed.). 1989. *Agroforestry systems in the tropics*. Kluwer Academic Publishers, Boston, pp. 427–53.

King, K. F. S. 1989. The history of agroforestry. In Nair, P. K. R. (ed.). 1989. *Agroforestry in the tropics*. Kluwer Academic Publishers, Boston, pp. 3–11.

Kronick, J. 1984. Temporal analysis of agroforestry systems for rural development. *Agroforestry Systems* 2:165–76.

MacDicken, K. G., and N. T. Vergara. 1990. Introduction to agroforestry. In MacDicken, K. G., and N. T. Vergara (eds.). 1990. *Agroforestry: Classification and management*. John Wiley & Sons, Inc., New York, pp. 1–30.

Maranon, T. 1988. Agrosylvopastoral systems in the Iberian peninsula: Dehesas and Montados. *Rangelands* 10:255–58.

Nair, P. K. R. 1989a. Agroforestry systems, practices and technologies. In Nair, P. K. R. (ed.). 1989. *Agroforestry systems in the tropics*. Kluwer Academic Publishers, Boston, pp. 53–62.

Nair, P. K. R. 1989b. Classification of agroforestry systems. In Nair, P. K. R. (ed.). 1989. *Agroforestry systems in the tropics*. Kluwer Academic Publishers, Boston, pp. 39–52.

Nair, P. K. R. 1990. Classification of agroforestry systems. In MacDicken, K. G., and N. T. Vergara (eds.). 1990. *Agroforestry: Classification and management*. John Wiley & Sons, Inc., New York, pp. 31–57.

Newman, S. M. 1986. A pear and vegetable interculture system: Land equivalent ratio, light use efficiency and dry matter productivity. *Experimental Agriculture* 22:383–92.

Newman, S. M. 1990. Temperate agroforestry: Its role potential and recent advances in research. *XIX World Congress Report B*, IUFRO, pp. 282–91.

Orev, Y. 1988. Fodder and firewood for forest dwellers. *KIDMA (Israel Journal of Development)* 10(3):16–200.

Prinsen, J. H. 1988. *Albizia lebbeck*—a promising fodder tree for semi-arid regions. Nitrogen Fixing Tree Association, *NFT Highlights* 88-03, Waimanalo, Hawaii.

Raintree, J. B. 1987. *D&D user's manual: An introduction to agroforestry diagnosis and design*. International Council for Research in Agroforestry, Nairobi, Kenya.

Rocheleau, D., F. Weber, and A. Field-Juma. 1988. *Agroforestry in dryland Africa*. International Centre for Research in Agroforestry, Nairobi, Kenya.

Vergara, N. T. 1982. *New directions in agroforestry: The potential of legume trees*. East-West Center, Honolulu, Hawaii.

Vergara, N. T. 1985. Agroforestry systems: A primer. *Unasylva* 37:22–28.

Von Carlowitz, P. G. 1989. Agroforestry technologies and fodder production—concepts and examples. *Agroforestry Systems* 9:1–16.

Weber, F. R. 1986. *Reforestation in arid lands.* VITA Publications, Arlington, Virginia.

Wiersum, K. F. 1988. Outline of the agroforestry concept. In Wiersum, K. F. (ed.). 1988. *Viewpoints on agroforestry.* Agricultural University Wageningen, Netherlands, pp. 1–26.

Wood, P. J. 1990. Principles of species selection for agroforestry. In MacDicken, K. G., and N. T. Vergara (eds.). 1990. *Agroforestry: Classification and management.* John Wiley & Sons, Inc., New York, pp. 290–309.

Young, A. 1983. An environmental data base for agroforestry. *ICRAF Working Paper* 5, Nairobi, Kenya.

Young, A. 1985. Land evaluation and agroforestry diagnosis and design: Towards a reconciliation of procedures. *Soil Survey and Land Evaluation* 5:61–76.

17 Windbreaks Plantings and Sand Dune Stabilization

The use of drylands that further reduces the limited cover of vegetation can cause wind erosion and, in some cases, the formation of sand dunes. Wind erosion is a natural feature in these environments, largely because the rainfall is too low to support an adequate cover of protective vegetation. Of particular interest to foresters and other resource managers is the planting of trees and shrubs to reduce the detrimental effects of prevailing winds that often characterize dryland environments. Windbreak plantings and the establishment of a vegetative cover to stabilize movements of sand dunes are frequently implemented to control wind erosion.

Initially, processes of wind erosion are discussed briefly in this chapter, so that the roles of windbreak plantings and sand dune stabilization can be understood better.

WIND EROSION

Erosion and deposition of soil by wind modifies the terrain of many dryland regions and, in doing so, results in losses of productivity. In contrast to water erosion, to be discussed in Chapter 18, wind erosion is more diffuse and generally occurs where winds are prevalent and vegetative cover is sparse. The areas of the world that are susceptible to wind erosion are delineated in Figure 17.1. Although many of the areas depicted as susceptible to wind erosion are drylands, some areas are not. Areas that experience both excessive winds and agricultural cultivation are susceptible to high rates of wind erosion.

Processes of Wind Erosion

Hudson (1981) recognized five forms of wind erosion that can either overlap each other or occur simultaneously. Vegetative cover, parent rock and soil material, and the velocity of wind collectively affect the processes that lead to the following forms of wind erosion:

- *Detrusion*, the wearing away of rock and soil by suspended soil particles.
- *Abrasion*, the wearing away of rock and soil by larger soil particles skipping or bouncing along the surface of land.

323

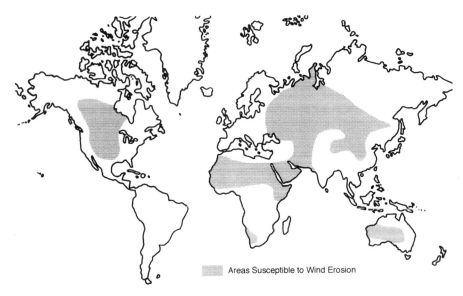

Figure 17.1. Areas of the world that are susceptible to wind erosion (adapted from Hudson 1981)

- *Efflation*, the removal of fine particles by actions of wind.
- *Extrusion*, the rolling away of large particles of soil.
- *Effluxion*, the movement of intermediate-size soil particles (sand) by saltation.

When vegetative cover is absent and, as a result, the soil surface is exposed, wind erosion is governed largely by wind velocities and the size of soil particles. The quantity of soil moved by wind is proportional to the wind velocity and the square root of the diameter of the soil particles, as described by Schwab et al. (1966):

$$S = (V - V_o)d^{0.5} \tag{17.1}$$

where S = Quantity of soil moved
   V = Velocity of wind
   V_o = Minimum wind velocity required to move soil particles with a diameter, d
   d = Diameter of soil particles

It can be seen in equation (17.1) that the size of the soil particles is important in estimating the quantity of soil moved by wind. Depending upon the size of the soil particles, one of the following types of soil movement can occur (Hudson 1981):

- *Suspension*, which moves small particles of soil ≤ 0.1 mm in diameter for great distances, as evidenced by dust storms.
- *Saltation*, in which soil particles from 0.05 to 0.5 mm in diameter are suspended for relatively short periods of time and distance, moving by skipping or bouncing along the surface of land.
- *Creep*, which is movement of larger particles of soil, 0.5 to 2 mm in diameter, along the surface of land by a rolling action without suspension.

After wind erosion begins, it becomes somewhat self-generating and requires a considerable effort to control. The velocity of wind required to dislodge and start a soil particle in motion is greater than the velocity required to keep that soil particle in motion. Each soil particle that is moving acquires energy from the wind. This energy is transferred to other particles on the soil surface upon impact of the first particle at the surface and, in the process, initiates the movement of the other soil particles.

Wind erosion has resulted in large quantities of soil moving great distances throughout the world. It is recognized that the Loess Plateau in China and the loess soils of the midwestern United States are soil deposits from wind erosion. Unfortunately, there is little information on rates of wind erosion or amounts of soil deposition. One estimate of the latter was obtained from measurements of windblown soil deposited on snow surfaces in Iowa (Hudson 1981). Here, 450 kg/ha of soil deposition were determined to have originated in Texas, nearly 800 km away.

Prediction of Soil Loss by Wind

The complexity of processes and factors involved has limited the development of physically based methods for predicting soil erosion by wind. However, wind tunnel studies supported by limited field experiments have led to the synthesis of the Wind Erosion Equation, expressed as:

$$E = f(ICKLV) \qquad (17.2)$$

where E = Soil loss by wind erosion
I = Erodibility of soil, or vulnerability to wind erosion
C = Local wind condition factor
K = Soil surface roughness
L = Width of field in the direction of prevailing winds
V = Vegetative cover factor

Equation (17.2) is somewhat analogous to the more widely used Universal Soil Loss Equation (USLE) that is applied in predicting surface erosion caused by rainfall and overland flow of water (see Chapter 18). Unlike the USLE, however, the wind erosion factors in equation (17.2) are not multiplied together but require graphical and tabular solutions that consider the interactions of processes and factors.

The relative rates of wind erosion from a vegetated surface and bare ground are shown in relation to annual precipitation in Figure 17.2. In climatological regions with relatively high annual precipitation amounts, there tends to be a greater vegetative cover, reducing susceptibilities of soil to wind erosion. When vegetative cover is lost, however, the rates of wind erosion often increase dramatically. Areas with higher annual precipitation generally are more susceptible to erosion by actions of water than wind.

Vegetative cover also affects wind erosion by altering velocities and patterns of wind flows. The structure of vegetation and its influence on wind velocity profiles, therefore, become a factor affecting wind erosion. It is here that use of trees and shrubs as windbreaks comes into play.

Reviews of wind erosion prediction methods and the effects of soil characteristics by Hagen (1991) and Zobeck (1991) provide insight into factors that should be considered in development of improved predictions of wind erosion. Hagen (1991) listed the soil properties that affect erodibility as follows:

- General properties, including surface wetness, bulk density, and roughness or microrelief of the soil surface.

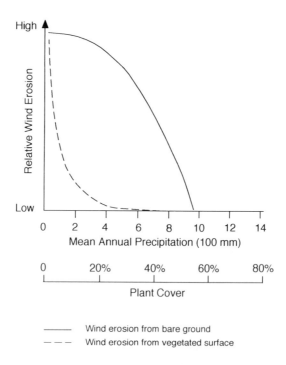

Figure 17.2. Relative rates of wind erosion from a vegetated surface and bare ground as a function of annual precipitation (adapted from Heathcote 1983)

- Soil aggregate properties, such as particle size distribution, stability when soil is dry, and density.
- Soil crust properties, for example, thickness, stability when soil is dry, loose soil above, cover fraction, and density.

This listing and the requirements for solving equation (17.2) suggest that considerable information about soil properties and wind conditions at a site must be known to estimate wind erosion. Such information often is lacking, particularly for noncultivated areas in which there has been little research or measurement of wind erosion.

Effects of Wind Erosion on Productivity

Although rarely quantified, wind erosion can reduce soil productivity in many dryland regions of the world. Hauck (1985) estimated that nearly 25 percent of the land area of Africa north of the equator and about 35 percent of the land area of the Near East are affected adversely by wind erosion. The drylands in Africa have received widespread attention because of droughts and soil losses, and the accompanying famines that reoccur. Dregne (1990) reported that wind erosion in the vicinity of Medenine, Tunisia, has caused large areas of blowouts of soil between shrubs and the hummocks around them and, as a result, has reduced productivity of the land in excess of 25 percent.

Wind erosion, also prevalent along much of the Sahelian region of West Africa, is particularly acute in Mali (Example 17.1), but quantitative data on the amounts or effects of this erosion are sparse. One fact that cannot be ignored, however, is the prevalence of dust storms that can last for several weeks in the region.

Example 17.1

Effects of Wind Erosion in Mali, West Africa (Dregne 1990)   Wind erosion in Mali has degraded lands by means of a process that locally is called "wala-wala." Cultivated lands subjected to wind erosion experience a condition in which the finer textured *B horizon* of the soil profile becomes exposed at its surface. This horizon becomes hard upon drying, making the surface difficult to plough by either hand or animal traction. This hard layer also has low infiltration capacities, which causes more overland water flow when rainfall occurs and, therefore, less soil moisture is available for agricultural crops. The result is a loss in productivity. To remedy this situation requires intensive efforts to reduce wind erosion and renovate the soils so the agricultural crop productivity can be enhanced.

WINDBREAK PLANTINGS

Harsh environmental conditions and the shortage of water in dryland regions are intensified by strong winds. The level of agricultural and livestock production and the living conditions of people often can be improved by planting trees and shrubs in protective windbreaks, which reduce wind velocities and, as a result, the degree of wind erosion. *Windbreaks* are woody, nonwoody, or nonvegetative (board or rock walls, earthen banks, etc.) barriers established to protect a site from wind flows. In this book, an emphasis is placed on the use of trees and shrubs in windbreak establishment. Windbreaks are considered synonymous with *shelterbelts* in this chapter.

Benefits

In addition to reducing wind erosion, a primary objective of windbreak plantings is to protect agricultural crops and grazing livestock from the detrimental effects of wind. The production of agricultural crops frequently is increased, in large part due to a lessening of evapotranspiration rates. Livestock production also can be increased because the animals are sheltered and, as a consequence, not subjected to stresses of hot, dry winds. Other benefits of windbreaks include moderating the extremes in air temperatures and increasing aesthetic values in areas where the occurrence of trees and shrubs are scarce.

Protection and other benefits offered by windbreaks often are combined with potentials for the production of primary wood products by selecting appropriate tree and shrub species for windbreak plantings. In many instances, the protective and productive functions of these barriers are combined into sustainable *agroforestry*, a land management strategy that was discussed in the previous chapter.

Favorable environmental effects must be weighed carefully against the value of the scarce water resources in situations where water is limited and windbreaks must be watered. Adverse environmental effects also can occur if trees and shrubs comprising the windbreaks harbor birds, insects, or diseases that are harmful to agricultural crops. *Symbiotic relationships* (in which two dissimilar organisms live together in close association) between the pests of agricultural crops to be grown and the possible alternate hosts of the pests must be investigated thoroughly before selecting the tree and shrub species for windbreak plantings.

Competition Between Windbreaks and Agricultural Crops

Windbreaks are living barriers that can compete for soil moisture and nutrients with agricultural and forage crops growing near to the roots of trees and shrubs in the windbreaks. The yields of agricultural crops also can be reduced by allelopathy by tree and shrub roots, and by shading (Kort 1988). The magnitudes of decreased yields are dependent upon the tree and shrub species involved, the type of agricultural or forage crop, and the geographical location. Reductions in yields of agricultural crops because of windbreak competition generally are found in a zone between 0.5*H* (*H* = height of windbreak) and 2*H*, when they occur (Lyles et al. 1984, Read 1964, Stoeckler 1962).

Windbreak competition often is reduced by root pruning. This task can be accomplished by digging trenches or using specialized equipment. The effectiveness of root pruning depends largely upon the rooting characteristics of the trees or shrubs within the windbreak. Reductions in yields of agricultural or forage crops because of windbreak competition usually is more than offset by increases in crop yields beyond the zone of competition. Windbreaks should not be planted if such is the case.

Basic Design Criteria

Three *zones of influence* are delineated when planning a windbreak planting: a *windward zone* from which the wind blows; a *leeward zone* on the side where the wind passes; and a *protected zone*, that area in which the effect of a windbreak is felt. The relative widths of these zones are dependent largely upon the orientation and patterns of windbreaks with respect to prevailing winds, the height of the barrier, its density, and the spacing within and between windbreaks and their internal structure.

Orientation and Patterns   When planning windbreaks, the direction of the prevailing wind must be considered. For maximum effect, a windbreak should be established perpendicular to the prevailing wind. This orientation minimizes the number of windbreaks needed to protect a site. Terrain that slopes into the wind should be avoided, as a windbreak on this site only deflects the wind flow upward. Windbreaks with a clear vertical side provide best windspeed reduction.

To protect a large area, a number of separate barriers can be established as components of a windbreak network. When the prevailing winds in an area are mainly in one direction, a series of parallel windbreaks that are perpendicular to that direction can be established. In some cases, dense barriers are planted across major wind directions and less dense windbreaks are planted across minor wind directions.

A checkerboard pattern is required when winds originate from different directions. Before establishing windbreaks, however, it is important to make a thorough investigation of local winds and the relative strengths of these winds. On rolling terrain, the barriers are more effective when planted along ridgetops. A compact barrier in *U*, *V*, *X*, or square configurations can be used for sheltering livestock. Windbreaks planted around buildings are often in L-shaped patterns across the prevailing winds. A compromise may be necessary to account for both the direction of prevailing winds and the cultural and physical characteristics of an area being protected.

Height of the Barrier   The area in the protected zone of a windbreak is proportional to the height of the barrier. Therefore, the number of windbreaks that are required to protect a designated area of agricultural or forage crops is related

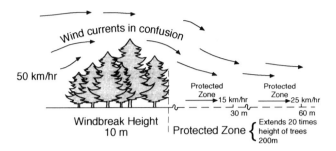

Figure 17.3. Effects of a windbreak on wind velocity (adapted from Forbes 1961)

directly to the height of the tallest trees or shrubs in the windbreaks (Finch 1988). It generally is thought that a windbreak of optimum density protects an area over a distance up to its own height ($1H$) on the windward side and up to 20 times its height ($20H$) on the leeward side, depending upon the strength of the wind, as shown in Figure 17.3. The tallest and best adapted species should be selected in establishing a windbreak to minimize the number of windbreaks required.

Density   The effectiveness of a windbreak is influenced greatly by its density. If a windbreak is a solid barrier, the wind flow will pass over the top of it and cause turbulence on the leeward side because of the lower pressure on that side. This results in a comparatively limited zone of effective shelter on the leeward side in comparison to the zone that a "moderately permeable" windbreak creates. When a barrier is permeable to wind, however, the flow of wind is separated, with part of it deflected upward and part of the flow penetrating through the barrier. The difference between a solid barrier and a "loose" barrier is illustrated in Figure 17.4. Optimum permeability generally is from 40 to 50 percent of space, corresponding approximately to a density of from 50 to 60 percent in vegetation (Hagen 1976, Hagen and Skidmore 1971).

Spacing and Structure   The spacing of trees and shrubs within a windbreak row depends largely upon the tree and shrub species planted, the desired barrier density, the number of rows in the windbreak, and the type of management followed once the windbreak is established. Planting stock generally is placed close together to obtain early closure. As trees and shrubs mature, every other plant can be removed by thinning. The final spacing within a row usually varies from 2 to 6 m for medium to tall trees, from 1.5 to 2.5 m for small trees, and from 1 to 2.5 m for shrubs. Narrower spacings generally are used in one-row plantings. Spacing between the rows in a windbreak often ranges from 2 to 6 m.

    A windbreak must reduce the flow of wind along the ground and diffuse upper wind flows. Rarely can both of these wind flows be affected significantly by one-row windbreaks. For maximum protection, therefore, a barrier ideally should con-

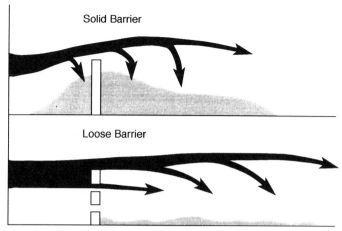

Figure 17.4. A solid barrier deposits soil materials closer to the barrier, while shallow, wide deposits of soil result from a loose barrier (Note the drifting in front of the solid barrier.)

tain a combination of different species of trees and shrubs. Low, dense trees or shrubs are established in the outside windward side, followed by medium-size trees and, finally, taller trees whose crowns break up the upper wind flows into eddies. A similar pattern is planted on the leeward side, when spacing permits. If this is not possible, at least the last row on the leeward side should be a low, dense coniferous tree or shrub species.

Windbreaks that follow the above pattern will develop into a triangular cross section, with the tallest trees in the center flanked by medium-size trees and shrubs on the edges. Rectangular cross sections also can be adequate for windbreaks of from two to four rows, providing at least two of the rows have foliage to the ground.

How wide a windbreak should be depends largely upon the amount of land that can be devoted economically to the planting of the windbreak and the number of rows required to maintain the desired barrier density. In many instances, narrow windbreaks of moderate density can be as effective as wide barriers and have an advantage of occupying less land.

In general, windbreaks of up to five rows are effective and not difficult to maintain. In considering their total economic worth, however, an account also should be taken of the potential multiple benefits of the barriers. In addition to the wind protection provided, wood products, fodder for livestock, and food and cover for wildlife can be provided. Windbreaks of more than five rows can be desirable for these considerations. At the opposite end of the spectrum, one-row windbreaks can be risky because holes can develop and funnel wind onto the agricultural or forage crops being protected.

Species Selection

Tree and shrub species to be used in windbreaks should be well adapted to the soils and climate of the area. In addition, the trees and shrubs selected for windbreak plantings should possess the following characteristics:

- Resistance to the force of winds.
- Rapid height growth.
- Straight stems, wind firmness, dense and uniform crown formation.
- Deep root systems, which do not spread into agricultural fields or pasture-lands. (Laterally rooted species can compete with agricultural crops and forage resources they are suppose to protect.)
- Resistance to drought, diseases, insects, and other pests.
- Appropriate phenological foliage characteristics, for example, leaves throughout the year or only part of the year.
- Value for wood or nonwood products.

Although the use of one tree or shrub species simplifies the subsequent management of windbreaks, it is not often that one species will have all of the above characteristics. Also, as previously mentioned, a combination of two or more tree or shrub species frequently are needed to provide adequate protection. For example, in many instances, the form of *Acacia* makes it useful for planting in the outer rows of windbreaks, while the inner rows often consist of tamarisk and *Eucalyptus*. A single tree or shrub species, particularly one that sprouts after cutting, such as *Eucalyptus* or neem, sometimes can be managed to provide the necessary vertical shelter by alternatively cutting the outer rows and allowing the uncut trees or shrubs to complete the shelter.

A listing of tree and shrub species suited for windbreak plantings in many of the dryland regions of the world is found in Appendix II. As a matter of policy, however, authorities in the locality should be consulted before an extensive planting program is undertaken. In recent years, efforts have been initiated to genetically improve trees and shrubs to be planted in windbreaks (Cunningham 1988), but this work has been limited to only a few species.

Planting Techniques

Planting techniques for windbreaks are similar to those used in other tree and shrub planting programs in dryland regions. Hand planting is common, although mechanized planting machines and cultivators might be justified in extensive windbreak-planting programs. As the trees and shrubs in windbreaks require high survival rates and uniform and rapid growth, watering or supplementary irrigation can be required during the establishment and initial growth phase. The soil should be "well prepared" and a permanent source of water must be assured, however, for watering and irrigation to be successful. A water transportation and application system also must be planned. The number of waterings and the amount of water applied depend largely upon the climate, tree or shrub species, and soil type. To illustrate this point, about 6 applications of 10 L for each seedling probably is sufficient to ensure survival in a sandy loam area with a dry season of 8 months receiving 150–200 mm of precipitation.

Gaps in plantings cannot be tolerated. Replacement planting should be considered when trees or shrubs are lost, especially in cases where the elapsed time from the original planting is relatively short and, therefore, replanting will allow the general integrity of the windbreak to be retained.

Management Considerations

That windbreaks are effective in improving the livelihood of people is demonstrated by many reports of net increases in agricultural crop production as a result of windbreak plantings (Kort 1988). The effects of windbreaks on cereal crops, forage crops, and arboriculture in Mediterranean climates, in which there is a long history of windbreak plantings, are shown in Table 17.1. However, windbreaks can become ineffective, even when the barriers have been designed properly, if they are managed poorly.

The management of windbreaks should focus on maintaining and improving the growth and vigor of individual trees and shrubs, and the structure of windbreaks in their entirety, so that they function as effective barriers in reducing wind velocities (Salem 1985). Management practices that are prescribed to meet these and other objectives of windbreak plantings involve the timely applications of cultural treatments, rehabilitative measures, and renewal prescriptions.

Cultural Treatments As trees or shrubs in a windbreak mature, they change in shape and appearance, which often necessitates some form of cultural treatment to ensure continuation of the sheltering effect. Pruning might be used to stimulate height growth; eliminate multiple stems and leaders; remove branchwood that has been damaged by wind, insects, or disease; or provide release for adjacent rows in multiple-row windbreaks. Many species prune themselves naturally when growing in close association, while others, such as poplars, can require regular pruning to obtain clear stems free of branches. Trees and shrubs that coppice readily generally require the most intensive pruning schedules.

The removal of trees or shrubs by thinning can be required to keep a windbreak at the desired barrier density. Thinning also tends to increase diameter growth, which is necessary to increase the volume of trees or shrubs significantly. Sanitary thinnings are necessary to remove dead, insect-infested, or diseased trees or shrubs. Individual trees and shrubs are selected for cutting on the basis of their condition—that is, spacing, vigor, wood product potentials, and so on. The removal of trees or shrubs involved either *low thinning*, to eliminate those that have been suppressed, or *high thinning* to reduce competition within dominant classes.

In multiple-row windbreaks, in addition to considering removal of individual trees or shrubs, the complete removal of one or more rows also can be an option.

TABLE 17.1. Effects of Windbreaks on Cereal Crops, Forage Crops, and Arboriculture in the Mediterranean Climate

Locality	Bioclimatic Zone	Type of Windbreak	Crop	Difference in Yield (% of Control)
		Cereal Crops		
Egypt	Arid	*Casuarina*	Irrigated Wheat	
			straw	102
			grain	94
	Arid	*Casuarina*	Irrigated Corn	
			straw	97
			kernels	94
Yugoslavia	Semiarid	Mixed	Rainfed Wheat	
		deciduous	dry summer	115
		species	wet summer	123
		Forage Crops		
Egypt	Arid	*Casuarina*	Irrigated *Trifolium*	117
Tunisia	Arid	*Arundo*	Irrigated Potatoes	200
	Semiarid	*Arundo*	Rainfed Beans	110
	Semiarid	*Arundo*	Rainfed Tomatoes	171
		Arboriculture		
Argentina	Arid	*Populus*	Irrigated Vines	146
United States	Arid	*Eucalyptus*	Irrigated Oranges	124
Egypt	Arid	*Casuarina*	Irrigated Vines	100
Israel	Arid	*Cupressus*	Irrigated Grapefruit	115
Tunisia	Semiarid	*Cupressus*	Irrigated Oranges	132

Source: Adapted from the Food and Agriculture Organization of the United Nations, 1985).

The removal of entire rows in a multiple-row windbreak is prescribed frequently to increase diameter growth rates and to develop denser and more vigorous crowns of trees and shrubs in the residual rows. A schedule of the timing and intensity of the treatment must be specified, regardless of the purpose of thinning.

Cultural treatments are dictated largely by a need to attain the desired barrier density and species composition of the windbreak. Because pruning and thinning involves the removal of woody parts, fuelwood, other wood products, or fodder, benefits can be obtained through this process (Example 17.2).

When a windbreak has been established on lands where livestock are allowed to graze freely, protection of the barrier can be required. Grazing can reduce the foliar density of the lower 2 m of a windbreak, and soil compaction resulting from livestock can reduce the vigor and life expectancy of the windbreak (Dronen 1988). Protection can be achieved by planting thorny vegetation in the windbreak or using a barbed-wire fence along the edges of the barrier.

Example 17.2

Harvesting of Fuelwood from Windbreaks in the Majja Valley, Niger, West Africa (Persaud et al. 1986)   Neem (*Azadirachta indica*), a tree introduced into West Africa from India, has been planted for a number of years in windbreaks of two rows in the Majja Valley of central Niger (Examples 6.3 and 12.2). Ten years after the initial plantings, villagers on whose land the windbreaks were planted began to harvest fuelwood from the oldest windbreaks. It became necessary, however, to ascertain the "best" method of harvesting fuelwood while retaining the benefits of the windbreaks in controlling wind erosion and increasing yields of millet and other cereals.

Methods of harvesting fuelwood tested included pollarding all trees in both rows of 100 m segments of the windbreaks, pollarding all trees in only one row of 100 m segments, pollarding one tree in four in both rows of 100 m segments, and removing branches overhanging the alleys from trees in both rows. The effects of these harvesting methods from wind erosion were compared to an uncut control.

The results from these tests were inconclusive and, to some degree, confounded because wind in this area tends to blow from many directions. However, the harvesting of fuelwood by removing the branches overhanging the alleys, while not yielding the quantities of fuelwood as the other methods, maintained protection on the site to a greater extent than other harvesting methods. It appears possible, therefore, that limited fuelwood amounts can be harvested from windbreaks in the Majja Valley without seriously compromising the effectiveness of the barriers in controlling wind erosion.

Protection from fire, insects, and diseases also must be considered. Windbreaks in particular areas can concentrate fuel accumulations, insect populations, and diseases. Plans to control or contain such damaging agents should be developed and understood by managers (Dix and Harell 1991).

Rehabilitative Measures   Rehabilitative measures are applied to a windbreak that becomes ineffective because of reduced foliage density. Two commonly employed techniques are additional plantings and the pruning of established trees or shrubs to stimulate coppice growth.

Gaps in a one-row windbreak can be filled by additional plantings, although this rehabilitative measure is less effective as the barrier becomes older and, as a result, size differences between the original and replanted trees or shrubs become greater. A multiple-row windbreak of low density can be rehabilitated by planting additional rows of small trees or shrubs within or outside of the established rows. Windbreaks in which densities become too low because of ineffective small trees or shrubs or browsing damage by livestock or wildlife often can be improved by cutting windbreak vegetation back to the ground to secure coppice growth. However, the effectiveness of this technique depends upon the coppicing characteristics of the species involved.

Renewal A windbreak has a life that is dependent on the status of trees or shrubs of which it is composed. After trees or shrubs start to decline in growth and vigor or begin to die—even preferably before this stage is reached—a renewal program should begin. Felling rows on the leeward side and then replanting them often is recommended to renew a windbreak consisting of many rows (Salem 1985). If the windbreak consists of one-row, a new row can be planted parallel to the old one, and when it has matured, the old one is removed. To renew narrow windbreaks arranged in a network, new windbreaks can be planted between the existing barriers, which then are removed when the new windbreaks become effective.

Renewal cycles for windbreaks depend largely upon the growth rate of trees and shrubs comprising the barriers, especially in terms of height and the desired extent of the *protected leeward zone*. It was stated earlier that a windbreak of optimum barrier density can protect an area of up to $20H$ on its leeward side. Therefore, the extent of the protected leeward zone is related directly to the height of the barrier. In planning a windbreak planting, a decision initially should be made about the ultimate width of the protected leeward zone. If, for example, the planned width is 200 m, this means that when the height of the tallest trees in the barrier is 10 m, the protected leeward zone will be $20H$. The elapsed time required for the tallest trees to reach 10 m in height after the windbreak has been planted, in effect, is the "targeted" renewal cycle. It must be emphasized that this renewal cycle is only an approximation to be used in the planning process. The uniformity of height growth, the number of rows in a windbreak, the cultural treatments imposed, and the potential demands or markets for the trees and shrubs removed in the renewal are among the many factors affecting the actual renewal cycle.

Another consideration in designating the width of the protected leeward zone and its renewal cycle is whether the barrier is a component in a network of parallel windbreaks. When this is so, the spacing between the windbreaks in the network also must be planned. In many instances, the planned spacing is the ultimate protected leeward zone, in which case the renewal cycle of the windbreaks in the network is based largely upon the same factors as mentioned above. However, studies have shown smaller reductions in wind velocities between the second, third, and successive barriers in a network (Heisler and DeWalle 1988, Woodruff and Zingg 1955) because of the turbulence created by the first windbreak, which presents the second barrier with a wind flow that is more turbulent than the flow toward the first barrier, and so on.

SAND DUNE STABILIZATION

Sand dunes are formed when winds blow regularly over poorly vegetated lands. Sand dunes and other aeolian deposits are shaped and then reshaped into complex

forms not only because of wind but also because of the nature of the ground surface, topography, vegetation on the site, and size of the sand grains (Mabbutt 1972,
Ghose 1985). Observations of aerial photographs and satellite imagery indicate
that a variety of sand dune forms are found throughout the world. A classification
of common sand dunes is presented in Table 17.2.

Sand dunes that are not covered with vegetation, or otherwise stabilized, move
in the direction of the wind at a speed that can approach 10 m annually, endanger-
ing forests and woodlands, grazing lands, agricultural crops, irrigation canals,
urban areas, and roads. To prevent this encroachment, it is necessary that sand
dunes be stabilized in some way. Stabilization has been achieved through use of
petroleum products spread on the sand dune, chemical mulches and sealants, and
diversion fences made of wood panels, stone, or soil. Another method of sand dune

TABLE 17.2. A Classification of Sand Dunes

Sand sheets
Minor dunes
  Sand ripples
  Granule ripples
Free dunes
  Simple dunes
    Crescentric dunes or barchan
    Longitudinal dunes
    Transverse dunes
  Compound dunes
    Linked barchan
    Linked longitudinal ridges
    Reticulate dunes
  Complex dunes
    Barchanoid forms
    Longitudinal forms
    Transverse forms
    Peaked forms
Dunes related to obstacles
  Topographical barriers
    Leeward accumulations
      Sand shadow
      Sand drift
      Lee dunes
    Windward accumulations
    Climbing and falling dunes
    Anchorage by vegetation
      Isolated mounds
      Transverse ridges
      Parabolical dunes
      Longitudinal ridges

Source: Adapted from El-Ariss (1988) and Ghose (1985), by permission of the
Food and Agriculture Organization of the United Nations.

stabilization, and that stressed in this chapter, is to establish a protective vegetative cover on the dune. Planting of vegetation, including trees and shrubs, is often the best and most permanent method of sand dune stabilization. Before a protective vegetative cover can be established, however, it is necessary to prevent the movement of sand long enough to enable the vegetative cover to become established. Preplanting barriers are constructed for this purpose.

Preplanting Barriers

Sites that are subject to sand dune encroachment generally cannot immediately be stabilized by the establishment of a vegetative cover because of possible exposure of the root systems of the vegetation to blowing sand, injury to these plants from abrasive actions of blowing sand, or the burying of plants by sand. Therefore, preplanting barriers are built to reduce the velocities of wind at the sand dune surface. Locally found materials commonly used for erecting the barriers include twigs from trees or shrubs, grass sheaves, old railroad ties, poles, and earthen ridges.

Various approaches are available in establishing preplanting barriers (Kaul, R. N. 1985b). Barriers can be established in parallel lines when the prevailing wind is from one direction. When the wind blows from different directions, a checkerboard pattern is used. The distance between parallel lines of preplanting barriers or the size of the checkerboard depends upon the wind velocities, steepness of the site, and form of sand dune. Preplanting barriers normally are built 1 year before a planting program begins, regardless of the scheme employed.

Artificial dunes, called *foredunes*, are erected along coastlines as barriers to prevailing winds in stabilizing *coastal sand dunes* (FAO 1989). The foredunes should be constructed about 50 m from the floodline and approach 10 m in height to stop advancement of coastal sand dunes. Foredunes also are used in stabilizing *inland sand dunes*, where a specific source of blowing sand is present. In this latter case, the foredunes are created at the windward end of the sand dune.

Species Selection

The process of planting trees or shrubs to stabilize sand dunes should include species trials in planting programs to evaluate tree and shrub species for long-term use. The species to be utilized in sand dune stabilization obviously must be drought resistant. Other desirable characteristics include:

- Well-developed root systems that are capable of deep vertical penetration to reach lower soil moisture layers. (Root systems of considerable horizontal spread also are advantageous to take maximum advantage of limited precipitation amounts.)
- Wind firmness, that is, the capability of withstanding high wind velocities without being uprooted.

- Being able to withstand high and low temperature fluctuations; abrasive actions of blowing sand particles; and salt spray for sites near the sea.
- For sustainability, trees or shrubs that are able to regenerate vegetatively, either through suckers or sprouts are preferred. (Harsh environments that are associated with sand dune formations often severely limit the possibilities of achieving successful regeneration by the planting of seedlings.)

As with windbreaks, sand dune plantings can have multiple benefits. In addition to stabilizing the movement of the dunes, the trees and shrubs planted often are harvested for fuel, poles or posts, fodder, or other types of woody and nonwoody products (Kaul 1985a, Salem 1985). Unfortunately, knowledge of these utilization possibilities is inadequate for many species of trees and shrubs that have potential for sand dune stabilization. Studies on species-site relationships are required before successful implementation of large-scale sand dune afforestation efforts can occur. Examples of trees and shrubs suitable for sand dune stabilization are listed in Appendix II.

Planting Techniques

To achieve high survival rates, planting of bare-rooted stock should be scheduled after the onset of the rainfall season, when the sand is wet. In many situations, a better strategy is to plant either container plants or cuttings of plants that regenerate vegetatively. In practice, it often is necessary to plant relatively large containerized trees or shrubs close together, 1×1 m, on the windward side, but they can be planted farther apart, 2×2 m, on the sheltered side (Kaul, R. N. 1985a). The planting depths vary with species but should be as deep as possible to tap the maximum soil moisture.

Watering or irrigation can be required to help the plants survive until they have sufficiently deep root systems. It generally is advisable to only water or irrigate at weekly intervals during the first 2 or 3 months after planting at a weekly interval, if water is not available in adequate quantities for irrigation on a long-term basis.

If soil fertility is limiting, fertilizers can be applied to enhance the establishment and subsequent growth of trees and shrubs (Kaul, R. N. 1985a). Inorganic fertilizers containing nitrogen in the form of ammonium sulfate have proven successful most generally, with lower responses to phosphate and potassium. Organic fertilizers also are used.

Management Considerations

Management of sand dune plantings consists largely of protecting the vegetation from livestock and other damaging agents and, when needed, applying cultural treatments to maintain the vegetative cover. If the trees and shrubs planted for sand dune stabilization can provide fuelwood and other wood products to rural people, management should consider these objectives as well (Example 17.3).

Example 17.3

Fuelwood Production on Sand Dunes in India (Kaul, O. N. 1985)   Shifting sand dunes in western India have been stabilized, to varying levels of success, by afforestation techniques developed at the Central Arid Zone Research Institute (CAZRI), located at Jodhpur. In addition to their function in stabilizing sand dunes, tree species like *Prosopis juliflora* also can be used for fuelwood. When this species is planted on sand dunes in areas where annual rainfall is from 150 to 250 mm and adequate soil moisture is available, nearly 15 t/ha of fuelwood has been produced at the end of the first 5 years after planting.

Other tree species planted in sand dune stabilization with reported fuelwood potentials include *Prosopis cineraria*, *Acacia tortilis*, and *Calligonum polygonoides*. Yields of fuelwood vary with the species and age of the trees and location, however.

Rehabilitative measures and renewal of vegetative covers also are scheduled as necessary to ensure sustainability.

Protection and Cultural Treatments   All livestock movement and other traffic should be eliminated in the initial stages of sand dune stabilization. Afterward, a deferred grazing system, discussed in Chapter 2, may be desirable to reduce the "harmful" effects of livestock. Protected passages for livestock should be established when necessary. Fire is often a concern because of a rapid desiccation of litter and annual foliage (Dalal 1985). Therefore, plans for fire control, for example, the establishing of a permanent network of firebreaks, can be required. Protection from insects and diseases also can be required.

Although cultural treatments generally are minimal, weeding occasionally becomes necessary, especially when competing vegetation is vigorous and trees and shrubs must be released to grow. Hand weeding is preferred to avoid problems of machinery traction in the sand. Thinnings normally are not prescribed, except in situations in which the initial planting is close or fuelwood or timber production are included in management objectives (Kaul, R. N. 1985b). More study is necessary to schedule thinnings in relation to the optimal use of the limited soil moisture amounts.

Rehabilitative Measures and Renewal   Rehabilitative measures, including additional plantings of trees or shrubs, or encouraging coppice growth, can be required when a cover of trees or shrubs becomes ineffective in stabilizing a sand dune. The renewal of the vegetative cover is necessary when trees or shrubs decline in vigor and begin to die. The criteria for specifying the renewal cycle are based upon the silvical characteristics of the species of trees or shrubs planted, knowledge of the original effectiveness of the sand dune stabilization effort, and whether fuelwood or other wood products also are produced.

SUMMARY

Wind erosion is common in dryland environments, especially in situations where the land use has reduced the protective vegetation. Windbreak plantings often are made to lessen the detrimental effects of wind erosion. The purpose of this chapter has been to provide sufficient information so that you should be able to:

1. Describe the general process of wind erosion.
2. Discuss the benefits that can be obtained from windbreak plantings.
3. Explain the design criteria for windbreak plantings.
4. Discuss the cultural treatments, rehabilitative measures, and renewal of windbreak plantings.

The establishment of a vegetative cover of trees and shrubs to stabilize sand dunes also can be helpful in controlling the damaging effects of wind. After you have completed this chapter, you should be able to:

1. Discuss the role of preplanting barriers in establishing a vegetative cover for sand dune stabilization.
2. Describe the desirable characteristics of trees and shrubs to be planted for this purpose.
3. Explain the protection and cultural treatments, and rehabilitative measures and renewal of trees and shrubs planted to stabilize sand dunes.

REFERENCES

Cunningham, R. A. 1988. Genetic improvement of trees and shrubs used in windbreaks. In Brandle, J. R., D. L. Hintz, and J. W. Sturrock (eds.). 1988. *Windbreak technology*. Elsevier, New York, pp. 483–98.

Dalal, S. S. 1985. Management of forested dunes. In FAO. 1985. Sand dune stabilization, shelterbelts and afforestation. *FAO Conservation Guide* 10, Rome, pp. 97–102.

Dix, M. F., and M. Harrell. (eds.). 1991. Insects of windbreaks and related plantings: Distribution, importance, and management. *USDA Forest Service, General Technical Report* RM-204.

Dregne, H. F. 1990. Erosion and soil productivity in Africa. *Journal of Soil and Water Conservation* 45:431–36.

Dronen, S. I. 1988. Layout and design criteria for livestock windbreaks. In Brandle, J. R., D. L. Hintz, and J. W. Sturrock (eds.). 1988. *Windbreak technology*. Elsevier, New York, pp. 97–102.

El-Ariss, S. R. 1988. *A broad perspective of sand dune forms, wind regimes, and fixations.* Master's Thesis, University of Arizona, Tucson, Arizona.

FAO. 1985. *Arid zone forestry programmes: State of knowledge and experience—an overview.* FAO, Rome.

FAO. 1989. Arid zone forestry: A guide for field technicians. *FAO Conservation Guide* 20, Rome.

Finch, S. J. 1988. Field windbreaks: Design criteria. In Brandle, J. R., D. L. Hintz, and J. W. Sturrock (eds.). 1988. *Windbreak technology.* Elsevier, New York, pp. 215–28.

Forbes, R. G. (ed.). 1961. *Forestry handbook.* The Ronald Press Company, New York.

Ghose, B. 1985. Geomorphology of desert dunes. In FAO. 1985. Sand dune stabilization, shelterbelts and afforestation. *FAO Conservation Guide* 10, pp. 27–39.

Hagen, L. J. 1976. Windbreak design for optimum wind control. In Tinus, R. W. (ed.). 1976. Shelterbelts on the Great Plains: Proceedings of the symposium. *Great Plains Agricultural Council Publication* 78, pp. 31–37.

Hagen, L. J. 1991. A wind erosion prediction system to meet user needs. *Journal of Soil and Water Conservation* 46:106–11.

Hagen, L. J., and E. L. Skidmore. 1971. Windbreak drag as influenced by porosity. *Transactions of the American Society of Agricultural Engineers* 14:454–64.

Hauck, F. W. 1985. Soil erosion and its control in developing countries. In El-Swaify, S. A., W. C. Moldenhauer, and A. Lo (eds.). 1985. *Soil erosion and conservation.* Soil Conservation Society of America, Ankeny, Iowa, pp. 718–28.

Heathcote, R. L. 1983. *The arid lands: Their use and abuse.* Longman, London.

Heisler, G. M., and D. R. DeWalle. 1988. Effects of windbreak structure on wind flow. In Brandle, J. R., D. L. Hintz, and J. W. Sturrock (eds.). 1988. *Windbreak technology.* Elsevier, New York, pp. 41–69.

Hudson, N. W. 1981. *Soil conservation.* Cornell University Press, Ithaca, New York.

Kaul, O. N. 1985. Forest production on sand dunes. In FAO. 1985. Sand dune stabilization, shelterbelts and afforestation. *FAO Conservation Guide* 10, Rome, pp. 87–95.

Kaul, R. N. 1985a. Afforestation of sand dunes. In FAO. 1985. Sand dune stabilization, shelterbelts and afforestation. *FAO Conservation Guide* 10, Rome, pp. 75–85.

Kaul, R. N. 1985b. Sand dune fixation and afforestation: Traditional procedures for dune fixation: The hedge system. In FAO. 1985. Sand dune stabilization, shelterbelts and afforestation. *FAO Conservation Guide* 10, Rome, pp. 65–69.

Kort, J. 1988. Benefits of windbreaks in field and forage crops. In Brandle, J. R., D. L. Hintz, and J. W. Sturrock (eds.). 1988. *Windbreak technology.* Elsevier, New York, pp. 165–90.

Lyles, L., J. Tatarko, and J. D. Dickerson. 1984. Windbreak effects on soil and wheat yields. *Transactions of the American Society of Agricultural Engineers* 20:69–72.

Mabbutt, J. A. 1977. *Desert landforms.* Australian National University Press, Canaberra.

Persaud, N., S. Long, M. Gandah, and M. Ouattara. 1986. Influence of wood-harvesting method on wind protection between rows of neem (*Azadirachta indica*) plantation in Niger, West Africa. In Hintz, D. L., and J. R. Brandle (eds.). 1986. International symposium on windbreak technology. *Great Plains Agricultural Council Publication* 117, pp. 211–12.

Read, R. A. 1964. Tree windbreaks for the central Great Plains. USDA Forest Service, *Agricultural Handbook* 250.

Salem, B. B. 1985. Management and renewal of shelterbelts. In FAO. 1985. Sand dune stabilization, shelterbelts and afforestation. *FAO Conservation Guide* 10, Rome, pp. 133–36.

Schwab, G. O., R. K. Frevert, T. W. Edminster, and K. K. Barnes. 1966. *Soil and water conservation engineering.* John Wiley & Sons, Inc., New York.

Stoeckler, J. H. 1962. Shelterbelt influence on Great Plains field environment. *USDA Production Research Report* 62.

Woodruff, N. P., and A. W. Zingg. 1955. A comparative analysis of wind-tunnel and atmospheric air-flow patterns about single and successive barriers. *Transactions of the American Geophysical Union* 36:203–08.

Zobeck, T. M. 1991. Soil properties affecting wind erosion. *Journal of Soil and Water Conservation* 46:112–18.

18 Soil Erosion and Control Measures

Erosion through the actions of wind and water is an inevitable occurrence in dryland regions, largely because these environments are not always able to support an adequate cover of protective vegetation. The combined actions of wind and water are particularly devastating on areas with sparse vegetative cover, as illustrated in Figure 18.1. Land use practices that further reduce vegetative cover tend to accelerate erosion.

This chapter discusses accelerated soil erosion and the means by which such erosion can be minimized. Emphasis here is placed on soil erosion processes involving actions of water and the methods of controlling these processes by vegetative management practices and other means.

There are two reasons for considering soil erosion in relation to dryland forestry practices, both of which are linked intrinsically. First, forestry and other natural resource interventions can be threatened directly by soil loss, which, in turn, limit the potential of a site to grow trees, shrubs, and other herbaceous plants. Soil erosion must be prevented whenever possible and controlled when necessary to sustain plant productivity. These actions lead to the second reason to include the topic of soil erosion in a discussion of dryland forestry practices. In themselves, dryland forestry practices can be planned and implemented specifically to prevent or control soil loss from a site. When this is the case, the forestry practices play more of a protective role than a productive one. The maintenance of a vegetative cover, often including trees and shrubs, is generally the more permanent approach to meeting this goal and also the focus of this chapter.

PROCESSES OF SOIL EROSION

Erosion involves the processes of detachment, transportation, and disposition of soil particles. Raindrop impacts and subsequent overland water flow resulting from excess rainfall are the agents of erosion and transport in the case of soil erosion through the actions of water. *Detachment* is the dislodgment of soil particles from the soil mass by erosive agents. *Transportation* is the entrainment and movement of soil particles, at this point referred to as *sediment*, from their original locations. Sediment in surface runoff then travels overland from upslope sources to its place

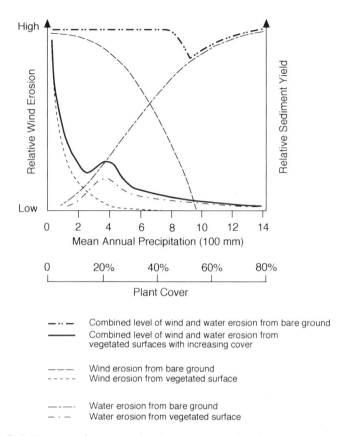

Figure 18.1. Relative rates of water erosion from a vegetated surface and bare ground, and the combined relative rates of wind and water erosion from a vegetated surface and bare ground, both as a function of annual precipitation (adapted from Heathcote 1983)

of *deposition*, which can be the toe of slopes, in stream channels, on flood plains, or in reservoirs. Some of the sediment is deposited only temporarily. When this is the case, subsequent storms, often several years later, can re-entrain the sediment and move it farther downslope. Eventually some, but not all, of the sediment reaches the ocean.

There are three soil erosion processes on upslope sites, specifically *surface erosion*, *gully erosion*, and *soil mass movement*. These erosion processes can occur singly or in combination. At times, it is difficult to distinguish or separate these basic types of erosion, because in reality there is a continuum of forms, and it is difficult to determine whether the erosion taking place is the result of the natural geological processes only or because of an acceleration of these processes by poor land management practices.

PREVENTION OF SOIL EROSION

General approaches to preventing excessive soil erosion in the first place should be considered before discussing the specific kinds of erosion and erosion control measures. Preventing loss of soil by avoiding the conditions that cause erosion or minimizing them when they occur is the most economic and effective means of combating soil erosion. To this end, land managers must consider carefully the actions of water on a land surface in relation to each land management decision made, whether this decision concerns the implementation of soil conservation techniques, water resource development, fuelwood or other forest management practices, grazing of livestock, or agricultural cropping. Situations in which soil erosion is likely to occur and, therefore, should be avoided in developmental interventions include sloping sites with shallow soils, soils with low permeabilities, and situations in which the denudation of vegetation is likely to occur.

The maintenance of protective vegetative cover is the best means of preventing soil erosion in most situations, although retaining an adequate vegetative cover cannot always be relied upon in dryland regions. In preventing soil erosion, therefore, simple measures should be taken to maintain the soil surface in a condition in which it readily accepts water. The more water that infiltrates into the soil, the better the chance of sustaining plant growth and, as a result, a protective vegetative cover. Included among these preventative measures are:

- Avoiding land management practices that reduce infiltration capacity and soil permeability.
- Maintaining a vegetative cover for as long as possible each year.
- Retaining vegetative cover on hilltops or steep slopes and restricting or eliminating livestock grazing on these areas.
- Locating livestock-watering facilities in relation to source areas for surface runoff.
- Carefully laying out and constructing roads and trails, especially on sites where water flows are likely to become concentrated.
- Applying appropriate erosion-control techniques and cropping procedures in agricultural fields.

A principle that illustrates the importance of preventative measures is that of the *critical point of deterioration*. This principle states that, for every site, there exists a point of deterioration because of erosion beyond which further deterioration occurs even more rapidly and that natural stabilizing forces are incapable of overcoming this (Satterlund and Adams 1992). A representation of this principle on a "moderately stable" site is shown in Figure 18.2. In general, this principle applies largely because accelerated erosion deteriorates a site at an ever increasing rate unless the processes are reversed.

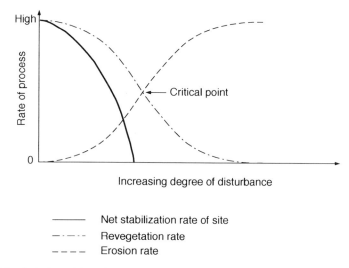

Figure 18.2. Relation of deterioration of a "moderately stable" site by erosion to the rate of revegetation (adapted from Satterlund, D. R., and P. W. Adams, *Wildland Watershed Management*, 2nd ed., © 1992 John Wiley & Sons. Reprinted by permission of John Wiley & Sons, Inc.) (At the critical point in deterioration, accelerated erosion becomes self-sustaining, and the site cannot recover by the natural process of revegetation. To the right of the critical point, deterioration continues to completion. To the left, a site recovers its stability at an increasing rate.)

SURFACE EROSION

The high rates of surface erosion that characterize dryland regions help explain the often shallow soil depth and lack of development of *A horizons* that are typical of many drylands (Thames 1989). Nutrients and organic materials can be removed by surface erosion from upland areas as quickly as soil is developed from parent materials. Surface erosion frequently is the reason that erosion pavements dominate soil surfaces in sparsely vegetated areas.

Processes

Surface erosion involves detachment and subsequent transportation of soil particles and small aggregates of soil from land surfaces by the collective actions of raindrops striking a land surface, thin films of overland water flow resulting from excessive rainfall, and concentrated flows of surface runoff. This type of erosion causes formation of rills and small gullies on the land surface. *Rill erosion* produces the largest amounts of soil loss worldwide (Brooks et al. 1991). Minute rills, formed simultaneously with the first detachment and transportation of soil particles, meander over the land surface, obscuring their presence from observation. This process leads to *sheet erosion*, which is the movement of a semisuspended layer of soil particles over the land surface between the rills. Sheet erosion, also termed *inter-rill erosion*, and rill erosion collectively represent the processes of surface erosion.

As overland flow becomes concentrated and moves downslope, the turbulence of the flow increases, which increases the velocity and mass of the sediment moved in the water. The resultant increases in kinetic energy causes even greater dislodgment and transport of still larger soil particles. When surface runoff carries a large amount of sediment, the abrasive actions of the load adds to the erosive power of the runoff. Soil loss can be excessive when intense rain falls on steep, unobstructed slopes with a sparse vegetative cover.

Methods of Control

A number of actions can be undertaken to control accelerated surface erosion once it has started. These general actions include:

* Protecting the soil surface against the energy of rainfall impact.
* Increasing the roughness of the soil surface and, as a result, reducing the velocity of surface runoff.
* Shortening the length and reducing the inclination of slopes to lessen the energy of overland flow and concentrated surface runoff.
* Improving infiltration capacities of the soil and, in doing so, reducing the quantity of surface runoff.
* Preventing concentration of overland flow to reduce the possibility of subsequent formation of gullies.

Surface erosion is controlled by minimizing the impacts of rainfall, preventing overland water flow and concentrated surface runoff on sites where surface erosion is potentially a problem, and combinations thereof. In large part, surface erosion can be prevented or minimized with appropriate vegetative management practices, including the management of grazing by livestock and the layout of roads and trails. After erosion is accelerated, mechanical methods also are used, although these methods eventually must be accompanied by vegetative methods of control. Mechanical methods often are the first step in controlling surface erosion until a protective vegetative cover can become established.

Vegetative Management Practices The most effective long-term methods of controlling surface erosion are based upon establishing and maintaining a protective cover of vegetation. In addition to reducing the impacts of raindrops and the flow of water on the land surface, evapotranspiration by the vegetation reduces the quantity of water stored in soil between rainfall events, resulting in more storage for rainfall and, therefore, less surface runoff. Furthermore, soil erodibility is lessened by the network of plant roots, and soil structure is improved through the addition of organic material. That vegetation cover is effective in controlling rates of surface erosion is illustrated in Figure 18.3 and Example 18.1. After excessive

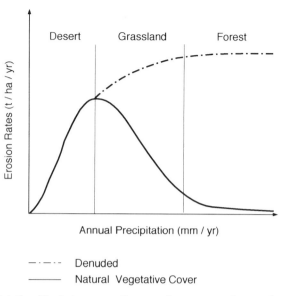

Figure 18.3. Relationship between surface erosion rates and annual precipitation for different vegetative covers and denuded land conditions (adapted from Brooks et al. 1991, Hudson 1981)

areas of mineral soil become exposed to the impacts of falling raindrops and flowing water, soil erosion is difficult to reverse, in most situations.

Individual plant species have different attributes in surface erosion control, different site requirements for growth, and different requirements for cultural treatments. Therefore, knowledge of plant species that are suitable for erosion control is important. Examples of trees and shrubs for this purpose are found in Appendix II and elsewhere in the literature (Nair 1989, Rocheleau et al. 1988, Weber 1986). Guidelines that specify plant species, site preparation methods, and seeding or planting techniques for local areas often are available.

Dryland forestry practices that minimize the destruction of ground vegetation and litter accumulations generally reduce the force delivered to the land surface by rainfall. In harvesting trees and shrubs for wood products, for example, operations in which individual or small groups of trees or shrubs are removed, rather than clearing large areas, should be implemented. Retaining residual strips of trees, shrubs, and other vegetation perpendicularly to the slope can reduce downslope movement of soil particles. Strips of vegetation adjacent to and upslope from stream channels also can be employed to protect streams.

Grazing Management While livestock production is essential to most local and regional economies in dryland regions of the world, overgrazing by livestock that removes excessive amounts of vegetation and compacts the soil can increase sur-

Example 18.1

Surface Erosion in Africa Increases Drastically after Removal of Vegetative Cover (Harrison 1987) What protects Africa's vulnerable soils from highly erosive rainfall is vegetation. Tree, shrubs, and herbaceous plants break the force of raindrops. Their root growth, plus activities of earthworms and termites they foster, creates thousands of pores and channels through which water can infiltrate into the soil. But, when vegetation is removed, the soil is exposed to the erosive power of rain. The increase in surface erosion after removal of vegetation can be spectacular. In one series of studies, the annual rate of soil loss from forests was nil—a mere 30–200 kg/ha. Annual losses from agricultural cropland was nearly 90 t/ha. From bare soil, a common situation on agricultural lands at the start of the rainy season, the rates of annual soil loss ranged from 10 to a massive 170 t/ha. Soil that took hundreds of years to form would wash away in one year at this latter rate of surface erosion.

face erosion. Some forms of grazing management is necessary, therefore, to achieve sustainable resource management on most drylands.

One method of controlling surface erosion resulting from grazing activities is limiting forage use by livestock. Forage use is controlled by reducing the numbers of livestock or controlling the distribution of livestock (Branson et al. 1981, Child et al. 1987). In many instances, reducing the number of livestock is difficult to achieve. Pastoralists generally are reluctant to reduce their livestock numbers because of the uncertainties of livestock production in dryland environments. However, the distribution of livestock often can be altered through the placement of water developments, salt blocks, and fences. Alternative grazing systems also can be employed to control the distribution of animals, as discussed in Chapter 2.

Surface erosion on grazing lands is often a result of deterioration in vegetative cover from past misuse on many sites. Grazing lands in poor condition can be rehabilitated in some situations by the reseeding and fertilizing of forage plants. Occasionally, mechanical methods also are needed to reduce surface erosion and improve the success of revegetation efforts. Importantly, no one method of improving the condition of grazing lands will be successful without accompanying proper livestock management practices.

Layout of Roads and Trails Excessive soil erosion can result from the improper layout and construction of roads and trails. Roads and trails are necessary to the infrastructure of many developmental activities, but their impacts on surface erosion can be greater than all of the other land management activities considered. No other activity requires such extensive and concentrated soil disturbance.

Some surface erosion will result from nearly all types of roads and trails. Therefore, the objective is to reduce the level of this erosion to the extent possible. To accomplish this, road or trail networks should be located to minimize the extent of exposed soil and disturbed areas and away from stream channels and gullies. Steep gradients should be avoided, because these sites are less stable than lesser slopes, exhibit excessive soil exposure to erosive actions of water from cuts and fills, and concentrate water more quickly than on less steep slopes. Many potential surface erosion problems from roads and trials can be eliminated in the planning stage before construction is initiated.

Mechanical Methods   The purpose of mechanical methods of controlling surface erosion is to promote infiltration and reduce runoff and consequent soil loss by retaining water on-site until a vegetative cover can become established. It is important, therefore, to evaluate the site in terms of its potential for sustaining a vegetative cover after mechanical methods become ineffective. The more effective mechanical methods include contour furrows, contour trenches, fallow strips, pitting, and basins (Branson et al. 1981, Brooks et al. 1991, Wiedemann 1988). The method ultimately selected depends largely upon the surface runoff potential of the site. A combination of mechanical methods often is prescribed, but the establishment of the protective vegetative cover should follow as quickly as possible regardless of the method.

Contour furrows, small ditches from 20 to 30 cm in depth that follow contours, break a slope length into segments and provide storage depressions for surface runoff. The furrows, usually constructed with a single-blade furrow plow that builds berms on the downslope side, form miniature terraces that hold water in place until it infiltrates into the soil. Furrows are most effective if the spacing between them is less than 2 m. However, the spacing pattern depends upon the degree of slope steepness.

Furrows must be placed on the contours. Otherwise, they become drainage ditches that concentrate runoff and accelerate soil erosion rather than prevent it. The effectiveness of furrows is increased, and the improper alignment of furrows with contours can be corrected by constructing crossbars within the furrows at intervals of from 1.5 to 10 m. In essence, the furrows then become a chain of small basins. If one basin fails, water in adjacent basins will be held in place. Contour furrows often fail because they do not follow the contours, the vegetative cover was not established successfully, and follow-up maintenance was not achieved.

Trenches are used on slopes too steep for contour furrows. There are two types of trenches, a *shallow outside type*, in which excavated materials form barriers to overland water flow, and a *deeper inside type*, in which the excavation retains most of the overland water flow. In general, the outside type of trench is suitable for slopes up to 30 percent and the inside type for steeper slopes up to 70 percent. Both types of trenches are expensive to build, require special machinery to construct, and must be designed to handle large flows of water. The failure of a trench on an upper slope could have a "domino effect" on trench failures downslope.

Revegetated strips have proven successful in controlling surface erosion on level to gently rolling landscapes by breaking the length of an obstructed slope. These strips are about 1 m wide, parallel to the contour, and cultivated to remove unwanted vegetation, loosen the land surface, and prepare a seedbed for planting. The original vegetation is left between strips until the newly planted vegetation becomes established. New strips then are tilled and planted, and the process is continued until the area that is subject to surface erosion has been rehabilitated. Conventional tillage equipment can be used for this technique.

Pitting is a technique of digging shallow depressions into the land surface to create storage for the surface runoff, promote infiltration, and facilitate revegetation in dryland regions. Pitting of extensive areas requires a tractor and a *pitter*. A conventional disk plow can be modified readily into a pitter. The number of pits required is estimated by dividing the calculated surface runoff from a *design storm* by the storage capacity per pit. Pitting generally is effective in controlling surface erosion on slopes of up to 30 percent.

Basins, which are similar to pits in design but larger, are usually about 2 m long, 1.8 m wide, and 15–20 cm deep. However, basins that are constructed manually require a large labor force. Therefore, basin-forming machines have been developed for use in large-scale operations.

Measurement of Surface Erosion

Surface erosion rates can be estimated by several field methods, including the use of plots, stakes, or measurements of natural landscape features.

Plots The most widely used method of estimating surface erosion rates is to directly measure the amount of soil that washes away from plots. To obtain this estimate, collecting troughs are sunken along the width of the bottom of the plots. Walls of plastic, sheet metal, plywood, or concrete are inserted at least 10 cm into the soil surface to form boundaries of the plots. The collecting troughs empty into a tank, in which both runoff and sediment are measured. Sometimes, these tanks are installed with continuous recording instruments so that rates of flow also can be measured. In other instances, the total volume of water and sediment is measured after individual rainfall events.

Plots vary in size from microplots of from 1 to 2 m^2 to the "standard" plot of 6 × 72.6 ft (approximately 2 × 22 m), that is, the 0.01-acre (0.004-ha) plot used for the Universal Soil Loss Equation (USLE) discussed later. Microplots are less expensive for multiple comparisons of vegetation, soil, and land use. However, larger plots provide more realistic estimates of surface erosion, because these plots better represent cumulative effects of increasing runoff and velocity downslope. Plots larger than the "standard" produce large volumes of runoff and sediment that are difficult to store. In these cases, devices that split or sample a proportion of the total water and sediment can be used, allowing larger plots to be used to quantify effects of large-scale land use practices.

Stakes Insertion of stakes into the soil can be used to estimate soil losses and sediment depositions that occur along hillslopes. A metal nail with a washer commonly is inserted into the soil, and the distance between the head of the nail and washer is measured. This distance increases as erosion continues, because soil that supports the washer is washed away. If the washer causes a pedestal to form immediately beneath the washer because of the protection from rainfall impact, measurements must be made from the nail head to the bottom of the pedestal. A benchmark should be established in close proximity of the stakes to provide a stable point of reference, and the stakes should be marked clearly for relocation.

Erosion stakes normally are arranged in a grid pattern along hillslopes. Repeated measurements of the stakes through time furnish information about the changes in soil surfaces that result from soil losses and depositions. This method of estimating surface erosion is inexpensive, but it presents some difficulty in converting the measurements obtained into actual soil losses in quantitative terms.

Natural Landscape Features Estimates of surface erosion sometimes can be made from measurements of natural landscape features, for example, from pedestals. Pedestals often form beneath clumps of perennial grasses, dense trees and shrubs, or other areas that are protected from impacts of rainfall. The distance from the pedestal top to its bottom increases as erosion removes soil from around these features. Repeated measurements of the heights of residual soil pedestals provide estimates, as described above.

A key to this approach is to relate the measurements obtained to a benchmark. Sometimes, the amount of soil that has eroded away from the roots of trees or shrubs can be estimated by repeated measurements of the soil surface and a point on exposed roots or from a nail driven into stems of the plants.

Prediction of Surface Erosion

Surface erosion is predicted from empirical relationships, physical processes, or a combination thereof. The empirically based Universal Soil Loss Equation (USLE) is used throughout the world to predict surface erosion, or more precisely soil loss (Elliot et al. 1991). The USLE predicts sheet and rill erosion with the following relationship:

$$A = RKLSCP \tag{18.1}$$

where A = Average annual soil loss (t/ha/yr)
R = Rainfall erosivity factor
K = Soil erodibility factor
L = Slope length factor
S = Slope steepness factor
C = Cover management factor
P = Supporting practice (conservation) factor

The USLE was developed for agricultural croplands and, as a consequence, had only limited use in predicting surface erosion from natural forests, woodlands, and grasslands until sufficient empirical field investigations were carried out to modify

Example 18.2

Estimation of Soil Erosion Rates by Applying the Modified Universal Soil Loss Equation (MSLE) (Brooks et al. 1991)   Surface erosion (sheet and rill erosion) rates were estimated for a 12,000 ha watershed in the Loukos Basin, northern Morocco, by applying the MSLE. Based on previous studies in the area and interpolations of tables published by the U.S. Soil Conservation Service (1977), the values necessary for applying the MSLE were $R = 400$, $K = 0.15$, $LS = 10$, and $VM = 0.13$ (a 30 percent ground cover of grass with a 25 percent canopy of tall weeds). Therefore:

$$A = RK(LS)(VM)$$
$$= (400)(0.15)(10)(0.13) = 78 \text{ t/ha/yr}$$

Total erosion from the watershed was 936,000 t/yr. Revegetative measures, as part of a watershed rehabilitation project, are anticipated to result in the following:

1/2 watershed area = 25% forest canopy with a 60% ground cover of grass
1/2 watershed area = 80% grass cover with a 25% short-shrub cover

These changes in vegetative cover are expected to reduce surface erosion, estimated by the MSLE with appropriately modified *VM* factors (U.S. Soil Conservation Service 1977), as follows:

$$A \ (1/2 \ \text{area}) = (400)(0.15)(10)(0.041) = 24.6 \text{ t/ha}$$
$$A \ (1/2 \ \text{area}) = (400)(0.15)(10)(0.012) = 7.2 \text{ t/ha}$$

The surface erosion rates for the rehabilitated watershed, therefore, is estimated to be 190,800 t/yr, a reduction of 745,200 t/yr.

the USLE for applicat⁚ .ns in these ecosystems. In these modifications, the *C* and *P* factors are replaced with a vegetative management (*VM*) factor (Example 18.2). The modified USLE considers the following (Dissmeyer and Foster 1985):

- Height and density of the vegetative canopy.
- Amount of bare soil on the site.
- Soil reconsolidation that considers whether disking, root-raking, or other forms of tillage have taken place.
- Organic content of soils.
- Effects of fine rootlets in the upper soil layers.

- On-site depression storage, which relates to the roughness of soils.
- Residual binding effects that consider prior land use.
- Other tillage or conservation practices in place.

Models have been developed to predict surface erosion from individual storms. These models require that runoff be estimated, with this estimate either used with the R factor in the USLE or replacing it with an alternative. One model, described by Elliot et al. (1991), uses the *KLSCP* factors of the USLE, but estimates soil losses from a single storm, as follows:

$$Y = 11.8(Qp)^{0.56}KLSCP \qquad (18.2)$$

where Y = Sediment yield (t/ha)
Q = Storm runoff
P = Peak discharge

There are a number of process-oriented erosion prediction models that are at different stages of development and testing. The purpose of these models is to relate the hydrologic processes and erosion processes in a realistic spatial and temporal setting. However, none of these models has emerged as a standard to the extent that the USLE and its modifications have become.

GULLY EROSION

Uncontrolled surface runoff, once it becomes concentrated, is capable of creating the spectacular gully formations that are commonly found in many dryland regions of the world. A *gully* is a relatively deep, recently formed eroding channel on hillslopes and valley floors where no well-defined channels previously existed. Water flows in these channels are ephemeral. The formation of gullies can be the result of soil mass wasting, although it is more often that gullies develop because of concentrated surface runoff on hillslopes with little vegetative cover and highly erodible soils. Gullies are common on sites subjected to land mismanagement.

Processes

Gullies form when the surface water becomes concentrated and overland flow occurs over a *nickpoint*, an abrupt change in elevation and gradient of the land surface that leads to increased velocity and turbulence of the water flow (Figure 18.4). Situations that result in accelerated flow velocity over bare soil can degrade the soil surface and begin processes of gully formation.

Once gully formation is initiated, there are two processes involved in gully erosion, *downcutting* and *head cutting*. Downcutting is the vertical lowering of a gully bottom, leading to gully deepening and widening. Headcutting is the upslope

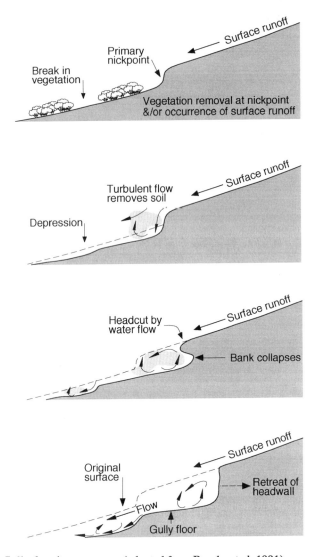

Figure 18.4. Gully-forming processes (adapted from Brooks et al. 1991)

movement of the gully into headwater areas, a process that increases the number of tributaries. Gully-forming processes generally move toward the attainment of a dynamic equilibrium at early stages of gully development. As gullies become older, however, they become more like a river. Active gully formation can be reinitiated following a period of stabilization by changes in vegetative cover, patterns and amounts of surface runoff, and landform features. It must be recognized that development of gullies is rarely an "orderly" process that moves from one condition to an advanced condition in sequence.

Gully erosion is prevalent in dryland regions where soil compaction and vegetation removal have resulted in concentrated surface runoff. However, subsurface
water flow also can dissolve, dislodge, and transport soil particles. In situations
where large subterranean voids are present in the soil, *nonmatrix flow* can occur.
When this flow becomes turbulent, as opposed to laminar, *matrix flow*, it is called
pipe flow. Soil pipes can grow to attain diameters in excess of 1 m, in which case
the soil above them often collapses. This process then can lead to formation of
gullies, often resulting in greater soil erosion than the actual pipe flow itself.

After gully erosion is initiated, it is difficult and expensive to control. Severely
gullied lands can threaten valuable forests, woodlands, plantations, livestock
grazing lands, agricultural fields, and cultural improvements such as buildings or
roads. Gullied watersheds also can be a major source of sediment or flood-level
water flows that threaten the production of farm lands or operational lives of irrigation works and reservoirs. Large-scale gully control efforts usually should be
undertaken only when the costs of control are less than the probable benefits.

Methods of Control

To be effective, gully control must stabilize the slope gradient and nickpoints.
Permanent gully control is obtained only by returning the site to a "good hydrologic condition," which necessitates the establishment and maintenance of a protective cover of vegetation, not only on severely eroding sites, but also on areas
above where surface runoff originates (Brooks et al. 1991, Heede 1976).

Establishment of Vegetative Cover On sites in which a vegetative cover will
grow rapidly, slope gradients can be controlled by the establishment of plants,
often without the employment of structural measures. The most effective vegetative cover in gullies is that comprised of a high density of rapidly growing relatively short plants with deep, dense root systems. Tall, flexible grasses and other
herbaceous plants are less suitable, as these plants are forced down on the gully
bottom under the impact of water flow, creating a smooth interface between the
flow and original stream bed that increases velocities of runoff.

Trees and shrubs can restrict the flow of water and, at the same time, cause a
diversion of water against stream banks. Where these restrictions are concentrated,
the water can leave the original gully, developing new gullies and headcuts from
where the flow reenters the original channel. However, trees and shrubs can be
planted on low sloping gradients in wide gullies to form "live dams" to accumulate
sediment by reducing runoff velocities.

Establishing vegetation can take considerable time on actively eroding sites.
Therefore, mechanical methods or control structures might be required to stabilize
a site for a time sufficiently long for vegetation to become established. During this
time, it is necessary to exclude livestock from the site and to follow up with strict
grazing controls. In no instance should structural measures be considered as a permanent solution to the control of gully erosion, regardless of how well they are
constructed.

Structural Measures   Structural measures can be necessary if conditions do not permit the immediate establishment of a vegetative cover. These measures are required at critical locations where stream channel changes take place. Such locations are nickpoints, headcuts, and gully reaches close to the gully mouth, where deepening, widening, and deposition frequently alternate with different regimes of water flow. Normally, these critical locations can be identified easily.

An effective structural design will help to establish and maintain vegetation in a number of ways. If the gully gradient is stabilized, vegetation can become established on the gully bottom. Stabilized gully bottoms make possible the stabilization of stream banks, since the toe of the gully side slopes is at rest (Heede 1976). This process can be accelerated mechanically by sloughing gully banks at sites where steep banks prevent vegetation establishment. However, banks should be sloughed only after the bottom is stable.

Vegetative establishment also is accelerated if large deposits of sediment are allowed to accumulate in the gully above structural works. Such deposits increase the soil water storage capacities and decrease channel gradients, as discussed in the following reference to *check dams*.

One structural measure that often is considered in attempting to control gully erosion is the construction of check dams. The purpose of a check dam is to replace the v-pattern of channel bed erosion with a broader channel bottom that is formed by the retention of sediment and other debris behind the dam (Hattinger 1976). In this way, the tractive forces of the erosion processes are reduced. Another important effect is to support the toe of steep slopes by sediment depositions and, in doing so, protect against undercutting of the slope.

Check dams often are required to control gully erosion when the erosion has caused advanced stages of degradation (Hattinger 1976, Heede 1976). In essence, check dams are barriers placed in series in an actively eroding gully to trap sediment that is carried down the gully during surface runoff events. The sediment that is deposited behind a check dam:

- Develops a new channel bottom with a gentler slope than the original gully bottom, reducing the velocities and erosive forces of gully flows.
- Stabilizes side slopes of the gully and "encourages" adjustment to their natural angle of repose, reducing further erosion of channel banks.
- Promotes the establishment of vegetation on the slopes and channel bottom of a gully.
- Stores and slowly releases water in such a way that the local water table is raised, enhancing vegetative growth outside of the gully.

Check dams can be built of loose rock, rock bound by wire mesh, or nonporous materials such as prestressed concrete (Heede 1976). Logs and small branches in combination with loose rock also have been utilized, although this approach often is not recommended because these materials do not remain in place long enough.

When wood rots, it causes changes in the conformation of the check dam, which can result in a new cycle of erosion.

Check dams should be located at the points predicted to be the toe of the sediment deposits backed up behind the next dam downstream. Check dams also should initially be constructed at the top of a gully, and then successive check dams built downslope. The ratio of the slope of the sediment deposits to the slope of the original gully bottom has been estimated at between 0.3 and 0.65 for sandy soils, and between 0.6 and 0.7 for fine-textured soils (Brooks et al. 1991). The steeper the original gully gradient, the smaller the ratio of aggraded slope to original slope. Headcut areas above the uppermost dam in a series should be stabilized with riprap materials or loose rock.

SOIL MASS MOVEMENT

Soil mass movement, also called *soil mass wasting*, is potentially an important type of erosion in steep, mountainous country. Soil mass movement, which involves erosion processes in which cohesive masses of soil are displaced, can be rapid, as is the case with landslides, or it can be slow, as with slumps and soil creeps. The types of soil mass movement are shown in Figure 18.5. The activities of people can accelerate the processes of mass movement.

Processes

Soil mass movement is the instantaneous downslope movement of soil, rock, and debris through the force of gravity. Soil mass movement occurs on hillslopes where *shear stress factors*, or forces that promote failure, become large in relation to *shear strength factors*, which represent the resistance of soil to failure. These conditions are found in steep mountainous areas that experience high intensity rainfall events. The stability of soils on hillslopes can be expressed in terms of a safety factor (F) as follows:

$$F = \frac{\text{Shear Strength Factors}}{\text{Shear Stress Factors}} \qquad (18.3)$$

Safety factor values of $F < 1$ indicate high probabilities of soil mass movement, while values of $F > 1$ suggest little risk of failure. In many respects, however, this relationship is more conceptual than mathematical in its application and interpretation.

Forces that promote soil mass movement increase, in general, as the slope and weight of the soil mass increase. Bedding planes and fractures, addition of large amounts of water to the soil mantle, and undercutting in road construction are common causes of increased shear stress (Brooks et al. 1991, Swanston and Swanson 1980). Resistance of soil to failure is determined by a complex set of relation-

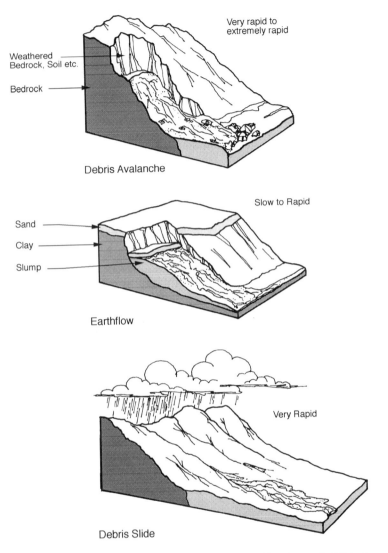

Figure 18.5. Types of soil mass movement (adapted from Brooks et al. 1991, Swanston and Swanson 1980, Varnes 1958)

ships involving the soil and inclination of the hillslope and the strength and structure of underlying rock. Cohesion of soil particles and *fractional resistance*, the latter being a function of the angle or internal friction of the soil and effective weight of the soil mass, between the soil mass and sliding surface are the major factors affecting shear strength. Shear stress and shear strength factors are dependent, in large part, upon the physiographical characteristics of a hillslope.

Methods of Control

Vegetation with deep, dense root systems, such as trees and shrubs, contribute to the fractional resistance of a sloping soil mass. Trees and shrubs help to stabilize soils up to 1 m in depth by vertically anchoring themselves into stable substrate (Brooks et al. 1991). Plants with fine to medium root systems provide lateral strength, also improving slope stability. The removal of soil water on a hillslope by evapotranspiration can result in lower water pore pressures, reduced weight of a soil mass, and reduced chemical weathering. The root strength characteristics of many tree and shrub species and the high evapotranspiration values of most forests, woodlands, and plantations suggest that such vegetative cover is better than herbaceous cover in reducing soil mass movement. Properly planned and carefully implemented forestry practices, therefore, are important to the control of soil mass movement.

Most commonly, road construction and the harvesting of trees and shrubs have the greatest land use impacts on erosion processes that lead to soil mass movement (Brooks et al. 1991, Hattinger 1976, Hudson 1981). Undercutting of slopes and improper drainage of roads are major causes of accelerated soil mass movement, necessitating a minimum of earthwork and the proper design and control of drainage in road construction. In reference to harvesting practices on steep slopes, the removal of trees or shrubs from a hillslope must be done in a manner that will maintain stability of the soil mass. Areas that naturally are susceptible to soil mass movement should be avoided altogether. Similar considerations also must be taken into account in the removal of trees and shrubs in the conversion of a site from a forest or woodland to agricultural crops of forage plants. In many instances, it is necessary to retain a cover of trees, shrubs, and other herbaceous plants on steep slopes to reduce the hazard of soil mass movement.

EFFECTS OF SOIL EROSION ON PRODUCTIVITY

The ability to reduce accelerated soil erosion, so that the long-term productivity of the land is not impaired, is one of the challenges confronting natural resource managers in dryland environments. To determine the effects of wind and water erosion on soil productivity requires an understanding of the relationships between rates of soil loss and the growth and subsequent productivity of plants through time. Unfortunately, these relationships are unknown in many cases and, of course, susceptible to the variations of rainfall that are found in dryland regions. Regardless of the setting, however, the effective root zone of the soil has to become diminished to the point at which plants can not grow at the same levels as those prior to erosion for long-term productivity of soil to become impaired. At some point, the loss of soil can become irreversible.

In most parts of the world, we simply do not have information about the reductions of productivity that have resulted from past erosion. As pointed out by

---

Example 18.3

Productivity Loss in Ethiopia Is Serious at a National Scale (Hurni 1986) Ethiopia is reported to have about 2×10^6 ha of agricultural cropland that has eroded to the point that the situation is considered irreversible in terms of long-term productivity. In northern Ethiopia, for example, 40,000 km^2 have become irreversibly degraded stone deserts. It has been estimated that total erosion damage in Ethiopia was about 30×10^6 in 1986 and is projected to equal 900×10^6 by the year 2035. These damages were estimated to be allocated as follows:

85% = Lost agricultural crop production, of which 45% was eroded so badly as to totally go out of crop production and 55% likely would lower crops yields
20% = Lost livestock production

Dregne (1990), information about erosion's permanent effect on soil productivity largely is anecdotal. Nevertheless, it appears that soil productivity loss is serious in many dryland countries of Africa, including Algeria, Ethiopia (Example 18.3), Kenya, Morocco, Nigeria, Tunisia, and Zimbabwe. Much of this soil loss occurs on agricultural cropland. Serious losses in productivity from degraded forests and woodlands, and overgrazed grasslands also are suspected but not quantified.

A problem of quantifying losses of productivity associated with soil erosion in dryland regions is confounded by the variability in annual and seasonal rainfall patterns. Production of natural forage plants and agricultural crops responds dramatically to shifts in rainfall amount and timing. The loss of productivity because of soil erosion is more subtle and longterm, and, therefore, easily masked by rainfall variability.

SUMMARY

Erosion of soil by the actions of water can be seen as surface erosion, gully erosion, and some types of soil mass movement on upslope sites. Improper land use practices that reduce the protective vegetation tend to accelerate soil erosion. After reading this chapter, you should have an understanding of soil erosion and control measures, and be able to:

1. Describe the processes of soil erosion by the actions of raindrop impacts and subsequent overland water flow.

2. Explain how land use practices and changes in vegetative covers influence the processes of soil erosion described above.

3. Explain and apply the Modified Universal Soil Loss Equation (MSLE) in estimating soil loss under different land use practices and vegetative cover conditions.

4. Describe how gullies are formed.

5. Explain the roles of vegetative and structural measures in controlling gully erosion.

6. Explain the meanings of *shear resistance* and *shear strength* as they pertain to soil mass movement.

REFERENCES

Branson, F. A., G. F. Gifford, K. G. Renard, and R. F. Hadley. 1981. *Rangeland hydrology*. Kendall/Hunt Publishing Company, Dubuque, Iowa.

Brooks, K. N., P. F. Ffolliott, H. M. Gregersen, and J. L. Thames. 1991. *Hydrology and the management of watersheds*. Iowa State University Press, Ames, Iowa.

Child, R. D., H. F. Heady, R. A. Petersen, R. D. Pieper, and C. E. Poulton. 1987. *Arid and semiarid rangeland: Guidelines for development*. Winrock International, Morrilton, Arkansas.

Dissmeyer, G. E., and G. R. Foster. 1985. Modifying the Universal Soil Loss Equation for forest land. In El-Swaify, S. A., W. C. Moldenhauer, and A. Lo (eds.). 1985. *Soil erosion and conservation*. Soil and Water Conservation Society of America, Ankeny, Iowa, pp. 480–95.

Dregne, H. E. 1990. Erosion and soil productivity in Africa. *Journal of Soil and Water Conservation* 45:431–36.

Elliot, W. J., G. R. Foster, and A. V. Elliot. 1991. Soil erosion: Processes, impacts, and prediction. In Lal, R., and F. J. Pierce (eds.). 1991. *Soil management for sustainability*. Soil and Water Conservation Society of America, Ankeny, Iowa, pp. 25–34.

Harrison, P. 1987. *The greening of Africa: Breaking through in the battle for land and food*. Penguin Books, New York.

Hattinger, H. 1976. Torrent control in the mountains with special reference to the tropics. In Kunkle, S. H., and J. L. Thames (eds.). 1976. Hydrological techniques for upstream conservation. *FAO Conservation Guide* 2, Rome, pp. 119–34.

Heathcote, R. L. 1983. *The arid lands: Their use and abuse*. Longman, London.

Heede, B. H. 1976. Gully development and control: The status of our knowledge. *USDA Forest Service, Research Paper* RM-169.

Hudson, N. W. 1981. *Soil conservation*. Cornell University Press, New York.

Hurni, H. 1986. *Highlands reclamation study, final report*. Vols. 1 and 2, FAO, Rome.

Nair, P. K. R. 1989. *Agroforestry systems in the tropics*. Kluwer Academic Publishers, Boston.

Rocheleau, D., F. Weber, and A. Field-Juma. 1988. *Agroforestry in dryland Africa*. International Council for Research in Agroforestry, Nairobi, Kenya.

Satterlund, D. R., and P. W. Adams. 1992. *Wildland watershed management*, 2nd ed. John Wiley & Sons, Inc., New York.

Swanston, D. H., and F. J. Swanson. 1980. *Soil mass movement*. Environmental Protection Agency, Environmental Research Laboratory EPA-600/8-80-012, Athens, Georgia.

Thames, J. L. 1989. Watershed management in arid zones. In FAO. 1989. Role of forestry in combating desertification. *FAO Conservation Guide* 21, Rome, pp. 211–33.

U.S. Soil Conservation Service. 1977. Procedure for computing sheet and rill erosion on project areas. *U.S. Soil Conservation Service, Technical Release* 41.

Varnes, D. J. 1958. Landslide types and processes. In Eckel, E. B. (ed.). 1958. Landslides and engineering practice. *National Academy of Sciences, Highway Research Board Specifications Report* 29, Washington, D.C., pp. 20–47.

Weber, F. R. 1986. *Reforestation in arid lands*. VITA Publications, Arlington, Virginia.

Wiedemann, H. T. 1988. Engineering systems for vegetative rehabilitation of arid lands. In Whitehead, E. F., C. F. Hutchinson, B. N. Timmermann, and R. G. Varady (eds.). 1988. *Arid land: Today and tomorrow*. Westview Press, Boulder, Colorado, pp. 871–81.

19 Rehabilitation of Saline Environments

It is well known that reductions in vegetative cover can lead to soil erosion and other forms of site degradation. What is not so well known, however, is that reductions in the vegetative cover also can lead to problems of salinity, especially in dryland environments. Reductions in vegetative cover leading to salinization often result from improper development schemes or excessive use of agricultural or natural resources on these fragile sites. The magnitude of these problems is illustrated by the fact that in excess of 9 million km^2 of land are salt-affected, with about 4 million km^2 being either dominantly saline or sodical (Malcolm 1989). These estimates are low because in some countries (e.g., Egypt and the Sudan) the extent of salinity is quantified only for irrigated areas, while other areas of salt-affected soils are known to occur. Extensive areas of salinity also are known to occur in countries such as Chile, Tunisia, and others, although reliable estimates are unavailable.

Until recently, the management of salt-affected lands has been restricted largely to establishment of salt-tolerant forage plants on affected areas for grazing by livestock (Armitage 1987, FAO 1989, Greenwood 1988, Malcolm 1989). Now, however, it is becoming more widely recognized that vegetation can be managed in ways that can lead to rehabilitation of saline environments, in addition to providing economic benefits. The possibilities for rehabilitation of salt-affected lands is increasing as a result. Knowing the causal relationships between vegetation management and salinity are necessary, therefore, to develop effective programs of rehabilitation.

The purpose of this chapter is to describe, in a general sense, the relationships between vegetation management and salinity and to outline methods of rehabilitation involving the planting of trees, shrubs, and other herbaceous species. Two types of saline areas are recognized. *Recharge areas*, where the causes of salinization occur, and *discharge areas*, where the effects of salinization occur. Each of these areas requires different considerations and rehabilitative measures. Rehabilitation of discharge areas is stressed initially in this chapter.

VEGETATION MANAGEMENT AND SALINITY

Engineering solutions were the mainstays of rehabilitation in the past, but they often were unsatisfactory because of their high costs, water shortages, material shortages, and other technical problems, including water quality, impermeable soils, and lack of dispersal areas (Malcolm 1989). An alternative to engineering solutions is to establish plants of sufficient salt-tolerances to survive on deteriorated saline sites. A prerequisite to this goal, however, is a general knowledge of the processes of salinization and the impacts of vegetative management on these processes.

Processes

Low rainfall and high potential evaporation rates in dryland regions means that most of the rainfall will be intercepted by the sparse plant canopies and then evaporated into the atmosphere, evaporated from soil surfaces, and lost through transpiration, processes that were discussed in Chapter 4. Under these conditions, only a small portion of the rainfall percolates below rooting zones of plants to water tables. Since water is the primary agent of salt movement in soil, it is the high rate of evapotranspiration in relation to the relatively limited percolation of water in soil that provides conditions for salt to accumulate and persist in the soil. Low-intensity, long-duration rainfall events, which are relatively infrequent in dryland regions, are needed for infiltration and percolation to occur which will move salt through the soil.

A question often asked is, *Where does the salt come from in the first place?* Salt is found naturally in rain, which contains small quantities of salt derived originally from oceans. Some of the salt that falls in rain enters the rooting zones of plants, where it is taken up in the transpiration process. Some of this salt is excluded by roots of plants and, as a result, accumulates in rooting zones within soil profiles (Greenwood 1988). Some dryland plants have evolved mechanisms that allow them to survive in saline soils and help them eliminate competition from other plants. Species of eucalyptus, for example, exclude salt in soil solutions through the transpiration process. Another example is salt-cedar (*Tamarisk* spp.), which exudes salt from glands in their leaves, resulting in salt accumulations on the soil surface.

When annual rainfall exceeds 900 mm, the salt concentration process essentially is equaled by leaching, which flushes salt to groundwater reserves. In regions with low rainfall, however, this equilibrium rarely occurs and, as a consequence, salinity can reach high levels in rooting zones of plants. To illustrate this point, in soils supporting natural forests in Western Australia, soil solutions have salt concentrations higher than that of oceans. The mass of salt approaches 9.5×10^5 kg/ha in some instances (Dimmock et al. 1974).

Impacts of Vegetative Management

Now, suppose that the leaf area of the sparse vegetation is reduced, such as that which occurs in the cutting of trees or shrubs for fuelwood or the overgrazing of forage plants by sheep, goats, or other livestock. When this happens, transpiration by the residual plants and plant parts will be less than vegetation in the pristine state, slowing accumulations of salt. The resulting higher soil moisture and increases in throughfall of rain through sparse plant canopies can increase recharge to water tables, causing them to rise into areas of accumulated salts in the soil on some sites. It is felt that although annual inputs of rain and, therefore, salt inputs remain unchanged, the stored salt will move upward in soil profiles with rising water tables (Greenwood 1988).

The above phenomenon can be explained through a *water budget*, the concept of which was described in Chapter 4. In a water budget, rainfall is partitioned into evapotranspiration, runoff, infiltration and percolation, seepages, and soil water storage (Brooks et al. 1991, Dunne and Leopold 1978). There are variations in the magnitudes of these pathway components from year to year, especially in dryland regions, although relative stability in the hydrologic cycle often is assumed in the long run and with pristine vegetation. The levels of water tables are relatively constant with this condition, but they rise and fall in response to the long-term precipitation patterns.

However, reductions in the leaf area of the vegetation, as might occur from the cutting of trees and shrubs or overgrazing of forage plants, also reduces evapotranspiration, with balancing increases in throughfall, runoff, infiltration and percolation, seepage, soil water storage, and, therefore, drainage to groundwater reserves. Water tables will rise, affecting the movement of stored salt upward (Example 19.1).

Alternatively, the leaf area on a site might increase as a consequence of planned management practices. Increases in leaf area can occur when managerial decisions are made to convert overgrazed land on which utilization of forage plants by livestock has reduced leaf area, root growth, and transpiration to agricultural crops or to reforest or afforest a denuded site. Regardless of the reasons for leaf area increases, salinization processes that were caused by the reductions of leaf area generally are reversed. Leaching will tend to decline, resulting in increases of stored salt.

Example 19.1

Rise in Water Table Following a Reduction of Leaf Area (Sharma and Williamson 1984) That permanent water tables can rise following a reduction of leaf area, in this case the leaf area of a forest, is shown by work of Sharma and Williamson in southern Australia, illustrated below. Matching levels of water tables on paired, initially forested watersheds diverged immediately following the clearing of one watershed for agricultural purposes. The water table level on the cleared watershed continued to rise for several years after treatment.

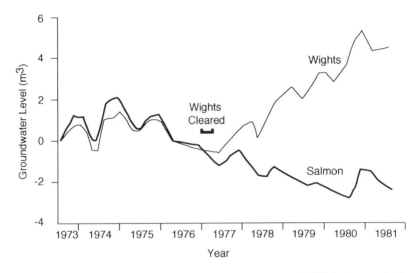

Changes in water table levels in forested (Salmon) and cleared (Wights) watersheds

One example that demonstrates the effects of changes in leaf area on salt storage is based on work of Peck and Hurle (1973), who measured the salt inputs in rainfall and salt outputs in streamflow discharges from 15 small experimental watersheds located in southwestern Australia. The measured salt balances on these watersheds are shown in Figure 19.1. On eight dominantly forested watersheds, the ratios of salt inputs to salt outputs nearly were balanced, averaging about 1:4. Comparable ratios averaged 5:1 on seven watersheds cleared of forests, indicating that the clearing of forests and, as a result, reducing leaf area can result in salt outputs greatly exceeding salt inputs.

Salt exclusion by vegetation causes salt to be stored in many soils (Greenwood 1988). Furthermore, it is the increased throughfall of rain from lower leaf areas that provides the additional water to mobilize the stored salt upward and also downslope, where it can form salt seeps and also enter streams. From these connections, therefore, one can conclude that vegetative mismanagement involving improper cutting of trees and shrubs for fuelwood or overgrazing by livestock can lead to salinization. On the other hand, it is possible that other vegetative measures, and particularly revegetation, might be able to rehabilitate salt-affected lands by reducing the amounts of mobilizing water. It is with this second proposition that this chapter now concerns itself.

REVEGETATION AND REHABILITATION

Evidence of successful vegetative management and rehabilitation of saline environments is rare, largely circumstantial, and limited in scope. Most of the examples

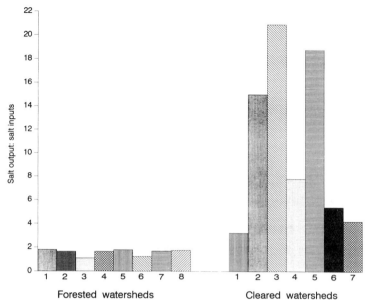

Figure 19.1. Salt balances on forested and cleared watersheds in southwestern Australia (adapted from Peck, A. J., and D. H. Hurle, "Chloride balance of some farmed and forested catchments in southwestern Australia," *Water Resources Research*, Vol. 9, p. 652, 1973, copyright by the American Geophysical Union)

of successes involve the replacement of shallow-rooted plants with low transpiration rates by deep-rooted species with high transpiration rates (Brown et al. 1983, Doering and Sandoval 1976). There is little documentation of successful rehabilitation through *revegetation*, although this approach to rehabilitation of salt-affected lands likely offers the most promise.

To rehabilitate saline environments by revegetation, a managerial strategy is necessary to discharge more water into soil bodies to lower water tables to safe levels (Greenwood 1988). In formulating this strategy, it is important that estimates be made of the following:

- Maximum amounts of water that percolate through soils but lowers water tables to safe levels.
- Quantities of extra water that reach the water tables after revegetation of salt-affected lands. (Hydrologists estimate increases in recharge of water tables following changes in vegetative cover by measuring responses directly in water tables, using water budget changes, tracer techniques, or plot studies.)
- Interception of rainfall by plant canopies, evaporation from soil surfaces, and transpiration by species that are included in revegetation measures. (Methods for measuring interception, evaporation, and transpiration, discussed in Chapter 4, serve these purposes.)

Methods for revegetation of saline environments can be prescribed from estimations of the above and consideration of other factors. Other factors to be considered include the purposes of rehabilitation programs, selection of plant species, methods of establishment, placement of plants on salt-affected landscapes, and costs of revegetation.

Purposes of Rehabilitation Programs

Revegetative programs to rehabilitate saline environments can serve a number of purposes in addition to rehabilitation. It is important, therefore, to establish clearly the purposes of a rehabilitation program in the beginning of the planning phase. In deciding upon the specific purposes, the following should be kept in mind (FAO 1989):

- Establishment of protective covers of vegetation on otherwise bare saline areas can contribute to a reduction of soil erosion processes. To illustrate this point, several *Atriplex* spp. exhibit prostrate growth habitats and stem layering, excellent characteristics for reducing soil erosion (Malcolm 1989). Moreover, layered stems are more able to survive intensive grazing by livestock.
- Trees and shrubs planted on salt-affected lands often are cut for fuel. Other herbaceous species planted primarily for forage production also can be utilized as a fuel. It is necessary, however, that appropriate compromises be found between rehabilitation and fuel production.
- Many salt-tolerant plants, including some tree and shrub species, can fill seasonal deficiencies in forage supplies and also provide valuable forage resources in periods of prolonged drought. Chenopod shrubs, for example, are planted on saline areas for this purpose (Greenwood 1988, Malcolm 1989). In some situations, these shrubs also furnish shelter for livestock.
- Bare salt-affected lands are poor habitats for wildlife in terms of providing required food, cover, and breeding areas. Planting of trees and shrubs, with *Atriplex cinerea* an example of the latter, provide food and cover requirements for specific wildlife species. Species planted primarily for fuel, including *Melaleuca* spp., also provide valuable wildlife shelter.
- There frequently are extensive areas around the larger cities in dryland regions that are salt-affected and unattractive. These areas, with airports, highway systems, and fringes of irrigation projects also are a source of dust, which blows through cities. Planted chenopod shrubs, such as *Atriplex cinerea*, can be a means of controlling blowing dust from these sites and, in doing so, improving local living conditions and aesthetic values.

It is fortunate that many of the above considerations can be translated into managerial goals and actions that are not mutually exclusive. In many cases, therefore, multipurpose rehabilitation programs are formulated.

Selection of Plant Species

Successful rehabilitation of saline environments through revegetation requires the careful selection of salt-tolerant plant species. Trees, shrubs, or other herbaceous plants can be selected for establishment, depending upon the management purposes and site conditions. On severely degraded sites, it might be necessary to plant *pioneer species* to ameliorate the sites sufficiently for more desirable plants, which become established subsequently (Malcolm 1989, NAS 1990).

A primary criterion in the selection of plants relates to the hydrologic task of reducing recharge of groundwater resources. An underlying requirement, consequently, is to select plant species with "superior" water-harvesting and evaporating surfaces (Greenwood 1988). With this in mind, the following statements can help in a plant selection process:

- Plants with shallow roots transpire less water than plants with deep roots, and, therefore, deep-rooted plants should be favored.
- Perennial plants should be favored over annual plants because annuals typically have smaller leaf areas, shorter leaf-cover durations, and shallower roots.
- Trees and tall shrubs should be favored over plants close to the ground. Elevated plant canopies of trees and high shrubs make better use of atmospherical advective energy, which leads to increased evaporation from wet leaves (intercepted rainfall) and higher evaporative demands (vapor pressure deficits).
- Deciduous plants transpire less water than evergreen plants, because the former have shorter leaf-cover durations, like annual plants do.
- Nonphreatophytes transpire less water than phreatophytes because of more limited water supplies. This situation can be modified if salinity in saturated soils is high, depths to phreatical surfaces are great (Van Hyleckama 1974), or the oxygen content is low.

It follows from the above that *halophytes* are important candidates for planting on salt-affected lands. Unfortunately, there have been limited analyses of comparative water use of halophytical vegetation. Nevertheless, increasing attention is focused on the use of these highly salt-tolerant plants for vegetative establishment in saline environments (Malcolm 1989).

Attention also must be directed toward the adaptations of plants to environmental factors, such as climatological conditions, salinity, and hydrology of the site, in selecting suitable species for planting on salt-affected lands (FAO 1989, Malcolm 1989). Trees, shrubs, and other herbaceous plants that have been grown successfully in saline environments are classified in relation to the climate and type of salt-affected lands in Table 19.1 (a), 19.1(b), and 19.1(c). This table is incomplete, although it illustrates a classification system that might be useful in generating lists of species that are appropriate for planting on particular saline

TABLE 19.1(a). Plant Species Grown Successfully in Saline Environments

| Climate | Type of Salt-affected Land | |
	Seacoasts	Endoreic (Closed) Basins
Warm-Mediterranean	*Sporobolus virginicus*	
	Atriplex cinerea	
	Atriplex paludose	
Dry-Steppe	*Iuncus acutus*	*Phragmites communis*
	Iuncus rigidus	
	Salsola tetrandra	
Dry-Hot desert	*Avicennia macina*	*Suaeda fruticosa*
	Aeluropus spp.	*Sporobulus marginatus*
	Sporobolus spicatus	*Aeluropus lagopoides*
	Suaeda menocia	
	Atriplex undulata	
	Atriplex amnicola	
	Atriplex canescens	
	Atriplex farinosa	
Dry-Cold desert		

TABLE 19.1(b). Plant Species Grown Successfully in Saline Environments

| Climate | Type of Salt-affected Land | |
	High Water Tables	Saline Seeps
Warm-Mediterranean	*Marieana brevifolia*	*Paspalum vaginatum*
	Atriplex amnicola	*Puccinellia ciliata*
	Atriplex undula	*Tamarix gallica*
	Atriplex lentiformis	*Agropyron elongatum*
	Atriplex nummularia	
	Halosarcia pergranulata	
Dry-Steppe	*Leptochloa fusca*	*Puccinellia distans*
	Salsola vermiculata	
	Atriplex halimus	
	Atriplex glauca	
	Atriplex undulata	
	Atriplex lampa	
	Suaeda fruticosa	
	Haloxylon schmidtii	
Dry-Hot desert	*Atriplex agrentina*	Tamarix gallica
	Atriplex boecheri	Tamarix pentandra
	Atriplex crenatifolia	
	Atriplex undulata	
	Aeluropus lagopoides	
	Sporodolus tremulus	
	Agropyron elongatum	
	Agropyron leucoclada	
	Salvadora persica	
Dry-Cold desert		

TABLE 19.1(c). Plant Species Grown Successfully in Saline Environments

Climate	Type of Salt-affected Land
	Uplands
Warm-Mediterranean	*Mairena brevifolia*
Dry-Steppe	*Atriplex vesicaria*
	Atriplex nummularia
Dry-Hot desert	
Dry-Cold desert	*Kochia prostrata*
	Aellenia subphylla
	Haloxylon aphyllum
	Salsola rigida

Source: Adapted from FAO (1989) and Malcolm (1989), by permission of the Food and Agriculture Organization of the United Nations

areas. The types of salt-affected land presented in the table likely need further refinement.

Relatively little study has been undertaken to determine which plant species are adapted to planting in saline environments in most countries with problems of salinity (Example 19.2). One exception is the work in the western United States (Barker and McKell 1979, McKell 1986, Richardson et al. 1979, Valentine 1971). Ultimately, the suitability of species depends largely upon the following considerations (Greenwood 1988, Malcolm 1989):

- Establishment, survival, and growth for the periods of time designated in the rehabilitation program.
- Production of vegetative biomass of sufficient quantity and quality.
- Sustainable growth and yield for fuelwood or forage production, when these are a managerial objective.
- Other environmental benefits, such as erosion control or soil amelioration.

Methods of Establishment

In discussing the methods of establishing plants on salt-affected lands, attention is focused on trees and shrubs in order to be consistent with the theme of this book. Those interested in the establishment of perennial grasses or other herbaceous plants in saline environments are referred to appropriate literature on this subject (Eakin and Reed 1966, Frost and Hamilton 1965, McKell 1986, Valentine 1971). In reference to trees and shrubs, these plants are established on salt-affected lands as seedlings, from cuttings or other vegetative plant sections, or through sowing of seeds.

The planting of tree or shrub seedlings is successful only if appropriate site preparation techniques are followed. Site preparation techniques should control groundwater where its presence can influence accumulations of salt on soil sur-

Example 19.2

Selection of Species for Salt-affected Areas (Malcolm 1989) Little work has been done to determine which species are adapted to salt-affected areas in most countries. Limited observations by a number of authorities indicate that salt tolerant plants can be grown outside of their original habitats or in different climates. For example, *Atriplex undulata* from central-western Argentina grows well in Mediterranean climates in southwestern Australia and on the Persian Gulf. *A. amnicola* from northwestern Australia grows well in southwestern Australia and the Persian Gulf. *A. canescens* from the southwestern United States grows well on the Persian Gulf but poorly in southwestern Australia. It also has been observed, in general, that species unaccustomed to frost likely are winterkilled when planted in colder climates. An urgent need exists, therefore, for coordinated programs to exchange seeds and other planting materials, conduct large-scale adaptation tests, describe site conditions more thoroughly, and develop a data bank about species adaptation to saline environments.

faces, encourage salt to move downward in soil profiles rather than to accumulate at the surface, or both (FAO 1989). The first situation is achieved by drainage, deep furrowing, or ridging, while the second need can be met by planting on *niches* where leaching of salt is ensured naturally or by artificially building planting niches on the sites where seedlings can become established.

An illustration of the "niche technique" is presented in Figure 19.2. This technique, employed widely in Australia, consists of making a series of furrows and ridges, with planting niches on the ridges (FAO 1989, Malcolm 1989). The furrows collect surface water, which then is stored in the soil close to plants in the niche, while the ridges allow plantings to be raised above ground level to avoid waterlogging and flooding, and to help in leaching salt from the niche. The niche also provides a sheltered planting site on which compacted sideslopes facilitate runoff concentrating in the niche. Mulching in niches promotes water penetration and leaching of salts, and reduces evaporation and crusting of the soil.

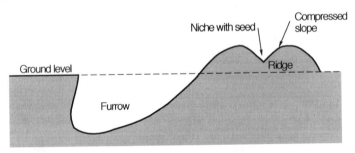

Figure 19.2. Furrow, ridge, and planting niche (adapted from the Food and Agriculture Organization of the United Nations, 1989)

Inserting unrooted cuttings or other vegetative plant sections of some tree and shrub species also is used in revegetation of some saline environments. However, inconsistent results about successes have been reported with this establishment method. Nevertheless, the method has been employed successfully in some situations when niches or similar site preparation techniques are used.

It is possible to establish a few tree and shrub species by the sowing of seeds (FAO 1989, Malcolm 1988). Strategies for successful seedings include the pretreatments of seeds to improve germination, mulches to modify soil temperatures and conserve water, and proper placement of seeds in soil. Establishment of plants from seeds faces a number of problems, which must be overcome because of:

- Low salt tolerances at time of germination.
- Poor utilization of limited rainfall.
- Temperature requirements for germination that are not attained normally.
- Poor soil structure.
- Insect attacks and diseases.

The best method of plant establishment is determined for each saline environment only by field testing and the evaluation of sites to be revegetated. After the method has been chosen, however, the following points should be considered (FAO 1989, Malcolm 1989):

- Possibilities of waterlogging, flooding, and erosion can be minimized by protecting the planting sites with appropriate soil conservation measures.
- Salt levels at the surface of soils can be reduced by cultivating the planting sites before initial seasonal rains to encourage infiltration water into the soils and to leach salts from topsoils.
- Planted areas must be protected from grazing by livestock and damage from wildlife activities.
- Protective measures should be implemented in areas where wind erosion is a problem.
- Monitoring is necessary for early detection of insect and disease problems. If they occur, these problems must be dealt with promptly.

Placement of Plants on Salt-affected Landscapes

When planning for the rehabilitation of saline environments, it is helpful to separate the affected landscapes into two recharge areas and discharge areas. The two areas are recognized in the planning process because they require different rehabilitative treatments (Greenwood 1988). Treatment of discharge areas often is deferred initially, but immediate treatment of recharge areas is mandatory. In general, there are two approaches to the rehabilitation of recharge areas:

- Plant species whose transpiration is only a little greater, relatively speaking, than that of plants to be replaced. However, these plants should be established on most of the recharge area to be effective.
- If the planted species have a "much higher" rate of transpiration than the original plants, the plantings need not cover the entire recharge area.

Successful revegetation of salt-affected lands is more effective on recharge areas largely because of the lower salinity (Greenwood 1988, Malcolm 1989). Revegetation is effective especially if rootings of plants reach into saturated zones of soil because of the permanent supplies of water. *Phreatophytes*, evergreen tree or shrub species with relatively large leaf areas, are an example of such plants.

There are several ways by which the plants can be placed in recharge areas, including one large plantation, several smaller plantations, agroforestry schemes, or "park-like" arrangements (Greenwood 1988). From a purely hydrologic standpoint, and if the roots of the plants are near or in water tables, the factor most limiting evaporation is atmospheric advective energy. On these grounds, therefore, the maximum dispersion of plants is the most effective placement. However, the land use and manner of managing plants often override this consideration of placement.

Costs of Revegetative Methods

The main costs of revegetation in salt-affected areas are those of plant production in nurseries; the labor required for planting; and fencing, when it is necessary to exclude livestock (Greenwood 1988). The lowering of costs is not necessarily a concern for tree or shrub seedlings that can be established satisfactorily by vegetative means or through direct seeding. When this is the case, costs of nursery operations are reduced greatly. The effective establishment of plants on salt-affected lands is achieved in some situations through the use of conventional crop-sowing equipment that has been modified specifically for this use, eliminating planting by hand labor. Unfortunately, fencing often is costly, although proper grazing practices can control livestock movements onto areas undergoing rehabilitation.

Frequently, the revegetation of salt-affected lands has been considered too costly, especially in situations in which labor costs are high. This situation is changing, however, with large-scale production of planting stocks, more efficient planting equipment, and improved rehabilitative methods that have increased probabilities of successes. In many situations, revegetative projects that had been abandoned or otherwise canceled because of costs should be reexamined, as their implementation might be feasible economically at this time.

TIME TO REHABILITATE SALINE ENVIRONMENTS AND LIKELIHOOD OF SUCCESS

Rehabilitation of saline environments usually requires several years, as it takes considerable time for trees and many shrubs to attain their maximum evapotranspirative capacities (Greenwood and Beresford 1979). On the other hand, annual crops reach their maximum potentials in the year of sowing. However, even when full evapotranspirative capacities are reached, evidence of rehabilitative processes might not be detected for a number of years.

Two processes must take place before saline environments again can support salt-sensitive vegetation (Greenwood 1988). First, the raising saline water tables must be checked and, eventually, begin to fall below levels of salt that are stored in soil profiles. Secondly, the salt must be leached from soil surfaces by rain for several years after the water tables have retracted to safe levels. Rehabilitation is expedited by evaporation, and one approach to achieving this is to increase the proportion of land treated.

A question commonly asked is whether it is possible to estimate beforehand the degree to which a proposed rehabilitative program will be successful. The estimation of success is dependent largely upon results of initial hydro-geological and vegetative investigations, which are costly and often require several years to complete (Greenwood 1988). Against this situation, however, must be placed needs for rehabilitation of salt-affected lands and frequent resistance to rehabilitation proposals by users of the land. Therefore, there often arises the multiple dilemma of delay, cost, uncertainty, and resistance, all of which have to be confronted and overcome. Otherwise, doing nothing will continue the devastation.

SUMMARY

In some situations, reductions in vegetative cover can lead to salinization in dryland environments. Through an understanding of the processes of salinization and the impacts of vegetative management on these processes, however, it might be possible to rehabilitate salt-affected lands by the establishment of salt tolerant plants. The purpose of this chapter was to present information necessary to understand and outline methods of rehabilitation involving the planting of trees, shrubs, and other herbaceous species. At this point in reading the book, you should be able to:

1. Explain the processes of salinization and the impacts of vegetative management on these processes.
2. Discuss criteria for the selection of trees and shrubs for rehabilitative programs.
3. Describe and explain the methods of establishing these plants.
4. Discuss the placement of plants on salt-affected lands for the purposes of rehabilitation.
5. Explain why it takes a relatively long time to rehabilitate saline environments.
6. Understand what needs to be considered in evaluating the benefits and costs of rehabilitating saline environments.

REFERENCES

Armitage, F. B. 1987. *Irrigated forestry in arid and semi-arid lands: A synthesis*. International Development Research Center, Ottawa, Canada.

Barker, J. R., and C. M. McKell. 1979. Growth of seedling and stem cuttings of two salt-desert shrubs in containers prior to field planting. *Reclamation Review* 2:85–91.

Brooks, K. N., P. F. Ffolliott, H. M. Gregersen, and J. L. Thames. 1991. *Hydrology and management of watershed lands*. The Iowa State University Press, Ames, Iowa.

Brown, P. L., A. D. Halvorson, F. H. Siddoway, H. F. Mayland, and M. R. Miller. 1983. Saline-seep diagnosis, control and reclamation. *USDA Agricultural Research Service, Conservation Research Report* 30.

Dimmock, G. M., E. Bettenay, and M. J. Mulcahy. 1974. Salt content of lateritic profiles in the Darling Range, Western Australia. *Australian Journal of Soil Research* 12:63–69.

Doering, E. J., and F. M. Sandoval. 1976. Hydrology of saline seeps in the northern Great Plains. *Transactions of the American Society of Agricultural Engineers* 19:856–65.

Dunne, T., and L. B. Leopold. 1978. *Water in environmental planning*. W. H. Freeman and Company, San Francisco.

Eakin, W., and L. W. Reed. 1966. *Establishing tall wheatgrass on saline soils in northwest Oklahoma*. Oklahoma Agricultural Experiment Station, Stillwater, Oklahoma.

Food and Agriculture Organization of the United Nations (FAO). 1989. Arid zone forestry: A guide for field technicians. *FAO Conservation Guide* 20, Rome.

Frost, K. R., and L. Hamilton. 1965. Basin forming and reseeding of rangeland. *Transactions of the American Society of Agricultural Engineers* 8:202–03, 207.

Greenwood, E. A. N. 1988. The hydrologic role of vegetation in the development and reclamation of dryland salinity. In Allen, E. B. (ed.). 1988. *The reconstruction of disturbed arid lands: An ecological approach*. Westview Press, Inc., Boulder, Colorado, pp. 205–33.

Greenwood, E. A. N., and J. D. Beresford. 1979. Evaporation from vegetation in landscapes developing secondary salinity using the ventilated-chamber technique. I. Comparative transpiration from juvenile *Eucalyptus* above saline groundwater seeps. *Journal of Hydrology* 42:369–82.

Malcolm, C. V. 1989. Rehabilitation of saline environments. In FAO. 1989b. Role of forestry in combating desertification. *FAO Conservation Guide* 21, Rome, pp. 183–99.

McKell, C. M. 1986. Propagation and establishment of plants on arid saline land. In Barrett-Lennard, E. G. (ed.). 1986. *Forage and fuel production from salt-affected wasteland*. Elsevier, Amsterdam, pp. 363–75.

NAS. 1990. *The improvement of tropical and subtropical rangelands*. National Academy of Sciences, Washington, D.C.

Peck, A. J., and D. H. Hurle. 1973. Chloride balance of some farmed and forested catchments in southwestern Australia. *Water Resources Research* 9:648–57.

Richardson, S. G., J. R. Barker, K. A. Crofts, and G. A. Van Epps. 1979. Factors affecting roots of stem cuttings of salt desert shrubs. *Journal of Range Management* 32:280–83.

Sharma, M. L., and D. R. Williamson. 1984. Secondary salinization of water resources in southern Australia. In French, R. H. (ed.). 1984. *Salinity in watercourses and reservoirs*. Butterworth Publishers, Stoneham, Massachusetts, pp. 571–80.

Valentine, J. F. 1971. *Range development and improvements.* Brigham Young University Press, Provo, Utah.

Van Hyleckama, T. E. A. 1974. Water use by salt cedar as measured by the water budget method. *U.S. Geological Survey, Professional Paper* 491E.

PART V

Implementing and Supporting Activities

20 Involvement of Rural People

The products derived from natural forests and woodlands and forest plantations provide people with essential goods and services, such as fuel for cooking and warmth, construction material for housing, and forage for cattle. Forests, woodlands, and plantations themselves help to provide clean water, protection against erosion and, in many areas, they provide shade from a burning sun. In many instances, these benefits are taken for granted. However, because of increasing population pressures and lack of appropriate forest management strategies, these benefits are no longer readily available.

Increasing pressures on forests, woodlands, and plantations for these and other benefits can result in a degradation of vegetative resources and an impoverishment of the land. Ultimately, the basic needs of people no longer may be satisfied, making the local poor even poorer. The situation can be countered by the improved management of natural forests and woodlands or the establishing of forest plantations in some areas. But, rural people often need guidance to integrate forestry into agricultural practices and to recognize that forest products and services can be as essential as agricultural products.

Many rural people have a tradition in agriculture that is not always matched by a similar attitude toward natural forests and woodlands, and forest plantations. This lack of tradition in forestry can be a barrier to the initiation of sustainable forestry projects on agricultural and grazing lands. However, this barrier often is removed by providing guidance through training and extension services, the education of people, and, most of all, by exhibiting the beneficial roles of trees and shrubs in demonstration plots that are established, for example, on a farmer's land.

A central purpose of rural development is to help people become self-reliant. However, rural development does not succeed unless it reflects the people's own interpretation of their needs, aspirations, and problems. In this respect, forestry must be forestry for people and, importantly, involve people. It must be forestry which starts at the "grass roots."

The dependence of rural people on forest products is discussed in this chapter in order to suggest that these people should become involved in forestry interventions. However, rural people often must overcome a number of constraints and conditions to fully realize the benefits of forestry. In many instances, it also becomes necessary to provide rural people with a form of external support to obtain their participation in forestry interventions and, in doing so, share in the benefits generated.

DEPENDENCE ON FOREST PRODUCTS

The importance of natural forests, woodlands, and forest plantations and the goods and services from these ecosystems to rural people is threefold (FAO 1985, FAO 1989a, Gregersen and Elz 1989):

- Trees and shrubs provide fuelwood and other goods essential to meeting basic needs at the household and community level.
- Forests, woodlands, and plantations furnish food and the environmental stability necessary for continued food production and security.
- Forests, woodlands, and plantations, and the products derived therefrom can generate income and employment in a rural community.

Fuelwood and Other Products

Wood is the dominant fuel for rural people in many countries and many of the urban poor as well, as discussed elsewhere in this book. Wood also is the principal material for constructing shelter and housing in many parts of the world. In addition, the role of trees and shrubs as a source of fodder is important. Many miscellaneous but needed nonwood products also are derived from forests, woodlands, and plantations (Example 20.1).

Billions of people use wood daily for cooking their food and maintaining warmth in the home. Wood is a preferred fuel because it can be used without complex conversion equipment. Wood frequently can be acquired at relatively little cost, often no more than the cost involved in gathering it. For the poor, there may

---

Example 20.1

Nonwood Products: Some Examples (FAO 1989a, McGinnes 1981) Utilization of native woody vegetation for nonwood products is important to the livelihood of people living in the dryland regions of the world. Foodstuffs, tannins, gums and resins, essential oils and extractives, and pharmaceutical products are only a few of the numerous nonwood products obtained from this woody vegetation. Although called *minor* forest products in many instances, they are vitally important to people and often constitute an important part of the total revenues derived from forests, woodlands, and plantations.

Of the 350,000 plant species that have been described by botanists, only 3,000 are reported to be sources of useful materials for people. Less than 100 of these plants are cultivated on a large scale, and none are xerophytical in nature. However, the search for native xerophytical plants of economic value has intensified greatly in recent years.

---

be no alternative to fuelwood. Even where alternatives are available, commercial fuels require cash outlays that generally are beyond the reach of the rural poor. One consequence of the growing rural populations in dryland regions is a relentless growth in the pressures on locally available forest resources and other sources of woody material. The collection of fuelwood extends, progressively, from gathering deadwood to lopping of live trees, felling of trees, total destruction of tree cover, loss of organic matter to the soil, and, eventually, uprooting of stumps and removal of shrubs. Subsequent to this, there is the diversion of agricultural residues and animal dung to fuel use, to the detriment of soil structure and soil fertility.

At the same time, steady disappearance of wood in the vicinity of a community of people frequently means increased social hardship. More time must be devoted to gathering fuel, often by women and children in many countries (FAO 1989b, Huston 1979). As the situation deteriorates further and households are forced to purchase their fuelwood, a heavy burden is placed on the household budget. Eventually, this shortage of fuelwood can affect the nutritional well-being of the people.

Food and the Environment

There are millions of people living in forests, woodlands, and plantations in dryland regions who are practicing shifting agriculture, also called *slash and burn* agriculture, to provide their daily food requirements. Traditional systems of shifting agriculture, which employ lengthy fallow periods under forests, woodlands, or plantations to restore the fertility of soils and are capable of supporting agricultural crops for only a limited number of years, largely have broken down. The growing population pressures and migration into forest and woodland areas by the people have forced a shortening of the fallow period to the point where it can neither restore soil fertility nor reestablish a usable forest crop.

Concurrent with the pressures on forests, woodlands, and plantations from shifting cultivation are pressures for the conversion of these lands for food production. This arises from the need of expanding rural populations for more land on which to grow food. Forests, woodlands, and plantations in many areas are the largest remaining "land banks," the one land cover that can absorb further large-scale extension of the area under agricultural crop production (FAO 1989b).

It has been estimated that the existing area of forests and woodlands in developing countries is reduced annually by 10–20 million ha. To the extent that this process releases land that can sustain growth of agricultural crops, it might be argued by some people that this loss can be acceptable. However, the pressures of growing populations over large areas force farmers onto soils that cannot sustain agricultural crop production and slopes that cannot be cultivated safely with techniques and resources available to these farmers. The consequences of these practices in terms of wind and soil erosion, silting, flooding, and drought are well known.

Income and Employment

It was pointed out in Chapter 7 that natural forests and woodlands, and forest plantations can give rise to cash crops. In addition to the income and employment generated by industrial exploitation, these ecosystems provide wood for local craftsmen. Throughout the world, furniture, tools, and fence posts are made locally within the community. These products, together with a variety of wooden handicrafts, frequently can be marketed outside the community as cottage industries.

In some countries, for example, Portugal, the forests, woodlands, and plantations held in the private sector often function somewhat like banks in the United States and cattle in Africa by providing a form of "capital" that can be liquidated in the future when the need arises. If this course of action is taken, however, it is important that "liquidation" does not result in devastating and permanent deforestation. Importantly, the forests, woodlands, and plantations should not be "mined" for short-term gains.

Forestry also can contribute to rural incomes in less direct ways. When other alternatives for raising incomes of the rural poor are not promising, the establishment of *fuelwood plantations* can provide a means to raise incomes by releasing dung and agricultural residues for reworking into the soil, thereby increasing the subsequent agricultural crop yields (FAO 1989a). In this way, forests, woodlands, and plantations can contribute to a more equitable distribution of income. In some situations, it might be easier to help the poor by providing them with fuel in the form of wood than with other benefits provided through taxation and redistribution.

CONSTRAINTS AND CONDITIONS

Where exploitable forests, woodlands, and plantations exist but do not fully benefit rural communities, the necessary adjustments in current forest management practices are often relatively easy to conceive, although they can be difficult to execute. The reintroduction of forestry projects can pose problems in areas where forests, woodlands, and plantations have been destroyed by rural people to make way for farming and livestock grazing. That this has happened should not imply that forestry is concerned only with planting programs. Much of forestry should be concerned with better management of natural forests and woodlands for the benefit of local people (Gregersen and Elz 1989).

Some of the possible responses to factors limiting implementation of forestry projects in rural communities are summarized in Table 20.1. These responses are discussed more fully below.

Competition for Land

Forestry tends to be practiced on areas with low population density, where the abundance of land permits integration of forestry with agricultural crop production

TABLE 20.1. Responses to Factors Limiting Implementation of Forestry Practices in Rural Communities

Factors	Possible Responses
Competition for land	
Competition for forest land	Intercrop trees and crops
	Allocate forest land rationally between tree, shrubs, and agricultural crops
	Improve nonfood benefits to affected communities, such as forest-food industries, nonwood product income, and social infrastructure
Competition for agricultural or grazing lands for afforestation	Plant trees or shrubs on roadsides, river banks, field boundaries, areas marginal for agricultural production, erodible lands unsuited for agricultural production or livestock grazing
	Improve productivity on arable areas to release land for growing trees and shrubs
	Plant multipurpose tree and shrub species to increase productivity
	Intercrop trees and shrubs with agricultural crops or combine with livestock grazing
	Introduce additional sources of income, for example, beekeeping
Timescale of forestry	
Output from trees or shrubs will not meet immediate needs	Plant multipurpose tree and shrub species to provide some early returns
	Provide financial support during establishment periods, paid employment, low interest loans, grants, or subsidies
	Introduce or expand complementary nonforestry sources of income
Risk that the producer will not benefit	Ensure security of tenure of land used for tree or shrub crop
Spatial distribution of benefits from forestry practices	
Benefits from production of wood may accrue, in part, outside of the community	Provide compensation that generates benefits elsewhere for those benefits foregone or inputs provided by the community
Seasonal shortage of labor	Adopt forestry practices that do not compete with peak demands for labor inputs

TABLE 20.1. *(Continued)*

Factors	Possible Responses
Lack of tradition in forestry	Provision of guidance and support through extension services, education of the people, technical advice and inputs, "grass-roots" training
	Demonstration projects

Source: Adapted from the Food and Agriculture Organization of the United Nations (1989a)

on some parts of the area or a use of some of the area for both trees and livestock grazing (MacDicken and Vergara 1990, Nair 1989). Typical of the integration of forestry and agriculture are shifting cultivation systems, with their fallow periods under trees. Pastoral-forestry practices, in which livestock graze among trees and shrubs, are an example of the second use. However, in many cases, these agroforestry systems are unable to withstand encroachment and increasing population pressure. An initial sign of breakdown frequently is the expansion of the intensive agricultural cropping component or livestock grazing at the expense of the extensive forestry component.

The competition between growing trees and shrubs and livestock grazing is more intense in areas where the population pressure is great and land is amenable to cultivation, even on a temporary basis. Even where the need to maintain land under a tree or shrub cover is evident, forestry frequently gives way to the more urgent needs of food production and security. A condition for introducing forestry into these situations is that it be accompanied by measures that provide the farmer or community with alternative ways of generating the necessary agricultural crop, livestock production, or income.

Dietary Considerations

Wherever a local economy is based on subsistence farming, the people's diet is an important factor in determining the land use. Its demands take precedence over those for wood. Diets that are based upon a single cereal obtained by alternating crop and fallow periods need a large area per household and, therefore, are likely to exclude a forestry component. Diets that require a higher content of animal products from livestock that graze in forests, woodlands, or plantations makes the regeneration of trees and shrubs almost impossible, especially when surplus livestock can be sold readily.

Dietary habits are among the deepest rooted elements in a way of life. In some cases, they are linked closely to cultural and religious beliefs. The introduction of new types of foods frequently is difficult and, as a consequence, must be pursued carefully. However, such an introduction can be important. When a greater variety of food is grown, it often is possible to rotate agricultural crops or integrate agriculture and animal husbandry, enabling more food to be produced on a smaller area. In this way, land can be released for forestry activities.

Direct competition with food production for land might be avoided by utilizing "unused" areas for forestry activities, if such areas can be found. Even in these areas, however, care must be taken to select tree or shrub species that are as productive as possible. Fast growing tree or shrub species are preferred, as well as those providing leaves, nuts, fruits, or bark for domestic use and for handicrafts.

The whole question of land use usually is confused by a lack of information about land capabilities and the factors needed for land-use planning. Unfortunately, the boundaries between areas that can support sustained agricultural cropping or livestock grazing and those areas that need to be devoted periodically or permanently to forest cover are seldom known.

Timescale of Forestry

Attachment to a particular diet and technique of food production is reinforced by considerations derived from the timescale of forestry in many instances. Many rural populations have developed a historical dependence upon the outputs of forests, woodlands, or plantations, largely because these ecosystems represented abundant, available, and local natural resources. As long as the wood products remained abundant, this process of exploitation could take place without regard to the relatively long time involved in producing wood of usable sizes. However, once the point is reached where wood can be supplied only by growing it, the time frame involved can become an important limiting factor.

The timescale of forestry frequently conflicts with the priorities of rural people. These priorities are focused logically on meeting basic present needs. Present needs are imperative, especially in subsistence situations. Land, labor, and other resources that can be devoted to providing the food, fuel, and income needed today cannot be diverted easily to the production of wood that will be available years into the future.

Forestry can continue to exist or be introduced at the community level only if it allows for the present needs of the people involved (FAO 1985, Gregersen and Elz 1989). If a local tree and shrub cover still exists, it can be possible to provide the same level of production in a less destructive way. In some areas, destructive local cutting of a forest, woodland, or plantation can be halted and reversed by concentrating the cut in designated areas and at designated times, thereby protecting the rest of the area so regeneration can occur. In other areas, forestry can be introduced in conjunction with other activities that secure income to meet the needs of a farmer until his trees yield products.

Spatial Distribution of Benefits

The spatial distribution of forest benefits are important in rural communities. To the shifting cultivator, the forest, woodland, or plantation is land upon which to cultivate food and cash crops, and is a source of fuel, building materials, fodder, and shade. The fact that the trees and shrubs that are utilized can provide raw material for an economically important industry is generally of little relevance to the shifting cultivator. To expect the cultivator to change his way of life to accommodate interests of others is unrealistic. Therefore, the buildup of more sustainable forestry systems will occur only when the community, in some way, benefits from the change.

A core of the problem for rural communities usually is that they derive insufficient benefits from the forest, woodland, or plantation. In general, this situation is attributable to conventional forest management objectives and administrative practices, such as an orientation of the natural resources toward conservation, wood production, revenue collection, and regulation through punitive legislation and regulation. Consequently, a task of a forester is to engage people more fully, positively, and beneficially in management, utilization, and protection. This task can take the form of greater participation by rural people in forestry work; development from the sale of miscellaneous products that can be produced in the forest, woodland, or plantation; or the allocation of forests, woodlands, and plantations for the concurrent production of wood and agricultural crops or forestry and livestock (Example 20.2).

The issue of the distribution of benefits also can arise with management that is designed to establish industrial wood crops through farming systems that grow trees or shrubs with food and cash crops. In themselves, trees and shrubs may bring no direct benefit to the farmer. Rather, the trees and shrubs often are viewed as an impediment that complicates this task. These systems will succeed only when the farmer perceives adequate compensation. Land, in itself, is not a sufficient inducement other than perhaps in the short term. It has been observed that multiple

---

Example 20.2

The Majjia Valley Reforestation Project, Niger (Harrison 1987) Harvesting of fuelwood from windbreaks in the Majjia Valley was described earlier in Examples 6.3, 12.2, and 17.2. The Majjia Valley reforestation project also represents a program in which rural people and government foresters worked together to achieve a common goal. The project began in 1974 when local villagers asked the local government forester if anything could be done to help them against the destructive wind erosion they continually faced. The forester, along with a Peace Corps volunteer, approached CARE for financial support to produce tree seedlings for the windbreak-planting program.

Foresters have powers to restrict harvesting of trees on farmers' land because all trees belong to the government of Niger. However, the forester in the Majjia Valley pioneered a "new approach" to forestry. Instead of being viewed as potential criminals in harvesting trees in the absence of authorization, the rural people became partners and principal beneficiaries of the project. Villagers dug planting holes in the dry season, after the forester chose locations for tree plantings. Paid nursery staff grew the tree seedlings. Local farmers were responsible for planting and protecting the trees against livestock. These tasks were taken on by paid guards when the farmers were not available. It was required that livestock stay away for 3 years after the trees were planted. Livestock owners, therefore, became the main losers in the project, with many selling their animals or simply moving away.

The total benefits of the project outweigh the costs. Windbreak plantings take up land, perhaps 15 in every 100 m, including the shade on each side of the barrier. But, even allowing for this loss, agricultural crop yields have increased by a reported 20 percent in comparison to similar lands unprotected by windbreaks. The windbreaks reduced soil erosion by lowering wind speeds and also prevented smothering of the crops by sand. These barriers reduced evaporation losses and increased the level of soil moisture for plant production. There also was less toppling of mature crops.

People in the Majjia Valley are aware of the benefits. In a survey of the project results, nearly 75 percent of the farmers indicated that the windbreaks increased food production. Farmers whose land was outside of the project area have expressed a desire to be included in the project. Additional benefits of fuelwood have begun to be reaped. In 1984, the earliest trees planted in windbreaks were pollarded and the wood given to village councils to distribute. However, the local chiefs gave much of the wood to their families or clients. Additional fuelwood was harvested in 1985, and another form of distribution was tried. One-third of the wood was given to owners of the field, one-third to woodcutters, and one-third to village councils. This latter distribution system has met with more success.

Contrary to what often has been claimed, the Majjia Valley reforestation project did not succeed *only* because of the high level of popular participation. True, the project was more successful than usual in West Africa, but it was still planned by government foresters and a foreign voluntary organization. It was executed largely by paid nursery staffs and guards, though these were recruited from local people.

The windbreaks were laid out with a disregard for their effects on the distribution of land. There was little compensation for the farmers who lost a considerable area. The method of distributing the fuelwood was decided, for the most part, by officials, not the local people, and still has not been resolved fully. When Majjia farmers are asked who owns the trees, they say, "the forestry department." And yet, the project did succeed. Though there was no formal consultation, people did ask for help, and the local forester responded. He gave them an insight into their problems and offered a solution to wind erosion, which was perceived as a serious problem by the villagers. The technology was appropriate and simple, and the tree species adapted to local conditions. The protection promised was delivered. Costs of the project to local farmers were relatively small, and the benefit of increased agricultural crop production was rapid and perceived by the farmers.

use systems tend to evolve over time into either settled agriculture, with a rejection of the associated growing of trees or shrubs, or full-time forestry employment.

Institutional and Technical Constraints

Sometimes, there is interest in forestry and no conflict with other aspects of the people's lives, but only a lack of organization or means. Areas that are marginal for agriculture also can be marginal for forestry activities. This situation is particularly the case in dryland regions, which tend to impose severe climatological constraints on the growing of trees and shrubs. The availability of labor can be a limitation, although labor is not necessarily a problem in most community forestry projects. The bulk of the forestry work falls in the slack season. Where there is a tradition of women working in the fields, this might release men for concurrent work in forestry. However, in dryland regions, the planting seasons for both agriculture and forestry are short and coincide with each other. As a result, the availability of labor for tree or shrub planting can be restricted, and, therefore, planning must allow sufficient flexibility to overcome this constraint.

Another constraint to the implementation of forestry in dryland regions is the associated costs. Successful tree- or shrub-planting programs often involve elaborate site preparation and planting techniques that require "sophisticated" and costly equipment. As a result, extensive planting projects can be beyond the capability and resources of the rural community. Therefore, forestry, as implemented by local communities, often must be confined to manipulation of existing vegetation, with plantation forestry undertaken only by the responsible technical branches of government.

Planting and rehabilitation practices on steep upland areas also are likely to present problems to rural communities. Where the problem is largely one of soil stabilization or the control of water runoff, the establishment of a tree and shrub cover on parts of the watershed usually must be accompanied by structural measures, such as the construction of terraces. Farmers will not have the resources or the technology to do this in many instances. To establish terraces, for example, they likely would have to forego one crop. Therefore, they will need a form of external support, such as credit and food aid.

Another institutional issue is land tenure. The patterns and traditions of use on communal land often make no provision for usages such as forestry, which require the setting aside of land for a particular purpose for relatively long periods of time (FAO 1989a). It can be difficult to introduce forestry prior to reform of land tenure or a change in land use in many situations. However, for success in forestry, farmers must have assurance that they will control the land on which trees or shrubs are planted (Example 20.3).

Frequently, the lack of a tradition in forestry extends beyond a simple lack of knowledge about growing trees and shrubs or an appropriate institutional framework within which to implement it. Usually, it contrasts with a "deep" tradition in agriculture. This contrast is reflected in the attitudes that people have toward

Example 20.3

Tenure Policy and Natural Resource Management in the Sahelian Regions of West Africa (Lawry 1989)   Sahelian states claim ownership of common property resources, including grazing land, forests and woodlands, fisheries, wildlife, and wetlands. An important effect of state ownership is that the local people cannot manage natural resources legally. Therefore, rural communities cannot assert control over natural resources in relation to outside users and, in many cases, how local residents use these resources. State strategies for natural resource management concentrate on enforcement of national legal codes and give little attention to developing economically viable management schemes that would have support of local users. This approach has contributed to a natural resource "free-for-all" and, in many places, increased resource degradation.

forestry, which are different than the attitudes toward agricultural crops and livestock. A forest, woodland, or plantation often tends to be seen by poor farmers as a "negative element" of the environment. To the settler, it is an impediment to the clearing of his lands and a haven for his enemies. These views can persist long after the forest or woodland has receded from the immediate vicinity of a farm or community. Hostility toward forests and trees can persist in areas that already experience shortages of fuelwood and building poles because of the damage done to agricultural crops by birds that roost in trees.

Other attitudes and behavioral patterns based upon that past also tend to be hostile to forestry. There is a widely prevalent attitude of wood as an abundant free material that can be collected at will. Seldom is there a good understanding of the role played by trees and shrubs in maintaining the fertility of the soil. There frequently is an inability or reluctance to recognize the consequences of soil loss and fuel shortages that will follow from continued destruction of adjacent tree and shrub cover. This feeling is without historical precedent for populations of many areas faced with the depletion or disappearance of forests, woodlands, plantations, and their outputs. There is nothing in these people's past that can give them guidance or that can forewarn them of what will happen until it does happen. Similarly, people seldom foresee the positive effects that forestry can bring.

It can be difficult for people to perceive beneficial effects of forestry until those effects occur. This situation is part of the long-term-short-term problem, where decision makers respond to short-term incentives to obtain immediate benefits for clients without recognition of long-term social and environmental costs. Rural people commonly must choose between short-term "profits" and long-term environmental stability and sustainability. Individuals tend to select the first option, while societies (of which the individuals also are a part) frequently opt for a longer viewpoint, hoping to ensure benefits for future generations.

There are constraints that prevent the acceptance of change by people, namely, the constraints that arise from inadequacies in the bureaucratic structure charged with this task. Some are faults that afflict most bureaucracies, such as rigid procedures, emphasis on interpretation of rules rather than on the rationale of the rules, inadequate training at lower levels, and arrogance of local officials. There also is the tendency for rural development efforts to become fragmented and dispersed among a number of "bodies" that fail to harmonize adequately and coordinate their efforts. It is important, therefore, that programs to encourage forestry in rural development do not contribute to this fragmentation. Forestry is only one part of a complex of different activities that are required for rural development. To be effective, its contribution must be integrated with the rest of the activities.

Finally, there are features of forestry that are not always conducive to effective impacts at community levels. The traditional preoccupation of forestry with conserving a forest, woodland, or plantation, combined with management objectives that focus on production of wood for industry are likely to be at variance with the needs of local people who live in and depend upon the forest, woodland, or plantation for their livelihood. This bias usually is reflected in the structure and staffing of forestry administrations and in the relative budgetary priorities of forestry. It also is reflected in the traditional training of foresters, who often find that they are not as well equipped to deal with people as they are with trees. The challenge to forestry of improving the condition of the rural poor can entail a radical reorientation that extends from policy formulations all the way down to its technical foundations.

ROLE OF INCENTIVES

Even though rural people may see the benefits of forestry, it can be difficult for them to become involved actively in planned interventions for a variety of ideological, legal, and economic reasons. It is frequent that people must be brought into forestry interventions as partners through directed efforts to "mobilize" their collective actions (Botero 1986). In general, there are three approaches to mobilizing rural people in forestry and integrating them into conservation programs:

- *Ideological motivation*—this approach includes "mass participation" of people on the basis of a religious, political, or ethical awareness and motivation campaign, or as part of ideological education.
- *Compulsory participation*—here, by means of regulatory measures, supervised credit, tied land leases, and other entitlements and rehabilitation schemes, people have no choice but to participate without much conviction and willingness. Otherwise, it might be argued, people can continue to suffer hardships. In some situations, however, compulsory participation can increase "hardships" to people.

- *Voluntary participation*—in this approach, an appeal is made to people in such a way that there is an "effective" response to action.

This chapter focuses on the third approach and, in particular, on the financial and economic incentives that are intended to motivate rural people and on the effective manner by which incentives are applied. A particular emphasis has been placed on farmers, particularly those at the subsistence level.

Justification for Incentive Schemes

Applications of incentives for forestry projects finds their justification in two basic arguments (Botero 1986). First, rural people, and especially farmers, might need a "big push" to obtain direct benefits from their participation in a forest management practice if the inertia of prior misuse of natural resources and underdevelopment are to be stopped. Second, conservation measures have beneficial effects on society as a whole and on the stability and "wise use" of a country's natural resources. Therefore, the costs of implementing conservation and restoration work should not be absorbed exclusively by the farmers.

Changes in land use and the implementation of forestry projects, soil conservation, and other conservation measures should benefit people in the form of goods and services in the area of influence. Therefore, it seems reasonable to expect that those who benefit will contribute to the financing of these programs. However, only rarely has such a "mechanism of transfer" of resources been established. In the absence of such a cost-sharing mechanism, society will need to share the financial burden through incentive schemes.

Farmers living at the subsistence level generally do not have the capital that is required to implement forestry projects and, furthermore, cannot afford to devote time to activities that will not bring immediate revenue. They also cannot afford to set aside portions of their land and take it out of agricultural crop production or livestock grazing without some form of financial support during transitional periods before forestry products are obtained.

A number of methods to assist the people through incentives is examined in the following paragraphs. However, there are risks involved in applications of incentives. A major risk of a poorly conceived or implemented incentive scheme is that it can be paternalistic. Incentives should not be regarded as a "gift," but instead as a cost-sharing arrangement that should "catalyze" the farmer's initiative, develop the farmer's managerial ability, and contribute to group action. A continued dependency of the farmer on incentives must be avoided. Self-reliance should be a basic target of any incentive program.

A few examples in which incentives have played a role in furnishing the support necessary to bring people into a forestry intervention and, at the same time, attain the desired objective serve as a prelude to a discussion of the types of incentives (Example 20.4).

Example 20.4

Types of Forestry Interventions: Some Examples

India

As part of India's social forestry programs, the direct involvement of rural people in raising, harvesting, and marketing of fuelwood resources is suggested in the belief that this work will increase employment. Villagers dig planting holes, transplant trees or shrubs to the planting site where they plant them, maintain them, and water them during periods of drought. In doing this, they either volunteer themselves for this work or become employed for wages when funds are available. As a direct monetary incentive, the villagers also are paid on the basis of survival of the trees and shrubs.

Niger

As part of the Majjia Valley reforestation project, villagers were promised fuelwood produced in windbreak plantings that they helped to establish and maintain. This promise was necessary to ensure the protection of the windbreaks from damaging by livestock. However, as the time to harvest the windbreaks approached, it became unclear whether the Government of Niger would allow villagers to exploit the fuelwood as promised. Although this issue has not been fully resolved, preliminary fuelwood cuttings of the windbreaks have been made available to the villagers through their respective chiefs.

United States

Incentives have been long used in the United States to provide external support to people engaged in small-scale forestry projects on their lands. These incentives, which are offered through federal, state, and local programs, include free planting stock and assistance in planting, credit against payment of taxes, and a form of cash payment for planting trees or shrubs rather than agricultural crops.

Types of Incentives

Incentives are measures that encourage a farmer, other rural people, and the rural community, collectively, to:

- Partially or totally absorb additional investments required in the implementation of a forestry project.
- Replace sources of income from traditional land use systems and techniques.

- Achieve sustained and, it is to be hoped, improved production and use of the natural resource base.
- Protect "endangered" goods and services, such as wildlife.

For convenience, the more commonly applied incentives in forestry can be classified as direct or indirect. *Direct incentives* improve production factors, living conditions, and investment capabilities of the farmer or community. *Indirect incentives* relate to policy measures that encourage conservation measures, such as monetary measures, tax exemptions, and the improvement of services. Examples of the many types of incentives that are considered in this classification framework are summarized in Figure 20.1 and elaborated upon below.

Direct Incentives in Cash   The most common direct incentives in forestry are *subsidies, payment of wages, subventions, credit, revolving funds,* and *cost-sharing arrangements* (Botero 1986). Subsidies are short-term and temporary measures, which should be applied carefully to help farmers in an adverse condition. In this sense, conservation work can be used as a relief and a compensatory tool. The payment of wages, one of the more common types of incentives, is applied for work on a farmer's land, on communal lands, on "state" land, and in areas affected by underemployment. With this incentive, farmers can involve members of their families and, when appropriate, the neighbors in a program.

Subventions, wrongly called subsidies in many countries, are nonrefundable governmental grants to encourage conservational work in the public interest. Subventions can cover 100 percent or less of the investment, but the farmers involved must comply with specified work norms and implemental needs. Credit schemes are only effective in situations where the people are responsible socially and economically. In addition to low interest rates and long periods for repayment, farmers will require a "grace period" corresponding to the time required for the realization of benefits. Small farmers in "marginal" conditions might not have access to credit schemes unless appropriate guarantee systems are established.

Revolving funds are effective incentives when the initial capital required for the incentives can be made available as a donation or as a long-term loan. Such funds can be managed by a rural community organization, if the community can undertake the responsibility, or by a banking institution, if there are risks of mismanagement. Cost-sharing arrangements vary considerably, but they generally follow one of two approaches. A government can allocate the total amount of capital required, implement the work, and recover its investment with part of the revenue from the improved practices, or people can work their land or the land of a third party, with the government providing capital.

Direct Incentives in Kind   These types of incentives include food, production inputs, tools and equipment, livestock and wildlife, animal feed, irrigation systems, use of water, technical advice, and transportation services. *Food for work* is one of the most widespread direct incentives in kind that is applied in forestry projects. In

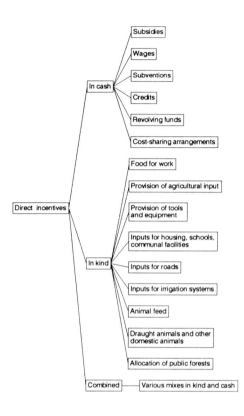

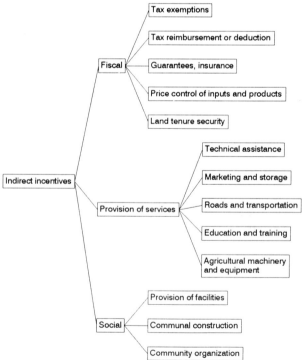

general, food rations are given in exchange for conservational and restorative work on a farmer's land, a neighbor's land, or public lands, or for the construction of roads, waterways, and communal facilities. Large incentive programs involving food for work are found in India, China, Pakistan, Ethiopia, and many other countries.

This type of incentive is most suitable when governments do not have the financial means to provide incentives in cash. However, this incentive should not be applied as a substitute for wages. Instead, it should be a tool to encourage rural people to introduce appropriate technologies. Innovative methods are needed to use food for work in forestry, for example (Botero 1986):

- Contracts setting goals in terms of physical outputs rather than people-days of work.
- Provision for long-term maintenance work, protection and silvicultural treatments, and other work extending beyond the period of the food for work project.
- Compensation for changes in land use practices and closing of areas to grazing to allow natural regeneration of a vegetative cover.
- Sale of food commodities to create revolving funds to establish community stores and to build facilities for use by the people in a community.

Fertilizers, seeds, pesticides, animal feed, hand tools, barbed wire, tree seedlings, and fruit trees are other direct incentives in kind that are use in forestry. Many of these incentives are coupled with food for work schemes. Water rights and low rates for water use in irrigation also can be applied to encourage conservational work. In some situations, fuelwood and other natural resources are offered as compensation for protecting against fire, controlling grazing by livestock, and eliminating wildlife poaching. Incentives in kind generally are most efficient when a comprehensive farm plan is prepared, and all of the required inputs for implementation and the necessary infrastructure are identified clearly.

Indirect Incentives Three categories of indirect incentives applied in forestry projects are *fiscal*, *provision of services*, and *social incentives*. To encourage forestry, a number of countries have formed legislation that exempts from taxation land and investments that "perform" a social function. This incentive can be a partial or total tax exemption, an exemption on land revenues, a deduction of investments from income tax, or similar fiscal benefits. In general, this type of incentive is applicable only to farmers who pay taxes. Therefore, it is the middle and large property holders who benefit from these fiscal measures. Other forms of indirect incentives to promote forestry practices include:

Figure 20.1. Examples of incentives (adapted from Botero 1986)

- Preferential rates or provision of services from public utilities, such as electric power, water for domestic or irrigation use, and storage and transportation of commodities to be marketed.

- Stabilization of prices for basic products or the purchase of production by a government to ensure adequate levels of income to farmers and to avoid exploitation by middlemen.

- Security of land tenure or long-term land allocation contracts, which allow for investment in conservation measures, therefore enabling farmers to obtain credit and to have access to other type of incentives.

- Technical assistance, training, and education to promote conservation.

- Community development efforts, including improvement of roads, rural electrification, water supply programs, construction of schools and dispensaries, development of sports facilities, improvement of housing, and fuelwood supply systems.

Introduction of Incentives

Although incentives of many types have been and continue to be applied to promote forest management practices, there generally is a need to refine incentive schemes to effectively attain two purposes. One purpose is compensation to farmers for the time and effort invested in applications of forestry-related conservation and land use practices that are beneficial to society as a whole. A second purpose is incorporation of poor subsistence farmers in "marginal" conditions into a developmental process by improving production factors and ensuring sustained productivity levels. Principles that should be considered in introducing an incentive program into forestry projects include (Botero 1986):

- Incentives to be promoted should be "well articulated" with other support elements in a rural development framework.

- Incentives in cash or in kind should have a catalytic role and, therefore, should be temporary until rural people and the community can acquire a degree of self-reliance through improved sources of income.

- Incentives should be applied through "grass-root" organizations to be more advantageous in terms of cost effectiveness. In addition, through this strategy, incentives will generate community initiatives and, sometimes, promote cooperative attitudes among the participants.

- Incentives should be introduced on the basis of local plans to ensure that people receive timely inputs to improved production as a trade-off to conservation work.

- Rural people in marginal conditions who do not have the "managerial abilities" to receive incentives in cash should be given incentives in kind.

- Fair cost-sharing rates should be established, considering neighboring farms, infrastructure and human settlements, and "common-property" natural resources.

- Supervision of the implementation of forestry projects should be effective and the flow of incentives should be efficient in order to ensure that the objectives of the practices will be fulfilled satisfactorily. To this end, assistance of community leaders is helpful.
- Recovery of resources invested in conservation incentives should not be expected in the short term. Revolving funds are an option to ensure further availability of incentives.
- Incentives should not be considered relief, governmental gifts, wages, or "pressure instruments." Participation should be voluntary and in "good terms" of partnership between governments and the rural people.
- Vital requirements to ensuring the success of an incentive should include stability of land tenure, appropriate marketing channels and prices for farmers' products, and well-organized "grass-root" organizations.

SUMMARY

Many rural people do not have a tradition in forestry. However, this frequent barrier to the initiation of forestry projects can be overcome, in many instances, by providing training and extension services, by the education of people, and by exhibiting the beneficial roles of trees and shrubs in demonstrations. Incentives also can be helpful in bringing people into forestry interventions. Key points that you should be able to explain after you have completed this chapter are phrased in the following questions:

1. How do natural forests and woodlands and forest plantations improve people's livelihood?
2. What are some of the limiting factors that people must face in considering the implementation of forestry projects in rural communities?
3. How can incentives be justified in mobilizing rural people in forestry and, as a consequence, integrating them into conservation programs?
4. What are the differences between direct and indirect incentives, and how is each applied?
5. What are some of the more important guidelines to follow in introducing incentives?

REFERENCES

Botero, L. S. 1986. Incentives for community involvement in upland conservation. In FAO. 1986. Strategies, approaches and systems in integrated watershed management. *FAO Conservation Guide* 14, Rome, pp. 164–72.

Food and Agriculture Organization of the United Nations (FAO). 1985. *The role of forestry in food security*. FAO, Rome.

Food and Agriculture Organization of the United Nations (FAO). 1989a. Arid zone forestry: A guide for field technicians. *FAO Conservation Guide* 20, Rome.

Food and Agriculture Organization of the United Nations (FAO). 1989b. *Women in community forestry: A field guide for project design and implementation*. FAO, Rome.

Gregersen, H., and D. Elz (eds.). 1989. *People and trees: The role of social forestry in sustainable development*. The World Bank, Washington, D.C.

Harrison, P. 1987. *The greening of Africa: Breaking through in the battle for land and food*. Penguin Books, New York.

Huston, P. 1979. *Third world women speak out*. Praeger Publishers, New York.

Lawry, S. W. 1989. Tenure policy and natural resource management in Sahelian West Africa. *University of Wisconsin, Land Tenure Center, Paper* 130, Madison, Wisconsin.

MacDicken, K. G., and N. T. Vergara (eds.). 1990. *Agroforestry: Classification and management*. John Wiley & Sons, Inc., New York.

McGinnes, W. G. 1981. *Discovering the desert*. University of Arizona Press, Tucson, Arizona.

Nair, P. K. R. (ed.). 1989. *Agroforestry in the tropics*. Kluwer Academic Publishers, Boston.

21 Monitoring and Evaluation

Forestry projects that contribute to sustainable development generate practices that use, affect, and are affected by the environment. The condition of the environment, in turn, affects the economic and social activities of people, and ultimately affects their well-being, as well. Often, the purpose of implementing forestry within an integrated managerial framework is to change land use practices and activities to improve the welfare of present and future generations of people without adversely affecting the environment. Unfortunately, linkages among forestry interventions, environmental systems, and the welfare of people are not well understood. Although we plan for particular resource and welfare effects when a forestry project is undertaken, because of uncertainly about our knowledge, we cannot be sure that the project will be carried out as planned or that the project will have the anticipated effects on the resources, environment, and welfare of people.

These and other uncertainties make it necessary to closely monitor and evaluate developmental projects and their effects on the natural resources, the environment being impacted, and the welfare of people to determine what changes in policies, practices, and activities may be required to meet desired goals. Monitoring and evaluation, therefore, must be an integral part of planning and management.

RELATION OF MONITORING TO EVALUATION

Monitoring is the systematic process of collecting information to provide a basis for adjusting or modifying a forestry project that already has been implemented, identifying "maintenance procedures" for project continuation, and improving future efforts. Monitoring should begin at the start of a project and continue throughout its duration. *Evaluation* is a process of appraising the results of a decision through both qualitative and quantitative monitoring activities. Evaluation is important in situations where there is little previous experience. Therefore, monitoring is the process of collecting information, and evaluation is the process of analyzing this information to determine the "worthiness" of the effort (Brooks et al. 1990). This information is valuable to many people.

Project managers need information about project activities, accomplishments, results, and impacts to manage effectively. Project personnel also need "early warnings" of potential problems in the performance of a project that could lead to failure of the project in meeting its goals and objectives. These potential problems must be known in time to take *corrective actions*, if possible. Project administrators need information to ensure project accountability. Project planners require information about the performance of ongoing projects to improve the planning for future projects and revise plans for current projects. Policymakers must have information to develop more effective policies related to forestry projects.

This chapter describes the nature of monitoring and evaluation, the design of monitoring programs, the monitoring of biophysical systems and socioeconomic impacts, and the design of evaluation systems. The importance of ensuring that the information obtained by monitoring and evaluation efforts is useful to planners and managers is emphasized. Suggestions as to how this can be accomplished also are offered.

NATURE OF MONITORING AND EVALUATION

Monitoring

Monitoring is the gathering of feedback information about project components, processes, and the activities for planning, appraising, selecting, implementing, and evaluating projects, as illustrated in Figure 21.1. Monitoring can be a onetime activity to record project accomplishments, for example, the number of trees

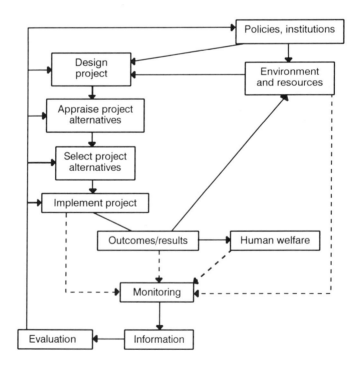

Figure 21.1. Monitoring and evaluation provide feedback information (adapted from Brooks et al. 1990)

planted in the project area or the length of road built to a specified standard in a specified time. Or, monitoring can be an activity in which observations are taken at stated intervals, such as hourly measurements of water flow in streams, annual deposition of soil in a reservoir, or annual incomes of rural people.

The monitoring of ongoing projects provides the information that is essential for management of the project. Information about the time expended on different tasks, the amounts of materials used, the financial and personnel records, and the records of individual and group accomplishments is helpful in the scheduling of work activities, the evaluating of work performance, and the providing of records of accountability to project administrators.

Monitoring of project outcomes and results, such as the number of planted trees or shrubs surviving, number of check dams built and the resulting decrease in sedimentation, or increases in agricultural crop yields, provides information that is essential for operational planning and subsequent project evaluation. Monitoring of the welfare of people helps to determine the magnitudes of gains and losses in health, education, and income. This information is needed to document project accomplishments and evaluate the project's benefits, costs, and social impacts. Monitoring of the changes in resources or the environment furnishes additional information about the impact of a project on the sustainability of project activities.

Observations obtained through the monitoring of biophysical and socioeconomic components of a project provide information about current or past conditions to meet the needs of project planners, managers, and others. But, actual observations are rarely in a form that is useful to planners and managers. Usually, these observations need to be evaluated before they can be used.

Evaluation

Evaluation is the process of organizing and analyzing the information obtained in monitoring to estimate the value of past activities for use in making decisions about future activities. Evaluations also estimate the value of past accomplishments to date for an ongoing project. Evaluations provide information about actual project achievements in the form needed by project planners, managers, administrators, and policymakers.

The terms *evaluation* and *appraisal* often are used interchangeably to refer to the establishing and comparing of project benefits and costs. However, *evaluation* refers to past activities, while *appraisal* refers to planned future activities. Using this terminology, one would say that an appraisal is made to estimate the value of future activities, such as weighing the expected benefits and costs of reforestation alternatives that are considered in the planning of a forestry project.

Monitoring and evaluation are not events that take place only once at a specified time during a project cycle. Instead, these events are part of an iterative, dynamic process. Monitoring and evaluation should take place throughout project planning and implementation. They provide feedback to project planners and managers to enable them to make changes in their plans and activities as they go along. One cannot specify the frequency for monitoring and evaluation, because that will depend largely upon the type of monitoring to be undertaken, its purpose, the technology used, and the resources available. Weather information, for example, might be recorded daily. Sediment accumulations on the bottom of a reservoir might be measured annually. Data about human populations and other census information might be collected once every 10 years. Monitoring and evaluation, therefore, provides a feedback mechanism, that is, one that furnishes timely information and is useful in guiding a project's direction as the project evolves. Monitoring and evaluation should be modified if they are not providing useful information.

DESIGN OF MONITORING PROGRAMS

Monitoring programs should serve the needs of the identified users. Collecting, processing, and storing information is expensive. Only the information that is actually needed, that can be provided to users at a time and in a form that meets their needs, and that will meet the needs of project planners, managers, administrators, and policymakers should be collected (Brooks et al. 1990). Each of these users has a need for a particular kind of information. One of the first considerations in designing a monitoring program, therefore, is to decide whose needs are to be met.

Monitoring programs must be linked closely to the people they are designed to serve. They should be interactive between those who have knowledge about monitoring technologies and those whose informational needs are to be met. The potential benefits and costs of meeting different informational needs must be considered in designing monitoring programs.

The design and organization of a monitoring program must be addressed early in a project's planning stage. The objectives, purposes, and inputs and outputs of the monitoring effort should be identified in the plan. Decisions must be made as to how the program is to be administered and who will do the monitoring. It must be determined whether those doing the monitoring are the same as those using the information obtained. If this is so, it helps to ensure that the information obtained will meet the needs of the user. One danger with this approach is that the monitoring program can fall into a routine collection of data for management purposes and, as a result, fail to provide the information that is needed to evaluate all of the effects.

Alternatively, monitoring might be carried out by an organization that is independent of the user. If monitoring serves a number of groups, this approach can be the most practical. A danger with this approach, however, is that the people responsible for monitoring can become so independent that they no longer serve the needs of specific users. Past experience indicates that large volumes of data that serve little useful purpose can be collected in the monitoring efforts. Monitoring activities also can be split so that some activities are performed by the users and other activities are performed by a group that is independent of the users.

In designing monitoring programs, informational needs are determined initially, after which priorities are established. With the informational needs and priorities in hand, the means of collecting specified kinds of information can be determined.

Determining Informational Needs

In determining informational needs, the users to be served by the monitoring program need to be identified. The users then must be consulted to determine their informational requirements. Those designing a monitoring program cannot assume that they know and understand the users' needs without a risk of designing an inappropriate program and collecting information that will not be used. File drawers and computer files are full of data and other information that were collected in the expectation that this information would be useful but subsequently never were used because they failed to meet the actual needs of the users.

With the users' informational needs known, it then becomes necessary to decide exactly what kinds of information will be obtained. If some of the required information already exists, it should not be included in the monitoring program. The benefits from the information must outweigh the costs of obtaining, analyzing, and providing it to users.

A goal of monitoring is not necessarily to provide the most detailed, accurate, and precise information possible, but to meet needs of the users effectively and efficiently. A good question to ask of users is, *How little information do you need to make a "reasonably" good decision?* Obtaining too much information in too much detail can interfere with decision making rather than help it. Users can suffer from "informational overload" by having so much information available that they cannot digest it all. It is better to spend more time on designing an efficient information system than trying to deal with information that needs not to have been collected in the first place.

Setting Informational-Needs Priorities

In establishing informational priorities, the costs of obtaining, analyzing, storing and retrieving, and presenting the information must be compared to the potential benefits of having the information. Those designing a monitoring program should recognize the time and costs of obtaining the information, training the necessary personnel, and writing the reports. Before the reporting requirements are imposed, the benefits of having the information and the alternative means of obtaining it should be studied. Furthermore, the monitoring and reporting requirements should be reviewed periodically to determine if the information is still needed or if the informational priorities should be modified.

Determining informational priorities is also an iterative, interactive process between those who will provide the information and the users. By themselves, these two groups may have limited effectiveness in establishing the informational priorities. Working together, however, they can be more effective.

Means of Collecting Information

Biophysical information for monitoring requires many types of instruments and sampling networks that ensure that the data to be collected make sense. Details about instrumentation and commonly employed sampling procedures for a number of biophysical data topics are available in the literature (Avery 1975, Conant et al. 1983, Ffolliott 1990, Kunkle et al. 1987).

Sampling procedures also are critical to socioeconomic data collections. Questionnaires or interviews with the inhabitants of the project area are common methods of obtaining information. However, it is important that the applications of these methods be thought through carefully, so that the information obtained is useful. For example, estimating the incomes of rural people can be accomplished with questionnaires or examinations of tax records. Questionnaires can be subject to reporting errors because of a reluctance of the people to disclose personal information, but tax records also can be inaccurate if information about incomes has been reported to hide tax obligations.

The required data already can be available from other sources for some kinds of socioeconomic information. For example, the records of registration of births and deaths, marriages and divorces, illnesses, taxes, transportation, business activities, organizational memberships, and special censuses often are available. One drawback with these records is that because they generally are maintained for other purposes, they may not contain the exact information that is needed for project planning, management, and evaluation (Hayes 1966).

The task of collecting information is made all the more difficult because only a few "standard" techniques for conducting monitoring programs are available. This deficiency is attributed largely to the fact that no single set of guidelines apply in all situations. As a consequence, one can find that the best allies are one's own creative instincts and those of others who are either cooperating with the project to be monitored or have confronted similar problems in other areas. A number of different monitoring approaches can apply in any situation, depending upon the objectives of the project and the circumstances in which the project was implemented. One or more of the following "categories" of measurements usually are included in a monitoring program:

- Direct measurements of inputs and outputs of the project, using the most appropriate mensurational techniques and procedures.
- Indirect measurements obtained through solutions of "predictive relationships" between inputs and outputs, when these relationships are available or readily defined for the project.
- Imputed measurements of changes in sustainability of the project and the welfare of people, both on and off the project area, as derived largely from "indices" of internal and external changes.

Information Management

Information is expensive to collect, analyze, store and retrieve, and evaluate. In designing a monitoring program, therefore, considerable thought should be given to how information is to be handled. A description of what data sets are to be collected and how the data will be processed, analyzed, stored and retrieved, evaluated, and ultimately presented to users should be part of the design. Information management, for example, through use of microcomputers, can be one of the most important parts of the monitoring program.

MONITORING THE BIOPHYSICAL SYSTEM

The purpose of monitoring the biophysical system is to determine whether the practices in a forestry project have had the effects intended. Figure 21.2 illustrates the types of biophysical monitoring that could be needed for this purpose. Importantly, the monitoring effort must have a specified purpose. If erosion control practices involving the planting of trees and shrubs are implemented to improve upland productivity and reduce downstream sedimentation, measurements of changes in erosion are needed. In addition, the changes in erosion must be related to both upland productivity and downstream sedimentation. This latter type of monitoring seldom is carried out, however.

To determine the effects of a forestry project on biophysical conditions, it is necessary to monitor the project area, where effects of the designated project can be measured. However, it also is desirable to monitor a control area, so that a com-

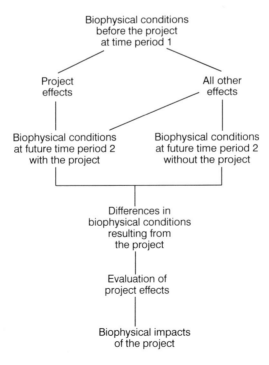

Figure 21.2. Comparing the impact of a forestry project on biophysical conditions (adapted from Olsen et al. 1981)

parison can be made of areas with and without the project, as outlined in Figure 21.2. In some situations, the "control" must consist of information obtained from the project area before the project was implemented. Comparisons then can be made between the "before" and "after" conditions of the project area. These comparisons involve some risks, for example, assuming that all of the conditions unaffected by the project (such as climatological patterns and nonproject land use activities) will continue to be the same after the project is initiated as they were before it was initiated. Nevertheless, this approach of monitoring can be the only practical course in many situations.

Considerations in monitoring the biophysical changes because of the implementation of a forestry project include clearly stating the objectives of the monitoring effort. It also is important to ensure that measurements made as part of the monitoring are useful and that the location, timing, and number of observations are compatible with the objectives of monitoring.

Types of Monitoring

Several types of monitoring can be carried out, each with its own purpose. Examples of these types, adapted from Ponce (1980), include:

- *Cause and effect* monitoring in a project is designed to quantify the effects of specific practices on the measurable outputs. Some questions that might be asked are, *Did the agroforestry practice implemented increase the production of fuelwood?*, and *Were erosion rates reduced?* This type of monitoring helps to answer the question of what happened and, in doing so, understanding why it happened.

- *Baseline* monitoring provides project planners and managers with reliable information about the variability of climatological, physical, and biological data. Baseline information helps people to better understand the variations in annual precipitation and the length of dry periods, what the extent of the differences in soil fertility is, and what the growth and annual yields of plants are. This kind of information is useful at early stages of project planning.

- *Compliance* monitoring is used to determine if specific criteria are being met. This type of monitoring provides information useful in the planning of future projects. Some questions to be answered are, *Are drinking standards being met?*, *Are farmers planting land for which they are receiving payment?*, and *Are limits to irrigation use being exceeded?*

Role of Simulation Techniques

Monitoring programs can be supplemented with models and simulation techniques. Microcomputers and accessible software programs help to estimate the future outcomes without the extensive data collections of the past. Monitoring also can help to calibrate and verify simulation models. Validated models then can be used at remote locations where complete monitoring programs are not in place. The details of simulation models and their uses are found in a number of references, including Hann et al. (1982), Rasmussen et al. (1985), and Roberts et al. (1983).

MONITORING SOCIOECONOMIC IMPACTS

Some forestry projects seek to protect the natural resource base and environment that people use to satisfy their needs and, as a result, enhance the welfare of people directly or indirectly. Other projects seek to directly change the way in which people use resources. Still other projects attempt to improve productivities of resources in meeting people's needs. Therefore, directly or indirectly, forestry projects are intended to affect people and their living standards.

Because these projects are "people oriented" in that they try to alter land use practices or change the effects of resource use on people, their managers must be concerned with monitoring changes in people's activities and in people who are brought into the project. Project managers must incorporate the collection, analysis, and evaluation of socioeconomic data topics into their monitoring programs. Similar to biophysical information, socioeconomic data must be collected so that differences between the before and after conditions can be used to determine socioeconomic impacts, as shown in Figure 21.3.

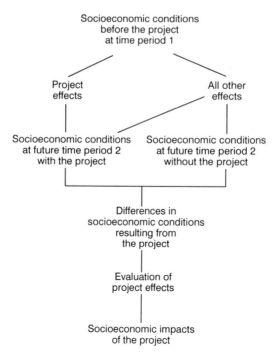

Figure 21.3. Comparing the impact of a forestry project on socioeconomic conditions (adapted from Olsen et al. 1981)

In achieving the above, some means of obtaining the information to establish the "before and after" conditions must be found. As with biophysical monitoring, rarely is it possible to monitor a "control" area for a project that exactly matches the project area. In many instances, it is most feasible to compare the before and after observations of societies being affected by the project. But, it must be recognized that changes are likely to have occurred in a society even in the absence of the project. Considerable judgment and experience is required to interpret and evaluate observations obtained in monitoring socioeconomic impacts.

Socioeconomic monitoring should not necessarily collect large amounts of data about a wide range of variables unless these data sets are required by law or needed by project planners, managers, and policymakers. To determine informational needs, a key is to identify *whom to ask*. For example, if the activity to be monitored is the responsibility of women and children, then women and children should determine the informational needs.

MONITORING PROJECT ACTIVITIES AND OUTPUTS

It is the responsibility of a project manager to achieve the goals and satisfy the objectives specified in the project plan. The manager is accountable for project expenditures and achievements. To be able to properly schedule project activities, manage people and funds effectively, and make "corrective" actions to change project directions when necessary, the project manager must have specific information about project activities and outputs (Brooks et al. 1990). Three forms of monitoring can be involved in obtaining this information:

- *Implementational* monitoring gathers information to answer the general question, *Did we do what we said we would do in the project plan?* Here, we seek to monitor project tasks and their performance to document actual accomplishments. This form of monitoring might rely largely upon records kept by project personnel, but it also should include some field checking to compare reports of activities accomplished with on-the-ground observations.

- *Effectiveness* monitoring gathers information to answer the question, *Did the project accomplish what we intended it to do?* Specific elements to be monitored are determined largely by the project goals and objectives. Here, changes in natural resources, environmental conditions, and socioeconomic conditions brought about by the project are monitored. In the context of sustainable development, this question might not be asked immediately after the project ends because some of the project benefits likely will accrue beyond the project's termination.

- *Validation* monitoring gathers information needed to check on the assumptions made in the project plan to answer the question, *Were the assumptions and information used in the project plan correct?* Variables to be monitored might be chosen to check on particular data sets and assumptions used in planning and managing the project that are thought to be relatively uncertain but that play a key role in the project outcome.

It generally is suggested that monitoring be integrated closely into the management of a project to keep close control of the information provided. The information collected must be processed, analyzed, and presented to the project planners and managers in a usable format and in a timely manner. Monitoring has little value if it provides wrong information or information at the wrong time.

DESIGN OF EVALUATION SYSTEMS

Evaluation systems are designed to meet the needs of the project planner, manager, and policymaker. It is essential, therefore, that evaluation procedures be designed as the result of a dialogue between the evaluators and users of the information to ensure that pertinent, timely, and useful information is provided. If evaluations are not "user driven" and designed to meet user needs, they are unlikely to be used. However, evaluation systems should be independent of the activities being evaluated to provide objective evaluations.

In contrast to monitoring programs, Casley and Kumar (1987) suggested that evaluations be undertaken at a central location, for example, in a regional or a national office. Reasons for this include:

• The high level of skills needed for evaluation for every project may not be available locally.
• Data sets needed for evaluation, particularly information on long-term resource, environmental, and socioeconomic impacts, may need to be collected in a time span that is longer than the project duration.
• It can be necessary to gather information beyond the "boundaries" of the project area in order to make comparisons.
• Standard methods of evaluation can be needed to facilitate comparisons among several forestry projects in a region, which might be difficult to achieve if each project conducted its own evaluation.
• An independent evaluation unit is likely to provide a more objective evaluation of a project than could the project personnel themselves.

Evaluations must be linked closely to monitoring, and the requirements of evaluations should be used to design the monitoring program. However, evaluations usually require additional studies to provide the information not obtained through monitoring. For example, monitoring can provide information about the extent to which a particular agroforestry practice has been adopted by the local people. But, monitoring is unlikely to explain why a particular agroforestry practice was not adopted by the people. A monitoring program usually is confined to determining what happened, while an evaluation often seeks to analyze a situation to determine why something happened and suggest what might be done to correct an "undesirable" situation. To do this might require a study to gather information not obtained by the monitoring program.

Evaluations are concerned with extracting the pieces of information that are essential for project management from a mass of data sets and presenting this information in a form that is easy to use. This task requires skill and an understanding of the data and information available, the methods of analysis, and the informational needs of the user. Information has little value if it cannot be used or has been received at the wrong time to be used. Therefore, attention should be given to the means by which the collected data are to be analyzed and how the information is presented to prospective users.

An evaluation of a forestry project should provide an objective analysis of the performance, effectiveness, efficiency, and impacts of the project in relation to the objectives. The evaluation attempts to:

- Critically reexamine, in light of subsequent developments, the project's rationale that was stated in the preparation documents.
- Determine the adequacy of a project to overcome the constraints on forestry activities, and, as a consequence, promote the desired changes.
- Compare actual achievements with targets set, and identify reasons for shortfalls or overachievements.
- Assess the efficiency of a project's procedures and the quality of the managerial performance.
- Determine the economic efficiency of a project.
- Determine the environmental impacts of a project.
- Present the lessons learned and the recommendations that follow from them.

The evaluation of a project, which can be formal or informal, can occur at a number of stages in the life of the project, including:

- During the project's duration, to determine the strengths and weaknesses of the project so as to provide a basis for "midterm" corrections of activities.
- At the termination of the project, to examine the overall project effectiveness and to provide information to improve planning of future projects.
- After the termination of the project, to evaluate longer-term impacts of the project in order to better judge the effectiveness of the project's sustainability in achieving desired changes in land use practices and people's living conditions and in identifying unexpected consequences.

Early Warning Signs

Evaluations are iterative processes that are carried out throughout a project's duration to provide feedback information to help in guiding the project's direction. An evaluation should help to determine how things are going and provide "early warning signs" of potential problems in carrying out project activities (Example 21.1). If potential problems are known in time, corrective actions can be taken.

Types of Evaluation

Four types of evaluation are common (Casley and Kumar 1987):

- A *continuous and ongoing* evaluation is often an informal type of evaluation that is conducted by project personnel to improve the planning and

---

Example 21.1

Some Examples of Early Warning Signs of Potential Problems in Dryland Forestry Projects

Category	Examples
Resource and environmental	Decreases in growth and yields of plant resources
	Adverse changes in plant species composition
	Lessening of livestock-carrying capacities
	Loss of soil resources to erosion
	Adverse changes in water yields, timing of flow, and water quality
	Loss of aquatic life
	Loss of biological diversity and ecological stability
	Loss of wildlife resource
Socioeconomic	Adverse changes in employment and working conditions
	Detrimental impacts on local cultural traditions
	Increase in local and regional vulnerability to external pressures
	Loss of political stability
	Decreases in public participation
	Adverse allocations of resources
	Lowering of the levels of production
	Loss of stabilities in incomes

---

management of an ongoing project. Results of this type of evaluation are used to better achieve the project's goals and objectives.

- A *midterm* evaluation is carried out after the initial phase of a project to determine how well the project is functioning. The performance of the project also is evaluated to find out how specified components are performing, to appraise their accomplishments, and to determine whether they are achieving their objectives on time. The results of this type of evaluation are useful in deciding whether major changes are needed in the project.

- A *termination* evaluation is conducted at the end of a project to document activities and accomplishments for use in the project's completion report. Here, the emphasis is placed on documenting what the project achieved in comparison with its original goals and objectives. Departures from goals, objectives, and other targets need to be explained and justified and the unexpected consequences described. Attention should be given to the chances of sustainability of the project's benefits after termination, with recommendations as to how benefits can be sustained. Termination evaluations are intended to provide information to improve planning of future projects. Therefore, unsuccessful components of the project being evaluated should be documented along with successful components so that we do not repeat failures of the past.

- An *ex-post* evaluation is conducted several years after a project has been terminated to document the long-term effects, accomplishments, and impacts of the project. The effects of many forestry projects continue after the project terminates. For example, forest and other vegetation planted to control soil erosion can provide lasting benefits for decades following establishment. Similarly, it can take years to evaluate the effectiveness of measures to control sedimentation. Only through long-term evaluation can long-term benefits and costs be identified and quantified. Unfortunately, ex-post evaluations rarely are reported in the literature, which is surprising because many of the benefits and costs attributed to forestry projects are long term in nature.

Evaluation, regardless of the type, focuses on different aspects of project management. Casley and Kumar (1987) mentioned three aspects of particular importance: *performance*; *outputs, effects,* and *impacts*; and *financial and economic efficiencies*. All of the project's activities should be evaluated to determine the extent to which each contributed to achieving the project's goals and objectives. This evaluation includes a review of goals and objectives, implementation problems, project inputs and services, project benefits, managerial performance, and financial performance. It is necessary to systematically obtain the information needed for evaluation from the start of the project to conduct a performance evaluation. This evaluation also can help a project manager to improve the managerial performance by indicating how the manager is to be evaluated in the future.

A project should be evaluated with regard to outputs, effects, and impacts. The project's activities might have been completed successfully, but the results obtained can be different than anticipated. Suppose that a project objective was to reforest a watershed, while the project target was stated in terms of planting a specified number of hectares with trees. Tree planting may have been completed successfully on time, but only a few hectares will have been reforested successfully if most of the trees subsequently died. It can be seen, therefore, that a project's target often is not stated in terms of the goals and objectives of the project. An evaluation is needed to determine if a project's activities actually accomplished intended goals and objectives. In addition, an evaluation is needed to determine what secondary, unplanned, unintended, and external effects and impacts occurred and, if they did, whether they resulted from the project activities.

A major focus of evaluations are placed on financial and economic efficiencies of a project. One of several measures of financial and economic efficiency is used for this purpose. Among these measures are *present net worth, internal rate of return,* and *benefit and cost comparisons.* A distinction is made between these measures of financial and economic efficiency, as pointed out in Chapter 9. This general subject has been addressed in detail by Dixon and Hufschmidt (1986), Gittinger (1982), Gregersen and Contreras (1979), and Gregersen et al. (1987).

From the above, it can be seen that evaluations can focus on different aspects of a project to meet different needs. An evaluation should not be undertaken simply for the sake of doing an evaluation, but should answer specific questions about a project and be focused on what the user wants to know about the project.

While people who are responsible for the monitoring and evaluation programs cannot ensure that the information they produce will be used in planning, managing, and administering projects, and setting policies, they can target those programs to meet informational needs of the users. Failure to involve the users in the design of monitoring and evaluation efforts, failure to obtain the needed information, incorrect data analysis, failure to provide the information in a form that can be readily used, and failure to provide the information when and where it is needed are "breakdowns" in monitoring and evaluation that almost certainly will ensure that the information produced will not be used. The best way to ensure that this does not happen is to meet the design criteria that have been suggested in this chapter.

One of the justifications for incorporating monitoring and evaluation into the planning of forestry projects is the often incomplete and uncertain knowledge about interrelationships among the project activities, the resource and environmental systems, and the impacts on the welfare of people (Brooks et al. 1990). We monitor and evaluate to obtain needed information about the "real world" as a project unfolds to improve our ability to manage the project and plan for subsequent steps. Unfortunately, almost any monitoring and evaluation effort that is designed also will be incomplete and imperfect. There are many possibilities for error, and the knowledge that we gain through monitoring and evaluation will contain uncertainties. The best strategy to follow, therefore, is to maintain a level of skepticism, not rejecting the information obtained unnecessarily but always checking and testing the information against common sense.

SUMMARY

Monitoring and evaluation should be integral parts of the planning and management of forestry projects in dryland regions. However, monitoring and evaluation are conducted for different purposes. *Monitoring* is the process of obtaining information to provide a basis for adjusting or modifying a project that already has been implemented, identifying procedures for project continuation, and improving future monitoring efforts. *Evaluation* is the process of appraising the results of a decision through the information collected through monitoring activities. At the end of this chapter, you should be able to:

1. Explain the relation of monitoring to evaluation and the nature of the two processes.
2. Describe the steps in designing monitoring programs.
3. Understand the differences in monitoring biophysical and socioeconomic impacts.
4. Describe the general design of evaluation systems.
5. List some of the early warning signs of potential problems in forestry projects.
6. Describe the different types of monitoring and evaluation.

REFERENCES

Avery, T. E. 1975. *Natural resource measurements.* McGraw-Hill Book Company, New York.

Brooks, K. N., H. M. Gregersen, A. L. Lundgren, R. M. Quinn, and D. Rose. 1990. *Manual on watershed management project planning, monitoring and evaluation.* ASEAN-US Watershed Project, College, Laguna, Philippines.

Casley, D. J., and K. Kumar. 1987. *Project monitoring and evaluation in agriculture.* Johns Hopkins University Press, Baltimore.

Conant, F., P. Rogers, M. Baumgardner, C. McKell, R. Dasmann, and P. Reining. 1983. *Resource inventory and baseline study methods for developing countries.* American Association for the Advancement of Science, Washington, D.C.

Dixon, J. A., and M. M. Hufschmidt. 1986. *Economic valuation techniques for the environment.* Johns Hopkins University Press, Baltimore.

Ffolliott, P. F. 1990. *Manual on watershed instrumentation and measurements.* ASEAN-US Watershed Project, College, Laguna, Philippines.

Gittinger, J. P. 1982. *Economic analysis of agricultural projects.* Johns Hopkins University Press, Baltimore.

Gregersen, H. M., and A. H. Contreras. 1979. Economic analysis of forestry projects. *FAO Forestry Paper* 17, Rome.

Gregersen, H. M., K. N. Brooks, J. A. Dixon, and L. S. Hamilton. 1987. Guidelines for economic appraisal of watershed management projects. *FAO Conservation Guide* 16, Rome.

Hann, C. T., H. P. Johnson, and D. L. Brakensiek (eds.). 1982. *Hydrologic modeling of small watersheds*. American Society of Agricultural Engineers, St. Joseph, Michigan.

Hayes, S. P., Jr. 1966. *Evaluating development projects*. UNESCO, Paris.

Kunkle, S., W. S. Johnson, and M. Flora, 1987. *Monitoring stream water quality for land-use impacts: A training manual for natural resource management specialists*. Water Resources Division, National Park Service, Fort Collins, Colorado.

Olsen, M. E., B. D. Melber, and D. J. Merwin. 1981. A methodology for conducting social impact assessments using quality of life indicators. In Finsterbusch, K., and C. P. Wolf (eds.). 1981. *Methodology of social impact assessment*. Hutchinson Ross Publishing Company, Stroudsburg, Pennsylvania, pp. 43–78.

Ponce, S. L. 1980. *Water quality monitoring programs*. USDA Forest Service, Watershed Systems Development Group, USDG Technical Paper 00002.

Rasmussen, W. O., C. T. K. Ching, L. A. Linden, F. A. Myer, V. P. Rasmussen, Jr., R. A. Rauschkolb, and C. S. Travieso. 1985. *Computer applications in agriculture*. Westview Press, Boulder, Colorado.

Roberts, N., D. Andersen, R. Deal, M. Garet, and W. Shaffer. 1983. *Introduction to computer simulation: A system dynamics modeling approach*. Addison-Wesley Publishing Company, Reading, Massachusetts.

22 Forestry Extension Programs

Extension programs provide the means to introduce practices of forest management to rural people and to disseminate technology that is appropriate to forestry projects in dryland regions. Extension programs are necessary to transfer knowledge related to forest management practices to the people who often are responsible for the implementation and maintenance of forestry projects on their own lands or lands owned or controlled by a community or state. Many countries already have a network of agricultural extension workers in place. People trained specifically in forestry extension are lacking in the networks of many countries, however. To remedy this situation, it frequently becomes necessary to establish forestry extension programs, staffed with workers specifically trained in forestry.

PURPOSES OF FORESTRY EXTENSION

Forestry extension has many purposes. A main purpose is helping rural people to examine their forestry needs and the problems that are affecting their livelihood. From this examination, extension then helps to determine the degree to which these problems can be solved through forestry-related activities within the range of the people's skills and financial resources (Sim and Hilmi 1987, Stymne 1984). At the same time, the viewpoints of the people should be made known to the political leaders responsible for formulation of laws and infrastructures so that policies are promoted that help people to realize their goals.

Emphasis must be placed on rural people themselves being able to recognize their needs and problems and, as a consequence, to decide to do something about them. Forestry extension helps to:

- Initiate dialogues through participatory approaches that facilitate recognition and definition of the people's needs and problems.
- Indicate a set of possible courses of action from which the people can select those most suited to the situation at hand.

It is not necessarily a purpose of forestry extension to provide a managerial organization to do things for people. Rather, the primary function of forestry extension workers is assisting people in doing things for themselves, viewing their situations critically, and helping them analyze their own abilities to meet their needs and alleviate the problems (Example 22.1). It is to be hoped that if people have successes in solving limited problems, they then will undertake more involved problems and, in doing so, gain experience to enhance the quality of their lives.

FORESTRY PRACTICES FOR EXTENSION

It is not the intent of this chapter to consider the "silvicultural" aspects of forestry extension, which differ from place to place largely because of vegetative, climatological, and soil features. However, there are forestry projects to which extension can be applied and, in doing so, provide benefits to people (Sim and Hilmi 1987, Vergara and MacDicken 1990). Examples of these forestry projects, many of which were the topics of earlier chapters in this book, include:

- Agroforestry in all its forms.

Example 22.1

Benefits of Forestry Extension Programs to Rural People (Sim and Hilmi 1987) A primary benefit of forestry extension programs is that they meet a need that people have defined for themselves and considered sufficiently important to devote their time and resources to satisfy. In doing so, the people may learn to cooperate, plan ahead to achieve their collective objectives, and obtain skills that can be applied usefully to improve many other aspects of their lives. In material terms, rural people's needs include:

- Fuel for cooking.
- Poles or small timbers for building purposes.
- Fodder for livestock.
- Fruit for consumption or sale.
- Shade or shelter for people or their animals.
- Employment from the manufacture of handicrafts.
- Cash income from the sale of surplus products.

Many of the benefits of forestry extension are difficult to measure and value, however. To illustrate this point, readily available fuelwood or timbers for building can lead to improved health and increased time for cultivation of food crops. Similarly, the establishment of fodder or shade trees for livestock can lead to higher values of animal products before a measurable benefit from tree products arises. If these situations help rural people to understand and appreciate interrelationships among forestry, agricultural crop, and livestock production, a more favorable viewpoint of forestry extension might be attained in the future.

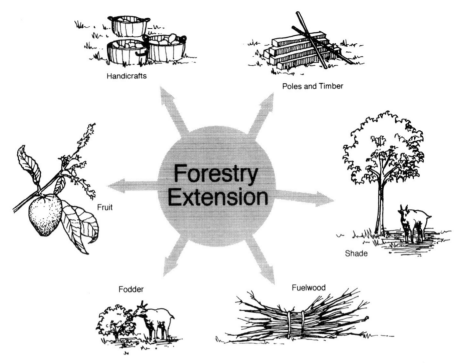

Forestry extension programs can bring a wide range of benefits to many rural people. By permission of the Food and Agriculture Organization of the United Nations.

- Management of community woodlots that meet the requirements of people for fuelwood, posts, and other wood products needed at the local level, especially when it is difficult to meet these requirements through agro-forestry efforts.
- Management of natural forests and woodlands held in common ownership or state or private lands that are subject to trespass, to minimize losses of vegetative, soil, water, and other resources that are basic to satisfying the people's needs.
- Erosion control to minimize loss of soils.
- Increasing available water supplies, water conservation measures, and watershed management practices.
- Management of amenity plantations for multiple purposes, to be undertaken by individual families around their homesteads or community groups in areas of public interest or concern.
- Small-scale, forestry-based enterprises, for example, production of charcoal, collection of honey, or supplying materials for local handicrafts.

COMMUNICATION

Forestry extension activities involve communication. The *communicative process* includes a communicator, in this case the extension worker, a message to be communicated, channels of communication, and a targeted receiver or group of receivers to whom the communication is sent, as shown in Figure 22.1. Barriers block the passage of a message in some instances. One example of a barrier is the suspicion that rural people often have of "strangers" and anything that they may say about the people's customs or ways of life. It is necessary, therefore, that the barriers be overcome to ensure the receipt of the message.

When the receiver responds to a message, this is termed *feedback*, which is the reverse of the communicative process. Feedback should receive as much attention as the message itself. A message that is not understood is valueless no matter how often it is repeated. The continued repetition of a message without modification can annoy the receiver and, as a consequence, prove to be counterproductive.

The channels of communication are classified as spoken, visual, and written. There also are combined channels, for example, a videotape or 16-mm film with a sound track. Combined methods of communication often are more effective than the use of any of the channels in isolation.

Sophisticated communication is not necessary and, in fact, can have a negative impact if not understood. Simple, clear, and concise messages can have greater impacts (Example 22.2). Line drawings can be as effective as glossy posters. The appropriateness of communicative channels must be considered to match the most effective method with a particular situation.

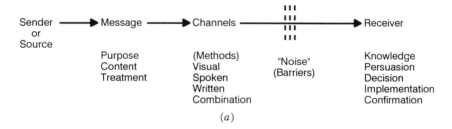

(a)

When the receiver responds to a message, this is termed feedback
and the S - M - C - R process is reversed.

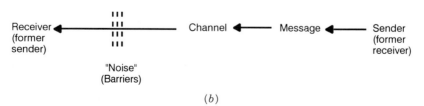

(b)

Figure 22.1. The communicative processes (adapted from Hunter 1973), by permission of the Food and Agriculture Organization of the United Nations

Example 22.2

The "Trees' Prayer" in Zambia: An Example of Effective Communication in Forestry Extension Activities To explain the many benefits and encourage proper use of trees, the Ministry of Lands and Natural Resources, through the Forest Department, posts the "trees' prayer" in villages throughout Zambia. This prayer, originally written in Portuguese, presents a message of conservation and management by telling people of the many roles of trees through the use of a poster, illustrated below.

> Ye who pass by and raise your hand against me,
> hearken ere you harm me.
>
> I am the heat of your hearth on the cold winter nights,
> the friendly shade screening you from the summer sun;
> and my fruits are refreshing draughts,
> quenching your thirst as you journey on.
>
> I am the beam that holds your house,
> the board of your table,
> the bed on which you lie
> and the timber that builds your boat.
>
> I am the handle of your hoe,
> and the door of your homestead,
> the wood of your cradle
> and the shell of your coffin.
>
> I am the gift of God and the friend of man.
>
> Ye who pass by, listen to my prayer—
>
> HARM ME NOT.

EXTENSION METHODS

Forestry extension workers provide people with the opportunities to learn about forestry projects and, simultaneously, stimulate people so that learning can take place. People pass through a series of stages in changing their ideas or practices. It is necessary, therefore, that forestry extension workers be familiar with these stages of the *adoption process*, illustrated in Figure 22.2. The extension methods selected for use must be linked to the stage of thinking of rural people. A key in the adoption process is moving through the *crossover threshold* of this process, from adaptation and trial to adoption and implementation (Rogers and Stonemaker 1971).

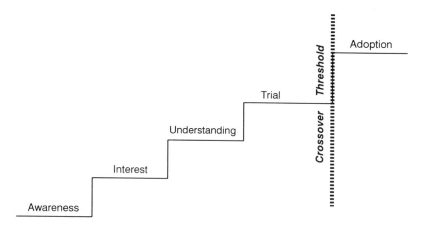

Figure 22.2. The stages in the adoption process (adapted from Rogers and Stonemaker 1971)

People learn in different ways, some by listening, some by seeing, and some by discussion. As a consequence, some extension methods are more effective than others in particular situations. For this reason, a variety of extension methods have evolved. The methods commonly used in forestry extension include:

- Individual and personal methods, including visits to a home or farm, receiving a person at an extension office or place of work, and informal contacts.
- Group methods, for example, open community meetings for all people, meetings for a group of people with specific interests, and meetings limited to selected individuals with responsibilities as leaders.
- Mass media methods to reach large numbers of people quickly, including use of circular letters, newspapers, posters, pamphlets and leaflets, fact sheets, displays, and radio and television.

The most effective method or combination of methods should be selected to accomplish the needed forestry extension activities. People generally learn most effectively through a combination of extension methods, if this is possible.

EXTENSION ACTIVITIES

A variety of extension activities can be used to introduce forest management practices to rural people. In large part, a responsibility of forestry extension workers is to select the most appropriate activity or set of activities that communicate the benefits of forestry projects to people. Activities most often employed in forestry extension programs are *educational campaigns, educational tours*, and *demonstrations*. The use of volunteer leaders to help conduct these activities allows more people to benefit from extension programs.

Educational Campaigns

An educational campaign implements a well-organized plan that encourages the adoption of a particular forest management practice. It is a teaching effort that is concentrated into a specified period of time. The central idea, that is, to adopt better practices, is kept before people during the entire time. People are shown repeatedly that "this" is a solution to a problem.

The more frequently people are exposed to a new idea, the more likely they are to adopt it. Educational campaigns apply this principle by focusing people's attention on a proposed forest management practice through the many methods of communication. People become interested because they continually see reminders that dramatize the issues of concern. To be successful, an educational campaign must:

- Offer solutions to a forestry-related problem that people recognize.
- Address a forestry-related problem that is important to a relatively large number of people.
- Offer a solution that people can and will accept.
- Emphasize only one idea at one time.

Educational Tours

One special type of educational campaign is an educational tour. An educational tour is a field trip organized by a group of interested people to observe situations or conditions related to specific forestry problems. Educational tours can be oriented toward one forest management practice and can include demonstrations of that improved practice. On the other hand, general educational tours can show several kinds of practices or demonstrations and their positive or negative outcomes.

Well-planned and conducted educational tours are effective forestry extension methods. However, educational tours might not be the most efficient method to disseminate information in remote areas with sparse populations.

Demonstrations

Forestry extension workers around the world have found that a demonstration is another convincing teaching method. In general, there are two types of demonstrations, *result demonstrations* and *method demonstrations*. The differences in these demonstrations reflect the purposes for which they are planned.

Result demonstrations are designed to show the advantages of improved forest management practices and applied scientific methods to everyday situations and to arouse the interests of people through displaying, side-by-side, traditional, and "more modern" forest management practices. Many rural people have improved their living conditions after viewing result demonstrations of a forest management practice. When a result demonstration is located on the land of a trusted cooperator, additional credence can be given to the practice or method.

Result demonstrations generally are effective because they build confidence in findings and facts, and in the extension worker who teaches them. These demonstrations also can localize research findings to the local conditions, appeal to the eye, develop local leadership, and strengthen extension teachings.

Method demonstrations are used to show a person or group of people how to do a job, step-by-step, until they have acquired the necessary proficiency. The people attending method demonstrations can participate in the activity, which results in more complete learning than listening passively to a talk. If properly conducted, method demonstrations often generate interest and enthusiasm in a forest management practice in addition to providing the skills required for its implementation.

Demonstrations of either type are more effective if the size of the learning audience is relatively small, permitting all of the people in attendance to hear and see what is demonstrated. Otherwise, they likely will become disinterested and might continue with current practices or adopt improper techniques. If large numbers of people need to be reached, therefore, multiple demonstrations offered in diverse geographical locations for ease of attendance can be effective.

Volunteer Leaders

Forestry extension workers can reach more people with the help of volunteer leaders. In many instances, an individual extension worker can be required to serve 1,000 families in many countries. Therefore, the needs of these families can be better met with use of properly trained volunteer leaders. In a one-half day period, for example, an extension worker can teach members of one youth club, who then can teach their parents and the members of 10 or 12 additional clubs. Instead of helping the members of only one club, the extension worker has multiplied the educational efforts.

Anyone in a village or rural community can be a possible leader. People become leaders when their ideas or actions influence others, or when they help other people obtain what they request or need. There already are people in most villages or rural communities with some knowledge and experience of the forest management practice in question. These people usually become the leaders.

Leaders typically fall into two groups, *formal leaders*, such as the chiefs, religious leaders, teachers, and the extension worker, and those who are leaders because of what the people expect of them. In this second group are many who likely might not consider themselves leaders. These people are called *volunteer leaders*, unpaid leaders, or informal leaders. Volunteer leaders are important for two reasons:

- Volunteer leaders are local to the community and usually remain there. Educating people who are willing to devote time and effort to plan and carry out the program provides immediate and, in many instances, continuing impact on the community. A trained extension worker can reach more of the people needing assistance with help from local volunteers.
- Local volunteer leaders likely are trusted more readily by their peers than a visiting forestry extension worker might be.

Involving volunteer leaders help forestry extension programs succeed. In essence, a forestry extension program planned in cooperation with volunteer leaders becomes the program of both the extension workers and the volunteer leaders who will work to make it successful. Importantly, volunteer leaders keep a program realistic and related to local needs and resources. Volunteer leaders not only channel information to people, they relay people's reactions back to the professional extension workers, permitting adjustments needed for the viability of the program. Such feedback is important for the success of extension programs.

ORGANIZING FORESTRY EXTENSION SERVICES

In organizing forestry extension services, both a *central-level office* and a *field-level organization* should be considered. Each of these two organizations has its own roles and assigned tasks, and can implement forestry extension programs effectively when the organizations are structured appropriately and integrated. A balance between the responsibilities and activities of a central-level office and a field-level organization must be attained, however, to ensure effective and efficient extension.

A Central-level Office

There likely is a need for a central-level policy-formulating and coordinating office in a forestry extension service. This centralized office can vary in size and function according to the extent to which forestry extension services are concentrated into a single agency or distributed among many agencies (Stymne 1984). However, at a minimum, there should be one high-level officer responsible for forestry extension.

Institutional Arrangements A choice must be made about whether the central-level forestry extension office should be placed under the agriculture administration or incorporated into the forestry administration. One argument in favor of placement in agriculture is that a network of agricultural extension workers already exists in many countries. Moreover, it can be difficult to distinguish between agricultural crops and forest crops in many instances, especially in agroforestry practices.

One argument against linking forestry extension too closely to agriculture is that agricultural problems, activities, and budgets frequently are so large that they overshadow forestry considerations. However, the linkages of forestry extension with the established forest administration can make specialized knowledge needed for silvicultural treatments and other forest management activities more readily available. On the other hand, one traditional goal of many forestry agencies is the protection of forest resources, and this can create attitudes and practices that make cooperation with farmers and rural people difficult.

There can be alternative institutions in which to coordinate forestry extension programs, however. These alternatives include ministries or departments for integrated rural development or the conservation of natural resources. An advantage of these types of affiliation is that forestry extension is likely to be accepted more easily as part of an integrated effort to involve people in forest management practices and conservation. Unfortunately, problems other than forestry can receive the most attention.

The question of what is the "best" institutional arrangement for a particular situation should be answered on a local basis. What is efficient, effective, and appropriate in one place, region, or country might not be so elsewhere and, therefore, should not be recommended.

Chief Officer and Resources Another decision confronting the organizing of forestry extension services concerns the level of the chief officer responsible for forestry in the central office. One option is having the chief of forestry extension report directly to a minister or upper-level department head who is on an equal level with the chiefs of forestry administration and agricultural extension. Another possibility is to place the chief of forestry extension under the chief of forest administration, with a status equal to that of the chiefs of research, development, and planning. A third option is to place the chief of forestry extension at the head of a functional forestry unit reporting, for example, to the chief of silvicultural operations or similar functions.

In general, the higher the chief officer responsible for forestry extension can be placed, the better will be the officer's access to top policymakers and the more evident will be the importance of forestry extension. A lower placement is an appropriate choice if better coordination can be obtained by attaching forestry extension to existing agricultural and natural resource administrative units. The chief of forestry extension also can be placed directly under the chief of a regional administrative organization. Because shortages in financial resources and trained personnel are common, such a strategy can be a better alternative to creating an entirely new organization that is dependent upon scarce resources.

Another question to be answered concerns the number and kinds of officers and the levels of financial and other resources that will be allocated to a central office responsible for forestry extension. The answer to this question depends largely upon the tasks to be carried out by the central office, the political importance attached to forestry extension programs, and the rate of expansion deemed possible in forestry extension programs. If the main responsibility of the central office is to provide ideological leadership and coordinate other agencies, only a few people with the capacities necessary for communicating with others are needed. Some authority should be given to the central office over financial resources that are allocated to different agencies for specific forestry extension activities.

The relationships of the chief of forestry extension to workers at the field level also must be established, especially in the case of a "straight-line" organization. The question of who supervises the field workers on a day-to-day basis is crucial. In many instances, this person is as critical to the whole forestry extension organization as the financial resources available.

Legal Assistance   One other function at a central office should be mentioned. Policies relating to forestry extension programs can lead, in some instances, to legal or regulatory complications. Laws concerning the ownership, the land use rights, and the sharing of proceeds from forestry projects may have to be passed to get people interested in acting as forest managers. Legislation can be needed for defining what is expected from the managers of different types of land and for protecting the rights of these land managers. Therefore, it often is important to include legal work as one of the primary functions of the central office for forestry extension.

Field-level Organization

Tasks of a field-level organization in forestry extension services generally focus on inducing people to take on the responsibilities for forest conservation, that is, the "wise use" of forest resources and to give people the required assistance to do so (Stymne 1984). Some of the responsibilities of a field-level organization, depending upon its relationship with the central-level office and assigned levels of responsibilities, include:

- Gathering information about land use patterns and problems, for example, estimating the needs for the production of fuelwood or other wood products.
- Preparing strategies and plans for improving both land use and resource consumption patterns.
- Managing and coordinating programs, and ensuring that the financial support from the central office and other sources are utilized effectively and in appropriate manners.
- Convincing local leaders, farmers, and other land managers of the needs for improved forestry practices and, when feasible, forestry initiatives.
- Identifying who is responsible for the management of land that has been mismanaged or neglected.
- Establishing and operating local nurseries, and organizing field planting efforts and creating demonstration plots.
- Providing assistance in marketing of forest-based products when there are opportunities to do so.

Structure of a Field Organization It is not necessary that all of the above responsibilities be carried out by a single field organization or that one field organization specialize in one or more of the tasks. In actuality, there are a number of means for establishing an organizational structure at the field level, including:

- Working within established agencies or local groups of interested people.
- Addition of personnel to existing agencies.
- Involvement in joint extension programs with different sponsoring agencies.
- Initiating special forestry extension activities.
- Establishing a more "self-contained" field-level organization for forestry extension.

Approaches to Forestry Extension A field organization should be created that can be effective with limited personnel and minimal imported materials in choosing an appropriate organizational structure for a forestry extension service. Duplication of human, technical, and financial resources should be avoided. The following are two general approaches to forestry extension work by a field organization:

- Implementing an extension program preconceived by a central government, for example, introducing an agroforestry practice, planting trees on communal lands, establishing village forests or woodlands, restoring watersheds, or replanting deforested areas.

  If the program implementation approach is taken, a field-level organization that is "uniform" from area to area, that is, a "straight-line" organization, could be established. The form that this organization takes depends largely upon the tasks to be accomplished. The organization should have enough qualified people, technical and financial resources, and administrative authority to do the work itself.
- Strengthening specific capacities of an area for development, for example, through programs for integrated rural development.

  If the capacity-strengthening approach is taken, a field organization must be adaptable to respond to local needs and opportunities for development. In other words, the organization should be "grass-roots" oriented.

Independently of the approach chosen, a linkage should be established between the units responsible for forestry extension programs in the field and at the central level. When a program is implemented at the local level, this link can consist of instructions and budgetary provisions originating from above, with information about progress and financial requests coming from below. If a diffuse set of organizations exists at the local level, all of which are supporting development efforts, there should be a procedure for the central office to inform itself about what is happening so that it can direct its own efforts to supporting the most promising developments. One effective approach to obtaining information is to have an employee working in the central office be involved in field activities. Field tours and inspections are other possibilities.

Administrative Considerations   When a field-level organization is established, it need not necessarily be a completely new creation. Instead, it often is fitted in as a component of an already existing network. If forestry is to become an "add-on" responsibility for an already in-place extension worker, it must be determined what current work responsibilities are to be dropped or what additional compensation is to be given the worker for the additional work. Any forestry extension activity contemplated, therefore, must be preceded by a careful analysis of what the network is or should be and where an addition would be of value.

One outcome of such an analysis might be that money for forestry extension programs is allocated to a private voluntary organization (PVO) working in the area rather than spending money on creating a new agency. In this instance, fiscal guidelines and reporting mechanisms must be in place and adhered to. Another outcome might be that the best use of resources for improving forest management practices in a particular area is the offering of training courses about specified topics to extension workers. Especially at the field level, the choice of organizational structure is a matter that relates more to outside forces than it does to meeting requirements within the organization itself.

TRAINING FORESTRY EXTENSION WORKERS

The selection, orientation, and training of forestry extension workers are essential to successful forestry extension programs. Selecting appropriate candidates for training and establishing appropriately structured training programs for staff members is important.

Selection of Candidates

Candidates often are selected from a staff of existing forestry agencies or institutions by voluntary transfers, or direct assignments to extension services. Those selected should have a background in forestry, which then is adapted to extension programs. However, these candidates can find it difficult to obtain the necessary support from and cooperation with rural people because of their previous forestry duties and attitudes toward the public (Sim and Hilmi 1988). In some instances, the candidates are distrusted and, as a consequence, unacceptable to people, severely limiting their effectiveness in forestry extension.

Other candidates selected might have little technical knowledge of forestry, but they may have been trained in agricultural extension. While it is easier to train these candidates in the responsibilities of extension workers, there might be a danger in "releasing" them to forestry-extension positions if they lack experience in forest management practices at the local level, which is a necessity in gaining the respect and confidence of the public (Sim and Hilmi 1988). In these situations, rural people can believe that they know more about the forestry-related subject in question than the extension worker, making it difficult for the extension worker to establish necessary working relationships with clients. Interestingly, experiences in much of the United States have been somewhat the opposite, however, with *paraprofessionals* trained as deliverers of specific information and practices to the public being effective in many cases.

It is a waste of resources for extension organizations to initiate training opportunities already available through established educational and training programs in forestry when these opportunities are available. An argument can be made, therefore, that the training of forestry extension workers can be facilitated by selecting candidates who already have an education or a training experience in forestry at the appropriate level and who also have the unique skills to become effective extension workers. It is to this kind of training that this chapter addresses itself.

Levels of Training

Training of extension candidates generally is considered at three levels, *vocational, technical,* and *professional* (Sim and Hilmi 1988). The participants, purposes, and contents differ with these three training levels.

Vocational Training Vocational training is targeted largely at "junior" staff personnel, for example, those assigned previously as forest guards or in equivalent positions. The purposes of this training are to provide competency in the concepts of forestry extension programs and to teach the roles of extension workers in these programs, and the contributions of forestry, agriculture, and other rural development interventions in improving living standards of rural people (Sim and Hilmi 1988). The means by which to establish working relationships with the public also are suggested, and general administrative procedures necessary to support rural people are introduced. Competency-based vocational training programs usually last a few weeks to a month.

Technical Training Technical training is designed for "senior" technical staff personnel who have completed some technical training in forestry and have had subsequent field experiences (Sim and Hilmi 1988). Such training introduces the philosophy and methods of extension and the socioeconomic conditions of the area in which the trainee will work. The roles, techniques, and problems of other agencies and organizations that are participating in rural development are explained in the hope that a level of integration can be achieved.

Skills in assessing local needs, the developing of extension programs to meet these needs, and the organizing of the appropriate staff to satisfy the objectives of these programs are developed in technical training programs (Sim and Hilmi 1988). Ways to introduce forestry concepts into educational curricula at primary and secondary levels often are included. The requirements of administrative organizations to effectively communicate in implementing the agreed to extension programs are explained. Training at the technical level can be three months or more in length, depending upon the prior backgrounds and qualifications of the trainees.

Professional Training Professional level training is structured for trainees with the qualifications for entry to professional levels of forestry agencies or other equivalent levels and with the sufficient experience to understand the administrative, fiscal, and field procedures in these agencies (Sim and Hilmi 1988). An introduction to the range of knowledge and skills necessary to function at the central level or field levels of a forestry extension service is presented in professional training. Communicative skills are studied in depth to promote more effective forestry extension.

The areas of knowledge relevant to extension and the areas in which research efforts can be needed to improve performances of extension services are reviewed in professional training. The planning and organizational requirements to enable extension services to function at all levels also are presented. Professional training generally requires a year of study at an educational institution that would award an appropriate degree or certificate of completion.

In countries without formal training programs in forestry extension, the levels at which extension training should be initiated must be decided upon. In most situations, a one-month vocational training program can be planned and implemented more quickly than training at the professional level. Furthermore, relatively large numbers of trainees can be accommodated at the vocational training levels and then deployed in the field by the time that the first professionally trained extension worker is available. However, the sequences in which the training at the three levels becomes established depends largely upon a careful assessment of local requirements.

EVALUATION OF FORESTRY EXTENSION PROGRAMS

It is difficult to know when forestry extension programs are successful. Only general criteria are available to evaluate these programs (Sim and Hilmi 1987). However, a number of critical questions can be addressed to help in evaluating the success or failure of forestry extension programs. These questions include:

- Are extension delivery techniques appropriate for the local community and intended audience?
- Is the extension working in cooperation with the related organizations and agencies involved in development?
- Are local leaders and representatives involved in setting priorities and in planning and evaluating activities?
- Is there a systematic method of rotating input from the community members participating in extension programs?
- Do extension staff and community members appreciate and relate to their respective roles and responsibilities?

- Are local facts and information being collected and analyzed before setting priorities?
- Is the extension field staff being updated about new knowledge and innovative techniques?
- Does the system of promotion in the extension program reward office work and neglect fieldwork, or is there a beneficial balance between the two?
- Is appropriately trained extension staff being recruited and kept?
- Are funding agencies and the participating people being kept informed about the progress of major extension objectives?

Informal and formal evaluations of the effectiveness of forestry extension programs should be continuing processes. Informal evaluations should be ongoing parts of extension programs and should include monitoring of human and material resources, program participation of community members, and observed attitudinal changes of rural people. Scheduling of formal evaluations depends largely upon the type of extension program considered, the duration of the program, and the manner in which the program is implemented. Formal evaluations can be scheduled at:

- The midpoint of a designated extension program to determine if people's needs are being satisfied, to provide the people with opportunities to reevaluate their needs, and to obtain information that can be used in modifying contents and methodologies for the remainder of the program.
- The completion of an extension program to provide an overall assessment of the program in terms of changes in knowledge, attitudes, skills, and aspirations in meeting the needs of rural people and to obtain information that can be helpful in the design of future extension programs.
- A 6- to 12-month period after the completion of an extension program to provide information about the effectiveness of the program after the people have had opportunities to incorporate the practices into their patterns of life, to observe the "end" results, and to furnish a mechanism for staying in contact with the rural people.

Evaluations must be built into extension programs, not added as an afterthought. A number of useful strategies for this inclusion in the planning process are available for this purpose (Bennett 1977, Hunter 1973, Sim and Hilmi 1987).

LIMITING FACTORS IN FORESTRY EXTENSION

There are many reasons for providing forestry extension services. Two of the more commonly mentioned are to address a particular forestry-related need or problem and to initiate efforts in situations where there has been a lack of rural development in general (Sim and Hilmi 1987). In reference to the latter, successful rural development can be limited by one or more of the following:

- Inadequate political commitment.
- Inappropriate market infrastructures and transportation systems.
- Insufficient applications of current technological knowledge.
- Inadequate financial resources.
- Inabilities to organize rural people into effective bodies for action.
- Inadequate educational facilities.
- Inabilities of rural people to internalize how such change will benefit them.
- Lack of rural people's family structures and sex roles.
- Lack of rural people's necessary standards of health to implement selected actions.
- Lack of physical skills and abilities to overcome local obstacles.
- Inabilities to mobilize and use local resources.

In many instances, such a listing of limiting factors is too superficial to properly assess the situation. Cultural and religious factors can be as important as economic and technical factors, although they frequently are more difficult to deal with. It is likely that forestry extension cannot address all of the obstacles to development in a region. Nevertheless, efforts in forestry extension can promote interest in a closer examination of local problems and a spirit of self-reliance in considering them.

One other factor, but frequently the *most* limiting one to successful forestry extension programs, is a failure to recognize the roles of women and children in forestry and, as a consequence, a failure to address these roles in the extension programs. Forest management practices in the dryland regions of the world in which women and children have significant roles include the gathering of fuelwood, the carrying of water, and the harvesting of agricultural crops in agroforestry schemes (Example 22.3). These roles frequently are overlooked in the planning of forestry projects, although they are *real issues* in many countries, especially where there are specified divisions of labor (Huston 1979, Njuki 1989, and Sokona et al. 1986). In more "blended sex-role" cultures, one might forget these roles and, as a consequence, place additional work on women and children if the forest management practices that are considered require labor-intensive changes. Forestry extension programs, therefore, must be sensitive to this possibility to be effective in delivering their message.

SUMMARY

Forestry extension programs transfer the knowledge of forestry projects and practices to the people who are responsible for the implementation and maintenance of the programs on their own lands or lands owned or controlled by a community or

Example 22.3

Women and Children: Food and Energy Providers in the Sahelian Region of West Africa (Sokona et al. 1986) It would be hazardous to attempt to define in detail the role of women and children in the rural areas of the Sahelian region, for these areas are inhabited by numerous social and cultural groups with varied traditions and ways of life. However, one can say definitely that women and children there fulfill the twin roles of production and reproduction and that these roles are determined for them mainly within a framework of a subsistence economy in which they are the heart of the family unit.

The drought that hit the Sahelian region in the early 1970s has disturbed social and economic structures and has rendered conditions of life extremely difficult to all people. The main consequences include:

- Acute food deficits since the early 1970s, with food production per capita continuing to decline.
- Lack of water because of the drying up of rivers and lowered water tables and, as a result, a decrease in food supplies in the vicinities of human settlements.
- Destruction of livestock.
- An energy crisis.
- A rural-to-urban migration of people, particularly men.

The combination of these phenomena has contributed to enlarging the role of women and children in rural settings. In effect, the drought of the early 1970s has brought on an abandonment of land by men who have migrated to urban centers in search of work. This migration, whether temporary or permanent, has increased the responsibilities of women and children in helping to maintain the family's economic status. These responsibilities lead women and children to be more active than is traditional, both at home and in the field, as they are often the sole family providers of food and energy, two essentials of life.

---

state. A main purpose of forestry extension is to help rural people examine their needs and problems. Forestry extension then helps to determine how these problems can be solved through forestry-related activities within the range of the people's skills and financial resources. After completing this chapter, you should have an appreciation of the importance of forestry extension and be able to:

1. Describe the communicative process and the barriers to this process.
2. Explain the meaning of the adoption process and the crossover threshold in relation to learning.

3. Discuss educational campaigns, educational tours, demonstrations, and the use of volunteer leaders in forestry extension activities.
4. Discuss the roles and assigned tasks of a central-level office and a field-level organization in a forestry extension service.
5. Discuss the training of candidates for forestry extension at the vocational, technical, and professional levels.
6. Describe the factors that can limit the success of forestry extension programs.

REFERENCES

Bennett, C. F. 1977. *Analyzing impacts of extension programs*. USDA Extension Service, ESC-575.

Hunter, A. H. 1973. *Agriculture extension: A reference manual*. FAO, Rome.

Huston, P. 1979. *Third world women speak out*. Praeger Publishers, New York.

Njuki, C. 1989. Problems of access to education and training for women in Africa. *CODEL News*, September/October 1989, pp. 1–2.

Rogers, E. M., and F. F. Stonemaker. 1971. *Communication of innovations: A cross cultural approach*. Free Press, New York.

Sim, D., and H. A. Hilmi. 1987. Forestry extension methods. *FAO Forestry Paper* 80, Rome.

Sim, D., and H. A. Hilmi. 1988. Forestry extension curricula. *FAO Forestry Paper* 85, Rome.

Sokona, Y., K. Traore, L. Bobo, D. Ireland, and M. Balde. 1986. Women: Food and energy providers in the Sahel. *Work in Progress* 10(1):9.

Stymne, B. 1984. Forestry extension: Organizing a programme. *Unasylva* 86:13–15.

Vergara, N. T., and K. G. MacDicken. 1990. Extension and agroforestry technology delivery to farmers. In MacDicken, K. G., and N. T. Vergara (eds.). 1990. *Agroforestry: Classification and management*. John Wiley & Sons, Inc., New York, pp. 354–73.

APPENDICES

Appendix I

Selected Conversion Factors from Metric to English Units

Quantity	Metric Unit	English Unit	Convert Metric to English Multiply By
Length	centimeters (cm)	inches (in.)	0.394
	centimeters (cm)	feet (ft)	0.0328
	millimeters (mm)	inches (in.)	0.0394
	meters (m)	feet (ft)	3.28
	meters (m)	yards (yd)	1.09
Area	square millimeters (mm^2)	square inches (in.^{2})	0.00155
	square meters (m^2)	square feet (ft^2)	10.76
	square meters (m^2)	square yards (yd^2)	1.196
	square meters (m^2)	acres	0.000247
	hectares (ha)	acres	2.47
	square kilometers (km^2)	square miles (mi^2)	0.386
Volume	cubic centimeters (cm^3)	cubic inches (in.^{3})	0.0610
	cubic meters (m^3)	cubic feet (ft^3)	35.3
	cubic meters (m^3)	cubic yards (yd^3)	1.31
Velocity	kilometers per hour (km/h)	miles per hour (mi/h)	0.621
	meters per second (m/s)	feet per second (ft/s)	3.28
Flow	cubic meters per second (m^3/s)	cubic feet per second (ft^3/s)	35.3
Mass	grams (g)	ounces [avdp] (oz)	0.0353
	kilograms (kg)	pounds [avdp] (lb)	2.20
	metric tons (t)	short tons (t)	1.10
Density	grams per cubic centimeter (g/cm^3)	pounds per cubic foot (lb/ft^3)	62.4
	kilograms per cubic meter (kg/m^3)	pounds per cubic foot (lb/ft^3)	0.0625
Force	Newtons (N)	pounds force (lbf)	0.00986
Temperature	Celsius (°C)	Farenheit (°F)	$t_F = (t_C + 32)/0.556$
Energy	joules (J)	British thermal units (mean) (Btu)	0.000947
	joules (J)	calorie (cal)	0.239

Quantity	Metric Unit	English Unit	Convert Metric to English Multiply By
Special conversion	square meters per hectare (m^2/ha)	square feet per acre (ft^2/acre)	4.36
	cubic meters per hectare (m^3/ha)	cubic feet per acre (ft^3/acre)	1.41
	cubic meters per hour (m^3/hr)	cubic feet per second (ft^3/s)	0.00981
	kilometers per hour (km/h)	feet per second (ft/s)	0.912
	liters per hectare (l/ha)	gallons per acre (gal/acre)	0.0890
	liters per second (l/s)	gallons per minute (gal/min)	1.75
	kilograms per hectare (kg/ha)	pounds per acre (lb/acre)	0.892
	kilograms per cubic meter (km/m^3)	pounds per cubic foot (lb/ft^3)	0.0624
	number per hectare (No./ha)	number per acre (No./acre)	0.405
	joules per gram (J/gm)	British thermal units per pound (Btu/lb)	2.36

Source: Adapted from American Society for Testing and Materials. 1976. *Standard for metric practice.* American Society for Testing and Materials, Philadelphia.

Appendix II

Common Tree and Shrub Species for Forestry Applications in Dryland Regions

Species	Fuel	Fodder	Additional Use and Remarks
Acacia albida	X	XXX	tannin from wood, soil improvement
Acacia aneura	XX	XXX	posts and poles
Acacia brachystachya	XX	X	wood durable, small wood items
Acacia cambagei	XXX		posts, termite resistant
Acacia cyanophylla	XX	X	sand dune stabilization, windbreaks and shelterbelts
Acacia cyclops	XX	X	sand dune stabilization
Acacia farnesiana	XX	XX	posts, tannin from bark, hedges
Acacia mellifera	XX	XX	roundwood, hedges
Acacia nilotica	XX	XXX	wood durable, building material, tannin from bark and pods, gum
Acacia senegal	XXX	XXX	soil improvement, agroforestry, gum arabic, roundwood
Acacia seyal	XX	XXX	wood hard, roundwood, gum
Acacia tortilis	XXX	XXX	posts, sand dune stabilization
Acacia victoriae	X	XX	
Albizia lebbek	XX	XX	lumber, furniture, soil improvement, leaves for manure
Anogeissus latifolia	XXX	XX	roundwood, gum, tannin, silkworms
Anogeissus leiocarpus	XX	XX	roundwood, tannin from leaves and bark
Argania sideroxylon	XX	XX	construction material, oil from seed
Atriplex canescens	X	XX	windbreaks and shelterbelts
Atriplex glauca		XX	
Atriplex halimus	X	XXX	windbreaks and shelterbelts
Atriplex indica	XX	X	poles, furniture, tannin, oil, windbreaks and shelterbelts, shade
Atriplex nummulria	X	XXX	windbreaks and shelterbelts, sand dune stabilization
Atriplex semibaccata		XX	
Atriplex vesicaria		XX	

Species	Fuel	Fodder	Additional Use and Remarks
Azadirachta indica	XX	X	poles, furniture, tannin, oil, windbreaks and shelterbelts, shade
Balanites aegyptiaca	XX	X	edible fruits, oil
Boswellia papyrifera	XX		Frankincense gum
Boswellia serrata		X	Frankincense gum
Brachychiton populneum		XX	windbreaks and shelterbelts
Brosium alicastrum	X	XXX	construction material
Callitris glauca	XX		resistant wood, posts, poles, housebuilding, windbreaks and shelterbelts
Cassia auriculata	X	X	tannin, tea, hedge plant
Cassia simiea	XX	X	roadside plantations, lumber
Cassia sturtii	X	XX	
Casuarina cunninghamiana	XXX	X	windbreaks and shelterbelts, shade
Casuarina equisetifolia	XXX		posts, poles, tannin, sand dune stabilization, windbreaks and shelterbelts
Ceratonia siliqua	X	XXX	honey, soil conservation
Colophospermum mopane	XXX	XX	roundwood, carvings
Conocarpus lancifolius	XXX	XX	poles, shipbuilding, shade
Cordeauxia edulis		XX	seeds for food
Cupressus arizonica	X		construction materials, windbreaks and shelterbelts
Cupressus sempervirens	X		carpentry, furniture, windbreaks and shelterbelts
Dalbergia sissoo	XXX		furniture, building material, posts
Desmoodium spp.		XX	
Dichrostachys cinerea	X	XX	posts, sand dune stabilization
Eucalyptus camaldulensis	XXX		lumber, honey, windbreaks and shelterbelts
Eucalyptus gomphocephala	XXX		construction material, windbreaks and shelterbelts, soil protection, roadside plantations
Eucalyptus salmonophloia	XX		wood durable, roundwood, windbreaks and shelterbelts, roadside plantations
Euphorbia tirucalli	X		hedges, windbreaks and shelterbelts, latex
Gleditsia triacanthos	X	XXX	wood durable, roundwood, windbreaks and shelterbelts
Haloxylon aphyllum	XX	XX	windbreaks and shelterbelts
Haloxylon persicum	XXX	XX	sand dune stabilization
Juniperus depeeana	XXX		posts, berries, wildlife food
Juniperus monosperma	XXX		posts, berries, wildlife food, windbreaks and shelterbelts
Juniperus osteosperma	XXX		posts, berries, wildlife food, windbreaks and shelterbelts
Juniperus scopulorum	XXX		posts, berries, wildlife food, windbreaks and shelterbelts

444

Species	Fuel	Fodder	Additional Use and Remarks
Leucaena leucocephala	XXX	XXX	roundwood, soil improvement
Parkinsonia aculeata	XX	XX	soil fixation, erosion control
Pinus halepensis	XX		construction material, resin, soil conservation
Pithecellobium dulce	X	XX	posts, edible fruits, tannin, shade, hedges
Prosopis chilensis	XXX	XXX	wood durable, posts, soil conservation, sand dune stabilization
Prosopis spicigera	XXX	XXX	soil improvement, agroforestry
Prosopis tamarugo	XX	XX	furniture
Quercus arizonica	XXX		
Quercus emoryii	XXX		posts
Quercus gambelii	XXX		posts
Quercus hypoleucoides	XXX		
Robinia pseudoacacia	XX	X	posts, soil improvement
Salvadora persica	XX	XX	edible fruit, seeds give fat, roadside plantations
Schinus molle	X		windbreaks and shelterbelts, shade plantings
Simmondsia chinensis		X	Jojoba oil from seeds
Tamarindus indica	XX	XX	roundwood, construction material, furniture, edible fruits, drinks
Tamarix aphylla	XX		turnery, carpentry, sand dune stabilization, windbreaks and shelterbelts
Tetraclinis articulata	XX		furniture, lumber, timber, resin, erosion control
Zizyphus jujuba	XXX	XX	agricultural implements, edible fruits, drinks, fences, shellac
Zizyphus spina-christi	XX	XX	posts, hedges, erosion control

XXX = High Value   XX = Good Value   X = Moderate Value

Source: Adapted from the Food and Agriculture Organization of the United Nations. 1989. Arid zone forestry: A guide for field technicians. *FAO Conservation Guide* 20, Rome.

INDEX